"Buchanan has searched the relevant l
ness in quest of a developed vision tha
and the subjective worlds. . . . For one wno has
in similar ways in other fields for fifty years, Buchanan's enthusiasm is
profoundly gratifying. It is hard to see what more can be asked of Whitehead before his thought will be recognized as having solved the need for
a unified cosmology."

—**John Cobb**, Claremont School of Theology, emeritus

"Ever found process thought—with the whole universe pulsing and sparkling in every quantum—a bit of a trip? John Buchanan confirms your
suspicion! This irresistibly readable narrative of psychedelic exploration
. . . opens a stunning new portal into our shared reality. We discover not
just a remarkably lucid introduction to Whiteheadian theo-cosmology,
but—aimed right at our self-destructive civilization—the chance of a
spiritual awakening."

—**Catherine Keller**, Drew University

"Occasionally, the story of a life is so well told that it draws you in, becoming your story. And occasionally, theory and personal experience are woven
together so tightly that each sheds light on the other. Here, *both* happen. In
understanding the author, one understands transpersonal psychology, process metaphysics, and (dare I say?) something of non-ordinary states, the
mystical quest, and God. The result is one of the most compelling accounts
of conscious and unconscious experience I have read in years."

—**Philip Clayton**, Claremont School of Theology

"In this remarkable book, Buchanan has systematically explored the main
theses of transpersonal psychology in light of Whitehead's process philosophy. Buchanan demonstrates that, when taken together, transpersonal
psychology and Whitehead's process philosophy complement and support each other astonishingly well. Moreover, he shows how transpersonal
psychology and Whitehead's philosophy could form the basis for a new
cosmological vision for our world."

—**Stanislav Grof, MD**, author of *Beyond the Brain: Birth, Death,
and Transcendence in Psychotherapy*

Processing Reality

Perspectives in Process Studies Series

Process Studies refers to a transdisciplinary field of study inspired by thinkers like Alfred North Whitehead, Charles Hartshorne, John B. Cobb Jr., David Ray Griffin, and many others. It's a perspective that has influenced many people around the world. The process-relational perspective is a framework for conceiving reality according to the principles of deep relationality, harmony, intrinsic value, and change. The implications of taking these principles seriously are far-reaching. From cosmology and metaphysics to ecology, psychology, religion, and beyond, the Perspectives in Process Studies book series engages a wide range of topics from a process-relational lens, harmonizing fragmented disciplinary thinking in order to develop integrated and holistic modes of understanding.

Series Editor:

Wm. Andrew Schwartz

Processing Reality

Finding Meaning in Death, Psychedelics, and Sobriety

John H. Buchanan

CASCADE *Books* · Eugene, Oregon

PROCESSING REALITY
Finding Meaning in Death, Psychedelics, and Sobriety

Perspectives in Process Studies Series

Cascade Books
An Imprint of Wipf and Stock Publishers
199 W. 8th Ave., Suite 3
Eugene, OR 97401

www.wipfandstock.com

PAPERBACK ISBN: 978-1-6667-0928-5
HARDCOVER ISBN: 978-1-6667-0929-2
EBOOK ISBN: 978-1-6667-0930-8

Cataloguing-in-Publication data:

Names: Buchanan, John H., author.

Title: Processing reality : finding meaning in death, psychedelics, and sobriety / by John H. Buchanan.

Description: Eugene, OR: Cascade Books, 2022. | Perspectives in Process Studies Series. | Includes bibliographical references and index.

Identifiers: ISBN 978-1-6667-0928-5 (paperback) | ISBN 978-1-6667-0929-2 (hardcover) | ISBN 978-1-6667-0930-8 (ebook)

Subjects: LCSH: Buchanan, John H. | Addicts—Rehabilitation—United States. | Psychotherapy patients—Biography. | Hallucinogenic drugs and religious experience—United States. | Hallucinogenic drugs—Social aspects. | Process philosophy. | Process theology. | Whitehead, Alfred North (1861–1947). | Grof, Stanislav, 1931–.

Classification: BT83.6 B90 2022 (print) | BT83.6 (ebook)

10/25/22

Contents

Series Foreword / Wm. Andrew Schwartz | ix

Acknowledgments | xi

1. Waking Up | 1
2. My Journey | 13
3. What Was I Thinking? | 31
4. Return to Experience | 54

   An Ineffable Interlude | 71

5. A Complex Amplifier | 75
6. A Process Theory of Nonordinary States | 93
7. My Big Trip | 108
8. Demystifying Mysticism | 134
9. Psychospiritual Transformation | 157

   A Personal Interlude | 173

10. Putting It All Together | 179
11. A Vision for You | 208

    A Final Interlude | 231

12. What Are We Going to Do? | 233

Glossary | 257
Bibliography | 267
Index | 277

Series Foreword

Perspectives in Process Studies

T he goal of this book series is to make accessible big ideas that are too often marginalized. By big ideas I mean ambitious, comprehensive, and fundamental questions about life, truth, meaning, and more. From cosmology and metaphysics, to ecology, psychology, religion, and beyond, the Perspectives in Process Studies series has been developed to engage a wide range of topics from a process-relational lens, harmonizing fragmented disciplinary thinking in order to develop integrated and holistic modes of understanding.

Process Studies refers to a transdisciplinary field of study inspired by thinkers like Alfred North Whitehead, Charles Hartshorne, John B. Cobb Jr., David Ray Griffin, and many others. It's a perspective that has influenced many people around the world. The process-relational perspective is a framework for conceiving reality according to the principles of deep relationality, harmony, intrinsic value, and change. The implications of taking these principles seriously are far-reaching.

By recognizing that all things flow, the process perspective represents an alternative to static ontologies of being. Interdependent moments of experience replace independent substances as the final real things upon which the world is made. By extending subjectivity to all living entities, process thought deems the natural world intrinsically valuable. Therefore, the process perspective is fundamentally an ecological perspective. Process thought naturalizes the supernatural and normalizes the paranormal, contributing to the development of a new cultural paradigm that can account for the kinds of experiences regularly dismissed by many other worldviews.

Deeply appreciative of the natural sciences, process thought uniquely integrates science, religion, ethics, and aesthetics. It portrays the cosmos as an organic whole analyzable into internally related processes. In this way, process thought offers a constructive postmodern alternative to the mechanistic model that still influences much scientific work and is presupposed in much humanistic literature. Articulating a relational worldview for the common good, process perspectives create positive social change toward an ecological civilization.

Books in this series combine academic rigor with broad appeal and readability. My hope is that this series will be particularly useful for students, scholars, and armchair philosophers and theologians. However, I also hope that those interested in process thought but intimidated by Whitehead's technical jargon will find value here. Some texts will be more technical than others, but together these volumes will reflect the depth and breadth of diverse perspectives in process studies.

Wm. Andrew Schwartz,

Series Editor, Executive Director, Center for Process Studies, Assistant Professor of Process Studies & Comparative Theology, Claremont School of Theology

May 23, 2022

Acknowledgments

As this book is based on ideas first developed in my dissertation, I want to start by thanking Robert Paul, my dissertation committee chairperson, advisor, and primary professor during my time at Emory University. Rebecca Chopp, my second dissertation committee member, generously shared her expertise on Whitehead and the philosophy of religion. The third member, Stanislav Grof, was deeply involved with the writing of my dissertation and along with his wife, Christina, led a psychological training group that fostered an atmosphere of intellectual and psychospiritual stimulation. David Ray Griffin—with whom I studied Whitehead and William James at the Claremont School of Theology—made many useful suggestions throughout the dissertation process and beyond. I also want to recognize my friend James Schofield, who, acting as a lay reader, helped me work through many difficult problems. And I would be remiss not to mention my Emory dissertation support group, who supplied much-needed solace and conviviality.

I next need to acknowledge those teachers who were particularly important to my education, especially pertaining to the ideas found in these pages. In this regard, I want to single out David Smillie, Marion Hoppin, and Don Homa at New College; David Galaty, Richard Logan, and Gilbert Null at the University of Wisconsin–Green Bay; Mike Arons, Jim Klee, Bob Masek, and Chris Aanstoos at West Georgia College; and at Emory University, Robert Paul, Bob Detweiller, and William Beardslee. Also deserving recognition are John Quiring, whose herculean efforts in the library at the Center for Process Studies greatly simplified my research, and Jean Houston, whose workshops and seminars served as a hotbed of ideas and inspiration during my tumultuous twenties.

As I worked on reimagining my dissertation for a wider audience, valuable suggestions and editing help came from David Ray Griffin; Bruce Cleary (who also proposed the final title); Elizabeth Gibson, who edited a late version of the manuscript; and Elizabeth Stemen, who provided extensive editorial assistance along the way. This book might still be residing solely in my computer if not for an invitation to be part of a book series being started by Andrew Davis and Andrew Schwartz at the Center for Process Studies. Wipf and Stock Publishers generously accepted the Andrews' recommendation of my manuscript and have proven a wonderful publishing house to work with. K. C. Hanson, Matthew Wimer, and Calvin Jaffarian provided support in all matters before and after submission of my manuscript and Jeremy Funk's careful copy editing added important final touches.

Friends who have "been there" for me during this long process include Jacky, Jim and Kylea, Chip, Marco, Wendy, Jack and Nancy, Kieu, Lenny and Elizabeth, Jonathan, Matthew, Cal and Liz, Alex, David T., Zhihe and Mei, Phillip Clayton, Catherine Keller, and Steve Odin, as well as others too numerous to cite here. I also want to acknowledge in a generic fashion my friends from Serenoa, Rancho Mirage, and Everybody's, and to thank the people at Remley and at Schaper, Benz, and Wise, as well as Sandy Ebrahimi, for all their help and guidance over these many years. I must also attempt the impossible task of adequately thanking my family for their love and support throughout the many twists and turns of my life. Included here are my sisters—Barbara, Nancy, and Linda—and their families; my most excellent stepfamily; my many aunts, uncles, and cousins; as well as my now deceased mother and father and grandparents, and of course Aunt Lorna.

Finally, I am eternally grateful for the unceasing encouragement to complete this project offered by John B. Cobb, Jr., Stanislav Grof, and David Ray Griffin. This support from my most important scholarly influences has been of inestimable value. While I take full responsibility for the final form and content of this book, I want to acknowledge that it would never have come to fruition without their guidance, as well as the encouragement and help of many other incredible colleagues and friends.

—— 1 ——
Waking Up

Over forty years ago, an epiphany from a psychedelic experience launched me on an intellectual and spiritual adventure. This book, in its way, is the culmination of an amazing journey. The pivotal moment occurred sometime in the spring of 1972, several months after my first experience with LSD, while walking through the living room of "The Apartment"—a run-down rental house in Neenah, Wisconsin, typically inhabited by teens escaping from family supervision. In the midst of this early LSD trip, I had a sudden and vivid insight: *the essence of psychedelic awareness lies at the intersection between psychology, philosophy, and religion.* More precisely, I envisioned psychedelic enlightenment as a direct experience of the hidden meaning that lies within the area shared by three overlapping circles, representing the domains of psychology, philosophy, and religion. Out of this innermost realm flow psychological insight, philosophical illumination, and religious revelation. It seemed crystal clear to me that the deepest experiences, questions, and feelings related to all three of these regions arise out of a common psychic space, and that psychedelics could open the door to the mysteries that lay at their heart.

While many of my psychedelic experiences did not involve this kind of decisive insight, they invariably involved a feeling that the depths of the psyche were opening up, and more of reality was starting to pour into conscious awareness. This "more" might manifest simply as a far richer perception and appreciation of colors and sounds. Or it might entail a surge of new insights about myself, my past, and my relationships—suddenly revealed with extraordinary depth and clarity. And then, if egoic consciousness released its grip even more fully, feelings from still greater depths might flow in, revealing an unexpected and sometimes unwanted panoply of images, entities, and revelations about a universe far vaster than previously imagined.

Although many of my psychedelic experiences were terrifying, I was also fascinated by what I was encountering. From an early age, I had been intrigued by extraordinary experiences and powers, be it in science-fiction stories of super intelligence, portrayals of magical powers, fantasy about other worlds and beings, accounts of mystical faculties, or just the superheroes of Marvel and DC comics. Now, much to my shock and delight, I had stumbled upon a little pill that brought these other dimensions within my grasp, or so it seemed. Needless to say, I wanted to learn all I could about this new realm that was being revealed to me.

Inspired by my psychedelic insight into the heart of reality, I started to study psychology and philosophy over the summer at a local community college and continued to focus on these fields throughout my rather protracted undergraduate and graduate careers. My search eventually coalesced into two streams of thought that have proven most helpful for understanding this realm of deep inner experience—and understanding most everything else, for that matter. First, during undergraduate school, I encountered transpersonal psychology: the study of extraordinary experiences such as mystical and meditative states, psychical phenomena, spirituality, and higher states of consciousness. Not surprisingly, transpersonal psychology has a lot to say about the psychedelic experience. In fact, one might say that transpersonal psychology *is* the study of the states of consciousness and the varieties of phenomena that appear during psychedelic journeys. These tend to fall within the domains of psychology, philosophy, and religious experience—just as I envisioned during my psychedelic epiphany. The theories of Stanislav Grof (b. 1931), especially his phenomenology of nonordinary experiences and his cartography of the unconscious psyche, play a central role in my understanding and contextualization of these phenomena.

Then, early in my doctoral studies, I was bowled over by the possibilities of *process thought*, especially as articulated in the speculative philosophy of Alfred North Whitehead (1861–1947), although the ideas of William James (1842–1910) were also influential. Whitehead is still not widely appreciated today, but he is certainly one of the great minds of recent centuries: a brilliant mathematician, logician, mathematical physicist, historian of ideas, philosopher of science and nature, and a metaphysician. Whitehead is probably most generally recognized as Bertrand Russell's teacher and collaborator on the *Principia Mathematica*. He was also a very humane being: the *Encyclopedia Britannica* makes the uncharacteristically sentimental claim that Whitehead was "universally beloved."[1]

---

1. Lowe, "Alfred North Whitehead," 636.

A major reason for my excitement over Whitehead's metaphysics was my rapid realization of how superbly his ideas could serve as a sophisticated philosophical foundation for transpersonal psychology and could provide a rational link between spiritual and scientific concerns. Whitehead took this linking or synthesizing function very seriously, as exemplified in this emphatic statement from *Process and Reality,* his magnum opus: "Philosophy frees itself from the taint of ineffectiveness by its close relations with religion and with science, natural and sociological. It attains its chief importance by fusing the two, namely, religion and science, into one rational scheme of thought."[2] This idea of fusing religion and science within one philosophical system, of course, has important implications for my "interdisciplinary" vision into the deep underlying connection between spiritual, psychological, and philosophical insight.

But my search, though crystallized and energized by a desire to understand the meaning of my psychedelic experiences, was broader in nature. I was also looking for a way to positively reconcile my psychedelic insights and experiences with a rational and scientific understanding of the world, and for a way to coordinate these exceptional experiences with everyday life and values. Whitehead's speculative philosophy—as an "endeavor to frame a coherent, logical, necessary system of general ideas in terms of which every element of our experience can be interpreted"[3]—seemed made to order for these ambitions as well. Articulating a worldview of this kind has proven very useful, intellectually and pragmatically. It has helped me live through, or become reconciled with, some of life's more difficult issues, which is an important test. For according to William James's pragmatic principle, if you cannot live it, it is meaningless.[4]

This book has evolved out of a desire to understand and come to terms with five pivotal events that were life changing for me in many respects. All five had major psychological and spiritual impacts. All raised important questions about life, the universe, and the nature of reality. They all

2. Whitehead, *Process and Reality,* 15.

3. Whitehead, *Process and Reality,* 3.

4. Readers will have to excuse my rather facile translation of James's views on the lived importance of truth and meaning. Citing a passage from pages 413–14 of James's *Collected Essays and Reviews,* Gerald Myers provides a more precise summary of James's view on this subject: "The single most important point in his version of pragmatism is that the meaning of a philosophical proposition resides in what it provides or predicts as a practical consequence . . .

"There can be no difference that doesn't make a difference . . . The whole function of philosophy ought to be to find out what definite difference it will make to you and me, at definite instants of our life, if this world-formula or that world-formula be the one which is true" (Myers, *William James,* 295–96).

influenced what I studied academically and experimented with experientially. And all of these pivotal events made essential contributions to who I was and who I have become. Echoing Kant's famous formulation, each of these events in one way or another woke me from my "dogmatic slumber," ushering in a new understanding of some important dimension of life and reality. There are many things to "wake up" from, and to, in this life—and it is often a major crisis that galvanizes the awakening.

These five pivotal events can be characterized and summarized by the nature of the crisis each induced and the kinds of questions each raised:

First, my father's sudden and unexpected death when I was eleven brought about an *existential* crisis: can one have a basic trust in life? I found myself faced with profound and difficult questions. What is the meaning and purpose in life, given the capriciousness and inevitability of death and loss? If there is a loving God, how can we reconcile this Love with such tragedy and suffering? Or as William James succinctly couches it, Is the universe friendly? In short, "Is it safe?"[5]

Second, discovering the effects of alcohol and drugs led me to an *epistemological* crisis: How do we know ourselves and the world? What does it mean for who we are that taking certain drugs dramatically changes our perception of the world? How malleable are the mind and emotions, and the world? Is how one *feels* the most important thing?

My early LSD experiences brought about a third, *metaphysical* crisis. What is Reality? Is there *more* to reality than our everyday world? How are mind, body, and the world interrelated? What are "altered" states of consciousness? What do spiritual intuitions of "higher" states of awareness mean?

My "Big" psychedelic experience paved the way for my fourth, *theological/cosmological*, crisis. What is the ultimate nature of the universe? How do we understand "mystical" experiences of God? What spiritual entities, forces, and dimensions might make up the universe? What constitutes an adequate cosmology?

Fifth, getting sober crystallized a *spiritual* crisis: What is the meaning and purpose of existence? How can the insights from extraordinary experiences be effectively reconciled with everyday life? How does one integrate all these dimensions into a unified life?

Olaf Stapledon (1886–1950)—British philosopher, psychologist, and my favorite writer of science fiction—sometimes speaks of the universe as a "beautiful and terrible" place. Besides the obvious implication that the

5. "Is it safe?" is of course the infamous, pivotal question of Schlesinger, dir., *Marathon Man.*

universe has a dreadful and frightening aspect, Stapledon is also using the word *terrible* to mean "awe-ful"—that is, inducing a terrifyingly powerful sense of awe. And although I mostly felt shock and grief at my father's sudden passing, this eventually turned to awe at the capriciousness of life and the frightening universe that had been revealed. Awe and amazement also accompanied my discovery of the power of alcohol and drugs to miraculously remove my anxieties and change my feelings (and to get me dreadfully ill, though that was just plain awful). I was far more overwhelmed and astonished by my first LSD experiences and, if possible, even more so by the psychedelic revelations of my "Big Trip." Although getting sober at age thirty-one was necessarily a slow process, it too started with a series of shocks accompanied by a growing sense of awe at my amazing good fortune in escaping an ugly fate and then finding many of the answers and the community I had been seeking.

As a search for knowledge of the nature and meaning of reality, this book is perhaps best understood, and told, in terms of a *quest*. This quest is not so different from those that have been undertaken by many of my generation, and those of many generations before us (and certainly those to come). The questions and ideas that emerged out of my experiences do not seem idiosyncratic but rather are almost prosaic in paralleling many of the key issues that have been troubling the Western world for at least the last several centuries, and some for much longer than that.

More importantly, I believe that these experiences, properly understood, point to some revolutionary possibilities—new possibilities that our troubled world desperately needs. What seems most important for our civilization at this critical juncture is acknowledging, understanding, and responding to our planetary crises of environmental degradation, resource depletion, overpopulation, ever-more dangerous wars, and the more general problem of how to reconstruct human society in relation to these multiple, overlapping challenges. I believe this will require, among other things, a spiritual and philosophical reenvisioning of ourselves, the nature of reality, and our place in the cosmos—for the old vision is faltering. Many of the ideas and tools for just such a new vision are found in the spiritual and scientific possibilities offered by transpersonal psychology and the novel metaphysics and cosmology of Alfred North Whitehead's process philosophy.

This new envisioning must be *experiential* at its roots. It both must be grounded in experiences that reflect and create this new vision and also must develop a coherent view of the universe based upon a new understanding of how *experience itself* is fundamental to all reality. By recapitulating my own intellectual and spiritual journey—and presenting the two revolutionary systems that I have found most helpful for providing theoretical and experiential guidance and synthesis—I hope to illustrate analogically the more general application and importance of these ideas for society at large.

I have chosen a semiautobiographical style for this book for two main reasons: first, to present the key philosophical issues and ideas as they pertain to my own search for meaning; second, to offer personal examples of the psychological and spiritual phenomena under consideration. These ideas and events provide an experiential touchstone for the theoretical explanations and speculations explored in this book. Such an exposition seems only appropriate when discussing Whitehead's philosophy, given that he considers immediate experience the foundation of all thought and philosophy. Staying close to experience also helps avoid the errors associated with what Whitehead calls the "fallacy of misplaced concreteness," that is, confusing abstractions with more basic underlying realities.[6]

In the field of transpersonal psychology, two outstanding works from the 1970s serve as precedents for this type of personal approach to introducing and contextualizing important theoretical material. *The Invisible Landscape,* by Terrance and Dennis McKenna, takes readers on a journey through the authors' psychedelic adventures in South America and then reaches incredible intellectual speculations into the source and meaning of these experiences, spelled out at the physiological, biochemical, metaphysical, mathematical, and mystical levels.[7] I was surprised—and delighted—to discover that the metaphysics used as a philosophical touchstone is none other than Whitehead's. Thus, I am happy to acknowledge the McKenna brothers as the first (as far as I know) to employ Whitehead's philosophy as a metapsychology for the transpersonal field. Even more impressive is that they wrote such a tour de force while still in their twenties—a tribute both to their brilliance and to the power of their psychedelically enhanced vision.

Michael Harner's *The Way of the Shaman* is another remarkable book that boldly begins with Harner's own adventures among the shamans of some indigenous South American tribes and the psychedelic initiations in which he eventually is allowed to participate.[8] By inviting readers into the heart of his own experience, Harner brings to life shamanic practices and helps readers to understand more intimately the lived meaning of the theories he proposes. When dealing with extraordinary intuitions and feelings, direct

6. While this approach may sound like an attempt to adopt a deconstructionist strategy of sorts, my sympathies lie primarily with the kind of constructive postmodernism that is allied more closely with Whiteheadian thought. But I think it is fair to say that both kinds of postmodernism understand the importance of narrative—and of telling a good story.

7. McKenna and McKenna, *Invisible Landscape.*

8. Harner, *Way of the Shaman.*

personal revelation of this kind is useful, perhaps even necessary, to help convey their stamp of deep meaning, importance, and reality.

The power of a personal narrative should not be taken lightly, as it is often the more intimate story that inspires the most interest. And interest is very important. Whitehead makes this rather extraordinary claim, especially for a logician, regarding *interest:* "But in the real world it is more important that a proposition be interesting than that it be true."[9] Whitehead immediately follows up this maxim about the importance of interest—which lures us into entertaining new possibilities—with the rejoinder: "The importance of truth is, that it adds to interest."[10] For the sake of the truth-value of Whitehead's ideas, and that of the other theories discussed in this book, I will do my best to entertain and interest readers as we plunge into the occasionally heady propositions and challenging ideas residing in Whitehead's process philosophy and Grof's transpersonal psychology.

By blending my life story with my life's work in the following chapters, I hope I have found an effective way of conveying the results of my quest into the nature of reality.

Chapter Summaries

To introduce the psychological, philosophical, and spiritual ideas that constitute the heart of this book, I begin by tracing in some detail those early life experiences that sparked my interest in such esoteric matters. In Chapter 2, where I offer an autobiographical account of the critical early events that shaped my life, I highlight the important issues and questions raised by these experiences, and I give a general context for the motivations underlying my quest for intellectual and spiritual understanding.

The first part of Chapter 3 encapsulates my intellectual journey through about twenty years of college. My purpose is not to impress—as if a twenty-year college career is something to brag about—but rather to convey the intellectual path I was pursuing and to indicate what I found most valuable in the theories and ideas I encountered along the way. The last part of Chapter 3 consists of a short explanation of why I find Stanislav Grof's work so important, along with a brief introduction to Whitehead's philosophy. The chapter concludes with a preview of some of the ways Whitehead's process philosophy might prove most useful to the field of psychology.

In the fourth chapter I revisit two of my key psychedelic experiences as a way of introducing some of Whitehead's central metaphysical and

9. Whitehead, *Process and Reality,* 259.
10. Whitehead, *Process and Reality,* 259.

cosmological ideas. I hope this approach helps readers more deeply appreciate how valuable Whitehead's philosophy can be for interpreting extraordinary experiences and understanding nonordinary states.[11]

I continue my explication of nonordinary states in Chapter 5 by
turning to some experiences from my stay at Castalia, a monthlong seminar on Hermann Hesse (1877–1962) and Carl Jung (1875–1961) that I
attended in Switzerland when I was twenty. Whitehead's analogy of the
human body/psyche as a *complex amplifier* is explored and extended in a
transpersonal direction. Following up on this line of thought, I examine
Whitehead's ideas on symbolism in Chapter 6, where I develop a more
complete process theory of nonordinary states.[12]

Chapter 7 starts with my most important psychedelic journey, my
"Big Trip" at New College. The ramifications of this powerful experience set
the stage for a discussion of Grof's levels of the unconscious and his findings on the furthest reaches of transpersonal experience. I then compare
these findings with process philosophy's theories on the ultimate nature
of reality, and consider William James's thoughts on the "compounding of
consciousness."

This Whiteheadian theory of nonordinary states and exceptional
experience is further expanded in Chapter 8 to explore and critique some
basic ideas and images associated with psychedelic and mystical experiences. Several common but problematic notions such as "oneness," "living in the now," and "everything is consciousness" are considered from
a Whiteheadian viewpoint in an attempt to both clarify their valuable
insights and point out potential misconceptions and misrepresentations.

11. I will be using the term *metaphysical* to indicate something that pertains to
the fundamental or essential nature of reality. With *cosmological*, I am referring to the
types of actualities, beings, and structures that make up the universe. I will try my
best to minimize specialized terminology and to explain my usage along the way. I
can still remember returning to the dictionary of philosophy in frustration, striving to
understand what new terms like *transcendental* meant, as I worked my way through the
Critique of Pure Reason in an undergraduate course on Kant. Readers may also consult
the glossary for explanations of my usage of special terminology.

12. The terms *nonordinary, extraordinary,* and *transpersonal* appear frequently
throughout this book. *Nonordinary* typically refers to those states and experiences that
fall significantly outside the normal range of everyday awareness. Stanislav Grof coined
the term *holotropic* ("moving towards the whole") to indicate those experiences that
potentially lead to enhanced psychospiritual integrity, in contrast to those nonordinary
states that do not provide authentic access to deeper realities (such as barbiturate intoxication or illness-related delirium). Since in these pages I am usually pointing to a very
broad spectrum of experience, I generally use *nonordinary* when talking about states
of awareness and *extraordinary* in reference to experiences and phenomena. The term
transpersonal overlaps with both these categories, once again denoting that which falls
outside or beyond what are considered the usual limits of everyday personal awareness.

The chapter concludes by examining the experience of enlightenment and its implications for living in the world.

Chapter 9 takes a look at the meaning of psychospiritual development. Included here is a discussion of enlightenment and death/rebirth, the problem of taking the notion of *maya* or illusion too literally, and some thoughts on the unusual phenomenon I describe as "enlightenment paranoia."

In Chapter 10, I try to pull things together by presenting a general outline of a process-transpersonal cosmology in order to address one more time my pivotal question: What is Reality? I indicate how Whitehead's ideas might influence particular fields of knowledge, as well as offer a unifying foundation for all of them. This falls into what David Griffin would call a "constructive postmodern project," versus a deconstructive one.[13] Such an undertaking seeks to construct a better metaphysical foundation for our shared worldview, attempts to discover closer approximations to the truth about how things really are, and is generally more concerned with putting things together than taking them apart. The chapter concludes with some speculations about the ultimate implications of this cosmological vision.

In Chapter 11, "A Vision for You," I speculate even further about the nature of our spiritual universe, as well as how a such a spiritual vision might help guide us through the difficult challenges that lie ahead.

Finally, Chapter 12 presents some *lived* applications of the provisional answers I have found to my pivotal life questions: existential, epistemological, cosmological, metaphysical, and theological. Seeing ourselves as *cocreators* of reality, a notion that Whitehead's philosophy can help clarify in important ways, plays an important role in addressing a number of these issues. I attempt to illuminate how process theology makes comprehensible mystical experiences of spiritual entities, including God, and also helps redeem the ultimate metaphysical evil: loss. The chapter closes with a discussion of the "final problem," and some possibilities for an *experiential* spirituality.

I have included a short glossary to indicate my intended meaning for certain terminology, some of which is specialized language from transpersonal psychology and process philosophy.

I recognize that certain aspects of my technical discussions of Whitehead's thought may not be of interest to some readers, while other readers may quickly tire of my personal accounts and stories. Thus I encourage readers to take what you need and leave the rest.

13. For example, see Griffin et al., *Founders of Constructive Postmodern Philosophy*, especially David Ray Griffin's introduction (1–42).

As this book emphasizes my personal experiences with extraordinary states of consciousness, I should make several points clear right from the beginning. First, although psychedelic substances acted as a major catalyst for opening me up to a wider range of experience and to a new type of questioning about the world, I have since learned both from my studies and from my own life that extraordinary states do not require any outside chemical stimulation. The vast majority of such experiences occur either spontaneously or through nondrug induction techniques such as ritual, prayer, meditation, rites of passage, vision quests, and sensory deprivation (although the balance may have shifted significantly since the advent of the widespread availability of psychedelics). Transpersonal psychology has thoroughly documented that these kinds of extraordinary experiences have appeared throughout history and have been cultivated in most societies around the world via many different modes of access.

The importance of my own nonordinary experiences is that at a relatively early age they brought into stark relief aspects of reality that I had previously ignored or disregarded (and might well have continued to overlook): the here and now, the intense value of Being,[14] the possibility of mystical intuitions of God, the creative activity of every moment, and the mysterious nature of reality and existence—to name some of the more significant. Extraordinary states are of particular interest because of the range of experiences they reveal, the deep feelings and phenomena and insights they access, and the crucial questions they raise. Of course, these same questions that emerge out of psychedelic states have also been raised for millennia by philosophers, mystics, and spiritual seekers.

But while all these experiences and questions appear independently of LSD and other psychedelics, these remarkable substances are an especially potent means of thrusting them intensely into the forefront of conscious awareness and of unleashing the unconscious depths. Some, myself included, seem to require this kind of powerful stimulation to rouse us from our dogmatic slumbers, in their many guises.

Some Words of Caution

As so much of this book highlights the awesome potential of psychedelic substances, let me balance this enthusiasm by pointing out the unfortunate

14. Readers should be aware that words closely linked to God in the process thought of Alfred North Whitehead, Charles Hartshorne, William James, David Griffin, and John Cobb Jr. (words such as "Being" in this sentence) will be capitalized whereas otherwise they will not be.

truth that there are real and significant problems with the manner in which psychedelics are used in contemporary culture. All readers should be aware of the possible risks of participating in psychedelic adventures as they are most frequently encountered in our society today.

First, although this situation is rapidly changing, involvement with psychedelic substances often includes a risk of serious legal consequences. Then there is the related problem of one's underlying anxiety about these potential consequences transforming into significant paranoia, justified or unjustified, while immersed in the intensified feelings of psychedelic intoxication.

Second, from a practical point of view, since psychedelics are widely manufactured or harvested without any sanctioned oversight, the purity and chemical composition of any street drug is at best uncertain. This is particularly problematic with psychedelics, since proper dosage is so important. And not knowing exactly what or how much one is taking does not contribute to a positive mindset for the psychedelic session, as it is difficult to fully "let go" into frightening feelings or memories if one retains any suspicion of being in real physiological danger from the drug itself.

Third, psychedelics are extremely powerful psychoactive agents and should be used very judiciously, and ideally in a sacred context. This has been well understood in traditional societies, where these substances are administered by shamans and priests in special rituals and rites of passage. This would generally involve an experienced guide to prepare the psychedelic substances and to monitor the experience, a safe and supportive setting, and special psychological preparations to insure a proper mindset for the session. When these conditions are not met, especially given our current social environment, using psychedelics can be a risky business. I know this all too well, as we shall see. While I was lucky enough to survive my psychedelic days relatively unscathed, there are those who have not been so fortunate. Many people have run into severe legal problems, have been exposed to contaminated drugs and unwitting overdoses, or have experienced unnecessarily difficult trips (and outright bad ones) due to faulty set and setting.[15]

That said, the psychedelic landscape is changing rapidly. Within the next few years, psychedelics may well become even more widely available for various medical and therapeutic purposes. I believe that this will be

---

15. In a short essay, Gael makes an important point about "bad" trips, by emphasizing that "difficult is not the same as bad." From this perspective, *difficult* experiences are challenging because they are accessing powerful and meaningful energies, memories, and potential insights, and thus hold great potential for psychospiritual growth. *Bad* trips, on the other hand, also contain great healing potential, but the underlying complexes remain unresolved or incompletely processed, thereby coloring the entire psychedelic journey in a negative light. See Gael, "Difficult Psychedelic Experiences."

highly beneficial, as these substances have shown great healing potential in areas that are typically recalcitrant to traditional treatment modalities. However, I am less certain about whether making psychedelics freely available to the public at large is necessarily the path to follow.

Subjecting the production and sale of psychedelics to simple government oversight would help alleviate concerns about proper dosage and purity and legal repercussions. But it would also open up extremely powerful mind-altering agents to a much broader audience without any guarantee of proper use or supervision. We have relatively few Western cultural equivalents to the shamans, gurus, and mystery schools and cults of old, though I suspect that modern correlates would soon emerge out of the shadows, as has already begun to happen. Nonetheless, I cannot help thinking that Timothy Leary was onto something fundamentally important when he reportedly said that he did not want any governmental agency telling him what he could or could not do with his own consciousness.[16]

16. For what may be the historical basis of this attribution, see the IFIF letter quoted in Pollan, *How to Change Your Mind,* 197.

— 2 —

My Journey

Loss

Alfred North Whitehead asserts, "The elucidation of immediate experience is the sole justification for any thought."[1] In the spirit of this valuable exhortation, we turn immediately to some of my early experiences that were in great need of just such elucidation, beginning with the most difficult challenge of all: my father's unexpected death.

Eleven years old is an especially difficult age to lose a father: young enough to still need the security of the family and to depend on parental guidance, yet old enough to absorb the finality of death—as much as any of us can. What made this loss even more shocking for me was the abruptness of my father's passing, along with the otherwise good news that my life had been rather idyllic up until then.

I grew up in a peaceful town in Wisconsin, situated near the tip of a large lake, in a region prosperous from the paper industry. Our house was located across the street from a beautiful park set on a small harbor that filled with sailboats in the summer. My parents were a well-off, well-educated, very well-meaning couple that did their best for my three sisters and me, and for the rest of our community. I was the youngest and the only boy, so life was pretty sweet. I enjoyed all of the small-town activities, but I especially loved our home, filled with books and games and toys and family and friends. I still fondly remember our backyard populated with dozens of multicolored tulips that my mother brought back from Holland, along with violets, lilies of the valley, bushes filled with lilacs, towering elms and evergreens, and, my favorite, the weeping willows. My feelings were much the same as Dorothy's on her climactic return to Kansas: "There's no place like home!"

---

1. Whitehead, *Process and Reality*, 4.

While I was in elementary school, my sisters slowly departed for private school and college, so by the fifth grade it was just my parents and me at home for most of the year. I began to get much closer to my father as we started doing more things together, such as hunting and fishing trips to northern Wisconsin. In the spring of 1964, Dad started feeling inexplicably weak and experienced some breathing difficulties, but an initial medical checkup showed nothing out of the ordinary. In early June, he went to the Mayo Clinic, where he was diagnosed with lung cancer and given six months to live. I first heard this news when I went to visit my father at our local hospital the day after I returned from a horse show in Milwaukee. I had won my first ribbon—purple for eighth place—and brought it to show to him. It was his forty-fourth birthday, and my mother remembers that he was very proud of me. Two days later, he died.

With my father's death and the seeming disappearance of my family, I felt as if I had been thrown into a cold, lonely world—my paradise lost. I do not remember much of that summer, except for a trip with my cousin Jonathan and his parents, with whom I was very close. We made the long drive out to Yellowstone National Park by way of the Black Hills and the Badlands, and then returned via the endless fields of the Great Plains. Looking at the boiling sulfur springs and steaming pools of Yellowstone, even an eleven-year-old could sense his inner desolation and loneliness being mocked by his surroundings on this road trip through the heartland of darkness and grief.

I remember making two drawings in art class the following autumn that captured my inchoate feelings to a tee. The first drawing was of a tornado; the second was of a leaf-bare tree that I could see in our schoolyard through our second-story window. Both pictures were done solely in black crayon. I could sense that these pictures flowed from some deeper place in me, although I was too shut down to really know from where. But it doesn't take Sigmund Freud (1856–1939) to figure out that I was suppressing deep feelings of grief and its concomitant fear, anger, and sadness.

Despite my anger and grief, I do not remember questioning my belief in God during this time; I suspect I clung to every shred of support I could get hold of. Hating or doubting God was thus out of the question. I do not remember blaming God either, for even though predestination is a traditional Presbyterian doctrine, I don't think I was taught in church or at home that God is responsible for everything that happens.

However, it is fair to say that I had experienced a massive *moral* and *existential* shock, even though much of it was pushed below the surface of consciousness along with my deeper feelings of grief. In an inchoate way, I had started a *search for meaning and purpose* in a world beset by loss and death. But at a conscious level, I was simply concerned with trying to hold myself together and get by. I remember praying every night: "Please, God, don't let anything happen to Mom. I just couldn't take it if anything happened to her!" My feelings toward religion must have been ambivalent at best, as I quit going to our Presbyterian church shortly after I was confirmed. (My mother said that once I was a member of the church, it was up to me to decide whether I attended or not. I have not gone to church regularly since.)

Science became problematic for me as well. It seemed like every year in grade school, my mother had tried to get me involved in a new area of scientific endeavor. One year it was astronomy, another oceanography, and in truth, it all fascinated me. Left to my own devices, however, I loved reading the *World Book Encyclopedia* and showing off newly acquired facts to my family. I remember quizzing them on how high the Empire State Building was—with or without the antenna tower—and proudly announcing its true height. Being the youngest, I suppose I wanted to know *something* that no one else in my family did. But after losing my father, I slowly began to see of what limited help such collected facts, scientific knowledge, or even my logical mind were for dealing with the really big issues of life. In these dark waters, they provided nothing solid to hold on to.

In retrospect, I was very fortunate during this difficult time—as I have been throughout my life. I had a large, caring family nearby and some very good friends, and we continued to live in the house and town I loved. These supports allowed me to keep myself together at a time when falling apart seemed too dangerous and all too likely. As time went by, I felt less anxious and more connected to things; I began to "fit in" again. Growing five inches between eighth and ninth grades helped a lot with the latter, as did participating in debate and drama—and, of course, so did the proverbial healing power of time. And I had some ego-uplifting accomplishments, such as winning several state equitation championships. But deep down, I was still scared, lonely, and pretty disconnected from myself and from the world.

When I returned home after a weekend away to find Dad dying in the hospital, it brought home all too vividly that loss and death are *always* lurking just over my shoulder and might well be waiting at the next turn. It is hard to feel safe and at home in light of this knowledge. The nascent question for me became, What is the meaning and purpose of life in light of death and loss? In a moving and disturbing song, "Dust," Fleetwood Mac starkly describes our unavoidable fate: to disintegrate in the grave, cold and alone.[2] These sentiments are in the same tradition as graveyard meditation in Tibetan Buddhism, skulls on the desks of medieval monks,

---

2. Fleetwood Mac, "Dust."

and Heidegger's notion of Death as the ultimate horizon of life that imbues existence with its deepest meaning and value.

Powerful ideas. But how *exactly* does one live and find meaning in light of the tragedy of Loss? William James saw this dilemma in terms of this question: Is the universe *friendly?* In its depths, does the universe care about and support us? James believes the answer to this critical question is yes, as does Alfred North Whitehead. But as they also fully acknowledge the reality of loss, suffering, and death, their answers are neither naive nor simple. Thus it took me quite a while to understand their perspective, and longer still to genuinely embrace it.

Hope

An unexpected moment of minor "self-transcendence" occurred during junior high, as my mother was dropping me off for school along with my friend, Tom—who, being adopted, understood far better than most my sense of unease around having lost a father. My stomach was aching badly (with fear), as it often did in seventh and eighth grades. I was trying desperately to figure out a way to avoid school that day, when I had a sudden epiphany: the purpose to my life could be to make *other people happy.* Being nice and pleasing other people had been a subtext of my family life (not so bad really, as family lessons go), so it is not surprising that this idea might occur to me as a reason d'être. More significantly, I think this simple revelation of purpose reflected a psychological movement *away* from my fearful self-preoccupation and one *towards* other people and the world at large, as well as the first powerful conscious response to my inner turmoil over whether life could have a valid meaning and purpose.

There were harbingers of hope of another kind from several unexpected sources in these years. In sixth grade, a number of my friends and I read with excitement and wonder Madeleine L'Engle's classic children's book, *A Wrinkle in Time.* Its story—of the socially misfit girl, Meg, and her genius younger brother, Charles Wallace, who voyage into transpersonal dimensions to rescue their missing father—struck a powerful chord, echoing my damaged inner landscape and depicting a mystically expanded universe capable of great adventure and healing. L'Engle's visionary writings helped me believe that radically new possibilities and answers might be revealed if only I could enter into a different understanding or sense of Reality—and that Reality was perhaps far *more* than I had so far imagined. Then, in junior high, the song "Incense and Peppermints," by the band Strawberry Alarm Clock, and the Beatles album *Magical Mystery Tour* spoke to me in strange and compelling ways, suggesting some subtle intimation of stranger things yet to come. And come they would.

The next big revelation happened at my middle sister's wedding reception, when I was fifteen. During the celebrations at our country club, I made the mundane yet to me astonishing discovery that alcohol could *change everything*. My cousin's reply when I asked him why he said I should try the champagne was extremely apt: "It will make you feel different." So I tried a glass, and then another, and then a lot more. Not only did it make me feel "different," but I felt good—*really* good. Loggins and Messina sing poignantly about always being afraid and alone,[3] and when I drank that champagne, I wasn't afraid or alone anymore. And I felt *good*—at least until I found myself throwing up in the men's locker room, in my mother's new Olds 98, and for the rest of the night in my bathroom at home. (Little did I know that this initial pattern of drinking to feel better, losing control, and getting sick would be paradigmatic for my future drinking career.) I had discovered a new purpose in life: to feel good and to *be* happy—a crude hedonism, one might say.

Beyond the incredible relief from anxiety and isolation that alcohol provided—a kind of solace that even I did not know how much I needed—another and more fascinating discovery revealed itself at the reception. I had discovered that it was possible to dramatically change and manipulate my state of consciousness, and thus my feelings and my world. This knowledge gave me a great sense of comfort, as well as a hint at a new kind of freedom. My *mode* of experience itself was vividly revealed to be susceptible to significant alteration. Moreover, I had found a way to directly impact and control these modes of feeling. That day at North Shore Country Club, I experienced a remarkable *epistemological shock*: *how* I know the world could radically change my experience of *what* is known and felt. Better yet, I could *make* those changes happen through alcohol (and, as I would soon find out, through other drugs as well).

I loved the excitement and sense of ease and freedom that came with drinking, and how it helped me fit in with a wider social circle and not care as much about possible rejection. I was also intrigued to discover that alcohol could induce a kind of religious feeling that I had not been aware of before (or for a long time, at least). Our Spanish foreign-exchange student, Álvaro, became greatly annoyed one night as I tried drunkenly to convey to him just how moved I felt listening to George Harrison's "My Sweet Lord," which really was bringing me to tears with its beautiful and powerful evocation of yearning for a connection with God. And alcohol

3. Loggins and Messina, "Back to Georgia."

seemed to reendow Christmas with the magic and beauty that I remembered from when I was very young. I loved feeling this blanketing sense of peace, warmth, and depth of meaning. Alcohol, it seemed, could expand or deepen my consciousness and shift my emotional state.

In short, alcohol transformed my social anxiety into a feeling of connectedness, or (more accurately) calmed my general fears and provided such a sense of well-being that my social, sexual, and existential anxieties became manageable or even inconsequential. Alcohol even rendered a primitive religious or mystical sense of oneness and peace and beauty.

During this same period, I was also looking into other ways of manipulating awareness, such as hypnosis and meditation, and I practiced Hatha Yoga quite seriously for several years. In my senior year, I started experimenting with drugs such as marijuana, amphetamines, and other kinds of depressants besides alcohol. These new experiences helped me realize that the range of possible states of consciousness, or modes of feeling, was far broader than those simply produced by alcohol or through natural variations in awareness.

A strange and frightening occurrence preceded, and in a way also inaugurated, my transition into drug use. One night in autumn of my senior year in high school, my shoulder started aching badly. The next day I went to see a doctor at the insistence of my aunt Lorna, an experienced nurse. When the doctor returned to the examination room after checking my chest X-ray, he asked if there was any history of lung problems in my family. As my thoughts rushed to my father's lung cancer, I felt so lightheaded that I had to lie down on his examining table. Fortunately, my diagnosis was only a partial lung collapse related to an earlier undiagnosed case of histoplasmosis. After two more partial lung collapses that fall, we decided to opt for a new surgical procedure that involved scraping the surface of my lung with a scalpel so that the resultant scar tissue would adhere to the lung's outer plural lining.

"The tube fell out, the tube fell out!" were the words that instantly brought me back to consciousness postsurgery. It turned out merely to be a nurse overreacting to the disconnection of one of the tubes from the fluid-collection apparatus that was draining my chest. My far ruder awakening was the discovery that with every breath and movement I was in agony. Apparently, the doctor thought it was better not to worry me in advance about the kind of pain I would be suffering with the cracked ribs and acute pleurisy resulting from the operation procedure. Every three or three and half hours I would wake up and start yelling for a shot of the synthetic morphine that they were using for pain "management."

On the third day, I had recovered sufficiently so that I did not pass out as soon as I was shot up with the painkiller. Instead, after receiving my morphine, I was able to continue watching Daniel Boone on the television, while appreciating fully for the first time the wonderful glow spreading through my body and pleasurable lethargy in my mind. Although my trajectory towards drugs was already well established by then, in retrospect, I believe my lung issues may have stirred up those dormant fears around illness and death related to my father. (I was in the same hospital where he had died of lung cancer.) And I had now learned how well drugs could serve to ease physical and mental pain.

I started smoking pot in the late winter of my senior year. Soon we were lighting up pipefuls on the roof of my house and while driving around town. And since Álvaro, our foreign-exchange student, looked like he might be twenty-one years old, we were adding a lot more hard liquor into the mix—and an occasional hit of speed soon followed. Despite various problematic and scary experiences and consequences, I loved getting high and felt like I was living la dolce vita.

However, the summer after graduation, my first experience with a powerful psychedelic agent, mescaline, gave me pause. While alcohol usually provided a sense (or illusion) of being able to manage my feelings and state of consciousness, at the end of my mescaline experience I felt a scary loss of control of both body and mind. After I had been tripping all night, we decided to go downtown for some snacks. On the way back from the store, as we drove down Wisconsin Avenue towards my house and into the sunrise, I suddenly felt oddly disembodied and experienced the frightening feeling that I no longer had any idea how to control my arms or hands—which was particularly unnerving since I was driving the car. We did get home safely; apparently I still had enough control for that. But I felt *very* strange and was panicked by the thought of "freaking out" if I were to let go deeply into my experience. I went up to my bedroom and thought I could hear my friends downstairs discussing whether "John was freaking out." (These psychedelic panics have a self-fulfilling element to them.) I called down to the friend who had the most experience with this sort of thing. To my great relief, he came right upstairs and quickly was able to calm me down, which is surprisingly easy to do if no one else panics and simple reassurance and guidance are provided. The rest of the mescaline experience fascinated me, however, as it represented the deepest alteration in my consciousness to that point, including heightened sensory and verbal awareness—for example, food tasted *so* good (even better than with marijuana)—and, to the chagrin of my friends, I made one bad pun after another all night long. But I was so shaken by the feeling of "losing my mind" that I avoided psychedelics for some time to come (not marijuana and hashish, however, which I have since learned qualify as minor psychedelics).

Breaking Through

The next fall I traveled abroad for three months with my youngest sister. Linda was five years older than me, very attractive, rather wild, and an excellent traveling partner. It was so easy to meet people wherever we went, as long as I was in her company!

I did so much drinking in Spain, our first destination, that I frightened myself into quitting for a while. You know you are heading for real trouble when the Spaniards you are partying with express concern about your drinking. By the time we got to Afghanistan, I was ready for something new on the drug front and quickly started smoking (and eating) hashish, with a little opium and cocaine thrown in for good measure. My introduction to coke came when some Westerners I had recently met at a restaurant in Kabul took me to a local pharmacy where one could purchase German pharmaceutical cocaine under the counter for twenty dollars a gram. Back in my room with these more savvy friends, I watched with some trepidation as the cocaine was being chopped up carefully on a mirror for what seemed like forever. Then I snorted a little through a rolled-up bill—after having blown my first lines all over the floor by exhaling at a very inopportune moment. The next thing I knew, I "came to" and realized to my amazement that we had all been talking and laughing for the last twenty minutes. It was at first a shock and then a wonderful relief to be free of my "self," or (more accurately) of my usual self-consciousness, for a period of time. How marvelous to be thrown beyond the personal and its attendant petty anxieties!

That first time was by far the best high I ever had with cocaine. This was so often the case with drugs (though not so much with psychedelics). The first time was best, and everything after was a disappointment by comparison: a futile attempt to recapture the thrill of that first high. I don't know if it is the novelty itself that is unrecoverable, or if the brain habituates that quickly to a particular chemical alteration, attenuating future highs. Or perhaps, in this case, it was just some really good coke!

The same reluctance I felt about trying cocaine led me to pass up my first opportunity to experiment with LSD—*that* still felt like it was too much for me. One day, out of the blue, one of the expatriot hippies in Kabul offered me some LSD, as I watched him practicing yogic postures in his room. When he attempted to overcome my resistance by suggesting that taking LSD could be a religious experience, I indicated my disdain. I remember explaining to him that past-life memories (something he said I might experience with LSD) were impossible since DNA could not record an individual's memories during their lifetime and thus there was no viable mechanism for memories to be transmitted "between lives." I believe his even-handed response conveyed something like, "You may want to loosen your grip a bit on logic and science," which naturally made me more defensive than ever. I felt both skeptical and uneasy about being challenged this way, and I was certainly in no mood to have someone try to change my mind about the effects of LSD—much less try to change my mind about trying LSD.

This encounter encapsulates the frequent struggle that went on between my rational side and the part of me intrigued by the transpersonal realm. For I was, and still am in many ways, enamored with a scientific and logical approach to things. However, I have slowly come around to the point of view described by Bill Wilson in *Twelve Steps and Twelve Traditions:* "I had a scientific schooling. Naturally I respected, venerated, even worshipped science. As a matter of fact, I still do—all except the worship part."[4]

I came to see that my deep-seated allegiance to scientific rationality, while good in itself, became problematic when taken to the extreme of *scientism*—that is, science as an idol. Here, the scientific attitude can transmute into a reflexive, sometimes even a fearful or angry repudiation of "unfounded" speculation. This kind of "obscurantism," according to Whitehead, holds shut the door to truly novel possibilities:

> The dawn of brilliant epochs is shadowed by the massive obscurantism of human nature . . . Obscurantism is the refusal to speculate freely on the limitations of traditional methods. It is more than that: it is negation of the importance of such speculation, the insistence on incidental dangers. A few generations ago the clergy, or to speak more accurately, large sections of the clergy were the standing examples of obscurantism. Today their place has been taken by scientists—
> By merit raised to that bad eminence.
> The obscurantists of any generation are in the main constituted by the greater part of the practitioners of the dominant methodology. Today scientific methods are dominant, and scientists are the obscurantists.[5]

4. Wilson, *Twelve Steps,* 26.

5. Whitehead, *Function of Reason,* 43–44. If Whitehead were still alive, economists might be his new choice for the chief obscurantists, since economics is a methodology that also dominates our society today.

The thorny dilemma here is that entering into the transpersonal realm requires a "letting go" or loosening of the egoic boundaries of the psyche, including its rational mental structures. However, once this is accomplished, there can be a (conscious and unconscious) temptation to shrug off or throw out these boundaries and structures altogether. This can lead to disastrous consequences for one's psychological life and can severely impede any personal or intellectual attempt to integrate transpersonal experiences into everyday reality—not to mention that throwing off these boundaries can make trying to understand transpersonal experiences from a scientific perspective nearly impossible. The subtle challenge is to temporarily transcend one's rationality and scientific beliefs, but then to return to them to help integrate the transpersonal experiences, remaining open to the possibility of making significant modifications to one's previous worldview as well. (Whitehead likens the speculative enterprise to taking off and flying above things to get a new perspective and fresh ideas, but then returning to the ground to rationally sort through and evaluate these new possibilities.)

Sometime in the January or February following my return from Afghanistan, around my nineteenth birthday, my curiosity about LSD overcame my qualms. A friend was able to find us some "purple micro-dot" (a small, usually potent pill), and we dropped the acid at my house early in the evening. Almost fifty years later, I still remember the night in vivid detail.

As we began to get off on the LSD—that is, to feel the mind- and pupil-dilating effects—we went down into the basement and started to play Ping-Pong. I was amazed at how *well* we were playing. It seemed almost impossible to miss the ball, which looked like it was moving in a series of stop-action photos, connected by blurry trails. I *felt* different, too. I could feel my body much more vividly: the warmth of my skin; the tension and aches of my muscles; the thickness of the air moving through my lungs; the raw pleasure of motion. To make things more interesting, we turned on a strobe, switched off the lights, and played Ping-Pong to the rapidly flashing light. Surprisingly, we performed just as well as before, and much better than usual, under those rather tricky conditions.

Eventually, the strobe effect began to get me off a bit too much—strobe lights can sometimes amplify the effects of psychedelics, I later learned—so I went upstairs to regroup. As I emerged into the sunroom, I noticed something strange about the ceiling light. It was one of those antique glass globes with multiple pyramidal projections, but normally it did not have red, yellow, and blue light streams circling around inside it! Even under other psychedelics, I was rarely prone to "visuals," so this took me by complete surprise; I felt like a new reality was opening up to me.

I wandered into the kitchen, where I saw my sister and a friend of hers talking. When they turned, I opened my mouth to tell them about what was happening to me—but nothing would come out. I guess there was so much feeling gushing through my body and so many ideas rushing through my mind that it was impossible to slow down enough to get hold of one thing to say. Or it could have been just the opposite: my mind completely stopped for a moment, which was so disconcerting for a thinker like me that I was stunned into silence. In any case, this frightened me in the same way that my mescaline experience had, where I felt I had lost connection between my mind and hands.

I was to learn later that the most frightening experiences often hold the most potential for learning, as they can push one beyond one's usual boundaries into the complete unknown. When these opportunities arise, it is especially important to have a safe environment and a supportive guide, so that the fear can be used to open doors rather than lock them shut. But being a psychedelic neophyte, I was freaked out by this disconnect between mind and mouth, so I fled back to the basement only to discover that my friends were gone. I ran up the other stairs and found the back door wide open, so I grabbed a jacket and ventured out into the cold winter evening.

The snowy night seemed magical. The falling flakes looked like stars moving through space; the snow glistened like tiny diamonds; the cold was sharply invigorating, unable to even slightly penetrate my newfound warmth. My friends were walking ahead towards the frozen lake, so I ran up from behind, my lungs unaware of cold or breath, and yelled just as I caught up with them. (I am not sure why I did that, except that I felt like surprising them—which I did!—and I felt incredibly full of excitement.) We continued out onto the lake, which is huge, and it seemed like I was suddenly out on the Arctic Ocean. We climbed onto an iceboat, and I could *feel* us sailing through ice-choked seas, the freezing wind in my face. It was like I had entered into another place and time; my imaginative powers must have been amplified uncannily.

I cannot begin to express how vivid and real this all felt. As many others have maintained, it is extremely difficult to convey the significance of psychedelic experiences. So much depends on intangible qualities such as heightened intensity and depth of feeling. Unless a new type of "object" or particularly vivid insight is encountered, most of the experience remains veiled in subjective qualities of awareness. I can say that I saw multicolored energy flows within the chandelier in our sunroom, or that the second hand on a clock slowed and finally stopped right before my eyes, or that I temporarily understood how a sine wave describes the fundamental structure of reality, but the felt importance and ramifications of these experiences remain elusive. This is, in part, because of a heightened sense of interconnectedness that causes each insight to reverberate throughout a much wider spectrum of ideas and memories—all of which is extremely difficult to recapture once one has come down from a trip, much less adequately convey to someone else.

Would it help to suggest that Olaf Stapledon's characterization of the universe as a "beautiful and terrible" place takes on a new concreteness and depth of meaning within the psychedelic experience? Seeing snowflakes floating like stars past the streetlights, hearing musical depths of harmonic contrast never before entertained, feeling an Oriental carpet become tactilely alive, perceiving directly how incense through scent and smoke induces religious states—all this amazing beauty and much more was revealed through psychedelics. Watching the sunrise after a night of tripping can be an almost painfully exquisite experience. Walking through the yard at dawn becomes a primordial exemplification of the sentiment expressed in Cat Stevens's "Morning Has Broken"—a walk through paradise.

And terror was now not simply about the evil of loss and isolation, much less any worldly threat, but the awe-full terror of encountering a universe much larger and more overwhelming than I could ever have anticipated—and of having the psyche flooded, engulfed, and swept away by these powerful feelings. Here, then, was my *cosmological* shock.

If my father's death shocked me out of my childlike sense of personal security and safety, then psychedelic experiences shattered my sense of intellectual complacency and emotional security based upon a hyperrational and rigid understanding of what the world was really about. Death had roused me from my "dogmatic slumber," but it also made me hold all the more dearly onto those egoic tranquilizers I still had at my disposal: intellectualization, repression, and mood-altering substances. Psychedelics jolted me out my desire, and my ability, to continue to doze in this egoic cocoon.

Up until my first full psychedelic trip, I was a skeptic like Dr. Holden, the cautious parapsychologist in the film *Night of the Demon* (my favorite movie about paranormal investigation), who must come to terms with the fact that the universe is far vaster and more mysterious than his rational mind had suspected. Like Holden, I was forced to take seriously the opinion of his Irish colleague, Professor O'Brien: "I am a scientist also, Dr. Holden. I know the value of the cold light of reason. But I also know the deep shadows that light can cast, the shadows that can blind men to the truth."[6]

My shift in thinking, from seeing drugs as merely altering reality to realizing that they may actually open *expanded access* to a larger reality, bears

6. Tourneur, dir., *Night of the Demon*.

directly on why Stanislav Grof prefers to use the term *nonordinary* rather than *altered* to describe states of consciousness. The term *altered* assumes implicitly that our usual, everyday perception of the world is normal (in the sense of being a yardstick for what is real). Anything that deviates significantly from that norm must be an error, delusion, illusion, or hallucination. *Nonordinary* is a more neutral term that allows for the possibility that such experiences may reveal new aspects of reality, or may allow us a deeper appreciation of the reality that we already know. In other words, nonordinary states can provide an *extra*ordinary view of reality.

At the beginning of my psychedelic experimentation, however, I was still uncertain about how seriously to take these radically new experiences. Particularly unsettling was the embryonic feeling that there was something very important lurking just below the threshold of consciousness that psychedelics were beginning to tap into. More eerily, I sensed there was something *driving* me towards whatever was waiting there. I finally asked my early tripping partner—who was a little more experienced and a lot more fearless with psychedelics—if he did not think that there was *something more* going on here than merely getting really high. "No," he said, rather emphatically. Actually, his reply was a great relief, because that *something more* also felt threatening in an uncanny sort of way. I was happy to feel free to focus primarily on the more manageable aspects of psychedelic experience, such as enhanced sensory perceptions, altered ideation, novel interpretations of reality, and the odd and surprising ways events unfolded and interacted.

Shortly after my first forays into LSD, an old friend appeared at my door with a special treat. Having discovered a new drug of interest, Chip had purchased a small supply and hitchhiked back to Neenah from his college in Eau Clare in order to turn me on. Although we were never really sure what was inside those large pink and white capsules (THC supposedly, a mixture of MDA and other psychedelics more likely), we spent the next three days flying high. As this was my first major drug run, by the third day I was pretty strung out. That afternoon, I remember listening anxiously to a song titled "DOA" (dead on arrival) and then to Ten Years After singing "Over the Hill" and "Hard Monkeys"—songs about the highly relevant topics of overdosing, addiction, and wanting to get clean. For a disturbing and frightening moment, I could see very clearly the troubled road I was heading down. But, as usual, the most I could muster was to take a short break from getting high before resuming my inexorable journey into regions unknown.

I was still torn between the feeling that there was something more *deep down* awaiting discovery—something even more than the multitude of psychological and spiritual insights that regularly offered themselves under psychedelics—and the desire to carelessly enjoy the amazing *outer* adventures that always materialized. Typically, a trip consisted of both: first, an initial period of "getting off" where I would isolate myself, often on the living room couch in the dark, and listen to music while I felt like I was losing my mind, dying, or being reborn—or perhaps all three. Then, after a certain threshold was reached or breached, I would slip more or less comfortably into a new psychedelic state of awareness and rejoin my friends to embark on some shared adventure.

For example, I remember listening to side one of Emerson, Lake, and Palmer's first album, while curled up on the couch trying to hold on to some part of my mind—letting go of ego control is never easy. First came the mind-blasting "Barbarian," then the monumental "Take a Pebble," whose lyrics seemed to mimic or generate the ongoing dissolution of my habitual psychic structures. The album side culminates with "Knife-edge," which ends with the music artificially slowing down to a dramatic standstill—and my mind and body, in vibratory lockstep, went sliding along with it into nothingness. *My* "knife-edge" with psychedelics was that terrifyingly fine line between maximal openness to the creative possibilities and shocking freedom of each new moment, and of being completely swallowed up by an uncontrollable flood of unconscious feeling.

I had to get out of there—wherever this "there" was. So, as soon as I returned from the abyss, I leapt off the couch and went into the sunroom, where it turned out my friends had just decided to go to the local YMCA dance. The next thing I knew, I was listening astonished to three lead guitarists blowing my mind in the dark at this silly little dance. Then, I found myself flirting with a cute girl who somehow could tell I was tripping merely by observing that my pupils were dilated to the size of dimes. This was typical of how things often unfolded: I would go inside myself until I freaked out, and then I would shift back to the outer world to escape into a (relatively) familiar landscape, thereby distracting myself from the overwhelming forces within.

An intense episode of Boris Karloff's *Thriller* series, which I saw when I was very young, captures beautifully this issue of deep inner exploration versus turning these powers out into the world. "The Cheaters" starts off in an attic workshop with a man examining a pair of eyeglasses. He rises and moves in front of a standing mirror and carefully puts them on. As he stares into the mirror, he begins to scream. The rest of the show follows the glasses as, by chance, they pass from hand to hand, resulting in the violent death of whoever comes into their possession. What makes them so dangerous, it turns out, is that wearing the glasses grants the power to know what others are really thinking. The first person who comes into their possession, a junkman, discovers that his wife is having an affair with their handyman. He can hear their thoughts: they hold the junkman in complete contempt and are planning his imminent murder. Fearful and enraged, he attacks them both with a crowbar. When immediately confronted by a mailman, who has overheard the attack, the junkman lunges in his direction shouting, "the cheaters!" The mailman is forced to gun him down.[7]

The glasses finally come into the possession of a writer who has been investigating their history for a book that he hopes will revive his floundering career. The writer tells his wife that they were misused by the other people who had briefly owned them; the glasses were not invented to read minds, but rather to look into one's *own* mind. The junkman killed his wife and her lover before grasping the danger inherent in knowing the thoughts of others. When he tried to destroy the glasses—which he called by their colloquial name, "cheaters"—the mailman shot him, believing he was coming after *him* with the crowbar, when in reality the junkman was trying to destroy the glasses.

In preparation for the final chapter of his book, the author takes his wife to the house where the inventor lived so he can re-create the original experiment. His wife asks what happened to the inventor after he tried on the glasses. To her horror, her husband explains that the inventor hung himself in the backyard. The final scene shows the wife pounding on the locked attic door, begging her husband to stop, as the writer puts on the glasses and stares with terror and revulsion at his image in the mirror, which slowly turns into the cruel, selfish, ugly monster that he really is inside. (Hopefully, this last part of the analogy has a happier ending when actual psychedelics are involved. Even though psychedelics did reveal highly distressing parts of myself and my past, I was in turn opened up to equally beautiful revelations and possibilities.)

Like these fictional glasses, psychedelics are most effectively used as tools for looking *within*. When we gaze into the outer world instead, we invite problematic projections and dangerous misunderstandings. More importantly, we miss an incredible opportunity for inner healing, self-exploration, and spiritual adventure. This is what I meant earlier about using psychedelics in a sacred context: for inner spiritual work. Continuing the *Thriller* analogy, if the writer had had spiritual guidance, he might have been able to stay with the experience of a (terrifyingly) heightened perception of his past sins and ego flaws and to move more deeply into the psychological structures behind them. Then perhaps the spiritual depths that had been previously obscured would have opened up, revealing a path to transformation and redemption.

---

7. Brahm, dir., "Cheaters."

I do not mean to imply that there is no place in the psychedelic experience for such things as a deep appreciation of the beauty of music, nature, and human relationships. These are appropriate and almost unavoidable dimensions of tripping, for there is much to be revealed about our perception, understanding, and appreciation of the world. But these extraordinary experiences of the world should not distract or deter us from the remarkable opportunity for inner exploration and growth that psychedelics hold.

What Is Reality?

What propelled me more strongly in the direction of this *inner* journey was finding my future tripping partners, Alex and Pat, on my back doorstep one early spring afternoon. They had both gone to high school with me, but I had not known either of them well, so their sudden appearance in my life was rather surprising. Still, I was quite accepting of mystery back then, so I went with the flow. Soon we were hanging out together a lot. We quickly formed that kind of deep bond that shared psychedelic experiences sometimes generate: one night tripping can seem like an endless Dantean journey through heaven and hell. We shared many such psychedelic adventures over the next six months.

Soon after this first encounter, Alex and I drove out to my family's country club for some drinks and conversation. We sat out on the terrace by the pool overlooking Lake Winnebago and contemplated life over some Harvey Wallbangers. Alex had grown up in New Jersey, so he was way ahead of most of us Midwesterners in the cultural scene. As the warm, mellowing influence of the Wallbangers took hold, I spoke hesitantly about my intuitions of there being *something more* to discover from psychedelics. Alex was not only right with me on this; he had done some serious thinking and reading about such deeper possibilities. I was thrilled to have found a fellow adventurer for a journey to the center of the mind. We soon found ourselves embarked on a psychedelic search into the meaning and nature of reality; we'd started on an "Amazing Journey."[8] I found myself reading Ram Dass's *Be Here Now*, and *The Psychedelic Experience* (Leary, Alpert, and Metzner's psychedelic rendering of the *Tibetan Book of the Dead*), and listening endlessly to the wonderfully eccentric cultural parodies on the albums from Firesign Theatre.

Firesign's album title *Everything You Know Is Wrong* humorously captures a certain state of awareness where the mind is highly receptive to new possibilities because the habitual defining structural patterns of the psyche

8. The Who, "Amazing Journey."

are temporarily released or diminished. In my case at least, these patterns were released with a combination of joy, horror, surprise, awe, and humiliation (in various measures) in discovering that my old ways of knowing and feeling mostly hindered me from actually seeing and knowing things the way they really are. Consider the impact of Thomas Aquinas's powerful mystical revelation near the end of his life. In its aftermath, Thomas said that everything he had previously known or written was mere chaff—this from a man whose writings were among the most influential of the Middle Ages. And he meant it: Thomas never wrote another word.

Until the first time I took LSD, I had considered my previous drug experiences to be exciting, freeing, and sometimes scary *alterations* of reality. Alcohol made me more relaxed, a little wild, and reduced my anxiety around social interactions like dancing and dating. Pot changed things a bit more, making the world appear somehow different or enhanced, especially my perceptions of music, food, nature, and people. But through all these alterations, I felt like I was just modifying or shifting my feelings, thoughts, and perceptions about the *same basic reality* that I had always known. LSD forced me to radically reexamine all my notions of *what reality really is*.

If alcohol provided a major *epistemological* surprise, then my LSD experiences constituted a full blown *metaphysical* and *cosmological shock*. My basic (metaphysical) assumptions about the nature of reality, and my (cosmological) assumptions about the structure of the universe were suddenly up for grabs. Even more threatening, my fundamental sense of identity was shaken at its deepest foundations, dramatically captured by the lyrics from "Knife-edge" by Emerson, Lake & Palmer. I found myself poised on that *knife-edge* between wildly novel feelings within me and a wildly shifting, new world without. And even the distinction between inside and outside could seem as nebulous as the lyrics from Yes's song "Perpetual Change" portray it.

These early psychedelic experiences engendered a new set of questions and problems: How are body, mind, and world related? Where do perception and imagination begin and end? What is consciousness? What are spirituality and religious experience really about? And how could these new experiences be meaningfully reconciled and integrated with my previous scientific, rational worldview, and with everyday life? It would take me over ten years to begin to discover a satisfying solution to this last question.

Somewhere during that mystical spring before heading off to college, I had the consequential moment of psychedelic insight described at the beginning of Chapter 1. While trying to grasp hold of the essence of the psychedelic state of consciousness, I suddenly *saw* that this type of awareness could be envisioned as the intersection of philosophy, psychology, and religion. I realize now that it was at this moment that my full interdisciplinary tendencies—as well as my central areas of interest—took root so strongly that even my doctoral-degree specialization would be interdisciplinary in nature, bringing together psychology, philosophy, and religion, naturally. For the rest of my academic career, I investigated these questions from a broad-based perspective, looking into whatever area seemed to hold most promise for shedding light on the depth experiences that arise out of nonordinary states of awareness. And it was the remembrance of this interdisciplinary project that served as a touchstone for my journey into sobriety. However, it would take a number of further psychedelic experiences—along with some other pivotal events—before I reached *that* jumping off point.

3

What Was I Thinking?

In the previous chapter, I related several key life events involving psychological crises that raised some serious questions. Starting in the next chapter, I try to show exactly how transpersonal psychology and process thought offer workable solutions to these questions and for many other important issues too.

This chapter reviews the most influential concepts and theories I investigated before finally settling on Grof's psychology and Whitehead's philosophy as the most useful approaches for understanding psychedelic experiences, as well as for making sense of our lives and the world at large. By examining what theories *almost* worked, and the ways they did not, I hope to highlight what I find so uniquely valuable about Whitehead's and Grof's ideas. After tracing the evolution of my thinking, I give a brief introduction to Whitehead's and Grof's theories in order to pave the way for the more in-depth discussions ahead.

This account intersects with a pivotal nonacademic event without which I would never have completed this journey of ideas, namely, being granted the gift of long-term sobriety.

What Almost Worked

Even before embarking on my formal higher education, I was looking to the academy for some snappy answers to these pressing questions. In the summer of 1972—inspired by my recent psychedelic insights—I signed up for an introductory course in philosophy and one on behaviorism at a nearby community college (unfortunately, the introduction to psychology class was at the same time as philosophy). It became readily apparent that behaviorism was not going to be very helpful for trying to make sense of my drug experiences or my other questions, although I did find reinforcement theory interesting—and more personally relevant than I realized at the time. A strict behaviorist approach, which deliberately ignores all internal mental phenomena, was the exact opposite of what I needed in order to investigate the full range of human experience.

It is not entirely surprising, then, that I ended up taking LSD the night before the behaviorism final exam, then blowing it off to hang out with my soon-to-be girlfriend in the school library where she worked. This episode might have served as a warning for how difficult it would be to combine academic study with frequent psychedelic explorations. Psychedelics are wonderful for opening up the mind and spirit. But especially when combined with other drugs and alcohol, they tend to make serious intellectual work problematic, to put it mildly. This mixture led me to drop out of undergraduate school eight times in eight years, before I finally got sober for the first time. Despite these repeated setbacks, a deep-seated drive to find some satisfactory answers to those pressing questions kept bringing me back to my formal studies.

My introduction-to-philosophy class was certainly more intriguing than behaviorism, but in comparison to the questions and ideas being raised by my psychedelic sessions, the discussions struck me as tame and simplistic. This may have been partly due to our teacher, who believed in some sort of scientistic philosophy. At the final class, he shared his favorite theory, which (if memory can be trusted) was that the only valid philosophical questions are those that science could, hypothetically, one day prove to be true or false. Since the *opposite* view—that philosophy should be most concerned with questions that science *cannot* adequately address—seems like more interesting territory for philosophical speculation, readers might be inclined to think that my memory had reversed his position. However, my recollection is supported by the example he gave: that life after death is a meaningless question for philosophy since it can never be proven true or false by science. Setting aside the question of whether the *most* interesting philosophical questions might be precisely those that are *not* decidable purely on scientific evidence, I felt compelled to take issue with his example simply on empirical grounds. I pointed out that in a hundred years from now a new "radio" might be invented that employs frequencies that allow us to communicate with the dead. After speaking with departed friends and relatives for years, a general consensus on the reality of life after death would certainly begin to emerge. The professor responded that such a machine was impossible, which seemed to me to be begging the question, not to mention highlighting a critical flaw in his approach.

In retrospect, both classes turned out to be quite valuable by indicating to me early on that a strictly scientific approach to psychology or philosophy would prove inadequate for answering the most difficult questions about the nature of human experience and expanded consciousness in a thorough and meaningful way. Nonetheless, I remained a rational empiricist in the broadest sense throughout my studies—seeking coherent, logical ways of accounting for all human experience, including the scientific realm.

I will not recount the full array of theories and ideas I entertained over my college years, given that they spanned nine years of undergraduate school alone! Instead, I will focus on the concepts and thinkers I found most relevant to my search. My intent is to convey how this wide range of ideas influenced my thinking, and why I ultimately found Whitehead and Grof's theories to be most valuable.

The New College Experiment

The next fall I started undergraduate studies at New College, a private three-year experimental school in Florida. And experimental it was: socially, intellectually, academically, and, especially for me, in the realm of consciousness. Part of the campus had been designed by I. M. Pei in a style that seemed very modern yet somehow also ancient. Across Highway 41, the rest of the campus lay on the grounds of the former estate of John Ringling's brother and sister, positioned between Ringling's Italianate mansion on the one side and the Ringling Circus Museum on the other. It was a weird and wonderful place, highly conducive to nonordinary experiences and populated with nonordinary people.

At New College I began to search in earnest for theories and systems of ideas capable of incorporating and interpreting the flood of ideas and insights that were coming my way both from my own experience and via the exploding cultural scene of the early 1970s. I looked most closely at cognitive and developmental psychology, the writings of Carl Jung, the psychology of dreams, and Buddhist thought—which I believed to be the most promising leads. Ironically, my first New College advisor, Douglas Berggren, was a philosopher who, as I learned much later, actually taught a class on Whitehead. But in retrospect I see that it was important for me to explore many things that did not quite work before I could fully appreciate what ultimately worked really well.

One of my first classes was with Ann Faraday, who had recently published *Dream Power*. Her multiperspective approach to dream interpretation deftly illustrated how things may have multiple meanings and causes—symbols in particular. More significantly, her theory gave me an initial sense of how conscious experience might arise out of a combination of past events ("day residue"), older memory patterns, and unconscious feeling, all creatively synthesized into meaningful symbols. This, in fact, is quite close to Whitehead's interpretation of experience in general, though I would not have been able to clearly articulate any of this at the time.

Developmental psychology also offered important insights into the unfolding and functioning of the mind. The theories of Jean Piaget (1896–1980) gave a picture of evolving mental structures or processes that grow in complexity through their interaction with the environment. My ventures into cognitive psychology also pointed to mental processes of great complexity and fluidity, but which were still only understood at a very basic level. While both developmental and cognitive psychology provided important clues about the general nature of mental activity, they had little to say about the dynamic processes of the *personal* unconscious. The overall scope of these fields was too narrowly limited—especially in light of my concerns about the meaning of altered states of consciousness.

Carl Jung, on the other hand, had much to say about the personal unconscious, and the collective as well. His prototypic example of plumbing one's personal depths to discover collective truths was, and still is, inspiring to me. Like many others, I was captivated by Jung's colorful and vivid descriptions of the psyche's inner landscape. And his more transpersonal notions of the archetypes and the collective unconscious as repositories of the symbolic and spiritual depths of the mind resonated with much of my psychedelic experience and helped validate the importance of the spiritual quest.

The same could be said of Eastern philosophy and religion, which addressed spirit and soul with a similar exquisite sophistication. I was particularly taken with Buddhism—I was reading *Three Pillars of Zen* my first term[1]—which seemed to offer the most straightforward path towards enlightenment. Also very important was Buddhism's superb analysis of the essence of momentary awareness as sheer becoming, and the Hindu philosophers' brilliant expositions on the ultimate nature of God and Cosmos. Their critique of ego delusion/illusion seemed in line with my psychedelic insights, but it also produced a quandary: how was I to work on dissolving my ego while also continuing my intellectual pursuits? This raised the more general question of the comparative merits of intellectual insight and knowledge versus direct intuitive understanding, a question largely resolved by my eventual realization that both are important and both have their place.

At the same time, Eastern thought often seemed obscure or opaque and ultimately incompatible with much of modern science and a rational understanding of the world. While we must learn from the past, we cannot

---

1. See Kapleau, ed., *Three Pillars of Zen.*

turn back the clock. Similarly, Jung's theoretical attempts to connect the individual psyche to the larger universe at times lacked coherence and veered off towards the mystical, in a problematic sense. Such crucial problems deserve as much clarity as possible.

It would be disingenuous not to mention my own limitations in the world of science, especially during a time when I was running so many chemistry experiments on myself! It became apparent that I was not cut out for hard scientific research when my rat escaped temporarily during one of its training sessions for my experimental psychology class. Recaptured after a forty-minute chase through the lab—an escapade I decided would be best kept between my lab partner, me, and the rat—my professor was later perplexed and chagrined that our rat was the only subject to demonstrate a zero learning curve. The poor rat may have been following all too closely in my footsteps; in my cognitive psychology class where I was a subject in a facial recognition experiment, I too scored at chance level. To be fair, I believe my poor performance was in part due to some native cognitive deficits, likely exacerbated by being high on something during the test.

These fiascos remind me of another at New College. This one occurred during the final exam for my philosophy of psychology class, which included the question: What comes first, philosophy of psychology or the psychology of philosophy? The day before the exam, I stayed up all night on speed trying to study. The following morning, I was largely incapable of thought or speech, a state hardly conducive for a one-on-one oral exam with my professor. Dr. Norton generously allowed me to substitute a take-home for my botched oral. Then a friend kindly offered to type up my answers and ended up helping with the writing as well. He took the approach my professor—who was a philosopher—was looking for: philosophy must come first since it defines the basic terms and articulates the presuppositions that will form the foundation for the scientific enterprise. While I thought all this was true enough at that time, and still do today, I also thought that psychology should come first in some important regards. First, the unconscious psychological orientation of the philosopher inclines him or her to certain biases and assumptions that deeply influence the shape of the philosophical system. (Jung and William James have made intriguing analyses of certain philosophers using this stratagem.) Second, the *conscious* psychological decisions and preferences of a philosopher are important for the same reasons, although less so as they are usually more out in the open. Third, and most importantly—as the Buddhists, Descartes, the phenomenologists, and Whitehead all have argued—the primary evidence for philosophy is to be found in human experience itself, the only part of reality with which we have direct, intimate contact. Thus psychology, understood as our own direct experience, becomes the necessary starting point of philosophical analysis.

These academic blunders and other drug-related misadventures motivated me to investigate alternative means of accessing "altered" states of consciousness: biofeedback, meditation, sensory deprivation tanks, Sufi whirling, and hypnosis were just some of the approaches I tried out. While I still relied heavily on drugs for my explorations, this approach of different *modes of access* to altered states seemed especially important. I also turned to various more or less contemporary writers for guidance in these regards, including John Lilly, Carlos Castaneda, Herman Hesse, Aldous Huxley, and Jean Houston.

Jean was about as close as I ever got to having a guru, inspiring me with her storehouse of fascinating ideas and stories combined with an unsurpassed intellectual fervor. *The Varieties of Psychedelic Experience,* written with her husband, Robert Masters, was the first academic work I encountered about nonordinary states, and it immediately taught me to appreciate the interdisciplinary approach they brought to the subject. I also was struck by their later book, *Mind Games,* which had a series of psychedelic-like explorations initiated through trance induction and guided imagery. Unfortunately, I was quite resistant to this particular mode of access, even when I very much wanted to "go under" and open up to these experiences. The shift into a nonordinary state could be a difficult process for me; even with psychedelics, it was often a painful and arduous transition. My suddenly heightened awareness of bodily tensions and energies along with the ambiguous emergence of powerful emotions and images was not welcomed gladly by my ego. (I can relate to the agonizing resistance Mr. Spock goes through when first infected by the "psychedelic" spores in the *Star Trek* episode "This Side of Paradise.")

I started studying seriously with Jean through her workshop intensives, which exposed me to an incredible array of ideas in psychology, philosophy, history, mythology, and religion. Her dramatic renditions of the speculations of Arnold Toynbee, Joseph Campbell, Gerald Heard, and Pierre Teilhard de Chardin provided an initiation into the history and evolution of human consciousness and spirit. Jean also introduced me to the writings of Olaf Stapledon and perhaps even Whitehead. Importantly, she put great emphasis on the psychophysical as well—for example, Feldenkrais Method, Alexander Technique, and neo-Reichian approaches—providing a badly needed grounding to my search, my body, and my psyche. Jean's primary aim, however, centered on creating a new guiding Myth or Story for our civilization, while mine at that time was more directed to understanding the workings and depths of the human psyche.

On, Wisconsin!

After five years at New College, I transferred to the University of Wisconsin–Green Bay, another school that had arisen out of the energy of the 1960s. Here I deepened my investigations in neurophysiology, personality and psychoanalytic theory, and clinical psychology. Philosophy likewise became a more serious subject of study. I was especially drawn to the Continental thought of Kant, Husserl, and the phenomenological tradition. At Green Bay, I was also introduced to a broader cultural-historical perspective, including Kuhn's ideas on paradigms and Marcuse's on repression and civilization.

Although I found Kant a difficult subject for my first deep encounter with philosophy, I dug in and became intrigued by his notion of human conscious experience as the product of the unconscious Mind's categorical organization of Reality. And despite his eventual rejection of the project of metaphysics, Kant's philosophy opened my mind to the possibilities of a broad systematic attempt to understand the character of reality, mind, and nature. However, Kant's radical disjunction between noumena and phenomena—between things as they are in themselves and our experience of them— struck even my philosophically naive mind as highly problematic. Once the universe is fundamentally rent asunder, all attempts to put Humpty Dumpty back together again become palliative at best.

Phenomenology's corrective for Kant's bifurcation of reality—namely, a radical "return to experience" as the primary source of philosophical evidence—struck me as very promising, as did its agenda to describe the fundamental structures and activities of phenomena as they arise in consciousness. After my encounters with systems that discounted experience in one way or another—such as behaviorism and the neural reductionist theories of that time—it was refreshing to find a theory that not only took experience seriously but also made it the primary focus and method of study. Phenomenology's emphasis on a type of introspection to investigate the nature and structures of consciousness was in some ways reminiscent of the Buddhist meditative technique of simply observing the flow of experience, although with different explicit goals. Ultimately, I found Husserl's—as well as much of the rest of phenomenology's—focus on "consciousness" too narrow. Also, its purely descriptive methodology proved too self-contained for my purposes, as it made it difficult to connect the phenomenological project to any broader scientific concerns or to develop the kind of large-scale synthesis I was looking for.

I was quite drawn to neurophysiology and neurology, which are of course foundational to psychology in a most basic sense. These subjects helped me more fully appreciate the astonishing complexity of the microscopic world, especially the intricate structures and entities that constitute the human nervous system. Consequently, I started to think more seriously about the central role that must be assigned to the organismic nature of things. As a primary substrate of human experience, any final synthesis must find a fundamental place for the cellular transmission of neural impulses and the even more complex activity occurring in the brain's neurons and processing centers. How was I to connect the disparate efforts of neuroscience and phenomenology, both of which seemed to be describing vital dimensions of human experience and of reality?

Regrettably, I have found that neuroscience's efforts have been unnecessarily limited in scope by a generally reductive methodology. How much can we really learn about the full range of human experience by observing what part of the brain lights up during a neurological scan, no matter how sophisticated the technology? This kind of reductive approach is partly natural to this field of inquiry and partly due to an overreliance on an outdated materialistic understanding of the human organism, to which I think Whitehead's philosophy of organism can provide a decisive alternative.

Although perhaps unwelcome to some, I must believe that this corrective would be well received by many neuroscientists. The contemporary understanding of cellular functioning seems much more amenable to a *process* view of cells and molecules as organic pulsations that feel and synthesize their internal and external environments. As for the higher psychological functions, a materialist neuropsychology can at best describe the primitive neural activity that informs the more complex syntheses occurring in the higher phases of experience, remaining mute on any possible downward causation from the psyche as well as on the psyche's own complex activities. But I am getting ahead of myself.

At Green Bay, I also encountered humanistic and transpersonal psychology. I greatly admired the vigorous attempts in these disciplines to deepen the field of psychology and draw on concepts and practices from Eastern and Western philosophy and mysticism. Broadening and softening the notion of scientific objectivity made a great deal of sense to me—after all, psychology is dealing primarily with human *subjects*. Humanistic and transpersonal psychology seemed to be struggling with many of the same paradigm questions that I was finding so challenging.

Down to Georgia

Having finally completed my undergraduate degree, I moved to Georgia to attend an unusual master's program that Jean Houston had recommended to me. My studies at West Georgia College, in a program specializing in humanistic and transpersonal psychology, naturally involved a wide range of humanistic psychology classes. I also continued my research into Continental philosophy, including courses in hermeneutics, Heidegger, Ricoeur, and Merleau-Ponty. Furthermore, at West Georgia I had the opportunity to take a more systematic look at Eastern religions and philosophies, as well as Jung and clinical neuropsychology.

As my studies progressed, various theoretical systems appeared quite promising for a time, but none of them seemed capable of putting it all together. Phenomenology, with its focus on conscious experience, still appeared unable to reach very far beyond this starting point—especially in regard to other dimensions of reality as they exist for themselves—or to break out of the hermeneutic circle arising from its preferred methodology of self-consciousness reflection. Merleau-Ponty seemed to be on the right track with his expansion into the phenomenology of the bodily unconscious, but phenomenology as a whole was still too academically isolated from the mainstream because of its methodology. I loved Heidegger's analysis of the nature and meaning of human existence and Ricouer's and Cassirer's insightful theories on the fundamental role of symbolism in human experience and culture. But the problem remained: how to connect their humanistic insights to the nonhuman world and the scientific project at large. And, unfortunately, Eastern religion and Eastern philosophy are simply not designed for, nor fully capable of, a deep interface with Western science, if left simply to their own theoretical resources.

At West Georgia, I became more deeply immersed in transpersonal psychology. This field was definitely most closely allied to my own quest, given its fascination with higher dimensions of experience, an expanded way of envisioning the scientific endeavor, and the attendant philosophical and religious questions. Here I discovered many like-minded thinkers such as Alan Watts (1915–1973), Abraham Maslow (1908–1970), Charles Tart (b. 1937), Stanislav Grof, and Ken Wilber (b. 1949), whose interests in these matters very closely paralleled my own. They too were attempting to understand the origin and meaning of transpersonal experiences by drawing on a wide array of philosophical, psychological, religious, and scientific theories.

But even the most comprehensive of their theoretical models—for example, those of Grof and Wilber—did not fully address all of my concerns. Grof's excellent psychology and cosmology seemed to lack the adequate metaphysical concepts necessary to deeply explicate the nature of the self and its mode of access to the world and to act as a basis for an interdisciplinary synthesis. While Grof did not neglect these issues, I thought his approach relied too heavily on some problematic concepts borrowed from Eastern thought, even when he connected these concepts with some promising ideas emerging in contemporary science: for example, holography.

As in much of New Age thought, the attempt to apply scientific metaphors to philosophic categories usually fails to do justice to the inherent complexities of either, while efforts to correlate modern theories and ancient Eastern insights usually result in construals of Eastern insights through scientific and philosophic categories for which they are inadequate or unsuitable. A similar general criticism might apply to Ken Wilber's writing, even though his efforts to create a grand philosophical synthesis showed impressive and far-reaching scholarship. While I greatly admired his work, I could not help thinking that something vital was missing from his metaphysical analysis, a lack reflected in various inconsistencies in his elaborate "theory of everything" and in a frustrating tendency to retreat behind the clouds of ineffability.[2]

Despite being exposed over the years to many inspiring subjects of study, I was not taken with every theoretical system that I encountered. I felt less affinity for structuralism, with its heavy focus on abstract relationships that tended to overshadow the importance of subjective experience and organic feeling. Likewise for analytic philosophy, whose painstaking analysis of language and unremitting clarity of statement seemed foreign to my interests. Nor was I strongly attracted to those kinds of postmodern thought that focus primarily on the *deconstruction* of human culture, rather than seeking a systematic way of accounting for the full range and character of human experience, especially as lived and felt. Psychedelics and my father's death had already taken things apart more than sufficiently; now I was looking for a new and vital way to put everything *back together*.

I am well aware that my cursory objections to so many major systems of thought may sound rather arbitrary and high-handed, especially to those who have found much merit in them. And I believe there is great value in most things, just as in most people, once you really get to know them. My critical comments in this chapter are not to disparage any of these theories—on the contrary, I found many of them to be among the most interesting and promising. My aim here is mainly to point out where

___

2. For more on my critique of Wilber's metaphysics, see Buchanan, "Whitehead and Wilber."

they were unable to fully address the key parameters and goals of my particular search.

Finally, I must add that while I am most enthusiastic about the possibilities offered by Grof and Whitehead's work, I still think of myself as a cognitive psychologist, a Jungian, a phenomenologist, a neo-Reichian, a Jamesian, and even a Stapledonian (if there is such a word). I have not left behind my admiration and gratitude for all that I have studied along the way, but I will focus here on those ideas that I have found most useful for answering my big questions about life and reality.

Fortunately for me, my advisor at West Georgia College was friends with an Emory University professor who taught in their Graduate Institute of the Liberal Arts. Mike Arons had sent a number of his graduates into Emory's rather unconventional PhD program, which turned out to be a perfect fit for my interdisciplinary interests. It was here that I had the good fortune to be introduced to process thought by one of Whitehead's own students, William Beardslee.

Emory—and Whitehead

The interdisciplinary department at Emory University, the Graduate Institute of the Liberal Arts, was located at the time in what was known as the Physics Building, along with the Department of Religion, oddly enough. A more concrete metaphor for my quest would be difficult to find: if only I could similarly discover a way to *intellectually house* physics, religion, and the many fields that lie in between them within a single structure! Then I would have the kind of unified picture of the universe and human experience necessary to integrate everything from my commitment to science and rationality to my interests in the most far-reaching transpersonal dimensions.

During my doctoral work at Emory I continued to investigate depth psychology and the psychoanalytic tradition, as well as taking assorted courses in mythology, symbolic anthropology, and literary theory—always searching for the missing piece to the puzzle. But I continued to be confronted by the now familiar shortcomings: post-Freudian psychoanalysis remained too limited in range and overly reductive; symbolic anthropology and mythology were (understandably) concentrated mostly on the human world and seemed to have little direct connection to the natural sciences. My search seemed so fruitless that while studying literary theory, I was sorely tempted to retreat into the arts and interpretation—and might actually have done so if I had demonstrated any significant artistic ability.

Then in my second semester at Emory, I made a remarkable discovery. My advisor suggested I might want to take advantage of a last opportunity to study with William Beardslee, an expert in Whiteheadian thought, who was retiring at the end of the year. As I spent the semester with Beardslee poring over the writings of Whitehead, and process philosophy and theology more generally, I came to realize, "This is exactly the approach I have been searching for all these years!" In Whitehead, I had found a rational, systematic way to make sense of the full range of human experience from the mundane to the transcendent: a set of fundamental ideas able to incorporate the theories of science, yet in tune with humanity's basic intuitions about everyday life, religion, and nature.

I was amazed to find a system that put *feeling* at the heart of reality, in the form of a momentary experiential event. And importantly for my psychological interests, these pulses of actuality were subtly interconnected through their "intuitions" of past events. I quickly saw that this provided a way of understanding how things are all connected yet have their own individual existence too. As I delved more deeply, I found that Whitehead's "speculative philosophy" allowed me to coherently think through such diverse issues as quantum theory, mystical experience, human perception, and mind-body interaction. This was all possible without reducing mind to matter, quantum reality to conscious observation, the universe to consciousness, or consciousness to neural activity. Whitehead's metaphysics showed how all these facets of the world can have their own actuality *and* be seamlessly interconnected within a rationally coherent picture of the universe. It was like stumbling upon a workable Unified Field Theory that includes human experience as an integral part of the field.

Perhaps the most remarkable thing was that I was actually able to absorb *any* of this at all. By that point, I had been slowly relapsing on Valium and codeine and pot for several years—having gotten sober shortly before my final year in Green Bay—and my concentration and memory were faltering. That summer I took some flying lessons but was unable to continue because it would take me most of the hour just to inspect the plane! Apparently, though, my interest in Whitehead's philosophy was so intense that in spite of this cognitive impairment I was able to absorb many of his ideas and establish a solid foundation in process thought. This was not easy—but being introduced to Whitehead's innovative philosophy rarely is.

A New Beginning

The full impact of my relapse caught up with me early in the fall. On my way to meet a professor for lunch to inform him I was withdrawing from school, I veered off the road, hit a bulldozer, and totaled my car—an accident that just might have been related to my having been up the entire night before doing drugs. Through a harrowing yet fortuitous set of circumstances, I found myself several months later in treatment at the Betty Ford Center near Palm Springs, California. This turned out to be an enormous blessing—in more ways than one. Besides saving my life and ushering me into sobriety, spending time in Southern California provided me with two other life-changing opportunities: first, an opportunity to continue my involvement with Whiteheadian thought and, second, the chance to study with Stan and Christina Grof. Thus, via the Betty Ford Center, I became deeply involved with three spiritually oriented communities, which together have provided secure homes for my recovery, my intellectual interests, and my transpersonal yearnings.

In the spirit of giving credit where credit is due and avoiding placing blame where is it not warranted, I want to acknowledge that it was my mother who at a critical moment suggested that I might consider going to the Betty Ford Center. Although it had been in operation for only two years, my mother was familiar with the center because her second husband had been closely involved with its inception. At one point when she was participating in the family program as part of my treatment, my mother was asked about the negative effects of my drinking. All she came up with was that sometimes I became too friendly with waiters and waitresses! Although my family knew that something was seriously wrong in my life, I did my best to keep them in the dark about the darker aspects of my addiction. When they offered help or tried to intervene, I would deflect and reject as only an addict can. Thus my newly found excitement and honest relief at my mother's offer to contact the center revealed a momentous change in my psychological outlook.

Following six weeks of both inpatient and outpatient treatment, I elected to stay on in California while I got my sobriety legs. After about six months in the desert, I "came to" and remembered that the Center for Process Studies, a Whiteheadian research and archival center, was located about an hour and a half west of Palm Springs at the Claremont School of Theology. Moreover, this was where my Whiteheadian teacher from Emory had retired to head up their Process and Faith program. The next fall and spring, I found myself doing off-campus study at Claremont, including courses on Whitehead and William James taught by David Ray Griffin, an outstanding expert in the field.

Similarly, one day out of the blue, it occurred to me that I had heard that Stan Grof, one of the top transpersonal psychologists in the world, was living and teaching at Esalen Institute on the Big Sur coast of Northern California. Grof's research and theory-building represented to my thinking the best synthesis of the various depth psychologies, incorporating the full spectrum of human experience and explicating the nature and function of nonordinary states of consciousness. Moreover, his clinical research provides the best mapping of nonordinary states of consciousness in the modern Western world. I also found Grof's writings personally reassuring because they indicated that my extraordinary experiences were not unlike what others have encountered during nonordinary states; even better, it turns out that these same kinds of experiences have appeared in most times and places throughout history.

Eventually I made the breathtaking drive up to Big Sur and spent three weeks at Esalen, considered by many the birthplace of the human-potential movement. My brief study with Stan and Christina Grof at Esalen eventually led me to participate in their first three-year training group in holotropic breathwork psychotherapy. This experience reinforced the critical realization that nonordinary states can be successfully accessed through *nondrug* methods, and that, in fact, most nonordinary experiences do not involve the use of artificial chemical stimulation. Our association eventually resulted in Stan becoming a member of my dissertation committee at Emory, and both Stan and Christina becoming dear friends of mine. This book is a direct consequence of that dissertation research, which also was focused on Whitehead's "philosophy of organism" and Grof's depth psychology.

In my dissertation, I tried to show how the theories of Grof and Whitehead complement and reinforce one another. Grof's work is especially important because it takes nonordinary experiences seriously and provides a *psychological* understanding of how they occur, as well as a phenomenology of what they are like. Whitehead's philosophy gives a *metaphysical* understanding of how nonordinary states might arise, shows how they are compatible with our everyday experience of the world, and offers a cosmology that is applicable to this entire range of experience.[3] These two powerful systems

3. I am not alone in this assessment of the amazing depth and breadth of Whitehead's cosmology. On the back cover of the fiftieth-anniversary edition of *Star Maker*— Olaf Stapledon's Whiteheadian-influenced vision of an ultimate cosmology—John Lilly, that most intrepid and seasoned explorer of nonordinary states, makes this powerful pronouncement: "*Star Maker* is the most influential book I have ever read. It shows me a God large enough to encompass everything I've thought and experienced." (Stapledon,

of thought—Grof's transpersonal psychology and Whitehead's process philosophy—provided me with the intellectual (and experiential) tools to start working on a synthesis of ideas capable of addressing those questions that had begun to emerge so many years before.

Paradoxically I now see that I could not really have known what I was looking for until I had found it. Just as each of my major life crises broadened my perspective on reality and opened new avenues of questioning, so each new system I encountered opened me to new theoretical possibilities—and to new problems. It was only when I stumbled upon Whitehead's philosophy that I finally encountered a deeply satisfying way of understanding all the questions that had defined my search—and of answering those questions as well.

What Did Work

Over the next few pages, I will briefly introduce some key aspects of Whitehead's philosophy in order to lay the groundwork for the more in-depth discussions to come.[4] While some of my later explications of Whitehead's ideas may seem unduly complicated, a solid understanding of his basic concepts and overall vision is necessary to genuinely appreciate the power and applicability of Whitehead's philosophy. My aim is to keep these discussions as nontechnical as possible, without losing too much of what is novel in Whitehead's thought. I hope readers will not be concerned if this first foray is difficult to fully absorb. The rest of this book is devoted to making these ideas more intelligible.

While there are many excellent introductions to Whitehead's philosophy, popularizing his ideas has proven problematic. His comprehensive and novel reenvisioning of philosophy is inherently difficult to convey simply or quickly. Whitehead's insistence on the importance of *coherence* between first principles means that they can only be fully understood in terms of one another. Since full comprehension of each principle calls for knowledge of the entire metaphysical scheme, Whitehead's philosophy must be introduced and learned in stages of ever-increasing depth. His magnum opus, *Process and Reality*, is criticized for its oblique presentation, when in fact Whitehead is intentionally employing multiple

---

Star Maker, back cover).

4. David Ray Griffin greatly influenced my thinking on how to organize the presentation of Whitehead's ideas in this section and throughout this book. However, I take full responsibility for any and all confusion or imprecision therein.

perspectives and contexts in order to produce a spiraling hermeneutical encounter with his unorthodox theories.

For those who think that novel, fundamental concepts can be explained without contextualization aside from purely logical-philosophical considerations, Whitehead has provided just such an abstract summary in the second chapter of *Process and Reality:* "The Categoreal Scheme." The remainder of his great work is spent fleshing out these primary notions, or in Whitehead's words, "has the purpose of rendering this summary intelligible."[5]

This unusual degree of conceptual novelty creates another problem for Whitehead, who is also criticized for employing too much special terminology. Whitehead did not do so lightly, but he was caught in a dilemma that he referred to as the "fallacy of the perfect dictionary": the erroneous belief that we already possess words for all necessary concepts and ideas.[6] Thus, when trying to introduce a fundamentally new metaphysical notion, one must choose between using a familiar term, like *feeling*, which will only partially convey the novel idea (and will in some ways mislead) or coining a new or less well-known term, like *prehension*, which will point more clearly to the novelty of the ideas embedded within, yet may produce confusion or engender the charge of obscurantism. By using an interplay of more and less familiar terms to describe his key metaphysical concepts, Whitehead attempts to mitigate this "perfect dictionary" dilemma. With this in mind, let us examine Whitehead's *prehension* a bit more closely, as well as consider his other fundamental metaphysical innovation: the *actual occasion*.

The answers to many, if not most, of my big questions are rooted deeply in Whitehead's generalization of *experience* to describe all actual entities in the universe—that is, making *all actuality* "experiential" in nature. This is accomplished in part through his special understanding of *feeling*. Charles Hartshorne hails Whitehead's novel use of *feeling*—or, more technically, *prehension*—as the "most powerful metaphysical generalization ever accomplished."[7] While *prehend* usually means "to grasp or seize," Whitehead employs the term more broadly to indicate the manner in which all events are able to take in or absorb aspects of the world, bringing that data directly into their own inner makeup. By envisioning all actuality as arising out of the *feeling of past feelings,* Whitehead unifies under one metaphysical concept nine key philosophical categories: causation, memory, perception, substance (as endurance through time),

5. Whitehead, *Process and Reality,* 18.
6. Whitehead, *Modes of Thought,* 173.
7. Hartshorne, *Creative Synthesis,* 107.

space, time, relation, self-identity, and the interrelations between God and World.[8] In short, all actuality creates itself by feeling the past and integrating this information into a new unity.

Along with Whitehead's notion of *feeling* or *prehension*, perhaps his other most important philosophical innovation is the *actual occasion: actual* because it fully exists; *occasion* because it is a momentary event. In a process similar to the one described by contemporary quantum theory, an actual occasion is an event that creates itself by drawing directly on data from past events to generate a new momentary unit of reality. Essentially Whitehead generalizes quantum theory and combines it with William James's insight that experience comes in "drops" in order to describe all actuality in terms of these momentary bursts of synthesized feeling. (For those familiar with Leibnitz, you could say that actual occasions are like his monads, except reconceived as momentary and supplied with open windows to the past.) Actual occasions are thus momentary events—but because they are composed of feelings, they are *experiential* events, or fleeting subjects. Everything actual in the universe is composed of, or found within, actual occasions, ranging from quarks to molecules to cells to human beings and even to any purely spiritual entities that may exist, including God.[9] This view of the universe as increasingly complex organismic societies results from another of Whitehead's generalizations: the extension of cell theory to all of reality.

The most primitive type of feeling in Whitehead's metaphysical scheme is the initial, direct *grasping* of data or feelings from past occasions of experience—that is, from past subjective events. This grasping represents a *direct flow* of past feeling into a new moment of reality. *Feeling* is more suggestive of the fact that every grasping of the past involves a particular way or form of *how* it was felt; *prehension* is more suggestive of the fact that each such grasping has an object—it is a feeling *of something* (of some

8. Hartshorne, *Creative Synthesis,* 107. (Griffin makes similar assertions in his writings.)

9. Hartshorne's modification of Whitehead's notion of God—from a single, never-ending synthesis of the universe to a series of actual occasions—is widely accepted by the process community. This caveat presents a good opportunity to extend a more general one: I am offering in these pages *my* understanding and interpretation of Whitehead's philosophy and process thought. For example, while I present what I take to be a coherent integration of Whitehead's mature position on the nature of God, other Whiteheadians prefer a version that sees an impersonal universe providing some of the functions otherwise ascribed to God, whether in the form of a Buddhist/Hindu collective unconscious or even a more starkly atheistic vision. Whitehead himself did not explicitly work God into his metaphysical thinking until relatively late in his career. Thus, there are various plausible ways that his basic ideas have been understood and employed. I am sharing here the way that I think works best philosophically and is most adequate to our experience at large, including the transpersonal.

aspect of a past event). The central point, though, is that all actual occasions are momentary experiences involving a synthesis of past events into a *new whole*. (Actual occasions and prehensions are discussed in a more evocative manner in the next chapter, as these concepts lie at the heart of the Whitehead's understanding of the universe.)

Such a system could be called *panfeelingism*, but *panexperientialism* is a more accepted global characterization. Either term, however, better reflects Whitehead's position than the more familiar usage *panpsychism*, which tends to suggest that reality is composed completely of individuals that are both conscious and enduring, as opposed to Whitehead's understanding of actual occasions as *momentary*, largely *unconscious* events. As in modern psychological theory, where for humans most experience is understood to occur at the unconscious level, this would be all the more markedly the case for the experience of those much simpler events that compose entities such as cells, molecules, and atoms—whose feelings (presumably) lurk in the remote unconscious depths. (It might be better to describe the experiential quality of very simple occasions as *nonconscious* rather than unconscious, especially since *unconsicious* suggests that conscious awareness might at times be present.)

It is especially important to emphasize that a process cosmology differs from most panpsychisms in that it does *not* attribute experience to all *objects* in the universe, only to all actual occasions. For Whitehead, experience (and thus the *potential* for consciousness) is limited to those momentary events that are unifying centers of activity, which would include such things as atomic, molecular, cellular, and human-level psychic events. Rocks and cars, on the other hand, while composed or aggregated out of atomic and molecular centers of feeling, do not possess a higher-order unifying psychic center and thus cannot be said to have their own experience or "psyches." Again: the atomic and molecular events that *make up* a rock, car, or table are composed of feelings and are thus experiential in nature; but rocks, cars, and tables *themselves* as macroscopic objects do *not* (presumably) have a unified center of (even unconscious) feeling or experience.

By attributing at least some modicum of feeling to all actuality, Whitehead's philosophy avoids the highly problematic hypothesis of an evolutionary "leap" from insentient matter to entities possessing life and experience. In a process metaphysics, even atomic-level occasions exhibit the fundamental action of *grasping and unifying the past into a new event* that is characteristic of living entities, and which for Whitehead is the ultimate origin of experience. Assumedly, such atomic- or subatomic-level "experience" would be so primitive as to defy normal human empathy. Nonetheless, its contrast with human experience is still merely one of intensity, depth, and quality, not an absolute difference *in kind* such as would exist between so-called insentient matter and experiencing or living beings.

In a Whiteheadian universe, there is nothing without inner activity— no dead matter and no empty space, no "vacuous actuality." All actual occasions are spatiotemporal events: space and time themselves are sustained by the universal field of ongoing events. This view stands in stark contrast to Cartesian dualism with its mental substances (minds) that are temporal but not spatial, and physical substances (the world of objects) that are spatial but not temporal (that is, which exist in a durationless instant). Whitehead's philosophy carves out a relatively unexplored metaphysical position, *pluralistic monism*: it is *monistic* in that all real entities are made up of the *same kind* of substance (experience or feeling); it is pluralistic in that there are *many different* entities in the universe. Such a Whiteheadian universe might evocatively be described as an *ocean of feeling*, with the momentary events like waves rising out of the depths (of the past).

Perhaps most controversial for contemporary science and philosophy is Whitehead's admittance of an Ultimate Actuality into the heart of his cosmology and metaphysics. Whitehead did not introduce the idea of God into his metaphysical scheme without deep and lengthy deliberation. He wrestled with religious matters throughout his life. Ultimately, his conviction that a coherent understanding of cosmological processes required a *source* of novelty and order beyond the observable physical universe inclined him to the position articulated in the final pages of *Process and Reality*. While Whitehead argues that we should reject many of the ways that God has been appealed to as an explanatory force, such as creation ex nihilo (creating the universe out of nothing) or as an all-controlling power, he does not think that we should necessarily reject the idea of a divine influence in the world.

Whitehead champions William James's position expressed at the end of *Varieties of Religious Experience*: talk of God is vacuous unless we can speak of real divine effects in the world. These chief effects, in terms of everyday human experience, are our *ideal impulses*. For transpersonal psychology, they are mystical intuitions of the divine. For the universal process, they are the novel possibilities that push ahead the evolution of complexity and order.

The "highest form of feeling"—to use Charles Hartshorne's poetic formulation—is God.[10] The God of process theology is similar to Plato's notion of a World (or Universal) Soul, paralleling another of Hartshorne's images: the Universe as the body of God. The guiding principle here is one of God as that ultimate series of moments of experience who completely

10. See Griffin, "Charles Hartshorne."

integrates and consciously synthesizes *all* past events. Although the entire past informs every new event, only God's moments of experience have sufficient depth, intensity, and complexity to fully incorporate the feelings of the entire universe.

This position should not be mistaken for pantheism, since God is *not* everything. Rather, God feels everything—and influences everything—but so does every other event in the universe. Hartshorne refers to this understanding of God and World as pan*en*theism. God is in everything, and everything is in God; but every event has its *own* moment of actuality, too. There is an everlasting flow of feeling between each of the universe's new momentary events and God's own moments of becoming. In his final lectures, William James argues against the notion of an Absolute that is *everything,* and thus ends up robbing the rest of reality of its . . . well, its reality. Whitehead adopts a view of God very similar to James: God is understood to be in an intimate and constant *interaction* with the rest of the universe, and vice versa.

Finally, by saying that experience or feeling is fundamental, process philosophy achieves a more *rational* worldview than those that start elsewhere. It is able to show how the truths of the natural sciences, the basic beliefs of the world's religious traditions, and our hardcore commonsense notions—those which in practice we cannot help believing—*all cohere.* (This coherence will prove extremely useful for my attempt to locate transpersonal experiences within a worldview congenial to scientific truth and the realities of everyday life.) Furthermore, process philosophy can show how these commonsense beliefs—beliefs in an external world, the past, other minds, causation, and ideal norms—arise *naturalistically* from the basic way we encounter the universe. This process perspective seems vastly preferable to those theories that construe these foundational commonsense beliefs merely as *irrational* opinions or beliefs (Hume, Santayana), as supernatural implantations (Reid), or as ad hoc consequences of "evolutionary theory."

The reader may well have noted that in this section, and in the last paragraph in particular, I have made some broad and so far unsubstantiated claims. Fear not; I attempt to establish their validity in much of the rest of this book.

Stanislav Grof is the other theorist who has proved invaluable to my search. His unsurpassed clinical experience with LSD psychotherapy—first at a psychiatric clinic in his native Czechoslovakia and then at the Maryland Psychiatric Research Center—combined with his supervision of tens of thousands of sessions involving nonordinary experiences induced through the holotropic breathwork technique that he created with his wife, Christina, give an unparalleled experiential foundation to Grof's theoretical work.

Articulated first in his groundbreaking *Realms of the Human Unconscious,* Grof's "cartography of the human psyche" charts the amazing phenomenology of nonordinary experiences revealed during his observations of psychedelic and breathwork sessions, running the full gamut of the psychical, paranormal, and mystical states described in religious, occult, and anthropological literature throughout the ages. Complementing this transpersonal phenomenology, Grof has developed a unified psychoanalytic theory of the unconscious, combining the work of Freud, Jung, Otto Rank (1884–1939), and Wilhelm Reich (1897–1957) into a multileveled, dynamic description of the unconscious processes, including a unique perspective on the origins and treatment of psychopathology. In addition, and critical for my concerns, Grof's theory of nonordinary states offers insight into *how* these experiences arise, their typical pattern of unfolding, and the potential value they hold for us as individuals and as a society.

In his last major lectures William James lauds two seminal thinkers, Henri-Louis Bergson (1859–1941) and Gustav Fechner (1801–1887), for expanding and deepening the range of evidence and theory, arguing that they point the way for the future of philosophy and psychology.

> I have now finished these poor lectures, and as you look back on them, they doubtless seem rambling and inconclusive enough. My only hope is that they may possibly have proved suggestive; and if indeed they have been suggestive of one point of method, I am almost willing to let all other suggestions go. That point is that *it is high time for the basis of discussion in these questions to be broadened and thickened up.* It is for that that I have brought in Fechner and Bergson, and descriptive psychology and religious experiences, and have ventured even to hint at psychical research and other wild beasts of the philosophic desert . . . It is as if the actual peculiarities of the world that is were entirely irrelevant to the content of truth. But they cannot be irrelevant; and the philosophy of the future must imitate the sciences in taking them more and more elaborately into account.[11]

Bergson's interests in a pervasive vitality in nature and the centrality of process find systematic explication in Whitehead's philosophy of organism; Fechner's late interest in an ensouled nature and universe (which is what so intrigued James) find empirical support and rigorous theoretical expression in Grof's transpersonal psychology. Process philosophy and transpersonal psychology both draw heavily from James, who is considered a prominent member of both camps.

11. James, *Pluralistic Universe,* 330–31 (italics original).

Thus, the two trends explored in this book—process thought and transpersonal psychology—can both be traced back to some final reflections of William James from about a century ago. I think it would be profitable to reunite these two schools of thought: profitable for both areas individually and for the unique region they can illuminate when united. Together, they point the way towards a spiritually informed *cosmology* for the twenty-first century.

To conclude, I offer this anticipatory summary of some of the most meaningful ways that Whitehead's philosophy might contribute to the field of psychology and towards a vision for an ecospiritual civilization:

1. By providing a coherent, unified metaphysical foundation, Whitehead's philosophy offers a single system around which to organize interpretation, experimentation, and exploration. Through this shared ground, psychology becomes functionally connected to the other social sciences, the physical sciences, and the humanities as well.

2. This unifying interpretive framework is applicable to psychological theories and concepts arising from Eastern and Western, as well as modern and premodern, cultural systems.

3. Process philosophy offers viable solutions for psychology's critical philosophical problems—such as mind-body interaction and epistemological concerns about perception and knowledge of the world.

4. Whitehead's metaphysics provides a coherent philosophical underpinning for basic psychological concepts such as the unconscious, repression, memory, feeling, consciousness, and the self. This coherence can help explicate how these key notions and processes interact and relate. But while it offers a metaphysical basis and cosmological clues regarding these psychological processes, Whitehead's system is open-ended as to the specific theories and activities involved in these processes—these being matters for future study and research.

5. The philosophy of organism makes comprehensible the relationship between mental and physical and illuminates how the human body can assume a central role in all areas of psychological theory. It also shows how to directly connect the notion of physical energy with the experience of human emotion, sensation, and creativity.

6. Whitehead's philosophy suggests a model for understanding many dynamics and meanings of psychological and spiritual development and transformation.

7. Whitehad's philosophy also offers plausible interpretations for a wide range of parapsychological and transpersonal experiences and gives a starting point for distinguishing between the various theories concerning the phenomena that arise from the depth unconscious.

8. Furthermore, Whitehead's philosophy describes a cosmology in which the transpersonal dimension is part and parcel of our world.

9. Mystical and religious experiences are recognized as having the potential to reveal important information about the nature of the universe.

10. God and other spiritual entities are restored as rational possibilities.

11. Whitehead's notion of "Nature Alive" and his theories on the organismic nature of the universe provide a firm basis for an ecological rapprochement with our bodies, the world, the universe, and God. In addition, Whitehead's envisagement of a creative, advancing universe of interlocking, organismic processes provides an initial model for an ecological psychology and an ecospirituality.

12. This view of nature also allows us to conceptualize how we are in the world and how the world is in us. Whitehead's philosophy can thus help to lay the foundation for more fully reconnecting us—individually and culturally—to nature and the universe.

13. And finally, within this view of reality, human life and Life in general become fundamentally imbued with deep Value and Adventure.

If I could convey the full implications of these points quickly and adeptly, this book would be short and sweet. Unfortunately, my elaboration of these ideas will require some time and toil. This hurdle is again reminiscent of *Process and Reality* itself, where Whitehead requires only thirteen pages to lay out the essence of his philosophy and then takes another three hundred twenty pages to explain what it all means. As with *Process and Reality*, we will need to come at these ideas from several different angles to even partially illuminate their subtleties and depths.

We now begin that adventure.

4

Return to Experience

Psychedelic Experience, That Is

In the last chapter, I described my search for answers to the key questions that had been aroused by certain pivotal events in my life. My at-times frantic pursuit of The Truth brings to mind an incident from my early college days, one that throws into comic relief the ultimate futility of such an undertaking.

Having moved off campus from New College, my girlfriend (and future wife), Susan, and I had become friends with a number of our often equally eccentric neighbors, including a wonderful elderly woman whose family sometimes came to visit. One day, her teenage grandson excitedly filled me in on his epiphany from a recent acid trip. Mark had been in the midst of a psychedelic crisis, frantically asking himself, "What is the Answer? What is the Answer?" Suddenly, a breakthrough came as he realized that the Answer is, "What is the question?" This revelation felt so profound to Mark that he woke up his father at three o'clock in the morning to tell him about this amazing insight. One can only surmise that his father was not quite so thrilled.[1]

As with many LSD-inspired insights, this one can be written off as trite, drug-induced nonsense—or one may try to enter into the depths

---

1. While Grof's cartography of nonordinary states is most concerned with delineating a range of possible transpersonal encounters, prominent in my experience has been a heightened ability to follow ideas and questions to their inexorable logical conclusions, or to the paradoxes that lie beyond. These trains of thought were nearly impossible to re-create after having come down from the effects of the drug. The most powerful fictional depiction of this process that I know of is the encounter with the "Destroyer" frequency in Piers Anthony's *Macroscope*. Here, those with sufficient intellect are guided through a geometrical/mathematical progression that ultimately leads to a final conclusion—so terrible? so overwhelming?—that typically the mind is shattered, leaving the person in a permanent vegetative state, or dead.

of feeling that made Mark believe it was so significant. First of all, this insight on the face of it holds some intriguing implications: The search for any particular answer or goal presumes a prescribed perspective, which both focuses and delineates the nature of the answer that is likely to be found. The answer sought is demarcated by the question raised, as well as limited by one's own intellectual parameters. More profoundly, when one deeply perceives that the intellectual search for answers is a self-contained, self-limiting activity—the only answers you will get are more intellectual thoughts—the mind may suddenly snap loose and let go into the deeper field of feelings and sensations underlying the ego and everyday reality, as can happen in response to a Zen koan. Then things become really interesting, as this newly freed-up range of awareness opens to things as they are beyond (or before) everyday social consciousness.

Although it is possible to make some interesting speculations about Mark's insight, most of his LSD experience must remain hidden behind its subjective veils. Likewise, while I realize that I will not be able to communicate the essence of my direct subjective experiences with nonordinary states, there are some important facets of these events that can be conveyed.

Two of my psychedelic experiences—which I will call Sine Waves and Blue Acid for reasons that will soon become apparent—provide an experiential context within which to explore more deeply certain aspects of Whitehead's philosophy. Sine Waves bears directly on my questions regarding the metaphysical nature of reality, offering a mystical entryway into one of Whitehead's fundamental metaphysical concepts: the *actual occasion*. Whitehead's vision of reality is one of quantum (i.e., unitary) bursts of what he calls feeling, with these bursts of feeling interflowing, interconnecting, and compounding to generate the complex social order of our universe, including its spiritual dimensions. I have found this unifying vision most helpful for understanding my major life crises and their psychological, philosophical, and spiritual ramifications. The second experience offers a glimpse into what can happen when the metaphysical veil is pierced. In Blue Acid, various aspects of Whitehead's approach to temporality are teased out, as well as their implications for science and the transpersonal realm.

Sine Waves

This return to experience begins with another epiphany from my early psychedelic days. One spring afternoon I was sitting in the shabby living room of The Apartment—the run-down house where my psychedelically inclined friends and I hung out—reeling from the effects of a powerful dose of LSD.

Suddenly, a vivid insight flooded into my mind: *the essential structure of all of reality is captured by the sine wave function.* This intuition seemed to hold such power and import that I rushed into the kitchen, found paper and pen, drew a sine wave, and tried my best to write down the essential ideas behind this revelation. Anyone who has taken LSD will understand how deeply motivated I must have been to attempt to carefully preserve this insight while in the midst of this intense psychedelic vision. They might also be able to guess that when I came down, my drawing and words were unable to rekindle the flame of illumination, which had faded along with the effects of the LSD. I would study that page from time to time, hoping that the full insight would return, for I continued to believe that something of deep significance had slipped from my grasp.

Only many years later did it occur to me that the sine wave image might correspond to Whitehead's *actual occasions* and to William James's drops or pulses of experience. Given what I know now, I believe that my vision of the sine wave, as a reflection of the essential nature of things, arose out of a psychedelically heightened intuitive access to the subtle flow of *actual occasions* that constitute the basis of all experience. The fundamental rhythmic patterning of my subjective vibrations or pulses of experience, taking in and releasing feeling in their binary dance, emerged into my consciousness in the abstract form of a sine wave, still saturated with a sense of the import of its origins in the metaphysical heart of reality.

This ubiquitous heart beats to the rhythm of the past flowing into the creation of each new moment, with that moment then emptying itself into future events. This movement constitutes the eternal rise and fall of the universal process that is reenacted by every occasion of experience. In each new pulse of actuality, the universe breathes in the past to form a new event, and then this event exhales itself into the future. Our beating hearts embody this pulsing rhythm of all creation; our breath incarnates the rhythmic process of taking in the world and releasing the transformed product back into the universe. Whitehead's philosophy articulates how these basic human rhythmic patterns find their direct parallels at every level of reality and in all actual occasions.

Let us examine more closely this rather odd term: *actual occasion.* As is usually the case with Whitehead, it means just what it says: an actual occasion is something that is fully real (actual) and a momentary event (occasion).[2] For Whitehead, the universe is composed entirely of these momentary events that *feel* and absorb the direct influence of the past and

2. Please take careful note that when I refer to an actual occasion as an event, I am using the term *event* to indicate a subjective occurrence, not something simply observed by a subject, like a wedding or a car crash.

integrate these feelings into a *new* unified event. Perhaps the most critical thing to notice about these actual occasions is that this integrative activity is a *subjective* process, which internally transforms the objective past into a new event. To get a sense of what I mean by feeling the *direct influence* of another event, consider how a memory or bodily sensation enters into our conscious experience. The feelings and images appear as an immediate and essential part of that moment of experience, as something *within*. The relationship is experienced as *internal;* it is part of us.

Since this process of self-creation involves a *grasping* of past influences, along with the selection and transformative integration of these influences into a new unity, Whitehead believes that actual occasions can most accurately be described as *subjective* in nature. It is important to note that in most cases these subjective experiences are very simple or primitive in nature—such as those occasions belonging to atoms, molecules, or cells—and thus involve no conscious awareness. But while these more simple events may be very different from what human subjects experience in their own direct awareness, their processes of self-formation still resemble a rudimentary subjectivity much more than they do insentient matter or "vacuous actuality," to use Whitehead's evocative phrase. All of nature is *alive*—at least in this most basic sense.

Significantly, Whitehead's theory of actual occasions is a *quantum* theory of reality—and consciously so. As a mathematical physicist, Whitehead was fully aware of the fundamental changes going on in post-Newtonian science. In fact, because he disagreed with how Einstein made space-time subordinate to the gravitational influence of matter, Whitehead developed a competing relativity theory that rivaled Einstein's mathematical predictions but differed in philosophical priorities by making *events* primary.[3]

All actual occasions—from the momentary events that make up quarks, electrons, atoms, molecules, cells, and the human psyche—are quantum pulses of synthetic feeling, according to process metaphysics. Some moments of experience are more wave-like; some are more particle-like. Enduring objects—temporally-ordered series of events, such as atoms, cells, and molecules—are more particle-like, drawing heavily on their own predecessors to sustain their basic structure. But, like all actual occasions, they also receive and transmit wave-like feelings from the larger universe.

---

3. Matter is a "quality" of events, and in his mature metaphysics the space-time continuum is generated by actual occasions. Events understood as actual occasions play a central role in Whitehead's incorporation of quantum theory into his larger philosophical scheme. See Epperson, *Quantum Mechanics,* for a full discussion of Whiteheadian theory and contemporary physics.

Since the moments of experience making up the human psyche are of the *same kind* of quantums of synthetic feeling that constitute the rest of the universe, one can begin to see how Whitehead's philosophy offers an incredible opportunity for psychology to make fertile cross-disciplinary connections with biology, chemistry, and even physics: the entities they study are all of the *same* fundamental nature and are explicitly part of the *same* quantum universe. But for Whitehead, these quantums are all composed of feeling or experience—albeit extremely primitive, nonconscious experience in most cases—with the potential for consciousness to accrue only to some higher-order occasions.[4] Primitive experience or feeling is ubiquitous throughout the universe, and thus there is no radical disjunction between mind and matter; between psychology, religion, and science; or in the evolution of higher forms of life out of Earth's chemical brew

Whitehead's cosmology offers a highly complex, yet unified and coherent vision of all actuality as *interflowing and interacting pulses of feeling,* generating in turn the vast array of enduring objects and the larger social groupings they form—rocks, plants, animals, stars—as revealed through the "transmutational" (i.e., synthetic integrational) powers of our senses, brain, and psyche.

Some nostalgic images from my hometown may help illustrate this quantum play of vibrational feeling. Every year, the harbor across the street from our house was the site of the Fourth of July fireworks, delighting the thousands gathered along the docks and the grassy slope leading down from Riverside Park. I wish I hadn't missed my one opportunity to see them on psychedelics, for I now look back on those bursting sky rockets as pyrotechnic representations of Whitehead's theory of *concrescence,* the process whereby the many feelings of past events are grasped and synthesized into a new occasion. This process is vividly illustrated by those colorful firework explosions producing a central burst that is quickly surrounded by a halo of smaller flaring lights. Likewise (albeit in reverse), each new moment of experience starts by pulling in the feelings of past events (the halo of sparkling lights), generating a new event that adds its fleeting moment of creative subjectivity (the central burst). Then, this new occasion "perishes" (like the fading fireworks), only to be incorporated into future moments, represented by the next explosion of fireworks that fills the sky, overlapping and subsuming the glowing remains of the previous burst.

In the daytime, this same harbor presents another suggestive image. As small waves move across the surface, and the sunlight reflects off the

---

4. Might brain waves thus be analyzed in terms of the complex interaction of the sine waves generated at the neural level *and* at the level of the unifying synthesis accomplished by the actual occasions of the human psyche?

water at a certain angle, the sparkles of light that rapidly appear and disappear across the flowing ripples conjure up Whitehead's notion of the *creative advance:* the everlasting process of the interacting, interpenetrating flow of actual occasions. New events burst into existence only to disappear into the future, thereby giving rise to the next wave of new moments of experience. Perhaps the mesmerizing rippling phenomena, like the mesmerizing fireworks display, owes its compelling quality in part to its ability to evoke a fleeting intuition of the metaphysical processes active within our own unconscious depths.

The same compelling quality applies to a final image from my childhood: glistening snowflakes floating past the window or streetlight at night outside our house. Growing up in Wisconsin, I had many opportunities to appreciate these hypnotic displays. Unique, beautiful, and momentary, fleeting snowflakes also resemble Whitehead's occasions of experience. Sparkling snow crystals flashing in front of the light only to disappear again into the dark serve to conjure up a vague recognition of that everlasting flow of momentary events passing rapidly in and out of subjective existence—the essence of the creative advance of our universe. Deep and mysterious emotions can be stirred by these worldly phenomena, which remind us of the depth of creative feeling lying below and within.

Let us now look more closely at the equally fundamental idea of *feeling,* or more technically, *prehension.* To properly appreciate Whitehead's revolutionary use of feeling as the fundamental element in experience and thus in the universe—it is important to understand that human *emotion* is only one manifestation of a much larger phenomenon. Even in conventional usage, the term *feeling* can mean many things: an emotion, an intuition, a hunch, a sensation of touch, a sense of movement in the body (feeling something moving up one's spine), and so forth. Nevertheless, *feeling* in its full Whiteheadian sense refers to something much broader and deeper. It is the source not only of emotion but also of memory, perception, thought, causality, and experience itself.

Our emotions tap into this deeper sense of feeling when they disclose their partial origins in the sensations flooding in from the body's various organs: fear roiling in the pit of the stomach, love warming the heart, the skin tingling with joy—assuming one is not so energetically blocked as to have completely suppressed such bodily awareness. *Memory* as a general phenomenon involves a direct feeling or grasping (prehending) of one's past moments of experience—rather than being founded solely on neural storage mechanisms, as reductively hypothesized by much of contemporary neuroscience. *Sensation* comes from *feeling the feelings* of the body's far-flung neural receptor events. *Sensory perception* arises out of the integration of primitive feelings (of qualities or what Whitehead calls data) that have passed from the world into the special sense organs, where they are focused and transmitted through the nervous system to be integrated in the brain and finally transmuted (synthetically condensed) within the human psyche itself into the highly refined feelings we know as conscious sensory perception. Thus, Whitehead's use of *feeling* at the heart of his metaphysics is both an acceptance of insights from the Romantic tradition as well as a deepening *and* rationalizing of their fundamental intuition of the central role of emotion in experience and the world.

I should confess here that the idea of a recovery of deep feeling holds a personal psychological appeal. I sometimes still tear up a bit at the ending of the *Star Trek* episode about the curious plant spores (psychedelics?) that infect the crew with a sense of belonging, joy, and deep emotional connection. As they leave the planet, having exorcised the alien spores—and the carefree joy—from their systems, Captain Kirk turns to Mr. Spock and observes that he has not said anything about his experience on Omicron Ceti III. Spock, who has returned to his normal condition of total self-control and suppression of feeling, replies, "I have little to say about it, Captain, except that for the first time in my life, I was happy."[5]

Like Spock, I also tend to strongly repress feelings, as borne out by my MMPI psychological testing at the Betty Ford Center. Their psychologist informed me that I had scored higher on the ability to repress and deny than anyone else in the two-year history of the Center. I like to think that my lengthy efforts at self-understanding and recovery of feeling have led me to discover modes of thought in Whitehead and transpersonal psychology that may be of value to others personally as well as for addressing the critical problems facing our society and our world—for this very lack of deep feeling and connection appears endemic to the modern world.

In Doris Lessing's brilliant space-fantasy novel, *Shikasta*, Lessing uses the acronym SOWF to describe the "vital air" that has been depleted from Earth, leaving the human race in a state of misery, confusion, and isolation. SOWF stands for "substance-of-we-feeling": the subtle connecting energy that "kept everyone safe and healthy, and above all, made them love each other."[6] Lessing later attributes our epidemic of drug abuse (and all other addictions as well) to this lack of SOWF, these substances being desperately needed by people "to dull the pain of their condition."[7] SOWF serves as an excellent metaphor for the vague but oh-so-important

5. Senensky, "This Side of Paradise."

6. Lessing, *Shikasta*, 73.

7. Lessing, *Shikasta*, 195.

felt intuition of our interrelationship with all Being and beings, which is grounded in the flowing interconnectedness of feeling that Whitehead places at the heart of all things.[8]

The issue of connectedness versus isolation is especially relevant to the problem of addiction, as *isolation* is perhaps the central emotional fact in the addict's life. One of Alcoholics Anonymous's (AA's) primary contributions to sober living is the sense of *fellowship* and *community* it offers, both through meetings and a spiritual program designed to restore the addict to their place in the world. More broadly speaking, I would suggest that this lack of an experiential connection—an absence of "we" feeling—is in no small part responsible for the discord and discontent in our world at large, impairing our ability to come together in good will to address the enormous challenges facing us. This is a big reason why Whitehead's notion that experience is rooted in deep, connecting feeling is so important. When combined with transpersonal psychology's methods for accessing these unconscious depths, it offers a path to recovery of our deeper selves and our connectedness to the world and one another.

Having journeyed far afield from my sine-wave epiphany, I now return briefly to examine some of the important facets of a Whiteheadian universe that arise out these vibratory events. Here we have a universe composed of interflowing, interacting, interpenetrating moments of experience: a vast *ocean of feeling*. These momentary subjective events, or pulses of feeling, come together to form many types of societies: "social networks," one might say. Thus, serially ordered societies—such as atoms, molecules, and human psyches—are made up of a simple temporal sequence of occasions: one atomic moment flows into the next, single file. Societies that are both temporally and spatially connected come in a variety of forms. There are those societies that inherit shared qualities among members but do not have an overall center of experience: rocks, tables, and cars fall into this class. Some societies have significant inner organization, but do not seem to have an *independent center* of experience. Although such matters must ultimately be determined through empirical verification, trees, plants, and planets are possible examples of tightly connected societies lacking a central intelligence.

Compound individuals[9] constitute an especially important kind of society: this concept is critical for understanding complex organisms in general,

8. There are both psychological and metaphysical reasons why our normal awareness of this innate connectedness is often vague at best. This crucial problem is examined further in subsequent chapters.

9. *Compound individuals* is a concept some find inherent in Whitehead's thinking, but the term itself was coined and fleshed out by Charles Hartshorne. It should be

and for clarifying such issues as mind-body interaction and the nature of human experience in particular. Compound individuals refer to societies organized in an interactive, multilevel manner so as to generate what might be called higher-order events within the society. Quarks combine to form atoms, atoms combine to form molecules, molecules combine to form cells, and cells combine to help form the human psyche. This simplification of the structure of *compound individuals* glosses over the important point that interactive flows of feeling are going on *between and within* all of the various orders of complexity. For example, while the human psyche's occasions are informed primarily by neural events and the psyche's own past moments of experience, data is faintly flowing into and out of the psychic occasions from the entire body's collection of atomic, molecular, and cellular events, as well as from the universe at large. In other words, there are not strict levels or divisions but rather interflowing and mutually informing varieties of social interaction and complexity.

The idea in process metaphysics of a *compound individual* is revolutionary in two ways (at least). First, all the entities involved in the compound individual are composed of bursts of creative experience; second, each higher-order enduring individual entails a *new series* of momentary occasions. For example, a cell is not merely the sum of its component quanta, atoms, and molecules. Nor is this "something more" merely a new set of qualities in the sense of the whole being greater than the sum of its parts. What *is* greater is the appearance of a *new series* of cellular-level actual occasions that are in vibratory interaction with all the cells' component events. This is one meaning of Whitehead's ultimate metaphysical principle: "The many become one, and are increased by one."[10] Initially, this can be a hard notion to get one's mind around—it was for me, anyway—especially when applied at the human level. The psyche is neither simply the sum of the brain's activities, nor, as some philosophers assert, another aspect of, or perspective on, the brain. Rather, the human psyche is composed of a *series of its own experiential events* that are in intimate interaction with the brain's neural events. This is where the implications become particularly interesting for our purposes. One important consequence for neurophysiology is that both bottom-up causation *and* top-down causation are going on constantly between the brain and the psyche.

---

noted that there is considerable difference of opinion among process philosophers as to where to draw the line concerning compound individuals arising out of their component events: might they start to make an appearance with atoms, with molecules, or simple cells or eukaryotic cells—or not until human psyches?

10. Whitehead, *Process and Reality*, 21.

This important point merits repeating. In process thought, the human psyche or soul is conceived of as a series of moments of experience that draw especially upon the already intensified feelings of its brain's neural matrix and from its own past occasions of experience. The psyche's events are *not* merely the brain's activity from another point of view; they are *not* the "mental" or "inner" aspect of the physical brain. Neural cellular events already have their *own* moments of subjective immediacy and are in constant feeling interaction with other neural cells *and* with the experiential occasions constituting the flow of the human psyche. Thus, the human psyche is made up of momentary experiences that exist independently of—though in extremely close interaction with—the brain. Furthermore, these occasions of the human psyche feel not only the events of their neural network, the rest of the physical body, and their own past; they also have direct, vague intuitions of the *entire world*.

This means that the psyche transcends the brain in two ways. First, the psyche has its own synthetic moments of experience that integrate the brain's neural activity. Second, the psyche's momentary occasions *also* create themselves out of direct feelings of their own past and *all* other past events as well. In fact, the entire past universe is felt by every new occasion of experience (although the actual contribution of data from most past events is trivial).

The human psyche's radical openness provides a basis for reconceiving ourselves as *internally connected* to our world, our universe, and all beings therein. This inherent and fundamental interconnectedness suggests that the widespread alienation and disconnection felt by most of modern civilization is situational in nature, not our basic existential condition. It also has important implications about the latent intuitive powers of the human psyche and what it is capable of perceiving. Both these possibilities are harbingers of hope for our world: the former offers an opportunity for establishing a deeper brotherhood and sisterhood (and, one might say, "naturehood"); the latter the possibility of true spiritual insight and mystical revelation.

A few points outlined in this and in the previous chapters bear reiteration, as they are particularly important for understanding Whitehead's most general view of the nature of our universe. "Nature Alive" is the title of a chapter in Whitehead's *Modes of Thought* (the previous chapter is called "Nature Lifeless"). In "Nature Alive" Whitehead argues that the universe is composed entirely of active, creative entities. There is no empty space or inert matter—no vacuous actuality, to use his evocative phrase. Rather, there are interflowing, interpenetrating moments of (mostly nonconscious) *experience*, understood as the active grasping and synthesizing of past events into new pulses of creative feeling.[11] While some have considered Whitehead's scheme to be a panpsychism, this can be misleading. Panpsychism often implies a universe made up of psyches or minds, while the basic entities in Whitehead's cosmology are neither enduring psyches nor minds. Rather, actual occasions are momentary bursts of creative experience—most of which are *entirely unconscious*. Even highly complex events are only sometimes crowned with conscious feelings. While calling Whitehead's system *panexperiential* is much closer to the mark than panpsychism, to some it might still suggest a dominant strain of consciousness in the universe. This is definitely not the case for Whitehead. In Whitehead's philosophy—in contrast to some New Age thought—everything actual is *not* consciousness. Rather, everything is *feeling*, bearing in mind Whitehead's special understanding of that term.

These ideas have a number of important implications. For science and philosophy, a panexperientialism of this kind provides a rational basis for taking human subjectivity seriously, instead of being caught up in an ongoing, futile effort to explain it away. This pervasive subjectivity, combined with Whitehead's notion of a direct experiential connection between all entities, makes possible not only a coherent theory of human sensory perception, but furnishes a mode of access for extrasensory perception as well. Understanding all actuality to possess a subjective dimension renders a more congenial and reliable foundation for ecological theory and an environmental ethos. Finally, a panexperiential view of the universe opens the door to the possibility of a wide array of authentic spiritual entities, encounters, and insights.

One such insight provides the context for the second part of this chapter. This unusual experience led me to start reconsidering my understanding of temporality—and terror.

Blue Acid

Coincidentally, I know the exact day of this most disconcerting psychedelic experience: May 28, 1972. Recalling the correct *year* is seldom problematic (though not always!), but as the only notes I remember keeping about my psychedelic trips were about the "sine wave" enigma, the closest I can usually come to pinpointing specific dates is the month and year. This trip was notable, however, for being on my mother's birthday, as well as for highlighting another enigma: *time*.

11. Whitehead, *Concept of Nature*.

On that eventful day, my mother was staying at the house of some old family friends who were out of town. Feeling nervous about being in their house alone, she had asked me to spend the night there too. Naturally I agreed and told her I would be over later in the evening. But there was a problem. Someone had gotten hold of a few hits of "blue acid" (referring to its color), and we wanted to try it out right away. It was late afternoon, so I figured if I took just a third of a hit, I would come down sufficiently by ten or eleven o'clock. Then I would head over and join my mother at our friends' house with no one the wiser. Unfortunately, my careful planning failed to account for the possibility that this particular batch of acid might be so powerful that a mere third of a hit would be the equivalent of several normal doses of LSD.

Oblivious to the explosion lying ahead, I went into the kitchen at The Apartment to perform the delicate operation of dividing a small pill into portions for Alex; my girlfriend, Carolyn; and me. As soon as I pushed down firmly on the pill, it split apart and shot wildly in unknown directions onto our kitchen's dirty, multipatterned linoleum floor. I froze in horror (oddly anticipating what was to come later), convinced those tiny pieces were lost forever. Completely ignoring my admonitions that searching was futile, with grave focus Carolyn studied the floor for a few seconds, then bent over and picked up one of the blue acid halves. The next moment, proving my fears to be totally unjustified, she spotted the other half too. Properly chastened, I quickly returned to the task at hand, breaking off bits to make roughly even thirds and then parceling them out to Alex and Carolyn.

We settled down to wait for the effects to come on. I was not expecting anything intense, but I knew I still had to keep an eye on the time. A funny thing I had already learned about psychedelics is that for much of the trip time seems to pass extremely slowly—perhaps because every moment seems so full and so fascinating. Then, before you know it, you suddenly realize that hours have gone by. So I told myself that I would have to pay careful attention to the clock and not forget my promise to leave by eleven at the latest.

The acid came on strongly. I decided I had better lie down on the couch and listen to some music, which, as usual, was being psychedelically deconstructed into subtle lyrical secrets and harmonic depths and tonal complexities. I had to keep reminding myself to check the small clock sitting on the table at end of the couch. Every time I came out of a psychedelic reverie to anxiously glance at it, less time had passed: twenty minutes, ten minutes, five minutes, two minutes, one minute, thirty seconds . . .

Finally, as I stared unblinkingly at the second hand, it started to slow down more and more, and then it *stopped!* The next thing I knew, I found myself standing in the kitchen, desperately grabbing Alex's shirt lapels, screaming, "What are we going to do?" I was in such a state of sheer terror that it muted any concerns about how I had gotten there or what I was doing in this disconcerting pose. Alex, always a calm port in the psychedelic storm, removed my clutching hands and said, "We're going to walk around the block." This seemed like an inane suggestion, since for me the world was falling apart. In confusion, I asked him why, to which he replied, "Do you have a better idea?" I definitely did not, so I decided to follow his. The next moment, as if on cue, Carolyn came dashing up in terror, begging to know what we were going to do. I said, "Take a walk around the block," and the same routine played out again, word for word—it was rather like being inside a Firesign Theatre skit.

So, outside we went. Across the street sat my old elementary school, and down the block was the police station. But my attention was riveted on the scene overhead. It was a starry night, in both the literal and van Goghian sense. The stars had transformed into shooting stars and were falling out of the sky. *All* light had been transfigured. Along with the stars cascading down upon us, the blinking light on the corner stop sign was projecting a solid cone of red as intense as a searchlight, radiating past us to the other end of the block. Between time "stopping," the stars falling, and the fear that things were completely crumbling inside and out, I was overwhelmed—yet extremely grateful to have some friends sharing this wild psychedelic ride.

Around the block we went. Reaching about the halfway point (even walking this far seemed like a grand adventure), we noticed several people coming towards us. Drawing near, they turned out to be some kids we knew who were a year or two behind us in school. We stopped to attempt a brief conversation and discovered that they too had taken some of the blue acid that night and had settled on the same emergency plan of a walk around block, which just happened to overlap with our route.

I have related this story primarily to introduce some aspects of Whitehead's notions of time and process, but I also want to indicate some of the unusual perceptions and compelling synchronicities that cluster around psychedelic experiences. And it should be noted that the nonordinary state itself often yields a magnified sense of import and secret meaning lurking behind and within these phenomena. I believe that this feeling of hidden meanings derives largely from a heightened access to the unconscious depths, where a wealth of philosophical, cosmological, and metaphysical insight lies waiting to be revealed. But when during psychedelic experiences this increased unconscious access is combined with a greatly enhanced ability to see *connections* between everything, there is a natural tendency to attribute creative but sometimes fanciful meanings to the vague feelings and data that erupt partially into conscious awareness, which are often then projected onto outside events.

We see this not only in distorted conceptions of time, but also in unusual visual phenomena that commonly occur during psychedelic experiences. The more dramatic so-called hallucinations of objects or entities not visible during ordinary experience are often explained as some amalgam of personal fantasy and cultural and archetypal symbolism flowing in from the unconscious. However, it is also possible that at times these visions may be informed by authentic intuitions of things beyond our ken. This possibility should not be ruled out prematurely. Perceptions of energy fields, auras, and other such phenomena, often reported in other cultures and supported by some scientific studies, must at least be granted some credence as more or less accurate renderings of psychical intuitions projected onto conscious sensory perception. And, as we shall soon see, Whitehead's theory of perception affords a mode of access to a much wider range of phenomena than is normally available to ordinary sense perception.

At the same time I suspect that some visuals such as trails or the shooting stars from my blue acid trip may derive chiefly from a psychedelically enhanced flow of visual data combined with an extended present—that is, elements from the immediate past stretching vividly into the present moment, creating an enhanced perceptible pathway between past and present perception. Nor do I harbor any strong conviction that my psychedelic vision of colored energy flows coursing through our garden-room chandelier revealed some hidden aspect of objective reality. More generally, though, I think it quite likely that the radiant auras emanating from animals and plants that are often observed during nonordinary states do represent remarkable glimpses into an intangible dimension of our world. I will not pursue these ideas further here, as I have little personal experience with such phenomena, but I think the topic of subtle energies will be an interesting and productive one for the future of process psychology in its transpersonal dimensions.

Whiteheadian metaphysics carries other important implications for our understanding of time. Although I have not referred to it as such, we have already encountered Whitehead's *epochal theory of time,* which simply refers to temporality arising out of interconnected, momentary units of experience. Actual occasions, in their moment of creative self-becoming, are *atomic* (thus "epochs") in the sense of being real, independent wholes. And yet, with the balance characteristic of Whitehead's thought, the independence of these wholes is complemented by their internal relationships with the rest of the universe. Each moment of experience arises initially out of its feelings of the past universe (interconnectedness), thereby creating its own unique perspective with its own temporal and spatial domain (independence), and then passes out of subjective immediacy to become another accomplished moment of reality to be felt by all future events (interconnectedness). Put more simply, the past floods in to create a new event, which then flows back into the universe to join the ocean of other past events. The whole universe unfolds in accord with Whitehead's primary metaphysical principle: the many become one, and are increased by one. Time is not a thing-in-itself within which events occur; rather, temporal process is itself constituted by this flow of events.

We have also looked indirectly at Whitehead's *asymmetrical theory of time*. Basically, time is considered asymmetrical in the sense that the past consists of completed events while the future exists as mere potential. That is, process flows in only one direction: from the past into the present towards the future. Let me elaborate. In Whitehead's view, the past consists of all accomplished fact, namely, those events whose moment of subjective immediacy has already become and passed into "objectivity"; their settled feelings now influence all newly arising moments of experience. The *present* is precisely those newly arising events in their actual becoming—in their moment of subjective creation. The *future* as such does not yet exist as an objective reality. Yet it does exist as a metaphysical necessity, in the sense that *some* future *must* exist, since the creative advance—the many becoming one and being increased by one—is everlasting and necessarily entails the creation of some kind of new events. Additionally, the influence of the settled events from the past sets some limits on what is to come and thereby delineates the future within certain parameters. Thus, in accord with our native sense of time there must be *some* future, while the past defines the *general* shape of things to come. In other words—in complete accordance with the way we live our lives—the past is what has been, the present is what is happening, and the future is what will be. That sounds reasonable, doesn't it?

This may sound trite or too general to be of much importance. But when we consider several notable consequences of this process approach to temporality, we begin to appreciate its significance. Adopting Whitehead's process view of the creative advance provides a straightforward basis for understanding the directionality of time—that is, of differentiating the past and future. This obviates the need to resort to awkward explanations such as locating this directionality within the law of entropy (that is, distinguishing the past from the future on the basis of the energetic running down of the universe). With Whitehead's metaphysical foundation for the directionality of time, human and cosmic evolution find a rational ground. Furthermore, thinking of time as a product of the unfolding advance of *all* events, rather than as only a manifestation of human experience, provides a way of accounting for the reality of temporal process throughout the history of the universe. This avoids the paradoxical conclusion sometimes propounded that time has only existed since the advent of human consciousness and its temporal awareness. (Of course, this *is* true of the unique human experience of time, but not of temporal process itself.)

Whitehead's understanding of time entails a grave consequence for theistic *and* atheistic determinist theories. Since the exact nature of the future is undecided—that is, not yet actual—future events *cannot* be known or predicted in advance with total certainty, even by a God or an ultimate supercomputer with complete information on all past events. This means that our common human experience of freedom and choice is not obviated by some ultimate deterministic mechanism at the heart of our universe; rather, freedom and choice are congruent with the metaphysical workings of temporal process (and Whitehead's other metaphysical principles).

This theory of time holds important consequences for transpersonal psychology as well. If Whitehead's speculations are correct, then clairvoyance, if it exists, must be seen as a limited and partial insight into *possible* future outcomes. On the other hand, Whitehead's metaphysics strengthens claims of the possibility of accessing and reliving experiences and events from the past, as all events continue to exist as objective facts whose data can be directly felt by new occasions. *Changing* past events themselves, however, would be considered a metaphysical impossibility—as would time travel in the literal sense—since this would involve altering *previously accomplished* events. Travel into a not-yet-existent future makes even less sense except as a more or less accurate imaginative exploration into future possibility. I hope no one will feel unduly constrained if this process perspective on the impossibility of literal time travel proves accurate. We still have hundreds of billions of galaxies each containing hundreds of billions of stars to explore, not to mention the more immediate adventures of exploring the nearly unlimited depths of our own unconscious experience, which itself opens up into the vast universal depths.

Looking back on my psychedelic experience of time slowing down and the second hand stopping, what do I make of that now? (Yes, I did check later to see if the clock was otherwise operating properly.) While the *experience* of temporal passage can be understood much more fluidly in process philosophy—time itself arises out of the flow of experiential events—the creative advance obviously was not brought to a halt by my altered state. The intensified breadth and depth of attention made possible through psychedelic influence, however, could have made the lived duration of each new moment *feel* longer and longer to the point of stretching my perception of time far enough that the second hand seemed frozen. Time distortion, of course, is commonly reported in psychedelic accounts.

Of at least equal interest is the question of what occurred to cause my momentary amnesia or blackout, followed immediately by an extreme state of terror as I found myself in front of Alex crying, "What are we going to do?" I see now that this may well have represented a partial encounter with *ego death*, or a venture into that empty space between moments of experience, a mystical state most carefully set forth in Buddhist writings. This terrifyingly fascinating experience returns us to the original problem: the genesis, meaning, and implications of mystical and psychedelic states. Whitehead's revolutionary theory of perception, as I will try to demonstrate in the next chapter, proves quite helpful for sorting out many of these perplexing issues.

An Ineffable Interlude

Before moving on to further psychedelic stories and theories, I will consider the problem of *ineffability* and some epistemological issues related to mystical experiences in general. What can we really know and communicate about these extraordinary happenings? I briefly alluded to this matter in Chapter 4 while discussing Mark's insight that the answer is, "What is the *question*?" But for those seriously concerned with this problem—some of whom may be tempted to cite Wittgenstein's famous epigram: "Whereof one cannot speak, thereof one must be silent"—a few more words seem in order.

After reviewing one of my essays, Will Beardslee, the teacher who introduced me to Whitehead's work, cautioned against sounding too definitive with my interpretations of mystical experiences, since many people consider them *ineffable* or at least largely indescribable. The difficulty in retrieving and expressing the essence of such states and insights recalls the story I told earlier about my first LSD trip. Having just watched in stunned rapture as colorful energy flows circulated through our sunroom's glass chandelier, I walked up to the kitchen doorway and encountered my sister and her boyfriend. I opened my mouth to share my amazement over this radiant vision and all the other novel ideas and feelings that were pouring through me, but *nothing would come out.* I was struck completely dumb (unable to speak), overwhelmed by this flood of new feelings. It was as if my mind was both empty and overflowing simultaneously. In any case, I was left speechless in the face of my first taste of a radically nonordinary state of consciousness.

This unusual state of affairs was highly disconcerting, as I had always taken pride in my mental control and verbal ability. I am reminded of that unnerving feeling whenever I hear Pink Floyd's song "Brain Damage," in which the institutionalized lunatic chuckles about being unable to say anything—and then pours forth demented laughter. The lunatic's frantic amusement at his inability to share his inner world painfully captures that sense of being so overwhelmed by images and feelings that reverting to normal discourse seems totally inadequate and absurd—in fact, hilarious in a terrifying sort of way. From a Whiteheadian perspective, this represents the psyche being flooded by intuitions derived largely from those prelinguistic, precultural feelings that lie at the unconscious depths of the psyche, resulting in an experience that is beyond language because so much of it is coming from outside one's usual ego boundaries.

From this experience—and from many other struggles with trying to describe, to understand, or even to remember psychedelic insights and states—I can well sympathize with those who believe that mystical experiences, especially the more powerful ones, are fundamentally beyond description or interpretation. Nevertheless, I hold that the problem of ineffability is only partly true in regard to psychedelic experiences. These feelings can be at least partially described and partially conceptualized. After all, *all* experience is in some final sense ineffable, especially those involving deep feeling, such as love, gustatory enjoyment, sexual pleasure, and so on. It would take a culinary expert or an artist to come anywhere close to capturing the raw experience of eating a grape. On the other hand, *some* interpretation, conscious and unconscious, is built into all human experience, as Whitehead so pithily points out: "If we desire a record of uninterpreted experience, we must ask a stone to record its autobiography."[1]

Of course, we all *do* try to describe our personal experiences and to make as much sense of them as possible. The same principle should hold for mystical experiences. Many mystical insights and feelings may remain beyond communication in their fullness or immediacy, perhaps to an even greater degree than with other essential experience involving deep feeling and sensation, since the objects and states of mystical intuitions lie far outside the range of everyday existence and the words designed to describe it.

Whatever the merit of this argument, I *needed* to try to make sense of my psychedelic exploits—partly through seeking out others who had written about experiences that were similar to my own. And I searched even harder to find a general system of thought capable of providing a theoretical context for such extraordinary happenings. Process philosophy has proven most helpful in this regard, as well as for sorting out the issue of ineffability. In Whitehead's view, while human experience is always heavily influenced by the culture and one's past, it is not solely determined by or completely derived from past cultural forms. All our experience arises out of direct unconscious perceptual access to "things in themselves."

1. Whitehead, *Process and Reality*, 15.

Drawing on Whitehead's categories, David Griffin makes a crucial distinction between what we *can* and what we *cannot* know about mystical experience—in this case, about the *Holy:*

> The *perceptual* meaning of the holy ... is the subjective form [i.e., *how* an object is felt] of a prehension [i.e., a "feeling"]. The holy in this sense, which is sometimes referred to as the "numinous," is indefinable. Like the color yellow, its unique quality can be grasped only by being experienced. As a *conception,* however, the term *holy* can be said to refer to *that which is of ultimate intrinsic worth, in relation to which everything else finally has its worth.* Each religion, in referring to the ultimate reality around which it is oriented as God, Allah, Nirvana, Emptiness, Brahman, the Tao, or the Mandate of Heaven, is referring to that which it *conceives* to be holy, which some of its adherents believe they have *perceived* to be holy.[2]

Griffin is certainly correct in that we cannot adequately grasp the direct perceptual experience of another—the quality of *how* that person experiences something—through any kind of linguistic description. But it is possible for anyone to try to describe, however incompletely, *what* they experienced and how they *understand* their experience and related feelings. These descriptions and contextualizations can be compared, compiled, and organized into theories of mystical experience.

I now return to Beardslee's suggestion that interpretations of mystical experience should avoid sounding too conclusive, keeping in mind the highly speculative nature of this subject. Good advice, indeed. Please take all my forthcoming interpretations of nonordinary and mystical states as formulations that I have found helpful in my life and studies—as suggestions about how these experiences might be coherently understood and integrated into a worldview not all that different from the one in which we live every day, but quite different from a world understood primarily in terms of matter in motion.

The nondefinitive nature of such interpretations, and the variability among these experiences themselves, is highlighted in this observation by John Fenton, an Emory colleague of Beardslee: "From a descriptive-interpretive scholarly point of view, there is no general key to the meaning of all mystical texts, and there is no intrinsic general ranking system for different types of mysticism. Nor is there a best, highest, purest, or most complete type of mystical experience. Such judgments are not

---

2. Griffin, *Reenchantment without Supernaturalism,* 252 (italics original).

phenomenological, they are theological."[3] This is one reason I find Grof's cartography of the human psyche so useful. It offers a descriptive categorization of transpersonal experiences drawn from a large pool of subjects' spontaneous encounters with the depth unconscious unleashed. Fenton's view is also a valuable corrective to the absolutist and hierarchic tendencies found in certain strains of transpersonal theory, as well as in some New Age thought and contemporary religion.

Even with all I have just said about ineffability being only *partially* true for mystical experience, I still find compelling this concluding observation from Olaf Stapledon's classic work *Star Maker* regarding the limits of finite consciousness vis-à-vis the deepest mysteries of the universe. Having spent the entire book building towards his final statement on the ultimate spiritual meaning of this universe, and all universes, he ends his astonishing vision of God, the "Star Maker," with this caveat:

> But this was not the worst. For in saying that the spirit's temper was contemplation, I imputed to it a finite human experience, and an emotion; thereby comforting myself, even though with cold comfort. But in truth the eternal spirit was ineffable. Nothing whatever could truly be said about it. Even to name it 'spirit' was perhaps to say more than was justified. Yet to deny it that name would be no less mistaken; for whatever it was, it was more, not less, than spirit, more, not less, than any possible human meaning of that word. And from the human level, even from the level of a cosmical mind, this 'more,' obscurely and agonizingly glimpsed, was a dread mystery, compelling adoration.[4]

I will not pretend to accomplish here what Stapledon's collective galactic minds could not! However, there exists a wide range of transpersonal experiences lying between the most basic spiritual intuition and the final nature of the Ultimate cosmic entity. Many of these, I think, are fair game.

3. Fenton, "Mystical Experience," 61.
4. Stapledon, *Star Maker*, 248.

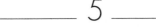

5

A Complex Amplifier

Theorists such as Ernst Cassirer have argued convincingly that it is our proclivity for symbolizing, or meaning making, that lies at the heart of what makes us human. We are *symbolizing animals.*[1] Whitehead goes even further, showing how *all* experience, even sensory perception, is inherently symbolic. Likewise his process metaphysics elucidates how this symbolization process itself is what *connects* us to a world beyond ourselves, rather than leaving us isolated in a world constructed entirely of subjective symbols. Whitehead's analogy of the human body as a *complex amplifier* serves as a unique grounding for his explication of this symbolizing capacity.

Jung, of course, devoted a great deal of effort to investigating the psycho-spiritual transformative power of certain symbols, especially those he termed archetypal. The transpersonal potential of symbols was brought home to me in a psychedelic experience I describe below.

Castalia

My journeys with psychedelics were as bewildering as they were illuminating, and so I was eager to discover what different writers and researchers had to say on this topic. One of the first and best books I came upon was Masters and Houston's *The Varieties of Psychedelic Experience.*[2] The title, of course, is a play on William James's *The Varieties of Religious Experience*, an appropriate reference in a number of ways—not least because in James's own book he describes using nitrous oxide to alter his own consciousness. Among other things, Masters and Houston's interdisciplinary effort brings together fascinating insights from psychology, philosophy, and mysticism,

1. Cassirer, *Essay on Man.*
2. Masters and Houston, *Varieties of Psychedelic Experience.*

meshing well with my intuition that psychedelics access the experiential intersection of these domains.

Apparently I had mentioned my interest in their work to my mother at some point, for during the spring of my first year at college, she alerted me to a monthlong gathering taking place in Switzerland the following summer called the Castalia seminar. Jean Houston was to be part of the faculty, along with other notables, including Harvey Cox, June Singer, and Michael Volin, known as the Yogi of Australia. The location of the seminar was near Lugano in Montagnola, on the grounds of The American School in Switzerland (TASIS), where all my sisters had spent some time and where I had once visited briefly. Near the home of Herman Hesse, the location was fitting for a conference called Castalia, after the fictional setting of his final novel and magnum opus, *The Glass Bead Game*.[3] The conference theme was Hesse's writings and Carl Jung, which of course allowed for a wide range of topics in the areas of psychology, philosophy, religion, myth, and literature. Not coincidently, Hesse and Jung had already become two of my favorite authors.

Jean Houston, as it turned out, was only scheduled to be at Castalia for a short time. But I was so eager to meet her that I was happy to spend a month at Castalia just to have this opportunity—which, incidentally, led to my eventual participation in a number of her intensive workshops. Jean turned out to be a fount of information and inspiration who helped guide my search and stabilize my life. There's no need to go into much detail on the seminar itself, which I found fascinating at the beginning, but somehow less so as the weeks went by and my drinking escalated—especially after locating a nearby source of gin. However, I do want to recount one day of particular consequence.

The day in question involved three events—all psychedelically enhanced—that culminated with me nearly leaving all I knew behind, or at least it certainly felt that way at the time. It all began rather benignly. While getting off on some LSD, I joined a small group of Castalians who were listening to a presentation by a beautiful Radcliffe student.

Her lecture, as I recall, was on the phenomenology of being *lost*. The exact timetable of that day is likewise lost in the mists of time. But as I was already beginning to feel the effects of the acid, I think it safe to say that it must have taken place sometime in the afternoon. All I really remember about her talk was that it felt eerily pertinent to my situation: both to my general sense of feeling a bit lost in life and to the more specific psychedelic sense of feeling my normal ego boundaries slipping away. Although this experience of losing

3. Hesse, *Magister Ludi*.

myself was always frightening, it was exhilarating and freeing at the same time. Thankfully, the cloistered gardens, beautiful buildings, and hillside setting overlooking Lake Lugano and the Alps provided a soothing and serene background to my growing psychedelic turbulence.

Tellingly, the more the acid came on, the less concerned I became with how appealing the lecturer was. In my case, at least, when under the influence of LSD, the powerful feelings surging through my body and soul overrode my normal urges for other kinds of exciting stimulation, even the erotic. Also, while in the grips of psychedelic intoxication, I often found it difficult to stay intentionally focused on anything for an extended time, as my awareness was largely at the mercy of deeper psychic currents. (This brings to mind an American I met in Afghanistan, who told me that he loved sex on heroin because he could go on and on, but he did not like making love on LSD, as he kept losing track of what was happening. On the other hand, Timothy Leary often describes the pleasures of psychedelic sex. But I suspect that such encounters occurred before or after the peak period of the acid trip—or perhaps I should say that I suspect this would be true for most people. Leary is somewhat of an anomaly, in many regards.) In any case, I left the lecture psychedelically charged and psychologically roused for the next event.

Jean Houston's workshop on "Your Death" met late that afternoon. Earlier in the day, Jean had asked me if her group could use the large balcony off my room, which overlooked the manicured grounds. I was happy to oblige. So, a little before sunset, about a dozen of us gathered in the fading light to imagine the circumstances surrounding our own death. I suspect Jean thought that a vivid confrontation with our existential boundaries would be a revealing psychological exercise. Our assignment was to describe in detail how we might want our own funerals or memorials to be carried out.

This became a deeply poignant experience, especially given my LSD-enhanced state of heightened emotion and imagination. Even more striking, though, was watching how others performed this task. Faces, when viewed psychedelically, often appear to be transparent masks, revealing both the surface charade and the hidden emotions within. Being privy to the naked psychic depths of others is a powerful experience—both fascinating and disturbing. Some were playful, some more serious, but all appeared to me to be consciously or unconsciously avoiding their deeper, authentic feelings about death. I departed this session emotionally primed by these recent confrontations with being alone and the prospect of my own death: two key issues for me—and for most people, I would hazard.

After Jean's workshop, the evening lecture was in the main lounge, where a German Egyptologist was giving a presentation on the meaning of the symbols of ancient Egypt. In a somewhat discombobulated condition, I stretched out on a sofa at the end of the large room. I sensed this was going to be a powerful talk. Hearing these ancient symbols colorfully described affected me strongly. Curiously, the lecturer's German accent seemed to add to the efficaciousness of his words. In fact, I began to feel that he was somehow *invoking* these symbols, that they were actually becoming alive inside of me in some palpable way. When he arrived at the symbol of the Snake, describing how its serpentine energies *rise up* into the sky, pulling one *up into the heavens* . . . well, I was right there along with him for the ride. I was slip sliding away to somewhere else with that snake, and with each passing second, I was climbing further and further from this reality. My entire world seemed to be rapidly fading away. When I realized that nearly everything was gone, and that I no longer could feel any sense of attachment even to my family—I could still vaguely remember them in some abstract fashion but felt no personal connection whatsoever—I suddenly became concerned about where this all might end up. I did not want to be discovered on that couch in a catatonic stupor, being trapped in some astral realm beyond my ken. The trouble this would cause for the Castalia organizers, and the pain that my family would feel, seemed unacceptable. This fate appeared to be a distinct possibility at the time, although in retrospect, this was more likely my ego grasping at straws to protect its already haggard boundaries. In any case, I pulled myself back from the brink somehow and struggled up to my room, where I lay in bed and held on for dear life until the psychedelic peak had passed.

Symbolism

Never before had I experienced so vividly the direct efficacy of what might be called a *living symbol*. It was as if some kind of "snaky" catalyst entered into my being and reshaped my psyche.

This encounter with the power of the symbol raised a number of questions, such as: How can symbols help transform inner experience in such a dramatic fashion? Also, if one does not believe that symbols are *all* there is to reality, then how do symbols mediate our interaction with a world *beyond* ourselves? From a transpersonal perspective, this problem becomes one of understanding how symbols might help *open up* experience to the deeper aspects of the universe. When I felt myself ascending towards some transpersonal realm, was this purely a subjective fantasy or hallucination? Or might my psyche actually have been opening up to a larger reality residing beyond the threshold of everyday awareness?

The larger issue at hand involves not only the psychodynamic and transpersonal power of symbols, but also what role symbolism plays in *all* experience. I believe that Alfred North Whitehead's philosophy holds the key to addressing these questions—and others as well—through his revolutionary theory of perception. Before examining Whitehead's theory, I want to relate a story about how Paul Ricoeur's views on symbolism have influenced my thinking.

While working on my master's degree at West Georgia College (now the University of West Georgia), it was my good fortune to take a course on Paul Ricoeur with Myron ("Mike") Aarons. Mike founded the humanistic psychology program at West Georgia and studied under Ricoeur while completing his doctorate in Paris. The main text for the class was *Freud and Philosophy*, Ricoeur's hermeneutic reading of Freudian theory.

As I pored over the course material the night before our final test, which was a group oral exam to be held at the house I was renting, I had a sudden epiphany about Ricoeur's theory of symbolic transformation. This rapidly evolved into a vision of how the chakra centers are symmetrically, but inversely, interconnected. The root chakra energy at the base of the spine transforms into the spiritual awareness of the crown chakra at the top of the head; the second chakra energy flows into the third eye; the energy from the solar plexus energizes the throat chakra; while the heart chakra acts as the center of transformation for the more primitive energies of the lower chakras as they transmute into higher spiritual feelings.

I do not know if this insight has any basis in reality, as impressive as it seemed at the time, but it did help me understand one of Ricoeur's central points: symbols act to transform emotions about a past object ("desire") into feelings about a present one. For example, if we take early childhood emotions related to one's mother—feelings of protection, warmth, love, envelopment, and a generally nourishing and supportive environment (ideally)—and redirect these feelings or qualities into some aspect of our adult life, we might obtain a symbol like Mother Earth, thereby generating a felt sense of the planet as a loving, nurturing environment that deserves our respect and care. On a more personal level, when we project our early feelings towards our parents onto a potential romantic partner, we are endowing these partners, for better or worse, with the symbolic possibility of rediscovering these long past feelings of ultimate intimacy. As Proust might have it, we attempt to recover lost time.

Stanislav Grof's accounts from psychedelic sessions provide vivid examples of these kinds of symbolic transformations of past experience. Under psychedelic stimulation, people frequently relive episodes from very early on in their lives, sometimes reportedly regressing all the way back to their birth and even into experiences from the womb, and thereby dramatically alter their adult orientation to objects in their life as well as to life in general.

While these findings fly in the face of the conventional medical view that prenatal neurons are not sufficiently myelinated to support memory consolidation, abundant psychological testimony and evidence call this mainstream position into doubt—as do recent discussions concerning some type of memory being present in simple organisms devoid of any nervous system at all. And as we have seen, memory, from a Whiteheadian perspective, is not based solely on brain storage mechanisms but rather involves direct feelings (prehensions) of past events.

When perinatal memories erupt into adult consciousness, they tend to give rise to experiences such as floating through the vast reaches of outer space, swimming through the ocean, or enjoying a tropical paradise. It is not difficult to see how the feeling-tone of these images flows easily out of the vicissitudes of intrauterine existence. At the other end of the spectrum, various manifestations of hell-like images—witches and demons, fiery torment, vast scenes of war and destruction—often arise to symbolically convey the painful and frightening experiences surrounding the more violent aspects of the birth process. Again, past feeling is symbolically transformed to create images and emotions in the present that capture the essential qualities of those memories.

Past feeling can pertain to more than just our personal past, or even our perinatal past. It can also involve intuitions into the broader depths of the universe. In Grof's research, the transpersonal dimension opens up into an astonishingly diverse realm of experiences, including past lives; direct insights into the structure and experience of animals, plants, and microscopic and inorganic forms; mythological and archetypal entities; parapsychological phenomena; mystical states; and more. But what do these extraordinary experiences mean? Are they real, in the sense of revealing objective information about our universe and the nature of reality? Or are they merely subjective imaginings that hold no broader cosmological or metaphysical implications?

If we are to take seriously transpersonal experiences—and everyday experience as well, for that matter—we require a theory of perception that coherently explains how objective reality enters into our personal experience, thereby obviating the modern paranoia that human consciousness is isolated within its subjective, purely symbolic moments of experience— what Santayana calls "solipsism of the present moment." This anxiety provides fertile ground for fictions like *The Matrix,* where the protagonist discovers that his whole world is a virtual reality. (The careful film viewer will, however, observe the plot holes that appear while trying to make a coherent story based on a notion that violates what David Griffin calls our "hardcore common sense"—in this case, our lived conviction that the world and other people are objectively real.[4])

Whitehead's theory of perception provides an excitingly novel understanding of how feelings from the immediate past of the *larger environment* and from the *body* are symbolically transformed into subjective experience, vanquishing the ghost of solipsism that has been haunting the West since Descartes's radical division of mind and matter. Equally important for my quest, Whitehead's theory also furnishes a rational, coherent interpretation of how parapsychological and mystical perceptions could provide real knowledge about the universe. The key idea, similar to the one described in Ricoeur's interpretation of Freud, is that feelings related to objects lying beyond everyday awareness are unconsciously perceived and psychically transformed to create new, relevant experiences in the present.

Metaphysics of Perception

A full account of Whitehead's theory of perception lies beyond the scope of this book. But residing within his complex theory are some foundational ideas that are highly relevant to the purposes herein.

A simpatico soul, Colin Wilson, makes the bold claim that *Symbolism: Its Meaning and Effect* is "not only one of Whitehead's most important books, but one of the most important books of the century."[5] While I would reserve Whitehead's *Process and Reality* for that particular honor, Wilson, unfortunately, is close to the mark when he states: "Whitehead has no gift for immediately seizing the attention."[6] So perhaps a brief introduction to Whitehead's ideas on perception from Wilson himself is in order, as *he* rarely has a problem generating immediate interest. This seems especially appropriate since Wilson shares a similar agenda to my own: employing process philosophy and transpersonal psychology to revitalize the intellectual and spiritual foundations of Western civilization.

In *New Pathways in Psychology*, Colin Wilson follows up a pithy summary of Thomas Reid's rebuttal of Hume's theory—that perception is entirely composed of "sense data"—with another pithy summary, this time of Whitehead's theory of perception.

4. Griffin, *Parapsychology, Philosophy, and Spirituality*, 101–3.
5. Wilson, *Below the Iceberg*, 119.
6. Wilson, *Below the Iceberg*, 119.

Whitehead argued that we have two kinds of perception, 'immediacy perception' and 'meaning perception', which operate together just as my two eyes operate to give me depth perception.
(Whitehead called them 'presentational immediacy' and 'causal
efficacy'.) Hume's 'string of perceptions' is immediacy perception; but more important, from the point of view of my will and
creative drives, is 'meaning perception'. Meaning perception
shows us what is important; immediacy perception shows us
what is trivial. One is a telescope; the other, a microscope.[7]

While Wilson has, in his inimical way, captured a key aspect of Whitehead's thought, some careful explication will be needed to illuminate
the full power of Whitehead's vision. Digging into Whitehead's theory
of perception will be worth the effort, for along with shedding light on
the origin of nonordinary experiences, it has important implications for
understanding the mind/body problem as well as how we can have real
knowledge of the world.

Whitehead's novel approach runs counter to most modern thought,
both scientific and philosophic, as he does not accept Hume's extreme
doubt—for example, doubt that humans have any direct experience of causality or knowledge of an outside world. Nor does he go along with Kant's
explanation that the constructive, synthetic powers of the unconscious
Mind are solely responsible for the world we consciously experience in its
causal, temporal, and spatial dimensions.

Whitehead argues that Hume's description of experience in terms of a
mere string of perceptions overlooks some crucial facts. For one thing, we
have direct experience of causality through our subtle awareness of the organic derivation of vision *from the eyes* or of hearing *with the ears*: our ears
tingle and our eyes vibrate with sensory feeling. And we feel pain and sexual
excitement flow through our bodies, not just register abstractly in our minds.
Very *short-term memory* is the clearest example of our retention of causal
feeling. We continue to feel music reverberating in our being as the chords
progress; we still have immediate possession of the first part of a sentence
while we take in the rest and can thus make sense of it as a unitary expression.
(And might psychedelic "trails" be the heightened or extended retention of
the visual data from just-past occasions of experience, like when I saw a stop-
action trail of Ping-Pong balls during my first LSD trip?)

Whitehead congratulates Kant on the fundamental discovery of the
constructive nature of Mind. However, Whitehead argues that it is the unconscious activity of creative synthesis that *produces* the unitary event—the

7. Wilson, *New Pathways in Psychology*, 56.

actual occasion—in contrast to Kant's notion of a unitary transcendental ego imposing structural order onto experience. (Kant starts with a one becoming many; Whitehead with a many becoming one.) Furthermore, rather than time, space, and causality being imposed by Kant's transcendental ego, for Whitehead, our experience of these basic relations occurs because they *exist in the real world* and enter directly into our experience as the universe floods into each new moment. This difference between Kant and Whitehead is of vital importance. Whitehead's theory eliminates Kant's radical disjunction between our phenomenal experience of the world and the noumenal realm of "things in themselves." By making the "things in themselves" at least partially knowable as natural constituents of our unconscious field of experience, Whitehead's approach overcomes this bifurcation between appearance and reality. Let us look more closely at how this plays out within a process model.

The novelty of Whitehead's theory of perception lies primarily in its metaphysical underpinnings. His overall view—that data are transmitted via wave-particles through the environment until received by the body and its specialized sense organs, then transmitted and augmented by the nervous system until they emerge into conscious human perception—is one largely shared by standard scientific theory. What remains mysterious in this standard account is *how* data are transmitted to and through the human organism; even more mysterious is how data enter *into* human experience. The source of this mystery, however, is not a mystery. It arises directly out of science's ingrained metaphysical prejudice for understanding phenomena in a materialistic fashion. This bias has so far at least made it impossible to coherently connect the world of material objects with the world of human experience, or (for that matter) to account for human experience at all. Whitehead's revolution was to devise an organic, experiential account of reality able to address just these points. While this account holds some surprising and possibly paradigm-changing implications, it does not run counter to contemporary scientific theory or empirical data, only to certain unwarranted extrapolations of these theories based on obsolete notions about the fundamental nature of things.

Whitehead's revised metaphysical fundamentals call for a new and primary mode of perception, where the past is felt *directly* by subsequent events. This conception provides not only a way of understanding the transmission of data between low-grade events—such as probability fields generating new quantum events—but also the mode of interaction between neural events and human occasions of experience: between the brain and the mind. This account also brings into play the possibility of a wide spectrum of parapsychological and transpersonal perceptions, as the human psyche is understood to be intrinsically open to receiving data from *any* other event in the universe. This chapter is titled "A Complex Amplifier" because this image captures powerfully Whitehead's notion of the human organism as a *reality resonator*, pulsing with the vibrational flow of the universe, as it receives past feeling and transmutes this energy into a novel perspective on the world. In this way, the human organism accomplishes in large what each actual occasion does in every moment: it creatively synthesizes its environment into new manifestations of actuality.

A Human Complex Amplifier

In his remarks below, Whitehead describes the foundations of human perception. Human sensory perceptual systems can be understood as *highly complex forms* of the more general phenomena of prehension, which goes on in every event. The human organism acts as a *complex amplifier* of the wider environment, providing an especially rich experiential matrix for its dominant occasions: the human psyche.

> This survey supports the view that the predominant basis of perception is perception of the various bodily organs, as passing on their experiences by channels of transmission and of enhancement. It is the accepted doctrine in physical science that a living body is to be interpreted according to what is known of other sections of the physical universe. This is a sound axiom; but it is double-edged. For it carries with it the converse deduction that other sections of the universe are to be interpreted in accordance with what we know of the human body.
>
> ... According to this interpretation, the human body is to be conceived as a complex 'amplifier'—to use the language of the technology of electromagnetism. The various actual entities, which compose the body, are so coordinated that the experiences of any part of the body are transmitted to one or more central occasions to be inherited with enhancements accruing upon the way, or finally added by reason of the final integration. The enduring personality is the historic route of living occasions which are severally dominant in the body at successive instants. The human body is thus achieving on a scale of concentrated efficiency a type of social organization, which with every gradation of efficiency constitutes the orderliness whereby a cosmic epoch shelters in itself intensity of satisfaction.
>
> The crude aboriginal character of direct perception is inheritance. What is inherited is feeling-tone with evidence of its

origin: in other words, vector feeling-tone. In the higher grades of perception vague feeling-tone differentiates itself into various types of sensa—those of touch, sight, smell, etc.—each transmuted into a definite prehension of tonal contemporary nexūs by the final percipient.[8]

I will attempt to unpack this important passage. In human perception, primitive bodily feelings stimulated by external events are channeled and amplified as they pass through the events composing the sensory organs and neural networks. In the actual moment of human-level perceptual experience, these rarefied feelings conveying data from the external environment are selectively prehended from the brain's neural matrix and synthesized into a new moment of human experience. This "new moment" belongs to the series of occasions that make up what we normally think of as the human mind, soul, or psyche. Thus, human perception arises primarily out of (1) multitudinous acts of miniperception that occur throughout the neurons of the sensory organs and the neural transmission systems, (2) the higher-order neural activity of the brain's perceptual centers, and (3) the final unification and synthesis that takes place in the dominant occasion of experience, which is a momentary manifestation of the human psyche proper.

However, the primitive perceptions ("physical prehensions") that facilitate the neural transmission of data and also initiate the dominant occasion's moment of experience must be carefully distinguished from the highly sophisticated moment of conscious sensory awareness that we normally equate with the notion of perception itself. Whitehead's theory of perception identifies *three major modes* of perceiving that help to clarify this important point.

Whitehead has developed special terminology to distinguish the two principal "higher grades" of perception from the more fundamental perceptual mode of *causal efficacy.* "Perception in the mode of causal efficacy" refers to the direct, unconscious perception of past occasions that occurs in all events during their initial reception of past feeling. The second basic mode Whitehead calls "perception in the mode of presentational immediacy": that is, sheer conscious sense perception. Presentational immediacy constitutes our experience of pure sensory perception understood in the traditional sense—that is, as awareness of uninterpreted color, shape, and sound. The third mode of perception, "symbolic reference," denotes our usual conscious mode of perception. It is a *mixed* mode in that it combines feeling and information derived from the two basic modes. This is what Colin Wilson refers to as "meaning perception" (though at times he seems

8. Whitehead, *Process and Reality,* 119.

to conflate symbolic reference with the function of causal efficacy—ignoring the fact that it is feelings from causal efficacy that provide the ground of meaning for symbolic reference).

The essential idea here is that symbolic reference arises out of the integration of the perceptual modes of causal efficacy and presentational immediacy. Feelings of causal efficacy, as our initial reception of data from other events, represent our primary mode of perception, while our conscious sensory awareness of the world is a secondary and derivative function. Our vague, feeling-laden direct perception of past reality (causal efficacy) is synthesized with the clarity of simplified conscious sense perception (presentational immediacy) to create a meaningful encounter with the world (symbolic reference).

I will elaborate a bit more, as Whitehead's theory and terminology can be confusing at first blush. Perception for a new "human-level event" (that is, for a moment of experience of the human psyche) begins with an initial flooding in of feelings from the immediate past containing information of the surrounding environment. These feelings involve especially the neural activity from certain sensory-processing areas of the brain. This flow of vast neural activity into the initial phase of a moment of human experience is an example of perception in the mode of causal efficacy. Through a process of abstraction, comparison, and synthesis, these feelings are focused into conscious awareness of an external realm of sensory presentation. In its pure form, this sheer sensory display—for vision, colored regions spatially organized—corresponds to what Whitehead terms perception in the mode of presentational immediacy. However, in nearly all cases, these two modes are combined to create our normal perceptual sense of a given world filled with familiar objects and entities calling forth emotional responses and appropriate actions. Via symbolic reference, the vague sense of derivation and feeling tone received from real entities in the world combines with the well-defined perception of a sensory array and spatial relations to create life's meaningful experiences of the world.

Of particular interest in this regard is the animal body and its role in perception. It is here that we have a direct, though usually vague, awareness of the role causal efficacy plays in forming our perceptual experience. We can sense the ear's effort to hear a faint sound or, as Whitehead suggests, feel our vision straining through fatigued eyes. It is in our bodies that we have a dim awareness of the route of inheritance that links together our prehensive grasp of the world with our highly sophisticated sensorial perspective. Consequently the human body enjoys a unique position vis-à-vis our meaningful lived-world: "the animal body is the great central ground underlying all symbolic reference."[9]

An example may help clarify how Whitehead's three perceptual modes operate in everyday life. Imagine that you return home at night and your dog runs up to bark hello. If all you experienced were a moving white area against a background of other colors in space, you would be perceiving almost fully in the mode of presentation immediacy. If you closed your eyes and tuned into your body's vague proprioceptive feelings and other bodily sensations, you would be perceiving almost completely in the mode of causal efficacy. And if you excitedly reached out to pet your beloved dog, happy to be back in the cozy hallway of your home, you would be experiencing the world through symbolic reference, the mode where we spend most of our waking existence.

This process of overlaying value-laden feelings upon the derivative clarity of conscious sensory perception to create a meaningful encounter with the world is symbolic exactly in the sense described early in this chapter. Feelings from past events are transmuted to endow meaning upon present experience (although in this case of conscious perceptual experience, the events in question are from the very immediate past). Transpersonal experience differs from our everyday symbolic experience in that it tends to employ more powerful symbolic contrasts in order to access feelings from past events lurking much further within the unconscious depths.

In addition to the fact that perception in the mode of causal efficacy directly connects us to entities beyond ourselves (thus providing an escape from solipsistic isolation, as well as an empirical access to outside reality and a practical notion of truth), what I wish to draw attention to is causal efficacy's *emotional basis*. In the following description, Whitehead evokes a picture of a universe based on *feeling*:

> The primitive form of physical experience is emotional—blind emotion—received as felt elsewhere in another occasion and conformally appropriated as a subjective passion. In the language appropriate to the higher stages of experience, the primitive element is *sympathy*, that is, feeling the feeling *in* another and feeling conformally *with* another. We are so used to considering the high abstraction, 'the stone as green,' that we have difficulty in eliciting into consciousness the notion of 'green' as the qualifying character of an emotion. Yet, the aesthetic feelings, whereby there is pictorial art, are nothing else than products of the contrasts latent in a variety of

9. Whitehead, *Process and Reality*, 170.

colours qualifying emotion, contrasts which are made possible
by their patterned relevance to each other. The separation of
the emotional experience from the presentational intuition is
a high abstraction of thought. Thus the primitive experience is
emotional feeling, felt in its relevance to a world beyond. The
feeling is blind and the relevance is vague.[10]

Here, Whitehead seems in tune with the mystic and Romantic intuition
of a universe flooded with flowing emotion. His emphasis on sympathy in
this respect is also reminiscent of (and a possible metaphysical grounding
for) Heidegger's use of the term *Sorge*, that is, "concern" or "care."[11] Also
relevant are the Soviet experiments involving recognition of color by the
sense of touch alone. This feat becomes more comprehensible in a context
where color is originally a "qualifying character of an emotion," rather
than an abstract visual component.[12]

It is precisely because perception in the mode of causal efficacy is
blind and vague (the opposite of clear and distinct) that both science and
philosophy have generally neglected its central role in human experience.
Their principal reliance on data derived from conscious experience has
engendered a prejudice favoring those features accentuated by presentational immediacy. This in turn, Whitehead argues, has led to a critical
misunderstanding of the true nature of human experience and of the role
of consciousness:

The organic philosophy holds that consciousness only arises in
a late derivative phase of complex integrations . . . For example,
consciousness only dimly illuminates the prehensions in the
mode of causal efficacy, because these prehensions are primitive
elements in our experience. But prehensions in the mode of presentational immediacy are among those prehensions which we
enjoy with the most vivid consciousness. These prehensions are
late derivatives in the concrescence of an experient subject. The
consequences of the neglect of this law, that the late derivative
elements are more clearly illuminated by consciousness than the
primitive elements, have been fatal to the proper analysis of an

10. Whitehead, *Process and Reality*, 162–63.

11. "Interestingly, Whitehead later [in *Adventures of Ideas*] used the English word
concern in a fashion somewhat similar to Heidegger's, probably without being aware of
Heidegger's use." Hartshorne, *Insights and Oversights*, 325.

12. Chapter 14 of *Psychic Discoveries behind the Iron Curtain* includes an extensive
discussion of Rosa Kuleshova and other individuals who have displayed exceptional
abilities in regard to "feeling" colors, reading through tactile imaging, and exhibiting
other unusual psychic sensory skills.

experient occasion. In fact, most of the difficulties of philosophy are produced by it. Experience has been explained in a thoroughly topsy-turvy fashion, the wrong end first. In particular, emotion and purposeful experience have been made to follow upon Hume's impressions of sensation.[13]

This emphasis on the priority of presentational immediacy has also contributed to the modern doctrine of a "lifeless" or insentient Nature,[14] by abetting a radical separation between an active inner mentality versus nature as inert matter. When we perceive the world in the mode of presentational immediacy, we "discover" a passive, lifeless, consolidated sensory array. This is due to the *transmutation* that occurs during the process of animal perception, through which the multiplicity, emotionality, and activity inherent to the world are obscured. ("Transmutation" is the process whereby a moment of experience combines the feelings from *many* prehended past events into one generalized feeling subsuming the entire group. For example, we see a green leaf rather than millions of molecular occasions exemplifying greenish feeling tones.) In contrast, the activity and aliveness of the world is revealed directly through feelings of causal efficacy. Western philosophy's penchant for starting its analysis of experience from the data presented by presentational immediacy—that is, from spatialized, conscious sensory imagery—has resulted in an unfortunate bias in its interpretation of the world: namely, a tendency to conceive of matter as dead or inert, and nature as passive, valueless, and exploitable.

Residing beyond the realm of such abstract philosophical or scientific analysis (and existential despair) exists a world full of inherent meaning and value—the "life-world" of phenomenology. We do not dwell in presentational immediacy but rather in a world revealed through the mixed mode of symbolic reference. Whitehead's notion of symbolic reference provides the foundation for his theory of symbolism and meaning. His theory of perception more generally helps ground us in a meaningful, enchanted world.

Before embarking on a deeper exploration into the nature of nonordinary states of consciousness, we return briefly to where this chapter began: the transformative power of symbols.

---

13. Whitehead, *Process and Reality,* 162.
14. Chapter 7 in Whitehead, *Modes of Thought* is titled, "Nature Lifeless."

Symbolism and Transformation

The role of symbols in psychospiritual transformation is cogently summarized by Roberto Assagioli: "Symbols as accumulators, transformers, and conductors of psychological energies, and symbols as integrators, have most important and useful therapeutic and educational functions."[15] Although probably implicit in Assagioli's statement, it is important to emphasize that symbols can play these same roles for spiritual and mystical experience. As we have seen, Whitehead's theory of symbolic reference provides an intriguing explanation of how symbols perform these functions. By acting as the mediating symbolic link between causal efficacy and presentational immediacy, "comparative" feelings—higher-level unconscious syntheses—facilitate the flow of primitive feelings (of Reality) into conscious perception and awareness. Symbols, when used properly, help conscious experience organize itself in such a way as to actualize an accurate emotional attunement with the depths of reality. Different types of symbolism attune us to different aspects of reality, in line with their particular signifying function. Borrowing one of Whitehead's examples, when we listen to an orchestra, our attention is on the emotional tones of the music, not the location of the orchestra; when a car honks at us, the situation is reversed—location and pragmatic meaning become paramount.[16]

A more immediately relevant example is provided by Steve Odin, who explains below how religious art is designed to attune conscious experience to the depth reality of religious feeling:

> In Shingon Buddhism, poetic forms such as the Ten Images or the varieties of *mandala* art are to be conceived as objects from sense-perception functioning as expressive symbols (*monji*) which refer to the formless void of emptiness (*ku*) and dependent coorigination (*engi*). However, from the standpoint of Whitehead's theory of symbolic reference, these images do not merely point to emptiness but actually lead to a unity of feeling between the symbol and the meaning of emptiness. By this view, there exists a common ground between our perception of emptiness and our perception of the images of emptiness, so that the symbol and the meaning of the symbol are fused by one intensity of emotion. Therefore, each image discloses the void just as the void reveals each image, such that symbolic form and formless emptiness shine forth through each other in a reciprocity of symbolic reference.

15. Assagioli, *Psychosynthesis*, 178.
16. Whitehead, *Symbolism*, 84.

> The major significance of Whitehead's theory of symbolic reference is that it undermines the false notion of symbolism in religious art whereby an aesthetic symbol merely points to the object which it symbolizes. Whitehead's view articulates instead *the genuine symbolic power of art as a bearer of ultimate reality.*[17]

Although Odin focuses his discussion primarily on the visual arts, both Whitehead and Hartshorne indicate that music is a particularly powerful medium for the symbolic transmission of feeling: "In hearing, the emotional content of sensation is easier to intuit than in vision."[18] And Whitehead writes that "music is particularly adapted for this symbolic transfer of emotions, by reason of the strong emotions which it generates on its own account. These strong emotions at once overpower any sense that its own local relations are of any importance."[19] In addition, music—through its forms of harmonic contrast—provides potential integrative patterns for the higher phases of concrescence, that is, for the more complex layers of unconscious and conscious integration.

Holotropic breathwork (the Grofs' method for inducing nonordinary states) takes full advantage of these properties, often starting off with drumming or other energizing music designed to provoke increased feeling in the mode of causal efficacy—that is, heightened unconscious stimulation. During the middle of the breathwork session, music with building intensity and crescendos is played to support and canalize the flow of unconscious feeling, and also to guide or structure the experience in the direction of transformation, synthesis, and resolution. The final part of the session usually involves peaceful music to help coalesce and integrate the shifts that may have occurred in the psyche's structure.

By facilitating the flow of emotions and deep feeling—and, in some cases, catalyzing a direct manifestation of particular features of reality—symbolic art functions both to induce nonordinary states and to direct awareness towards the realization of religious experiences. Reciprocally, nonordinary states themselves create a sensitized level of awareness that is much more susceptible to the subtleties of symbolic and religious art. In sum, nonordinary states can be induced by religious art, and they can open us to the reality and emotions carried within it as well.

This close alliance between symbolism and Whitehead's philosophy of experience should not be surprising, since his metaphysics is as closely aligned to aesthetic theory as it is to its other sources of inspiration:

17. Odin, "Postmodernism and Aesthetic Symbolism," 211.

18. Hartshorne, *Insights and Oversights*, 345.

19. Whitehead, *Symbolism*, 84.

quantum physics, propositional logic, and William James's psychology and
philosophy. The actual entity is conceived fundamentally as an *aesthetic
occasion* based on *harmonic contrasts* generating depth, breadth, and intensity of experience. (New Age and other mystical notions that conceive
of Reality as issuing from vibrational frequencies or harmonics might find
in Whitehead's metaphysics a sympathetic footing.)

Mandalas offer an example par excellence for illustrating this aesthetic
ideal. Great depth and breadth are obtained by patterning disparate elements
into a unified whole. Similarly, it is the *contrast* of images and colors that
creates the beauty of a painting or a sunset. Their harmonious splendor depends on proper contrast of elements, both physical and ideal. Deeply feeling
the harmony or beauty contained in each present moment is also in a sense
transpersonal, for one is focusing on the unfolding process of experience itself and thus temporarily suspending ongoing egoic concerns.

In this chapter, we have seen how symbols are able to recanalize or
channel feeling into new experiential understandings, perceptions, and
modes of awareness—as happened for me while I was listening to that German Egyptologist describe ancient religious symbols. We next consider
some of the broader implications that Whitehead's theory of perception
holds for nonordinary states and transpersonal experience.

6

A Process Theory of Nonordinary States

A ssuming Stanislav Grof is correct in his general hypothesis that LSD functions as an unspecific amplifier of unconscious processes, several related questions immediately come to mind. *What* kind of things can be accessed through these amplified processes, and *how* do these phenomena enter into human experience?

A Transpersonal Amplifier

Whitehead's novel theory of perception—delineating an additional *psychic* layer of complex synthesis and unification that complements the neural levels of perceptual processing—is incredibly important in its own right as perhaps the first philosophically and scientifically coherent account of its kind. However, for the purposes of this book, the most intriguing aspects of Whitehead's theory of perception have to do with its implications for transpersonal psychology. According to Whitehead, in addition to the energetic vibrations received via the sense organs and nervous system, subtle pulses of feeling from the *entire past universe* are able to enter directly into the formation of every new moment of human-level experience. This opens many avenues of thought previously blocked by the metaphysical orientations of the dominant scientific theories and philosophies of the modern era.

A very different picture of reality emerges when we envision the human psyche's unconscious depths reverberating with the pulse of the universe and suffused with feelings and data derived directly from the entities and processes that constellate our world. Admittedly, these extremely subtle prehensions rarely rise clearly into conscious awareness, appearing mostly in the guise of inchoate intuitions, dream images, or as incipient impressions haunting the minds of certain highly sensitive individuals. These subtle elements surface, often dramatically, during nonordinary states of consciousness, which are likely constituted partly by the flow of these transpersonal elements into conscious awareness.

If we expand Whitehead's notion of a complex amplifier to include the human psyche's ability to directly receive (prehend), highlight, and synthesize the pulses of feeling that flow in from the universe at large, we have a simple yet powerfully efficient model for understanding how many nonordinary experiences arise—and an excellent starting point for evaluating their meaning and significance. Furthermore, when we add to this picture Grof's characterization of psychedelics as "amplifiers or catalysts of mental processes," this model becomes even clearer.[1] Under the influence of psychedelics and through other techniques that intensify or amplify unconscious feeling, the flow of data from the past universe that usually remains far below the threshold of consciousness can suddenly thrust itself into awareness, providing a glimpse into things normally beyond the range of human consciousness—that is, phenomena from the depth unconscious and transpersonal realm.

In short, I am suggesting that the human body acts as a complex amplifier of the data and feelings flowing in from the immediate environment, and then the human psyche serves as a *secondary* amplifier performing two related functions. First, the psyche intensifies and transforms the data flowing in from the nervous system and brain; second, it intuits and amplifies the subtle feelings flowing in from the wider depths of the universe (especially its own past moments). When these "wider depths" include intuitions of entities and processes originating beyond one's personal history or local environment, then the psyche begins to function as a *transpersonal* receiver and amplifier. And since at its completion, each new moment of the psyche becomes a "superject"—that is, a completed event that in turn influences other newly forming events—the human psyche can also be characterized as a kind of *transmitter*, emitting waves of data-laden feeling. So from a Whiteheadian perspective, the technology of the radio may be a more apt metaphor for the psyche than the workings of a computer, given how the human body/mind acts as a receiver, amplifier, and transmitter of wave-pulses of feeling-information.

But why are we not more often, or even always, receiving conscious impressions of a transpersonal nature?[2] At least three factors could contribute to the suppression of the transpersonal depths. First, although I am not a fan of pulling evolutionary explanations out of a hat to justify how

1. Grof, *Beyond the Brain*, 29.

2. Of course, if we were, they would no longer be considered "transpersonal," that is, beyond or outside the range of everyday experience.

human beings "must" have developed, it does seem likely that to maximize survival of the species, it was critical for conscious awareness to attend primarily to the outside world as revealed through the physical senses. Seeing a lion or hearing a rattlesnake was more important to one's immediate survival than mystical revelations or archetypal visions.[3] Commenting on C. D. Broad's theory, Aldous Huxley makes a similar point in *The Doors of Perception:* "To make biological survival possible, Mind at Large has to be funneled through the reducing valve of the brain and nervous system."[4] (It should be noted, however, that most societies have created important rituals and ceremonies for accessing the transpersonal realm, be it for healing, helping with the hunt, tribal bonding, or purely sacred reasons.) Second, although this is slowly changing, modern Western society historically has not encouraged or gladly tolerated those individuals who embrace transpersonal phenomena, especially if such individuals proclaim the importance of such transpersonal experiences. In other words, there exists a strong cultural proscription around these phenomena, especially towards those who take them seriously. This is not the case in many other cultures, however, nor with children, who are granted much more leeway in exploring so-called altered states. Third, transpersonal experiences *can* be overwhelming and even potentially dangerous—especially if not properly supported within a ritual or sacred context—and are thus prone to be repressed by the individual's own defense mechanisms.

For these three reasons, and likely others as well, the ego tends to shield itself against transpersonal transgressions of its boundaries and province of control. Unfortunately, in modern societies this need for ego control often operates at a neurotic level, with well-placed caution being supplanted by irrational anxiety. I will say more about surplus repression later; for now, let us return to the idea of a *transpersonal* complex amplifier.

In an article about James Fadiman, an early LSD researcher, Tim Doody succinctly captures this point: "The psychedelics they ingested acted as a sort of antenna, allowing them to receive rather profound transmissions that they couldn't typically access during their ordinary states of consciousness."[5] It is easy to see how this kind of "ancillary antenna," receiving data and feelings from throughout the universe, has broad implications for understanding parapsychology, mysticism, and all manner of transpersonal phenomena. Of

---

3. On the other hand, it also seems possible that enhanced psychical intuition could provide a real evolutionary advantage by offering advance warning about dangers yet at a distance.

4. Huxley, *Doors of Perception,* 23.

5. Doody, "The Heretic," 70.

course, not all feelings flowing into our psyches are of an exotic nature; they come from mundane sources as well.

According to Whitehead, the occasions constituting the human psyche draw from several primary areas. From the body/brain itself arises a flood of enriched feelings that contribute heavily to the formation of thought, emotion, and perception. Another major source is the psyche's *own* past occasions, which convey memories and habitual experiential patterns. Much subtler in nature are the feelings flowing in directly from the surrounding environment, which form the immediate experiential basis for empathy, intuition, and potential parapsychological capacities. Expanding further into the depths of reality, we find feelings derived from the full range of existing entities and processes in the universe, providing the basis for transpersonal experiences of myriad sorts. Whitehead also describes an "initial aim" derived from feelings of God, which offers a possible direction of unfoldment to each new-arising occasion. What these transpersonal experiences *mean*, or imply about the nature of reality and our universe, will be considered later. First, I will consider more closely *how* nonordinary states arise.

For process philosophy, the entire past universe can broadly be conceived as the *depth unconscious* of each new occasion of experience, where each event receives and synthesizes this flow of past feeling into a new unity. The events making up the human psyche act rather like focused antennae, attuning themselves to favored wavelengths of past feeling at an unconscious level. Pursuing this metaphor a bit further, the human body/brain functions as an amplifier for selected "bandwidths" of past feeling, thereby making certain sense-related data a "dominant channel" for the events of the psyche—complementing the psyche's default setting to receive feelings from its own past events. It is hard not to think about oneself!

Besides being a source of personal memory, reinforced feelings from the psyche's historic route of occasions generate ongoing tendencies to experience reality within a particular established range. The flow of past feeling is "regulated" by these ego structures, understood as habitual formations in the experiential patterning of an enduring individual—in this case, the human psyche or mind. It is quite possible that nonordinary states arise through the interruption or release of these habitual personal and collective patterns, thereby allowing novel experiences to unfold more freely. Given the proper impetus, this process of unfolding happens quite *naturally* since—to repeat this crucial point yet again—the entire past universe potentially can flow into the unconscious experience of every occasion in every moment, and thus it is theoretically possible for any aspect of reality to rise up into conscious awareness. All that is required is the proper *opening*.[6] To understand more deeply how such openings might arise, we turn to what Whitehead refers to as the *concrescent structure* of the actual occasion, that is, the explicit process through which an event creates itself.

Concrescent Process and Nonordinary States

Whitehead's metaphysics offers a systematic framework for understanding how nonordinary states—through heightening perceptual depth and sensitivity and by creating novel structures and forms of experience—allow us to penetrate more fully into the nature of the universe and the underlying realities of human experience. His notion of causal efficacy is particularly critical for developing such a theory. It appears that most if not all methods for accessing nonordinary states directly or indirectly involve enhanced perception in the mode of causal efficacy—that is, heightened access to our direct intuitions of the unconscious depths. While stratagems may vary greatly, an underlying aim of these methods seems to be the increase in vitality, openness, connectedness, and depth of intuition that correlate with a heightened awareness of feelings from the mode of causal efficacy.

To delve more deeply into the nature of transpersonal phenomena, it helps to understand in greater detail Whitehead's understanding of *concrescence*. Literally, concrescence means a "growing together" of previously separate parts: "Concrescence is the *growing together* of a many into the unity of a one."[7] This term is used by Whitehead to indicate the process through which actual occasions create themselves: a process of receiving and synthesizing the feelings of past events into a new unity. Whitehead describes this process genetically—that is, developmentally—in terms of unfolding "phases of concrescence."

In the first phase, feelings from past events are directly replicated. The past flows into the present. In the second phase, pure potentials relevant to the data felt in the first phase enter the concrescence as *conceptual* feelings, that is, as possibilities relevant to how these feelings from past events might be synthesized into a new moment of experience. In the third phase, these potentials or possible forms of actualization are combined with the "physical" feelings from the first phase via a *unifying felt contrast*:

6. Regarding the notion of the human organism as a "transpersonal receiver," a dramatic fictional illustration of such an opening is found in Gerald Heard's classic short story, "Dromenon," in which a gothic cathedral acts as a sonic doorway, or a resonance chamber, into the depths of Reality. Heard, "Dromenon," 197–99.

7. Sherburne, *Key to Whitehead's "Process and Reality,"* 212.

that is, the direct feelings of past events are combined with relevant potentials or possibilities to create new patterns through a harmonizing
synthesis. For simple occasions, this terminates the concrescent process.
In more complex moments of experience, another phase of integration
occurs involving higher-order syntheses producing "intellectual" feelings,
including thought and conscious awareness.

To illustrate, consider a first glance at a painting of a sunset. The first
phase of concrescence would be a direct reception of the "color-laden" feelings from the brain's visual processing centers, along with a vague sense of
derivation from the general environment. In the second phase, certain data
from these feelings might be selected and accentuated by certain patterns or
forms for further refinement. In the third phase, the original feelings would
be synthesized with the more highly refined patterns from the second phase
to generate an awareness of these intensified, harmonious contrasts. Finally,
this sensory awareness might be crowned with a conscious sense and appreciation of the beauty of the overall effect of the painting. We should note
that this example presents a simplified picture in several ways. The psyche's
moments of experience are hypothesized to be only a tenth to a twentieth
of a second in duration. Thus any sense of appreciation or contemplation
would require a coordinated series of psychic events to sustain this extended conscious process. And of course these moments of creative psyche-level
integration are extremely complex in nature and so have much more going
on than the mere development of color and shape recognition.

Whitehead's theory of experience also helps explain why human
awareness is ordinarily blinded to most of the reality felt through "physical" prehensions (that is, our direct feelings of past events), and also why
enhancing awareness of feelings from the mode of causal efficacy through
nonordinary states can produce experiences and data of an extraordinary
nature. According to Whitehead's analysis,

> Consciousness only illuminates the more primitive types of
> prehension so far as these prehensions are still elements in the
> products of integration ... For example, consciousness only
> dimly illuminates the prehensions in the mode of causal effi-
> cacy, because these prehensions are primitive elements in our
> experience.[8]

Since consciousness arises only in the final phase of concrescence, if at all,
the dominating factors in consciousness tend to be the more highly sophisticated products of the later stages of concrescence, such as perceptions in
the mode of presentational immediacy and other clear and distinct ideas.

8. Whitehead, *Process and Reality*, 162.

Conscious awareness of feelings in the mode of causal efficacy are primarily vague and indirect, appearing most clearly in our perception of bodily feelings and in short-term memory—although even these are experienced through the filters of unconscious processing.

Whitehead's metaphor of consciousness illuminating elements of the phases of concrescence provides a simple way of visualizing how nonordinary states influence the concrescent process. During nonordinary experiences, the range of conscious illumination is extended further back into the earlier phases of concrescence, bringing into awareness elements and feelings that are normally relegated to the dark, unconscious depths. Thus, nonordinary states help reverse to some degree what Griffin refers to as "Whitehead's perceptual law" (as spelled out on page 162 of *Process and Reality*): "'that the late derivative elements are more clearly illuminated by consciousness than the primitive elements.'"[9]

This first formulation—that nonordinary states help the illumination of consciousness to reach more deeply into the earlier phases of concrescence—requires some qualification. According to Whitehead's theory, consciousness is the *subjective form* of "intellectual feelings" (that is, *how* intellectual feelings are felt). As intellectual feelings—and consciousness—cannot arise until certain types of processing have been achieved by the earlier phases of concrescence, it is technically inaccurate to visualize conscious awareness accomplishing its penetration of the unconscious depths by literally pushing back into the earlier phases of experience. However, this illumination of the unconscious dimensions of experience could be accomplished via a *more complete or intense appropriation* of certain aspects of the earlier phases by the final conscious integration, thereby enhancing conscious awareness of the more primitive elements of experience. In other words, rather than picturing the light of consciousness being cast further back into the unconscious during nonordinary states, I am suggesting that nonordinary states shift the concrescent process in such a way as to allow normally unconscious aspects of experience to flow more easily and completely into conscious illumination.

Process theology hypothesizes that full consciousness of the entire concrescent process is possible for at least one enduring actuality: namely, God. Thus, it is *also* possible that human beings (in a comparatively minor way) may be capable of a far greater awareness of the structure and content of the concrescent process than is generally acknowledged.

The nature of nonordinary states can be more fully appreciated by distinguishing between the sharply defined type of consciousness often depicted

9. Griffin, "What Is Consciousness?," 64.

in Whiteheadian theory, and a softer kind of "open" awareness frequently associated with nonordinary experiences. In this vein, John Cobb describes a *receptive awareness* that underlies consciousness and that is free from substantial symbolic ordering: "Conscious experience, then, includes both a diffuse receptive element and a significantly organized one."[10] Moreover, this receptive awareness is, according to Cobb, the more fundamental of the two modes of experience—metaphysically and genetically: "The evidence indicates that in the growth of conscious experience mere awareness is prior and primordial."[11] Thus, at the fringe of everyday consciousness lies a domain of experience belonging technically to the unconscious phases of concrescence. Cobb argues that this normally unconscious fringe can be actively attended to, or "cultivated," thereby bringing data from the margins into direct awareness without imposing a stricter conscious ordering upon it:

> It is possible to cultivate an awareness, even an attentive awareness, of these data that is free from such organization. Husserl's phenomenological method can be interpreted in these terms as can part of the technique of Zen Buddhism. All of this would be impossible if awareness were limited to what is significantly ordered.[12]

This suggests that we are on the right track in pursuing the possibility that during nonordinary states, modes of attention develop that facilitate an enhanced awareness of data or feelings from the earlier phases of experience, which usually are obscured by the organizational patterns and symbols of everyday conscious activity.

What I am proposing is that nonordinary experiences involve a heightened access to data and feeling from prehensions in the mode of causal efficacy. This interpretation applies both to the *data* revealed in such experiences, as well as to *how* nonordinary states are induced. The latter occurs in at least two basic ways. First, nonordinary states can arise by directly increasing unconscious psychic excitation and thus *breaking through ego structures* with increased flows of feeling. Examples of such induction techniques include psychedelic substances, dancing and chanting, and holotropic breathwork therapy. Second, nonordinary states can also be produced by *quieting the conscious mind*, thus making the ego structures more "porous" to feelings in the mode of causal efficacy rising up from the depths of experience. Examples of this approach might include

10. Cobb, *Structure of Christian Existence*, 27.
11. Cobb, *Structure of Christian Existence*, 27.
12. Cobb, *Structure of Christian Existence*, 26–27.

certain meditation techniques (such as transcendnetal meditation), sensory deprivation, and vision quests.

Varieties of Transpersonal Experience

Whitehead's metaphysical description of the concrescent process suggests the possibility of organizing nonordinary experiences into three basic categories. Although the groupings overlap somewhat, these distinctions may prove helpful for understanding why there occurs such a wide range of nonordinary experiences, and how they might come into being. The three categories are (1) enhanced awareness of feelings of causal efficacy emerging *within the mode of presentational immediacy*, (2) heightened awareness of the *entities* revealed directly through perception in the mode of causal efficacy, and (3) enhanced intuition of the *structure of experience itself.*

In this first category of nonordinary experiences, conscious perception of the world is enlivened and deepened by enhanced feelings of causal efficacy entering into perception in the mode of presentational immediacy. This heightened awareness of the qualities relating to the mode of causal efficacy—such as the intrinsic value, immanent activity, and interconnectedness of reality—produces a conscious perception of a world that is more alive and precious, and, in some way, deeply interrelated or "One." It is as if one's sensory perceptions were saturated with a heightened intensity and depth of feeling. Additionally, enhanced intuitions of God's involvement in the formation of every event may be transmuted into a conscious appreciation of a world filled by God's subtle presence. This sort of pantheistic (or more precisely, panentheistic) intuition may be reinforced by an increased awareness of the innate creative activity of all actual occasions, producing an apprehension of a spiritually vital world. Grof speaks of this kind of perception as the *immanence* of God or spirit in the world. Also belonging to this category would be experiences related to an intuitive sense of a hidden meaning or profound value that lies behind and informs the phenomenal world. In a nutshell, the everyday world becomes transformed into a place filled with wonder, aliveness, and a new depth of meaning and value.

While the first category involves the transformation and deepening of normal sensory perception, the second category is concerned more with the *specific data* revealed through our more fundamental mode of perception (i.e., causal efficacy). Instead of a flooding of conscious sense perception with the general feeling tones connected to the earlier phases of concrescence, in this second category, the individual opens up to a novel mode of encountering the universe that *transcends* normal sensory perception, although the data revealed may still be funneled through the familiar sensorial mediums. For example, perceptions of distant locales (remote viewing), data from other minds (telepathy), or even spiritual entities may appear as visual and auditory hallucinations—however, these are hallucinations only in the sense that the contiguous chain of physical events that normally mediates our sensory perception is incomplete.

The critical point here is this: if the image in question does in fact correlate significantly with a past entity, then the perception should not be considered hallucinatory, but rather a more or less accurate rendering of some actuality revealed through a perceptual mode other than normal sense perception. Thus, the second category is based upon *direct physical prehensions* of real entities and processes normally hidden from our conventional modes of sensory perception. In nonordinary states, data from these primitive feelings come into conscious awareness with enhanced clarity and intensity. Other possible examples of this type of phenomena include experiences of the body's energy fields, clairvoyance, perception of micro- and macrophenomena, and mystical and spiritual experiences involving individual entities. Grof's distinction of God as *transcendent* belongs to this category, in that here we are considering the possibility of direct nonsensuous perceptions of God, versus the generalized sense of God's presence flooding our everyday perceptual field as that is typical of the first category.

The third category involves enhanced awareness of the structure of experience itself. Here we find meditational techniques aimed at uncovering the most fundamental dimensions of reality—for example, certain Buddhist methods—that would seem to offer experiential access to Whitehead's "Category of the Ultimate": that is, to the problem of the One and the Many. In this third category, the central focus is not on any particular mode of perception or type of data, but rather on the nature of the concrescent process in its own unfoldment—that is, on unveiling the essence of human subjectivity. By Whitehead's account, the fundamental unit of the universe is the actual occasion, a burst of creatively synthesized feelings of past events. The actual occasion—the primary metaphysical reality of our universe—is the foundation of all human experience too. It follows that if human awareness can penetrate far enough into the depths of its own formative processes, it will encounter insights that transcend the merely personal and enter into the metaphysical. When subjective experience is stripped down to its essence, the bare bones of the universe's structure are also exposed. This is the domain of *metaphysical* knowledge.

In this discussion I have been focusing primarily on extraordinary experiences as they occur at the level of the human psyche. Obviously, alterations in processes at the neural level also have significant impact on how the events of the human psyche unfold and reorganize during nonordinary states. Most contemporary efforts to explain extraordinary experience have tended to concentrate mostly on such alterations in brain functioning to the neglect of the higher-level activity of the psyche. My attempt here is to fill this lacuna by demonstrating that it is possible to understand many facets of nonordinary experience by examining the psychological processes of the human psyche itself, especially when applying a Whiteheadian approach.

Parapsychological Phenomena

In the last section, I briefly mentioned some parapsychological phenomena that merit further discussion. The evidence for the existence of parapsychological abilities appears to be quite convincing, even from an experimental perspective, especially when meta-analyses of large numbers of studies are employed.[13] And everyday examples of apparent psychic phenomena abound. Since the anecdotal and experimental evidence so strongly indicates the existence of psi (i.e., parapsychological abilities, such as telepathy, psychokinesis, and clairvoyance), why is the reality of these phenomena so widely called into question, especially in the scientific community?

One likely reason is that clear and distinct, repeatable evidence is hard to come by, either experimentally or in everyday life. If these abilities really exist, why can't they be easily demonstrated within and outside the lab? Of course, this is why they are called extraordinary powers in the first place. If they were in obvious and regular use, then the question of their existence would not even arise, nor would they be considered extraordinary.

In fact, it seems that we *do* regularly employ telepathy, but it is usually cloaked under the guise of empathy or intuition. I expect that almost every reader will have many personal examples of knowing what another person is thinking or feeling, or what is happening to someone at a distance, with few if any direct physical clues on which to base these intuitions. What else is this ability to enter into another's psychic world than a sort of telepathic power, where we feel so clearly what another person is feeling?

Still, these everyday examples seem widely unconvincing to the modern scientific mind, and more surprisingly, so do the decades of positive results from experimental psychic research. I think we can assume with some confidence that a major reason for this dismissal is that the existence of psi powers goes against the unconsciously assumed metaphysics originally put in place partly to deny their very possibility. It is difficult to positively

---

13. See Griffin, *Parapsychology, Philosophy, and Spirituality,* chapter 2. Pages 83–85 deserve particular attention.

account for nonphysical causation or action-at-a-distance within a system that is *based* on rejecting these phenomena, by virtue of the position that all causality must be physical and mechanical in nature. This critical assumption is maintained despite the conspicuous exceptions of gravity, electromagnetic fields, and quantum mechanics, which are all somehow excused from having to cohere to these basic principles.[14]

This is one reason why Whitehead's alternative metaphysics is so important to the field of parapsychology. As we have seen, direct "feeling" connections between all entities are a basic premise of this philosophy. Thus telepathy ("feeling at a distance") is exactly the kind of psychic capacity we might expect to exist within a Whiteheadian paradigm, where *feelings* are precisely what enter into each new occasion of experience, forming its unconscious foundations. In this way, the feelings from other psyches might make their way into consciousness as intuitions of the emotions of those around us, especially those we feel close to. Thoughts, being more complex or abstract kinds of comparative feelings in Whitehead's system, might be expected to be more difficult to access via physical prehensions. And this is what we find in life: sensing another's feelings or emotions is much easier than tapping into another's explicit thoughts.

Within a Whiteheadian worldview, we might think of telepathy as a human occasion having a much greater than usual awareness of its unconscious connection to the feelings of another human's psychic events. We might also return to the analogy of the human psyche as an *antenna* receiving the subtle feelings of past events. Telekinesis, on the other hand, could be based upon *projecting* one's feelings into the constitution of future events. Both phenomena might be conceived of in terms of *attuning* one's own psychical events to the experiential occasions of another person or another object. Since occasions of experience can also be thought of as pulses or vibratory events, the notion of an attunement between events of this nature is not farfetched.

Here is one final word on psi phenomena. In transpersonal psychology, we sometimes find admonitions about the use or development of parapsychological powers. The source of this negative appraisal seems to lie in the writings of some Eastern sages who warn that these powers can serve as distractions or impediments on the road to enlightenment and should thus be shunned or ignored.

I see nothing wrong with exploring and developing these powers in a responsible way. Of course, psi abilities must be handled carefully, like

14. See Chapter 9 of *Parapsychology, Philosophy, and Spirituality* for a more detailed account of the historical origins of modern science's metaphysical commitments.

all powerful tools. But when treated as such, I do not think they need be feared as a distraction from other areas of psychospiritual development. And if we can find ways to harness these kinds of energies and abilities, they may prove surprisingly helpful in dealing with many of the problems that confront us now and in the future.

Further Thoughts

Transpersonal experiences, when understood within a Whiteheadian metaphysics, should be interpreted as having the potential to transcend the limitations accorded to human experience by a full-fledged cultural relativism—that is, the belief that all human experience is so hopelessly entangled in cultural and linguistic structures that the possibility of direct knowledge of objective reality is highly dubious. The symbolic order, as composed by language, society, and culture at large, does of course exert an enormous influence on how the world is consciously experienced—for, in Whiteheadian terms, it tends to dominate the propositional forms and comparative contrasts that structure the higher phases of concrescence. Nevertheless, perception in the mode of causal efficacy (the direct flooding of the past into each new moment) provides a constant and primordial source of prelinguistic, presymbolic feeling, and thus represents a direct mode of experiential contact with the universe that forms the basis of every new event.

Some important parameters governing this flow of primitive experience are (1) the openness of the initial phases of concrescence, (2) the availability of uninhibited feeling from the body and personal memory systems, and (3) the degree of flexibility and creativity in the higher phases of concrescence, which help facilitate the harmonious integration of feelings from the earlier phases and thereby elevate data out of the unconscious depths and into conscious awareness. Because they so strongly influence precisely these features of experience, nonordinary states are capable of furnishing an optimal environment for enhancing conscious awareness of various aspects of presymbolic reality.

Naturally, when nonordinary phenomena are rendered intelligible, either to oneself or others, abstraction and symbolism must enter into the picture, and these abstractions must be carefully scrutinized and evaluated. However, the key point is not whether culturally derived symbolism contributes to nonordinary experiences—with the possible implication that all information from nonordinary experiences must then be considered irredeemably tainted by the cultural symbolic order—but rather that *all* conscious experience (i.e., Appearance) carries within it elements of feeling derived directly from Reality (accomplished past events). What is important about nonordinary states here is that they help to raise these primitive feelings of Reality into conscious awareness, thereby both enlivening consciousness and affording the possibility of novel symbolic transformations that carry new insights regarding the depth dimensions of the universe.

By enhancing the flow of primitive feeling into conscious awareness, nonordinary states undo some of the natural repression related to "transmutation." Odin illustrates this point when he describes how mandala contemplation and creative visioning can enliven the field of consciousness with feelings of beauty and connectedness. The feelings of relatedness and vitality prehended from past actual occasions—which normally are lost through the transmutation (unification and simplification) of these feelings into clear and distinct perceptions—can be reinvested into conscious awareness during nonordinary states by flooding perception in the mode of presentational immediacy with causal feeling from the unconscious depths. This produces an experience in the mode of symbolic reference that is more vividly endowed with the aliveness, beauty, and meaning originally grasped by the physical prehensions, that is, by one's direct intuitions of the world.

Insofar as nonordinary states open up neglected modes of perceiving the world and offer an opportunity to transcend some of the frameworks imposed by our cultural conditioning, it is not farfetched to think of extraordinary experiences as *evolutionary openings* providing humanity with new perspectives on itself and its universe. (Openness is thus important from an intellectual, an experiential, and an evolutionary point of view.) This observation is in accord with William James's belief that the psyche, or consciousness, is itself an evolutionary agent.[15]

Finally, if the human brain is the most complex known organism in the universe, and if the human psyche draws upon this rich matrix in every moment to build its own experiential field and then adds its own intuitions, amplifications, and intensifications, is it not possible that the human psyche itself may represent the most sensitive and powerful instrument available for tapping into the subtlest aspects of reality? If so, the experiences of mystics and meditators may well offer crucial information about the deeper nature of our universe—information that of course must be carefully scrutinized, compiled, and compared with other reports of this kind, then correlated with other realms of evidence. This approach is in accord with the methods of

---

15. "Evolution meant for James not simply a biological progression from past to present to future but also the realization of potential in the immediate moment. Consciousness was a moving force in the evolutionary process." Taylor, *Exceptional Mental States*, 10–11.

speculative philosophy, which begins by drawing on the widest possible array of evidence revealed through human experience.

In Conclusion

Shortly after my Egyptian "snake ride" at Castalia, I asked Jean Houston if I could talk with her before she departed the conference, as she was only scheduled to be there for a few days. I told her about my search for meaning and attempts to discover the ultimate nature of reality. With some embarrassment, I also mentioned that I felt a compelling need to push myself until I reached "enlightenment," something I believed that I had glimpsed but failed to achieve the year before at New College.

Jean looked at me gravely and responded that it was dangerous to keep driving myself in this manner. She then said something along the lines of, "the brain is a delicate instrument," which along with some other admonishments, seemed to give me permission to back off of my mystical mission. This may well have saved my life, or at least my sanity, as I was stretched pretty thin at that point. Some years later, much to my surprise, I discovered that Jean had quoted, almost verbatim, a line from *A Wrinkle in Time,* my first transpersonal book, which I had encountered shortly after my father's death. Although my transpersonal journey had come full circle in a way, as it turned out, the journey was really more of a spiral. And there were still quite a few twists to go before I could fully turn my life around.

While this audience with Jean helped free me from the notion that I *had* to reach enlightenment, *or else,* psychedelics continued to evoke a powerful and compelling sense that everything in my world was "conspiring" to bring me to enlightenment—and very soon. At its extreme, I think of this as *enlightenment paranoia*, on which I will soon expound. But first I need to explain the origin of this overwhelming sense of impending illumination: my Big Trip.

— 7 —

My Big Trip

Here Comes the Sun

In the basement bar at the Castalia seminar, where I spent too much time with a glass of wine in hand, the jukebox often played a song that touched me deeply: "Question," by the Moody Blues. (Naturally, it is about the frustrations entailed in searching for "the answer.") Also receiving a lot of playtime was the Stones' "You Can't Always Get What You Want." That song was a favorite of one conference faculty member's son. That faculty member, Michael Volin, was billed as the yogi of Australia. One day, this rather wise and peaceful man annoyed and confused me with a comment to the effect that it would be good if I were a little more like his son, and his son were a little more like me. Apparently, he had observed that our song preferences also reflected a significant difference in our attitudes toward life. What I think he may have been trying to point out was that while he appreciated his son's devil-may-care attitude and my passion for enlightenment, in his opinion his son would benefit from being a bit more serious while I needed to lighten up. And what we both needed was more *balance*. Appropriately enough, "Question" is from the Moody Blues album *A Question of Balance*.

Of course, things were a little more complicated than that for me. My addictive nature pushed me toward pleasure and excitement, while my experience with psychedelics impelled me toward more profound questions. One memorable trip was primarily responsible for my almost desperate need to find *The Answer*, and to find it as soon as possible.

My most powerful and most important psychedelic session happened somewhere in the middle of my first term at New College. Early one evening, two friends and I split a couple of hits of blotter acid that had just arrived on campus. There followed that indeterminate—and sometimes interminable—period of waiting and wondering what, if anything, was going to happen. To distract myself, I walked over to a student's room in the next court where a small party was going on. While I was sitting around waiting to "get off," I noticed that the song playing on the stereo sounded strangely compelling—familiar, yet somehow different. As I listened, I realized it was the Beatles song, "Here Comes the Sun," from their *Abbey Road* album. There was something about that song . . .

Even though I did not recognize many of the people gathered at the party, I suggested to those around me that perhaps we should smoke some pot. To my surprise, and chagrin, no one had any (among my friends at the time, someone *always* had a joint). So, I got up grudgingly and walked back to my room, a little unsteadily, as I was definitely beginning to feel the effects of the acid. I returned to the party and produced a bag of pot . . . and, to my further chagrin, no one had any rolling papers or a pipe! Are they putting me on, I thought, or have I entered some weird other world? (In retrospect, it was simply a relatively *straight* world.) Well, back to my room I went, feeling even higher now, with the walk feeling correspondingly longer and "curiouser."

Tripping at New College often seemed like traveling back through time. The dorms, which were designed by I. M. Pei, conjured up powerful images of ancient civilizations, perhaps Sumerian or Old Testament days, replete with royal palm court, fountains, Escher-like stairways, and jigsaw room arrangement. Counterpointing this was the airport across the road, with its strange array of lights in the distance, and the pervasive tropical foliage that took on uncanny shapes and forms when viewed from under a psychedelic spell.

Returning to the party, having successfully negotiated this second and more arduous journey, I proudly produced the rolling papers and tried to find someone to finally roll a joint—but no one seemed to know how. With suspicions of some weird conspiracy passing through my mind, I attempted to roll some joints myself. This was not an easy task, as all doubt had been removed about whether I was going to get off well on this acid. But I settled down, focused, managed to roll a few joints, and started passing them around the room. People seemed excited and pleased, and I felt satisfied with a job well done.

Then I noticed that same song was playing again: "Here Comes the Sun." And it impacted me far more powerfully this time. Its simple words, which I had never *really* heard before, were dripping with deep significance as the music echoed through me, inducing a strange state of rapt attention. It's moving description of an endless, bitter winter struck at the core of my buried isolation and grief.[1] The subsequent lyrics, speaking of a return of warmth and joy, seemed to offer new hope for emotional and spiritual redemption, touching me at a profound level. And when the Beatles sang the refrain, the words seemed to portend the arrival of some actual light bearing tremendous significance. It seemed, until now, that I had completely missed the meaning of this song; I felt exhilarated and illuminated by its momentous message, which the music was reverberating deep within me.

Something told me it was time to leave. I threaded my way back through Pei's maze of dorm rooms and the central courtyard crisscrossed with those royal palms, feeling a new level of connection to everything. I looked up at the stars shining so brightly in the deep black sky and felt joy, wonderment, and powerfully alive. The evening belonged to that eternal time of mythic consciousness that Joseph Campbell describes so elegantly—I felt euphoric with anticipation of something great about to unfold. Then, as I was about to enter my dorm room, I suddenly experienced an incredible sense of being fully in touch with my own being, and my place in the universe, and I remembered the phrase: "Each man at one time in his life knows exactly who he is." This described my feelings perfectly . . . for about the next five seconds.

As I walked through the door, I was instantly accosted by my friend, Ann. I was surprised and taken aback, for not only did I have a mad crush on her, but she also seemed to possess almost supernatural powers of intuition. Ann immediately started telling me how she had been watching me truck around campus "like Mr. Natural," then led me over to my bed and had me lie down. She put *Abbey Road* on the stereo, then returned to my side and put her hand on my chest, whereupon I embarked on a journey from knowing exactly who I was, to discovering that there was infinitely more to know—and that most of what I thought I did know, was wrong.

As I struggled with bewildered amazement over Ann having chosen to play The Beatles' *Abbey Road*—and how it seemed as though her hand on my chest was subtly modulating my heartbeat and emotions—my experience began to resonate along with the themes and symbolic nuances of the music. As the second side of the album began playing "Here Comes the Sun," I felt more deeply and viscerally what I had experienced earlier at the party: the first verse captured my sense of being alone and frozen, deep down inside, since my father's death, while the third verse reflected the joy that was now being unlocked after years of cold and isolation. It is

1. Unfortunately, I could not obtain permission to quote any of the lyrics from "Here Comes the Sun" or other songs from side 2 of *Abbey Road*. Hopefully readers will be able to fill in the gaps in my descriptions of how the song's words impacted me that eventful night.

difficult to describe how the refrain about the impending approach of the sun affected me, on both a visceral and psychic level. Each time the line was repeated, the music added on another layer of complexity and intensity that energetically carried me into ever-higher levels of vibratory awareness.[2] And when I heard the line about spring's gentle thaw, I could clearly feel my body's long-held tensions and blockages melting away. What I did not realize was that much more was yet to be revealed. The words from "Here Comes the Sun" were literal portents of things to come.

The expansively beautiful song "Because" provided a much-needed respite, for the following track, "You Never Give Me Your Money," immediately inaugurated what might be considered a psychospiritual "life review." It opened with powerful, vivid imagery of climbing a mountain toward some numinous goal, while at the same time remembering with excruciating guilt the people I had hurt and wronged in my life. The lines from "You Never Give Me Your Money" triggered a mortifying process revealing the multiform ways I had disappointed and failed those I cared about most. Yet, I sensed that this process was simultaneously purging my ego, painfully melting away my old self, thereby preparing me for some impending spiritual revelation.

This ascent felt like approaching a new level of being that was somehow holy. The song "Sun King" particularly seemed to capture this experience of rising towards the heavens, while my concurrent associated imagery was reminiscent of that found in the astonishing climax of C. S. Lewis's book *Perelandra,* where Lewis's protagonist scales a sacred mountain to witness angelic beings inaugurate a New World and cross the threshold into a larger spiritual life.[3] My subconscious may have borrowed this imagery from Lewis, or it may have arisen from a similar archetypal source—who knows? The mind draws on a multitude of sources and levels in the creation of experience; this seems especially true for psychedelic visions.

Even as this painful cleansing of my past transgressions was preparing me for entering into some new level of being, a third strand of experience was emerging. Another type of visualization began to appear, not simply in my active imagination anymore, but projected right out in front of my eyes. In contrast to my inner archetypal vision, this outer vision was forming in the middle of my perception of the room. A circular space in the center of

---

2. The bridge's repeating lyrics have been described as taking "on the quality of a meditator's mantra." Everett, *The Beatles as Musicians.*

3. In this second book of Lewis's space trilogy, Ransom, Lewis's protagonist, journeys to Venus (Perelandra) where he battles evil and discovers more about the spiritual depths of the universe. Ransom's ascent of the sacred mountain and his associated spiritual encounters can be found in *Perelandra,* 191–222.

my visual field became like a three-dimensional viewing port, within which
a new type of imagery began to play out. (Those who remember the scene
portraying the fable of the fall of Woldercan in the film *The Seven Faces
of Dr. Lao* will have an accurate picture of the circular source of creative
imagery that came to the fore of my perceptual field.)

At first I was aware of moving through atomic and molecular-like
shapes. These shifted into more strand-like phenomena, accompanied by
a greater sense of motion as I seemed to journey into the depths of space.
I next became aware of some kind of extremely bright light obscured behind these strands or cords. Concurrent with this visual imagery was an
impending sense of final ego dissolution, promising to complete the ego
death initiated by my preliminary life review or purgatory experience. It
seemed the only way to push past and through these cords and other shapes
was by letting go completely of my own limited sense of self, whose core
inadequacies had just been so painfully laid bare.

As I somehow used my eyes to concentrate my *vibratory* efforts to reach
past these structures, which now appeared to be either molecular forms of
inner space or astronomical objects in outer space, I began to feel that the
blinding light radiating out from behind these phenomena was actually
a source of ultimate Consciousness and Being—God? If only I could *blast
through* these forms that somehow represented, or were correlated with, my
own egoic impediments and frailties, I would reach or connect with some
type of heightened consciousness or ultimate truth. This seemed of paramount importance, and I desperately focused my efforts to attain this final
breakthrough. I could see this Light blazing out from behind a final dark
cord, like the sun emerging from an eclipse, but here I reached my limit of
psychic penetration. I fell back into the room, shattered, as the vision faded,
listening to the end of *Abbey Road's* painfully beautiful "Golden Slumbers/
Carry That Weight." I felt I might be carrying this weight forever.

Following my return from the brink, there was a period of hearing
frequencies of sounds that I could only very occasionally decipher. They
seemed to have their source in some kind of vast telepathic network, operating at a level whose very existence I never suspected. I also perceived
people's faces around me in terms of archetypal patterns, like those represented in Tibetan Buddhist masks and drawings (or the bizarre faces on the
album cover for Pink Floyd's *Relics*).

Spiritually, I experienced an immense sense of failure and disappointment over my inability to reach a clear encounter with the Light. Psychologically, I felt humiliated and disoriented by these new and startling perspectives
on reality as well as by my prior naiveté and hubris. Physically, I was exhausted
and drained. While these intense feelings persisted for only a few days and

then slowly abated, this experience would not be forgotten and could not be ignored. I did not believe that every detail was true (so to speak), but I knew something of transcendent importance had been revealed.

This experience dealt me what might be called a profound *theological* shock—and a further cosmological shock as well. I had already discovered that extraordinary experiences could provide revelations about my inner reality and my state of consciousness, as well as offer dramatically different perceptions of the world around me. Now, my universe had been radically opened up to entirely other realms of existence, and much more importantly, the possibility of God as a conscious presence that could be directly experienced. My search for an adequate cosmological view of reality would now have to take into account these additional dimensions and possibilities of existence.

Mystical experiences of God do not represent breaking news for either the Western or Eastern spiritual traditions, and likewise neither does the possibility of astral realms (although this notion is more common in the East). Nonetheless, coming out of a liberal Presbyterian background, weighted heavily towards a rational and scientific worldview, I was shocked to discover that there might be a direct experiential basis for belief in God and other spiritual realms—that spirituality had objective dimensions far beyond the mere altering or deepening of one's own awareness, or transforming one's attitudes and actions in the world.

The rest of this chapter summarizes the major ideas I have found most useful for understanding the implications of my Big Trip. First, I briefly outline Grof's theory of the unconscious and how his approach helps tie together traditional and transpersonal psychological theories. This is followed by a detailed look at the three types of ultimate transpersonal experiences described in Grof's cartography of nonordinary states, as they apply both to my Big Trip and to the *ultimates* of Whiteheadian metaphysics. The chapter concludes with a discussion of Whitehead's reasons for including God in his final philosophical vision.

Grof's Theory of the Unconscious

Stanislav Grof's approach to understanding the human unconscious constitutes a powerful and effective synthesis of psychodynamic theories, phenomenological reporting and categorization, and experiential techniques. By presenting a spectrum view of the depth unconscious that connects the theories of Freud, Reich, Rank, and Jung, and Eastern psychologies, Grof provides an integrated system capable of interpreting an exceptionally wide range of psychological phenomena. Grof's theories are especially valuable for developing an adequate representation of the collective unconscious—one capable of incorporating the expanded range of phenomena encountered through psychedelics. Without an interconnected and open-ended theory of this type, many important phenomena are inevitably lost, ignored, misunderstood, or misinterpreted. As William James deftly put it, while arguing for scientific and philosophic openness to the cornucopia of evidence from psychical and transpersonal phenomena, "without too much you can never have enough, of anything."[4]

Grof finds it useful to discuss the dynamic unfoldment of unconscious material during nonordinary states in terms of four levels of experience: "(1) the sensory barrier, (2) the individual unconscious, (3) the level of birth and death, and (4) the transpersonal domain."[5] Phenomena from these "realms" of the human psyche may appear whenever the barriers between the ego and the unconscious are breached. The means and methods for accessing these unconscious regions are myriad.[6] Grof does not place much psycho-therapeutic significance on the phenomena manifesting from the sensory barrier realm, such as certain types of acoustic phenomena and varieties of often-fascinating eidetic imagery involving intricate shapes and patterns.[7] (In case readers are wondering, I have experienced eidetic imagery on numerous occasions, and it is very different from the visuals that characterized my Big Trip.) However, as Grof believes that they can, in part, be understood as reflecting the structure of "certain anatomical and physiological characteristics of the sense organs,"[8] sensory-barrier phenomena may be of special interest to psychologists and neurologists researching correlations between consciousness and brain structures.

The recollective-biographical realm, on the other hand, is of critical psychotherapeutic importance. This level of the unconscious contains a variety of repressed memories, emotions, and energies that have been explored and described by various psychological systems and psychoanalytic schools of thought—for example, by Freud, Reich, Adler, and Klein. Experiences from this level extend across the entire life span, from earliest childhood onwards. Grof, however, has found that physical traumas play a much more important role in the psychodynamic economy than is usually

---

4. James, *Pluralistic Universe*, 316.

5. Grof, *Beyond the Brain*, 93.

6. Grof, *Beyond the Brain*, 93.

7. Grof, *Beyond the Brain*, 93–95.

8. Grof, *Beyond the Brain*, 95.

acknowledged by most of these psychological systems.[9] This underestimation of the impact of life-threatening illnesses, accidents, and other injuries may be due to the widespread neglect of the psychological significance of the body at its organismic level of functioning.

Several things should be noted about the memories emerging out of the *recollective-biographical level,* especially in the course of intense psychotherapeutic work or during other nonordinary states. First, these memories are not merely remembered; they can actually be *relived.* This finding is in accord with Whitehead's notion that the past lives again during the formation of each new moment.[10] It would seem that in nonordinary states, the "immortality" of the past can be more clearly apprehended,[11] as the act of simple remembering intensifies and transforms into a full resurrection of the past. This may account in part for the therapeutic efficacy of what Grof calls *experiential* psychological techniques: by bringing unresolved situations fully and vividly into present awareness, a much more complete experiential integration of this material is realized than is usually possible in more intellectual or talk-based therapies. Experiences arising out of the recollective-biographical realm are self-selected for emotional relevance, and they tend to form what Grof has referred to as "systems of condensed experience" (COEX systems), similar to Jungian complexes:

> Another important distinction is that the relevant memories and other biographical elements do not emerge separately, but form distinct dynamic constellations, for which I have coined the term *COEX systems, or systems of condensed experience.* A COEX system is a dynamic constellation of memories (and associated fantasy material) from different periods of the individual's life, with the common denominator of a strong emotional charge of

9. Grof, *Adventure of Self-Discovery,* 5–6.

10. Note how both Grof and Whitehead come to similar conclusions about the possibility of bringing past events fully into the present. Grof writes: "In deep experiential psychotherapy, biographical material is not remembered or reconstructed; it can be actually fully relived. This involves not only emotions but also physical sensations, pictorial elements of the material involved, as well as data from other senses. This happens typically in complete age regression to the stage of development when the event happened" (Grof, *Beyond the Brain,* 96). While in the following quotation Whitehead may be thinking more of the immediate past, his general theory implies that *all* past events are available to human experience: "Thus the self-enjoyment of an occasion of experience is initiated by an enjoyment of the past as alive in itself and is terminated by an enjoyment of itself as alive in the future" (Whitehead, *Adventures of Ideas,* 193).

11. Whitehead uses the term "objective immortality" to indicate both the everlasting causal impact of every event, and also God's everlasting preservation of all accomplished fact (i.e., all completed events). For example, see *Process and Reality,* 347.

the same quality, intense physical sensation of the same kind, or the fact that they share some other important elements.[12]

In sum, nonordinary states allow the deep psyche to manifest repressed material that is psychologically important and ready for conscious processing. This material arises in the form of interconnected groups of memories and emotions, vividly recalled—thus facilitating the integration and resolution of these deep-seated blocks and complexes.

My guilt-laden regression through my history of betrayal provides a personal example of a COEX system. In this painful journey back through my life, I moved from my first lover, who I carelessly left behind when I went off to college, to earlier girlfriends I "used," then on to close friends I "abandoned," especially my dear friend Tom, who had been such a support in the years after my father died. We had become so estranged that he did not even discuss his plans with me before he ran away from home in high school. It seemed I had let down everyone in my life that I had once loved. (I recently had an insight that behind this COEX system lurks a fear of being abandoned myself, which produces a compensatory guilt and fear over failing others or letting them down. Unfortunately, I did not realize this at the time, for releasing that deep fear might have allowed me to go deeper into my Big Trip. It might also have altered the trajectory of several of my subsequent difficult friendships and intimate relationships.)

Grof's *perinatal* level refers to experiences related to the birth process.[13] For Grof, these experiences can hold peculiar psychological significance. Grof's research strongly supports Otto Rank's theory that the physical and psychological traumas accompanying birth underlie and feed into later life traumas, impacting powerfully upon the development of the personality and the formation of the defense mechanisms. In other words, the psychophysical trauma experienced by the organism at birth establishes a psychic predisposition towards certain types of complexes and character formations, and the unintegrated (but stored) energies and feelings from the birth trauma constitute a nearly endless supply of repressed dynamics that reinforce the crystallized personality structure. Hence, until these repressed perinatal energies are consciously integrated, the personality will remain recalcitrant to very deep psychological change—for these unrecognized, and thus unanalyzed, forces will continue to push the organism to continuously

---

12. Grof, *Beyond the Brain*, 96–97.

13. Those interested in the possibility of perinatal experiences might consult David Chamberlain's *Babies Remember Birth*; or the expansive collection edited by Fedor-Freybergh and Vogel, *Prenatal and Perinatal Psychology and Medicine*.

regenerate its current ego defense system, just as these forces inclined the organism to develop them in the first place.

Another personal example of a COEX system relates to my fear of suffocation. While this may be a justifiable concern, in my later life I developed a significant phobia of being in open water, such as when swimming or snorkeling out in the ocean. Looking back at my life for associated issues, one finds an ongoing inability to swallow pills; a period in my thirties where I woke up at night in a sudden panic, unable to breathe (once for several minutes); and for a time after my father's death I had episodes where I felt like I could not tell if I was getting enough air. Germane medical conditions would of course include my lung problems and surgery in high school, but I also had episodes of the croup when I was very young and now suffer from chronic asthma. Taken together, this represents a classic example of a COEX system, which manifested in my psychedelic and holotropic breathwork sessions in two ways. First, in psychedelic states, that sense of not knowing if I was breathing became very pronounced, especially early in the session, accompanied by a high degree of apprehension. During breathwork, primarily after I had weathered many sessions, a pattern developed where I would enter a very peaceful, almost unconscious, state, then suddenly jolt awake wildly in response to an overwhelming terror shooting through my body. Frustratingly, the source of this panic was blocked from view by my violently abrupt return to consciousness.

A conventional psychoanalytic interpretation might suggest that these symptoms are related to powerful repressed emotions from my father's death trying to reemerge but only manifesting as anxieties connected to the way he died. From a more Grofian perspective, the persistence and degree of terror presenting itself here might indicate an entire COEX system energizing, and probably founding, this suffocation issue. Suffocation experiences often appear in psychedelic sessions when reliving the birth process, as actual suffocation is a frequent companion of all stages of delivery due to various types of complications. As other frightening experiences around breathing issues arise throughout life, these tend to reinforce and build upon the original trauma, thereby expanding into a full-blown COEX system or what Jung called a psychological complex.

Reexperiencing and releasing the birth trauma and its secondary manifestations can engender remarkable psychotherapeutic transformation. The birth process lays the foundation for a lifelong orientation towards existence, as well as for a corresponding set of defense mechanisms to maintain this perspective—thus "protecting" the organism from perceived dangers correlated with the birth trauma. Consequently, the experience of consciously reliving one's birth provides the possibility of releasing the fear and pain at the base of the ego's defense mechanisms and thus radically altering one's relationship to reality. In its most powerful guise, this radical psychological shift takes the form of the death-rebirth experience.[14]

This experience of death and rebirth can, in turn, open up into an experience of the *transpersonal* level. In this way, the perinatal level acts as an interface between the biographical world and the transpersonal realm beyond. My archetypal imagery of climbing the sacred mountain to participate in the creation of a new world order contains elements of a rebirth experience, and ushered in the full-blown transpersonal aspects of my psychedelic session. One might also speculate that my guilt COEX, which correlated with attending Adam and Eve as they inaugurated their Eden, was based ultimately on a perinatal-level original sin—perhaps arising from a feeling of being expelled from the womb/garden when my mother used prescribed drugs to artificially initiate delivery, thus creating my feeling of primordial abandonment. You can see here how Grof's multileveled genetic approach can effectively combine Freudian biographical material, Rankian perinatal influences, and Jungian archetypal dimensions. Now let us look more closely at the vicissitudes of the transpersonal realm.[15]

14. More recently, Grof has had some reservations about how central a role to attribute to the perinatal realm. While I have often observed people go through nonordinary experiences that involved significant perinatal elements, in my own case such elements have been more ambiguous and difficult to distinguish as being definitely related to my birth process. Of course, many of the phenomena that Grof considers related to the perinatal realm are highly symbolic in nature and thus not always easy to identify as such. For example, I have had vivid experiences of seemingly battling for my life, as well as of death/rebirth struggles, and have also seen these widely manifested during others' holotropic breathwork sessions.

15. It is tempting to suggest a correlation between Grof's four stages of the basic perinatal matrices and Whitehead's four phases of concrescence. But if this correspondence is indeed significant, is this because the metaphysical structure is re-created at many levels of experience, or is the imprint of birth so fundamental that it widely permeates theory construction, especially when dealing with the most basic questions about the nature of reality? For example, the big bang theory of the "birth" of the universe seems to parallel human fetal development, where a tiny inseminated egg rapidly expands into a full-grown fetus that explodes out of the womb creating a new "universe." This takes us back to my New College professor's exam question concerning which should take priority: philosophy of psychology or the psychology of philosophy? Pierre Bayard, in his postmodern psychoanalytic reinterpretation of the detective novel, conceives a surprising similarity between theory construction and delusion—both being attempts to make meaning out of disparate phenomena (Bayard, *Who Killed Roger Ackroyd?*, 97–98). In fact, Bayard argues that such theory-constructive activity underlies the very creation of the self or subject. Thus, the connection between early experience and formal theory building becomes even more closely connected. The theories of reality (conscious and unconscious) that we have constructed to create ourselves—in order to make sense of the complex, confusing, and often overwhelming events of birth and

The Further Reaches of Experience

Drawing on decades of research, Grof has developed an extensive phenomenological mapping of the general range of transpersonal experiences that arise during nonordinary states of consciousness. Grof's transpersonal cartography—and especially his data from the following three categories—offers empirical support for two of Whitehead's more controversial views: that God is a *real Entity* within our universe, and that human beings could have *direct access* to God's being. Both of these prospects became issues of heightened concern for me following my Big Trip, for the blinding white light I experienced was not a metaphysical principle; rather, it felt like an overpowering Presence emanating from a conscious entity.

The hypothesized mode of access to God's experience would be via what Whitehead terms *hybrid physical prehensions,* acting in this case as a special type of "telepathic" communication: *telepathy* as mystical interaction and communion with God. "Hybrid" physical prehensions refer to a special class of those basic feelings or direct intuitions that arise immediately out of the present moment's connection to past entities. These feelings are called hybrid when they directly access a past event's complex higher-level feelings, rather than receiving the more general causal influence exerted by the fully accomplished event. According to David Griffin's analysis, "We can therefore take seriously claims for mystical experiences, understood as conscious experiences of a Holy Reality. The experience of God would, like telepathic interaction between humans, be present all the time; the only thing unusual about mystical experiences would be that in them this steady experience of God has risen to consciousness."[16] In other words, elements from our unconscious feeling connection to *all* past events may in certain occasions rise much more fully into conscious awareness, producing a telepathic or intuitive feeling when the moment of experience in question is another human being, or a mystical experience when the feelings originate from God. Neither of these modes of intuition is surprising in a Whiteheadian universe, where new events, be they the quanta of physics or the moments of human experience, arise out of a creative synthesis of the flood of energy/feeling from past events.

Grof delineates three kinds of transpersonal experiences that appear to access the ultimate depths, or heights, of reality: experiences of the Demiurg, of Cosmic Consciousness, and of the Supracosmic Void. These three categories are described as the most powerful and personally

early childhood—could hardly avoid being deployed when as adults we seek to understand the nature of the universe.

16. Griffin, *Parapsychology, Philosophy, and Religion,* 58.

significant mystical experiences in Grof's cartography. To a significant degree, they correlate with Whitehead's portrayal of the two basic aspects of God (the primordial and consequent natures), as well as with Whitehead's ultimate metaphysical principle: Creativity.

Experience of the Demiurg and of Cosmic Creation

Let us turn first to Grof's description of the Demiurg[17] to see what characteristics relating to God are reported in this category of transpersonal experience:

> In this type of experience, the subject has the feeling of encountering the *Creator* of the universe, or even of full identification with him. This can be accompanied by extraordinary insights into the process of creation, its motives, specific mechanisms, purpose, and problems. On this level, the Creator usually has many personal characteristics, although not necessarily an anthropomorphic form. It is possible to sense the forces that underlie and initiate the process of creation. Various subjects identified them as overabundance of generative energy, irresistible artistic impulse, boundless curiosity, passion for experimentation, thirst for knowledge or self-knowledge, pursuit of experience, immense love that wants to be expressed, or even flight from monotony and boredom . . .
>
> The Demiurg can be seen as the supreme force of existence, comparable to the concept of God in different religions. However, in some instances, it is one of the creators of many universes, or the creator of many universes.[18]

These qualities correspond quite closely with Whitehead's speculations about God's nature, purpose, and motivations. Regarding God's primordial nature, Whitehead writes:

> The primordial appetitions which jointly constitute God's purpose are seeking intensity, and not preservation . . . His aim for it [for all finite occasions] is depth of satisfaction as an intermediate step towards the fulfilment of his own being. His tenderness is directed towards each actual occasion, as it arises.
>
> Thus God's purpose in the creative advance is the evocation of intensities.[19]

17. *Demiurg* usually has an *e* on the end, but Grof uses this alternative spelling in *Adventure of Self-Discovery. Demiurge* often refers to the creator of the universe.

18. Grof, *Adventure of Self-Discovery,* 142–43.

19. Whitehead, *Process and Reality,* 105.

Comparing Whitehead's speculations with Grof's descriptions, it seems plausible that transpersonal intuitions of what Whitehead characterizes as God's search for richness of experience through the promotion of intense, novel experiences among its creatures might be consciously perceived by a human subject as the Demiurg's "boundless curiosity," "passion for experimentation," or "pursuit of experience."[20] Vis-à-vis the Demiurg's "immense love" and "artistic impulse," Whitehead's image of God's attitude towards the world includes the qualities of tenderness, patience, and wisdom: God "does not create the world, he saves it: or, more accurately, he is the poet of the world, with tender patience leading it by his vision of truth, beauty, and goodness."[21] Even though in Whitehead's philosophy God is not the *sheer* creator of all that is, God *does* exemplify the "aboriginal instance" of creativity, acts as the storehouse of all potential forms, and "is the lure for feeling, the eternal urge of desire"[22]; thus, God might well be perceived during extraordinary experiences as possessing what Grof describes as an "overabundance of generative energy," or as the "Creator of the universe."[23]

Before moving on to Grof's other two categories of ultimate mystical insight, I will describe how I understand the deepest levels of transpersonal experiences. Drawing upon Whitehead's image of consciousness "illuminating" the earlier phases of concrescence, I like to think of mystical encounters with aspects of God's being in terms of *Illumination*: referring to both the objective content and the subjective quality of the experience. This image can be particularly useful for clarifying the basic processes underlying the extraordinary phenomenology associated with mystical intuitions of God. To illustrate this point, I begin with Grof's account of a subject's high-dose LSD session, which Grof uses as an exemplar of an encounter with the "Demiurg":

> What followed was a tremendous expansion of consciousness. I was out in interstellar space witnessing galaxies upon galaxies being created right in front of my eyes. I felt that I was moving faster than the speed of light. There were galaxies passing by me one after the other. I was approaching a central explosion of energy from which everything in the universe seemed to originate. It was the very Source of all that was created. As I moved closer and closer to this area, I felt the incandescent heat emanating from it. It was a gigantic furnace, the furnace of the universe.

20. Grof, *Adventure of Self-Discovery*, 142.

21. Whitehead, *Process and Reality*, 346.

22. Whitehead, *Process and Reality*, 344.

23. Grof, *Adventure of Self-Discovery*, 142.

The sensation of heat was growing to unbelievable pro-
portions, as was the intensity of the light. I recognized that the
burning I was experiencing was the burning of the Purifying
Fire. As I moved closer, I sensed that my identity was shifting
from being the manifestation of this Energy to being the Energy
itself. It seemed that I momentarily entered the very core of this
Universal Furnace of cosmic creation. The experience was ecstatic and filled me with a sense of Infinite Power.[24]

This account typifies a tendency for subjects in mystical states of this
type to "symbolize" their approach to God's being in terms of moving towards, and sometimes into, a source of "hypercosmical light." In *Star Maker*
(which I had not read before my own encounter with the hypercosmical
light), Stapledon describes this experience:

For now it seemed to me, it seemed, that I suddenly outgrew
the three-dimensional vision proper to all creatures, and that I
saw with physical sight the Star Maker. I saw, though nowhere
in cosmical space, the blazing source of the hypercosmical
light, as though it were an overwhelmingly brilliant point, a
star, a sun more powerful than all suns together . . . And in that
moment I knew that I had indeed seen the very source of all
cosmical light and life and mind; and of how much else besides
I had as yet no knowledge.[25]

In both these examples, readers may notice definite similarities with certain
facets of my Big Trip.

Another example of this "hypercosmical light," this time drawn from
nothing less than Timothy Leary's first LSD experience, may help suggest
the power and prevalence of this kind of imagery:

It came sudden and irresistible. An endless deep swampy marsh
on some other planet teeming and steaming with energy and life,
and in the swamp an enormous tree whose roots were buried
miles down and branches were foliated out miles high and miles
wide. And then this tree, like a cosmic vacuum cleaner, went
ssssuuuck, and every cell in my body was swept into the root,
twigs, branches, and leaves of this tree. Tumbling and spinning,
down the soft fibrous avenues to some central point which was
just light. Just light, but not just light. It was the center of life. A
burning, dazzling, throbbing, radiant core, pure pulsing, exulting
light. An endless flame that contained everything—sound, touch,

24. Grof, *Adventure of Self-Discovery,* 143.
25. Stapledon, *Star Maker,* 218–19.

cell, seed, sense, soul, sleep, glory, glorifying, God, the hard eye of God. Merged with this pulsing flame it was possible to look out and see and participate in the entire cosmic drama.[26]

Masters and Houston provide another example of *illumination,* also from an LSD session, in which the subject had, in these authors' opinion, an authentic mystical experience. In this case, even though the phenomenology is somewhat different from Grof's example, we again find a radiant light or fire accompanying a sense of flowing towards and entering into God's being. The account is reported in the subject's own words:

> Although consciousness of self seemed extinguished, I knew that the boundaries of my being now had been dissolved and that all other boundaries also were dissolved. All, including what had been myself, was an ever more rapid molecular whirling that then became something else, a pure and seething energy that was the whole of Being. This energy, neither hot nor cold, was experienced as a white and radiant fire. There seemed no direction to this whirling, only an acceleration of speed, yet one knew that along this dynamic continuum the flux of Being streamed inexorably, unswervingly toward the One.
>
> At what I can only call the "core" of this flux was God, and I cannot explain how it was that I, who seemed to have no identity at all, yet experienced myself as *filled with God,* and then as (whatever this may mean) *passing through* God and into a Oneness wherein it seemed God, Being, and a mysterious unnameable One constituted together what I can only designate the ALL.[27]

From a Whiteheadian perspective, this variety of illuminative experience might originate when primitive unconscious feelings of God's presence suddenly heighten dramatically in intensity and start to dominate the pattern of *concrescent*—that is, to influence the design governing how the event shapes and creates itself. This vastly increased flow of primitive yet highly charged feeling *floods* the subject with emotions and intuitions related to God's being—which is archetypically experienced as a numinous, intense source of light and energy through which aspects of God's essence and experience are revealed. On a more technical note, a critical juncture in this process might involve a shift from hybrid to pure physical prehensions of God, resulting in an even more forceful and complete reception of God's nature. Also, the subject's sense of inexorably streaming

26. Leary, *High Priest,* 246.
27. Masters and Houston, *Varieties of Psychedelic Experience,* 308.

or speeding towards God, or Being, may reflect the psychophysical sensation of prehensions of God pouring into one's concrescent structure with greater and greater intensity and thus pushing or aiming the subject into an ever-increasing awareness of God's presence.

In describing illumination, I have concentrated on the early phases of concrescence, that is, the early stages in the formation of a moment of experience. However, the higher phases of symbolic and intellectual activity undoubtedly play a crucial role by creating harmonizing contrasts capable of maximizing the depth, breadth, and intensity of feeling. Also, I should emphasize that while I refer to this type of experience as *symbolic,* this term is not intended to impugn in any way the illuminative experience's capacity to reveal accurate information about the actual nature of the cosmos. For, in Whitehead's metaphysics, *all* higher experience is symbolic, in one way or another, including sensory perception.

By this hypothesis, differing levels of approach and opening to God will tend to reveal varying aspects or dimensions of God's being. Illumination begins with a powerful sense of expansion and acceleration beyond one's usual physical and psychological boundaries, and a penetration into and towards the deepest dimensions of reality. As one approaches this numinous source, experiences of the Demiurg—that is, God perceived as an *independent entity*—dominate conscious awareness. As one passes *into* this Light, or Source of Being, experiences relating to identification with God's inner subjective nature become predominant. Grof's next two categories offer evidence of these deeper penetrations, or openings, into God's essential Being and provide further support for Whitehead's analysis of God's nature into *dipolar* aspects, namely, God's primordial and consequent natures.

Experience of Cosmic Consciousness (or Universal Mind)

As with experiences of the Demiurg, encounters from Grof's category of Cosmic Consciousness offer not only a fascinating phenomenological portrait of mystical experiences of God, but they can also help us explore the adequacy and accuracy of Whitehead's theological speculations. Grof distinguishes these two closely related categories by describing cosmic consciousness in terms of moving beyond a personal deity involved in active creation and towards a timeless, abstract, all-encompassing Mind. To a Whiteheadian, this dichotomy sounds quite familiar: Grof's phenomenological data from this category concerning encounters with a universal mind parallels Whitehead's theory of a *dual-nature* God. I would suggest further that this extraordinary group of nonordinary experiences may shed light on a specific aspect of God's primordial and consequent natures in their active involvement with the creative advance of the universe.

Even though the contrast between God's primordial and consequent natures is ultimately an abstraction from the *essential unity* that characterizes all actual entities—including those constituting God—the distinctions Whitehead draws between these two aspects are very important for articulating the multiple facets within God's totality or wholeness of Becoming. For example, God's primordial nature, as the source and valuing of all potentiality, is infinite, "free, complete, primordial, eternal, actually deficient, and unconscious." On the other hand, the consequent nature "originates with physical experience derived from the temporal world, and then acquires integration with the primordial side. It is determined, incomplete, consequent, 'everlasting,' fully actual, and conscious."[28]

That is a mouthful! In short: God's primordial nature is a value-weighted storehouse of all possibility or potential form, while the consequent nature represents God's ongoing, moment-to-moment interaction with the universe of finite events.

Grof's exemplar transpersonal experience from the category of Universal Mind offers some support for Whitehead's theological speculations and provides an intriguing clue about the character of God's experience. This excerpt is from the report of a subject who had a deep transpersonal experience under the influence of ketamine, a powerful inducer of nonordinary states and out-of-body experiences.

> What I was experiencing now was new and very exciting. It seemed that true evolution was a real possibility and that each of us could play an important part in it. This evolution would lead into dimensions that I was not aware of in my everyday life and that I had not discovered in my previous nonordinary states of consciousness.
>
> The movement was becoming faster and faster, until it reached what seemed like some absolute limit . . .
>
> When the limit was transcended, the experience shifted dimensions in a way that is difficult to describe. Instead of movement in space, there seemed to be immense extension of consciousness . . .
>
> Here seemed to be all the creative energy and intelligence of the universe as pure consciousness existing beyond time and

---

28. Whitehead, *Process and Reality*, 345.

space. It was entirely abstract, yet containing all the forms and secrets of creation.[29]

Here in a single transpersonal session, we see two very different impressions concerning the depth nature of reality: on the one hand, an evolving universe with the prospect of real novelty and adventure; on the other, an eternal envisagement encompassing all forms and possibilities. Intriguingly, these two aspects also characterize Whitehead's theory of a "dipolar" God, whose consequent nature actively participates in the evolving universe, while the primordial nature represents God in solitary "contemplation" of the total order of potential forms.

From a Whiteheadian perspective, this subject's experience might represent a mystical penetration into God's being, such that, initially, an intuition of the evolutionary impetus and world participation of God's nature is revealed, followed by an even deeper revelation concerning God's primordial envisagement of the realm of pure potentials. The subjective character of this realm, however, according to this subject's report, is *not* unconscious, although it is "entirely abstract." This suggests that God's full nature—as embodied within God's consequent synthesis—includes within itself a *conscious vision* of the otherwise unconscious primordial envisagement. This would serve to enrich God's final satisfaction through the depth and intensity provided by this ultimate contrast between sheer possibility and accomplished fact.

The above example gives a feel for how the findings of transpersonal psychology might be used to flesh out Whitehead's bare-bones account of the spiritual dimensions of the universe, as well as to provide an empirical check on the accuracy of his speculations.

The Supracosmic and Metacosmic Void

At the furthest reaches of mystical illumination into the nature of the universe, experiences occur that Grof describes in terms of the *supracosmic and metacosmic Void*. The data from this category point to the possibility that these experiences are the result of transpersonal encounters with the *primordial nature of God* and its primordial embodiment of *creativity*. In the following quotation, Grof summarizes the core of these ultimate transpersonal experiences:

> The experience of the Void is the most enigmatic and paradoxical of all the transpersonal experiences. It is experiential

29. Grof, *Adventure of Self-Discovery*, 146–47.

identification with the primordial Emptiness, Nothingness, and Silence, which seem to be the ultimate cradle of all existence. While it is the source of everything, it cannot be derived from anything else; it is the uncreated and ineffable Supreme. The terms supracosmic and metacosmic used by sophisticated subjects to describe this experience refer to the fact that this Void seems to be both supraordinated to and underlying the phenomenal cosmos as we know it.

The Void is beyond space and time, beyond form of any kind, and beyond polarities, such as light and darkness, good and evil, stability and motion, and ecstasy or agony. While nothing concrete exists in this state, nothing that is part of existence seems to be missing there either. This emptiness is thus, in a sense, pregnant with all of existence, since it contains everything in a potential form.[30]

Numerous points of commonality exist between Grof's portrayal of the metacosmic Void and Whitehead's explication of God's primordial nature. For example, God's primordial nature is devoid of consciousness, while the Void is experienced as primordially empty and silent. The primordial nature is "all-embracing, unbounded by contradiction";[31] the Void is "beyond polarities." God's primordial nature is "atemporal" or "eternal," and "deflected neither by love, nor by hatred, for what in fact comes to pass"[32]; the Void is beyond space and time, and beyond good and evil. There are further correlations between these two notions: God's primordial nature is described as the "unlimited conceptual realization of the absolute wealth of potentiality,"[33] but is deficiently actual; the Void is "pregnant with all of existence, since it contains everything in potential form."[34] And while the primordial nature transcends the actual universe, it also enters into every occasion, just as the Void is "supraordinated to and underlying the phenomenal cosmos."

Given these considerations, we can venture the following hypothesis. Certain extraordinary experiences involving the "Void" can be understood to be transpersonal encounters with the *primordial nature of God* (as illuminated, of course, through heightened hybrid physical prehensions and facilitated by a peculiar level of openness and effective contrast in the higher phases of concrescence, in Whiteheadian lingo).

30. Grof, *Adventure of Self-Discovery*, 147.

31. Whitehead, *Process and Reality*, 348.

32. Whitehead, *Process and Reality*, 344.

33. Whitehead, *Process and Reality*, 343.

34. Grof, *Adventure of Self-Discovery*, 147.

Whitehead's metaphysical notion of *creativity* represents another point of similarity. Regarding the fundamental relationship between creativity and God, Whitehead writes, "The primordial nature of God is the acquirement by creativity of a primordial character."[35] That is, the primordial nature's *envisagement or valuing* of pure potentials provides the fundamental shaping of the raw creativity that fosters every moment of actuality. Transpersonal illumination of this primordial character of creativity might generate experiences such as those described by Grof in relation to the Void: experiences of the "primordial Emptiness, Nothingness, and Silence, which seem to be the ultimate cradle of all existence. While it is the source of everything, it cannot be derived from anything else; it is the uncreated and ineffable Supreme."[36] Even though *creativity* as a thing-in-itself is an abstraction,[37] it nonetheless represents the fundamental metaphysical activity of the universe. Creativity is the "universal of universals,"[38] namely, the process whereby the many become one and are increased by one.[39] Consequently, transpersonal perception of this Ultimate universal as revealed through its primordial embodiment may inspire a mystical sense of connection to the "cradle of existence" and to the "uncreated and ineffable Supreme." Direct intuition of the creativity embodied within God's primordial nature could be experienced also as a kind of *emptiness*—for creativity, in Whitehead's system, constitutes the "formless ground of all existence" and is thus equivalent to "'emptiness' in Buddhist language."[40]

Interestingly, according to Grof, the Void is "the ultimate source of existence," and the Universal Mind is its first manifestation or formulation.[41] Moreover, "the Void and the Universal Mind are perceived as identical and freely interchangeable; they are two different aspects of the same phenomenon."[42] This rather paradoxical situation can be resolved by Whitehead's notion of a dipolar God, whose primordial nature is the storehouse of all possibility and the primordial embodiment of Creativity, and whose consequent nature is the conscious realization and transformation of the primordial nature's influence on the world process. In Whitehead's view, the

---

35. Whitehead, *Process and Reality*, 344.

36. Grof, *Adventure of Self-Discovery*, 147.

37. Whitehead, *Process and Reality*, 7, 222.

38. Whitehead, *Process and Reality*, 31.

39. Whitehead, *Process and Reality*, 21.

40. Beardslee, "Process Thought on the Borders," 232.

41. Grof, *Cosmic Game*, 6.

42. Grof, "Realms of the Human Unconscious," 97.

primordial and consequent natures really *are* "two different aspects of the same phenomena": namely, God.

Since Creativity as the "universal of universals" occupies such a central place in Whitehead's metaphysics, it is important to appreciate the unique perspective that he offers on this underlying reality. Most philosophies have something that serves as the Ultimate Reality behind or beyond all the actual things of the world. For many, this is called pure Being and is often described by mystics as the Void or Emptiness. Whitehead differs by selecting "Creativity" for this ultimate—as the essential process whereby past events come together to form a new moment of actuality. This creative process, constituting the essence of all actual occasions, is instantiated in every event. Thus, it is not difficult to imagine that a mystical experience involving this fundamental activity that characterizes every moment of one's life might widen into the insight that this same creativity is intrinsic to *all* actuality. This creative essence of sheer becoming is often described as formlessness or emptiness, but is better understood in the Whiteheadian view as *openness*. However, since the creativity inherent in every event is subject to the guiding influence of God's primordial nature, mystical experiences of "pure becoming" may carry within them elements and intuitions of God's primordial nature. In this way, transpersonal experiences of the Ultimate Reality (Creativity) may often coincide with experiences of the Ultimate Actuality (God).

Whitehead's Envisagement of God

Transpersonal psychology views mystical experiences of God as phenomena of pivotal importance, deserving of serious philosophic and scientific consideration. My *theological shock* from encountering a godlike presence during my Big Trip left me of a similar mind. Once I had accepted that mystical experiences of God do occur—as is surely the case, whether or not one considers them veridical—and more importantly had felt the power and weight of such an experience, the problem of reconciling the possible existence of a Higher Power with the rest of my knowledge and beliefs became paramount. This is where *process theology and metaphysics* have proved so valuable.[43]

---

43. Let me remind readers that I am presenting here a contemporary process account of this topic—an account that follows Hartshorne's interpretation of God as a series of actual occasions, rather than Whitehead's own theory of God as a single, never-ending process.

Process thought provides a rationally coherent mode of access not only for mystical intuitions of God but for transpersonal and parapsychological experiences of many shapes and forms as well. In Whitehead's vision, the universe is composed of *layered organic environments* that are *intrinsically permeable* to intuitive perception based on the direct flow of past events into present experience. This bears repeating: the universe in all its glory and detailed nuance is inherently open and accessible to all events in general and to human intuition in particular. As we have seen, Whitehead's theory of perception makes comprehensible *how* transpersonal experiences can disclose real knowledge of the universe and its depths. We are *not* trapped in a material universe with only sensory perception to tentatively connect us to a hypothetical outside world through our epiphenomenal consciousness—that would be a sad state of affairs indeed.

Whitehead has several important reasons for including a vision of God in his final cosmology—for believing in a highest "form of feeling." Conforming to traditional piety is *not* one of them. First among these reasons is our direct experience of *ideals:* we have a conscience. Their efficacy in our lives means that these ideals must come from *somewhere.* According to his Ontological Principle, only real entities can produce real effects. For Whitehead, the most logical source of these intuited ideals is God's primordial nature. Second is the testimony of those religious experiences where one seems to become conscious of a wholly loving, compassionate Presence, which can be understood as the feeling of the divine compassion for the creatures (i.e., finite actualities).

However, unlike some New Age thinkers, Whitehead does not rely *primarily* on the testimony of mystical experience for his arguments in favor of the existence of God or other spiritual entities. He is too much of a realist about the limitations of such evidence, despite its strong emotional appeal and the strength of character of many of the individuals providing such accounts. Third is our dim but persistent sense that everything we do somehow *ultimately* matters. Fourth is the belief that there is such a thing as *truth*—which is unintelligible, as Nietzsche saw, if there is nothing but a multiplicity of finite perspectives. Finally, and perhaps most tellingly, we find remarkable *order* in a world composed (on Whitehead's account) of a vast plurality of partially spontaneous centers of feeling—an order that he felt strongly indicated some *central coordinating influence.* It is striking that a universe supposedly made up of randomly interacting particles has over eons generated ever-greater complexities and levels of organization, rather than descending into greater chaos or merely maintaining stasis.

This raises an important question: How might God *influence* the world to help bring about this degree of order, yet not quash the possibility of freedom and choice? Here Whitehead is in close agreement with Plato's account of the divine element in the world in terms of "persuasion." Since, according to Whitehead, God is the *chief exemplification* of metaphysical principles, not the glaring exception, God's interactions with the world must be similar in nature to the kinds of interactions attributed to all the finite events. Whitehead's theory of causation is cast in terms of the *conformity* between the feelings of past events and how they initially enter into new occasions. In other words, through a transfer of feeling/energy, past events directly impress themselves on the formative stages of new occasions, thus producing a "conformal" influence from the past onto the present.

Whitehead sees God's influence on the world similarly. We directly *feel God's feelings* (the Divine Eros for us), and because we feel them conformally (in the initial phase of experience), we have an impulse to act in accordance with them. As a result, we have a feeling of conscience when we do not follow the aim derived from our prehensions of God.[44] Moreover, since all events, including human occasions, have an initial feeling of God, our deepest levels of experience arise out of a vague but ever-present intuition of God's love.

The crucial point is that God's influence is understood as *persuasive,* not coercive. Thus, God's initial aim for us can be neglected or ignored if we so desire. This is a major reason—along with the creativity inherent in every event—why real freedom and choice can exist: God acts persuasively rather than controlling our every move. God's persuasive influence *does* provide an impetus towards greater order and intensity in the universe. However, this influence acts like a gentle ongoing push in that direction rather than like a puppet master pulling all the strings.

This idea of a *persuasive* influence is central to the process solution to the problem of evil, which presents a major stumbling block for many who might otherwise be inclined to believe in the possibility of God. (Take, for example, the withering attack that Dostoevsky lays out against the reality of a benevolent God in the story of "The Grand Inquisitor.") Simply put, the question is: If God is all good and all-powerful, why do bad things happen to good people—or to anyone, for that matter? Moreover, a completely omnipotent, omniscient God creates a real problem for the issue of free will. If God controls everything we do and knows everything that will happen, it is difficult to make any room for real freedom or real choice. Many moderns are not satisfied with the explanation that God works in mysterious ways, or that we must rely on faith in such matters. On the other hand, there are

44. For example, see Whitehead, *Modes of Thought,* 102, where Whitehead says that the feeling of ideals—of ideals entertained, ideals defaced, and so forth—is our experience of Deity.

those so attached to idea of power that if forced to choose between an all-good God or an all-powerful God, they opt for omnipotence. But the options are not really that straightforward.

Drawing on Whitehead's philosophy, David Griffin has worked out a process approach to the problem of evil that hinges on what it means for God to be omnipotent. According to Griffin's approach, God is as powerful as any entity *could be* in a universe where creativity is shared between God and its creatures. (And really, when you come down to it, if all the entities in the universe except One are powerless, then it does not take a very powerful Being to rule supreme.) Free will is the human experience of this shared creativity. God acts persuasively to bring about the best for every occasion of experience, but each event contributes its own impress on its final outcome. Thus, the creatures' capacity to exercise free will means that less than optimal choices, resulting in evil, are possible. There is also the evil that results from incompatible and competing actualities, such as damage from storms or killing other beings for food; God's lack of coercive power combined with the desire for a complex world means that such realities often exist.

A process answer to the problem of evil is that God is as powerful as a supreme being could be in a world with *real Adventure*. God also *is* all good. God works persuasively for the best future for the world and lovingly preserves all that has been, thereby saving the universe from what Whitehead considers the ultimate evil: *loss*—that "the past fades."[45]

This leads us to a crucial point of emphasis concerning God's place in the universe: process theology is a *naturalistic theism*. God is *not* considered a supernatural entity existing outside the universe or exempt from its laws. As mentioned earlier in this chapter, "God is not to be treated as an exception to all metaphysical principles, invoked to save their collapse. He is their chief exemplification."[46] Thus God works *within* nature; the reason mystical experiences can reveal God is that God is part of the *same* universe that we inhabit. God is exceptional not by being above physical laws or outside the universe, but by being the most all-encompassing, all-loving spiritual entity *in* the universe. Many in the process community believe that Whitehead's metaphysics, even his theological speculations, can be coherently merged with contemporary scientific theory and evidence (though some modifications to current scientific models might be necessary both in underlying principles and in certain outmoded ideas about theory and practice). For example, while God does not coercively direct evolution, God does participate in the cosmological unfoldment. As in all matters, God's primordial nature supplies new forms

45. Whitehead, *Process and Reality*, 340.
46. Whitehead, *Process and Reality*, 343.

and possibilities, gently luring the universe towards novelty, more complex orders, and greater intensities of experience.

Hopefully, this chapter has given readers a sense of how transpersonal psychology and process thought have helped me to understand and integrate the shocking impact of my most powerful psychedelic experience. While my own mystical experience of a theological nature was pivotal to my taking these matters seriously, the broad experiential confirmation from Grof's work and the intellectual understanding provided by process thought were vital for working out a satisfying worldview that included a Higher Power.

The next chapter considers mystical experiences more broadly and examines several New Age and mystical insights from the perspective of the Whiteheadian, transpersonal cosmology being developed in these pages.

8

Demystifying Mysticism

Introduction

One sunny afternoon at the Castalia seminar in Switzerland I was sitting on a grassy knoll next to a young man who was in the midst of a psychedelic euphoria. Looking out into the distance, he proclaimed, "It's all One." Curious, I inquired *exactly* what he meant by that emblematic, and rather enigmatic, statement—much to the apparent annoyance of the woman sitting on the knoll with us. Although a coherent answer was unlikely to be forthcoming, I could not help asking, as I was anxious to understand what he was actually experiencing. The idea of Oneness seemed tantalizingly suggestive *and* problematic even back then.

I have felt similar consternation when people talk about reaching a "new level of consciousness," as my bewitching friend Ann had once put it in describing an awakening she had one evening on a beach in Sarasota. This phrasing made it sound like a distinct plane of reality had been entered into, rather than merely some new insight achieved. My judgment in this matter was somewhat biased, as at times I had felt on the brink of some kind of permanent transformation of consciousness—which, disappointingly, never quite materialized. I have since come to believe that it is a mistake to try to draw such explicit experiential boundaries (especially when elsewhere espousing "no boundaries"). Systems that emphasize stages and levels tend to exacerbate a common tendency to think of things as rigidly separate rather than as interpenetrating. This tendency to think of things rigidly can result in, among other things, seeing oneness in terms far too absolute—in terms that relegate individuality to insignificance or illusion, or that at least unfairly privilege the One over the many.

Whitehead's philosophy proves extremely helpful for interpreting and sorting out many of the metaphysical claims and intuitions that commonly arise out of extraordinary states, such as "the One" just described. This chapter appraises several problematic and often confusing transpersonal New Age "truisms," while trying to illuminate what might be going on in authentic mystical experiences—in particular, how we might understand them from a Whiteheadian perspective.

Some may wonder about Whitehead's stated objective of "demystifying mysticism," as it can sound like he might be trying to minimize the importance of mystical insight, or make it fit into convenient or reductive categories of thought. That Whitehead has no intention or desire to denigrate or discount mysticism is evident from this more complete statement found on the last page of *Modes of Thought*:

> If you like to phrase it so, philosophy is mystical. For mysticism
> is direct insight into depths as yet unspoken. But the purpose
> of philosophy is to rationalize mysticism; not by explaining it
> away, but by the introduction of novel verbal characterizations,
> rationally coordinated.[1]

Whitehead, in fact, does not wish to explain away experience of *any kind*; like William James's, his is a *radical* empiricism. *All* experience is important for philosophical consideration, including the mystical and transpersonal in their myriad shapes and forms. Experience as such is philosophy's alpha and omega: "The elucidation of immediate experience is the sole justification for any thought; and the starting point for thought is the analytic observation of components of this experience."[2]

This brings to mind a conversation I had with a fellow student while waiting in the office of the Graduate Institute of the Liberal Arts at Emory. She had just gotten out of a class on postmodern theory and was excited about all the theories they were exploring—except the "constructive postmodernism" described in David Griffin's book, to which she took strong exception. As I had recently been studying with David out in Claremont and admired his brand of postmodernism, I asked what she found so objectionable. Apparently, she considered Griffin's approach too rational and logical—not at all like the multiperspectival, deconstructionist postmodernisms that appealed to her. She was writing her thesis on the waterways of Florida, with an eye on highlighting the meandering courses of natural rivers as opposed to the rigid, artificial structure of canals. While I too love free-flowing rivers, the proper comparison in this case, I think, is whether you would rather travel on them with a map that is organized rationally, or

1. Whitehead, *Modes of Thought*, 174.
2. Whitehead, *Process and Reality*, 4.

one that has been so radically deconstructed that one direction is ultimately the same as any other. The latter might be fun for a short trip when you don't care where you are going, but in the long run, the former provides a much better understanding of the ecosystem and a chance to explore it more fully and effectively. Likewise, Griffin—and Whitehead—is trying to construct the most accurate and comprehensive maps possible, to help us figure out both where we are and where we might be able to go.

Speculative philosophy—the method articulated and employed by Whitehead in *Process and Reality*—is the search for generalizations that apply to all of human experience and all of reality. For Whitehead, reconciling science and religion is the primary purpose of this speculative endeavor:

> Philosophy frees itself from the taint of ineffectiveness by its close relations with religion and with science, natural and socio-logical. It attains its chief importance by fusing the two, namely, religion and science, into one rational scheme of thought.[3]

On the one hand, process thought attempts to locate religious metaphor, theological conjecture, and mystical experience all within one rationally ordered set of ideas, thereby rendering them more comprehensible vis-à-vis science and everyday experience. On the other, it attempts to explain how religious symbolism might facilitate access to feelings from the depths that reflect authentic contact with spiritual entities, forces, and Being. Process thought, in this way, "rationalizes" mystical insight by treating it as a valid and valuable mode of perception into the universal depths and by making it coherent with the full range of human endeavor.

From the perspective of transpersonal psychology, religion was not originally conceived primarily as an abstract theory to answer abstract questions about existence or the nature of the universe, nor was it a method of maintaining the social order. Rather, formal religions evolved out of humankind's early efforts to make sense of the mystical experiences that emerge out of the unconscious depths and the insights they provide about the ultimate nature of reality. This view fits well with Whitehead's approach to philosophical analysis and with his understanding of religion, for both philosophy and religion arise out of direct human experience. Whitehead's philosophy is uniquely positioned to provide a rational and coherent interpretation of mystical experience, while neither discarding those qualities that make them such an important corrective to modern thought, nor undermining the vital advances made by modern science and reason. Let us look more closely at how this is accomplished.

3. Whitehead, *Process and Reality*, 15.

Mystical Experience in a
Whiteheadian Transpersonal Cosmology

My psychedelic insight at The Apartment marked the beginning of a lifelong investigation of that numinous space where psychology, religion, and philosophy overlap in mystical consciousness. Forty years later, I would summarize the meaning of my vision in this way. Psychologically, "holotropic"[4] states deepen and intensify experience, thereby increasing access to novel feelings and perceptions usually hidden in the unconscious depths, often leading to powerful revelations and original understandings. Theologically, sacred elements and dimensions of reality enter more fully into conscious awareness due to this psychodynamic shift, producing a variety of religious and mystical intuitions. Philosophically, this shift heightens direct perception into the nature of the universe and makes the metaphysical structure of experience more transparent to conscious awareness, thereby imparting sudden insights into the essence of reality.

In Chapter 6, I outlined how Whitehead's theory of perception provides a basis for distinguishing between three general types of information or knowledge that can be revealed through these nonordinary states, depending on what part of the experiential process yields most of the data. I will now elaborate on several implications of these distinctions by delineating three types of insights and intuitions that occur in transpersonal states.

The first type of knowledge produced by extraordinary experiences concerns the history of the individual and that person's most intimate environment. This would include personal and transpersonal memories and feelings, as well as data about the body and its various field manifestations, such as auras and energy fields. This might be referred to as *individual knowledge*—recognizing, of course, that this type of knowledge offers important clues for constructing theories about the nature of the human being in all its transpersonal complexities. Individual knowledge, then, represents a range of experiences that provide data relevant to the psychological exploration of the human psyche in its broadest personal manifestations, including perinatal and past life memories.

The second type of data revealed by extraordinary states might be termed *cosmological knowledge*. This category includes information about the history and nature of the universe, expanded to its broadest horizons, and the various entities and forces contained therein. The primary means of access to this data—as we have seen before—is enhanced awareness of perception

---

4. Once again, *holotropic* is Stanislav Grof's descriptor for those extraordinary states and experiences that facilitate psychospiritual growth; it literally means "moving towards the whole."

in the mode of causal efficacy. Most of Stanislav Grof's transpersonal cartography would fall under this category, ranging from experiences of animal and plant identification to encounters with mythological and alien beings to mystical experiences of deities, cosmological revelation, and God.

The final type of information involves *metaphysical knowledge*. This is, in a certain sense, information about a subjective process—but of a different order than what is referred to above as individual knowledge. When awareness penetrates far enough into the depths of its own self-formation, insight relevant to the basic structure of being/becoming itself can be revealed. From a process perspective, such insights arise because the human moment of experience is an exemplar of the fundamental makeup of every unit of reality. Thus, opening up to the essence of one's own becoming is simultaneously opening up to the metaphysical essence of reality. For Buddhism, it is the experience of Emptiness or Sunyata; for Whitehead, it is Creativity or Openness.

From the perspective of the philosophy of organism, a variety of mystical experiences or insights may result from accessing this deepest metaphysical dimension of reality. As we saw in the last chapter, mystical intuitions of this type may offer a deepened apprehension of Whitehead's Category of the Ultimate, the three components of which are "many," "one," and "creativity."[5] The ultimate metaphysical reality of each moment, of each here and now, is the process whereby the many past entities are creatively synthesized into a new one, and are increased by this one, which then joins the ranks of the many. When this never-ending process of creative activity is directly experienced as the foundation of one's own existence, it can be a moment of mystical liberation, beautifully expressed here by R. D. Laing:

> The experience of being the actual medium for a continual process of creation takes one past all depression or persecution or vain glory, past, even, chaos or emptiness, into the very mystery of that continual flip of nonbeing into being, and can be the occasion of that great liberation when one makes the transition from being afraid of nothing to the realization that there is nothing to fear.[6]

How are all these extraordinary experiences possible? As we have seen, Whitehead's philosophy describes a fundamental mode of perception that gives direct access to all past events. Such a mode of intuitive perceptual access to the hidden depths of the universe provides a basis for understanding how telepathy might be possible, as well as an analogous psychic access to

5. Whitehead, *Process and Reality*, 21.
6. Laing, *Politics of Experience*, 42.

other entities—potentially all past reality—including mystical experiences of God. This heightened depth of perception and intensity of awareness resulting from a flood of novel feelings rising up from the unconscious can in theory produce religious feelings of God as immanent *and* transcendent, of Nature as inspirited, and of the Universe as alive. And a Whiteheadian explication of this kind of direct perception into the metaphysical and cosmological structure of reality can give insight into the genuine meaning of such notions as Oneness, the Here and Now, and Enlightenment.

We will now consider how process philosophy can shed light on the meaning and implications of some familiar New Age adages.

Mystical Perceptions through a Process Lens

All Is One

We begin with the provocative revelation recounted at the beginning of this chapter: the intuition that "All is One." From a Whiteheadian perspective, of course, the basic insight is metaphysically accurate in that every occasion of experience does contain "everything" (i.e., feelings of the entire past universe) and does so by making it all "one" (i.e., one new unifying event). And this feeling that All is One could be reinforced through an enhanced awareness of the presence of the consequent nature of God—which consciously prehends and unifies everything in existence (in each moment)—leading to an experiential identification of sorts with this Universal feeling of Wholeness and interconnection. However, to conclude that each actual occasion is really *identical* with, or exhaustively encompassing of, the entire universe would be misleading. God, and all other entities, have their own *independent* moment of existence along with their interfused mode of being. Thus, all is one *and* all are many. This seemingly paradoxical position of *pluralistic monism* is how the philosophy of organism is able to make sense of a number of heretofore rationally irreconcilable insights from mystical states. The universe is composed of *many* events (pluralism), all of which have the *same* essential structure (monism).

What else might we say about this awareness of being "one" with everything—or feeling that All is One? Perhaps more explication of Whitehead's now-familiar metaphysical maxim (the many become one and are increased by one) is in order. Each moment of human experience is a creative unification of feelings from the past: the universe becomes condensed and synthesized into one moment of human being. In each moment, we are One with all that has been. This sense of derivation can be *felt*, and felt more strongly in nonordinary states when normally unconscious causal feelings are more easily accessible. But it should be emphasized that this sense of oneness *arises out of feelings from many past events,* and in the next moment this new "one" joins all other past events as fodder for the future.

The essence of universal process is this *flow of feeling* between the many and the one, and the one and the many. The sum of these pulsing moments of interflowing feeling *is* our universe. This, I suggest, is also the basis of the mystical intuition that *everything is connected.* While interconnectedness can also be consciously perceived and intellectually grasped, at its most fundamental level, the powerful mystical sense that everything is connected emerges out of a direct feeling of this creative process that is the very texture of the universe.

A major problem with taking the claim that All Is One in a literal way is that it may be seen as entailing the elimination of real others and even as a solipsistic worldview. Although David Hume's theory of perception implies just such a stance, not many people would be eager to defend this outcome—especially when arguing such a position leads to immediate self-contradiction (for *who* are you arguing with?). Whitehead's philosophy provides a novel alternative to Hume on this critical issue of how it is possible to have real experience of *other* beings; that is, how can something that seems to be outside of us appear *inside* our subjective moment of experience?

Paradoxically, when I have a moment of experiencing the world around me, everything I see, hear, and feel, is also *me*—the world that is *without* is somehow also *within*. A song lyric from "Perpetual Change" by Yes, one of my favorite progressive rock bands (wherein they talk about the flow from the outside to the inside and back again to the outside), nicely captures the essence of the process that helps resolve this paradox. Translating this into Whiteheadian terms, past accomplished fact (outside) flows into the newly forming event. These feelings are creatively synthesized into a new unity (inside) before feelings from that new event flow back out into future events (outside), thereby perpetuating this perpetual process of change—rather like my early psychedelic intuition of Reality being like a sine wave. By interpreting all events in terms of synthetic experiential activity, Whitehead makes the actual process of this interweaving flow of feeling comprehensible.

In this same way, Whitehead reconciles external and internal relations, as well as objects and subjects. In its moment of creative synthesis, the actual occasion is a *subject* forming itself out of its feelings of past events, which function as its *objects*. When its moment of subjective unity has been completed, it becomes a new object for future subjects. These feelings from past events constitute *external* relations, while the inner synthetic processes whereby these past events are felt and integrated are the *internal* relations. So, while our experience of the world is subjectively created, it is created *out of* feelings flowing in directly from the outside (that is, from past actual entities—real *others*).

Whitehead's system thus escapes the trap of solipsism. Philosophically, solipsism grows out of a misunderstanding of the true scope and nature of perceptual experience; psychologically, solipsism may arise in part from a sense of isolation based on a lack of *feeling* from the depth perceptual mode. This deficiency of feeling disconnects one from the world intellectually and existentially, and tends to leave one feeling lost and alone, or (as this condition is often described) alienated. A Whiteheadian solution to alienation would be reconnecting to those feelings, perceptions, and emotions that flow in from the unconscious depths and form the foundation of our being. This helps explain why Colin Wilson was so taken with Whitehead and Maslow's ideas: Process thought shows the philosophical way out of modernity's alienation and isolation; transpersonal psychology provides the experiential methods and maps to guide our escape.

To recap, Oneness may be seen as an overdetermined intuition into the nature of things, whose broader implications are often misapprehended. Process thought provides at least three ways that this sense of Oneness might be more coherently understood. First, it could involve enhanced perception into the intricate interconnectedness of the universe, epitomized by the flow of the Many becoming One. Second, Oneness could grow out of a subtle identification with God's consequent nature's moment-by-moment, unifying synthesis of all actuality. Third, Oneness could represent a heightened awareness of how each moment of subjective becoming feels and synthesizes the entire past into a new embracing One. As we shall see, another sort of spiritual insight can arise from intuitions into the essence of the concrescent process, resulting in the mystical experience of Openness or Emptiness, which might also be thought of as the oneness or unity of pure becoming.

There Are No Coincidences

Carl Jung's popular notion of *synchronicity* as an "acausal" ordering principle offers an appropriate point of departure for considering coincidences, connections, and causality in general. A prime example of synchronicity recounted by Jung involves a highly rational client whose intellectualism presented a formidable barrier to her therapeutic progress. One day, while the woman was describing a dream about being given a piece of jewelry shaped like a golden scarab, Jung heard a light tapping at the window. It was a beetle trying to get inside the room—one closely resembling the dream image of the scarab. Jung opened the window, caught the beetle, and handed it to the woman, saying, "Here is your scarab."[7] As one might imagine, this had a powerful effect on the woman's rigid belief in a perfectly rational order to the world. And rightly so, for this certainly seems to be a meaningful juxtaposition of events with no discernible causal connection—at least not a causal connection in the usual scientific sense.

When Jung speaks of an *acausal* ordering principle, I think he is pointing to the possible existence of an underlying design whose influence lies outside the realm of direct physical causation in the materialist or mechanistic sense. Under the rubric of synchronicity, Jung is experimenting with this notion of a deeper order or pattern that helps orchestrate our reality, an ordering somehow intimately involved with our psychic lives. So we should be careful not to assume that acausal means no cause; rather, we might think of synchronicity as pointing to causes or ordering principles that transcend the mechanistic or physical variety often depicted as billiard balls colliding.

What might Whitehead be able to tell us about coincidences, meaningful and otherwise, and especially about *nonphysical* causation? And what is a Whiteheadian to make of New Age sayings like "everything happens for a reason," and "nothing happens by accident"? First of all, coincidences *do* occur according to process philosophy—in fact, they occur all the time. Of course, in an ultimate sense nothing happens *by accident*, since all events are strongly influenced by the past. However, free choice, individuals working at cross-purposes, and the relatively blind actions of low-level entities—in combination—lead to all kinds of coincidences, accidents, and unplanned (and undesirable) events.

From a theological perspective as well, the oft-heard phrase "there are no coincidences" must be considered misguided at best, since the process God operates through persuasion rather than by coercive control. The apparent thrust of such maxims is that everything that takes place is determined, planned, or controlled, which I imagine is supposed to reassure us that our lives make sense and that we are in good (God's) hands. But this outlook also entails the unfortunate implication that we have little or no freedom, and worse, that all the horrible things that happen are part of what is meant to be. This prospect strikes me as far from comforting.

But what to make of Jung's scarab anecdote? While extraordinary coincidences and unlikely events occasionally occur spontaneously—against tremendous odds, someone eventually wins the Powerball jackpot—I think

7. Jung, *Synchronicity.*

Jung was on to a real phenomenon with synchronicity. In this regard, Whitehead offers an alternative causal principle, one that involves the "mental pole" of occasions of experience.[8] In a process metaphysics, physical causation is understood in terms of how new events initially conform to the feelings of past objects. But even though the past deeply influences the present, the new occasion can add novelty and creative imagination to how it synthesizes those conformal feelings. In addition, Whitehead hypothesizes that events can directly influence, and be influenced by, the more complex subjective activity of other entities. Among other things, we are talking here about the possibility of parapsychological influence or causation, such as telepathy and psychokinesis, where a contemporary subject taps into the mentality of another past or future event. (Tapping into a past event's mentality might appear as telepathy; direct influence on the mentality of an upcoming event might manifest as psychokinesis.)

Thus one way of understanding synchronicity is through psychical causation, in contrast to invoking some indefinite "acausal" principle. For example, psychical influences in the scarab story might include a telepathic sense of the beetle being nearby unconsciously stimulating the patient to relate that particular dream. In turn, Jung's intense focus on the dream image might have "persuaded" the beetle to fly over and bump against the window.

On a grander, more speculative scale, one could also consider the possibility of causal influences from other spiritual entities. The philosophy of organism allows for the potential existence of "purely spiritual beings,"[9] such as disembodied souls, guides, higher spiritual beings, or other entities reported in the psychical literature. Conceivably, one of these beings could involve itself in arranging for meaningful circumstances in order to assist people in their psychospiritual evolution.

There could be influence from the highest source as well. While process theology's notion of God does not allow for God's direct coercive involvement in worldly circumstances, God does offer in every moment a basic guidance for how things might best unfold to create the optimal experience. Some cases of synchronicity could involve a heightened

8. In *Process and Reality* Whitehead first uses "mental pole" explicitly on page 240, but he develops the concept in other places throughout the book. For example, on page 108, he writes that "Each actuality is essentially bipolar, physical and mental."

9. Whitehead uses this term in several places in his writings. In *Religion in the Making*, Whitehead states, "The doctrine here developed . . . is entirely neutral on the question of immortality, or on the existence of purely spiritual beings other than God. There is no reason why such a question should not be decided on more special evidence, religious or otherwise, provided that it is trustworthy" (107).

attunement to this *initial aim,* creating an ongoing sense of events unfolding in perfect harmonization.

I must caution, however, about falling under the spell of the kind of
hyperconnectivity that can occur in nonordinary states or in certain belief
systems. It is easy to see possible connections and meanings where they
do not really exist. A touching example of this tendency is found in the
documentary *Gimme Some Truth: The Making of John Lennon's "Imagine"
Album.*[10] At one point in the film, we witness an encounter between John
Lennon and a man who has been found trespassing at Lennon's estate. The
young, disheveled man seems to believe that some of the Beatles songs
are written *about him*—literally. For example, the young man says that he
thinks that *he* is the "boy" in the famous line from *Abbey Road* about carrying "The Weight." Lennon is direct with the man, asking how he (Lennon) could have written about someone he doesn't even know. Lennon
goes on to say that when he writes something, it is about himself, and
perhaps (if it is a love song) about Yoko. Then he asks the man if he is
hungry and invites him in for tea. The last scene shows the stranger sitting
at the Lennon breakfast table, relatively calmly eating some toast. Besides
the remarkable nature of John's response (caringly confrontational yet respectful), the thing to note in this encounter is the young man's conviction
that Lennon's song lyrics were somehow written *specifically* about himself,
the young man. This is a great demonstration of how, when people are
inordinately open to seeing connections between events, it is easy to see
ones that are not really there. At one end of the spectrum, hyperconnectivity can be a source of high creativity or amusing misunderstandings. At the
other end lies the world of schizophrenia.

When I was deeply immersed in my psychedelic days at New College, I
was particularly into Yes's 1971 song "Starship Trooper." Being curious about
the name of the final movement, "Würm," I looked it up in the dictionary
one day. It turns out *Würm* refers to the final glacial period in North America, particularly in Wisconsin. This struck me as a significant synchronicity,
as if the song was somehow intended for me, since I was from Wisconsin
and the Beatles line "the ice is slowly melting" from "Here Comes the Sun"
had been so powerful during my Big Trip. (The transpersonal implication,
if I recall correctly, was that these synchronicities were somehow related to
an unfolding plan that was guiding me towards enlightenment.) Years later,
I was able to ask Steve Howe, the guitarist for Yes, how they had come up
with the title "Würm." Howe told me that they had found it by chance going
through the dictionary—apparently without me in mind at all! As Lennon

---

10. Solt, dir., *Gimme Some Truth.*

says at one point in the documentary *Gimme Some Truth*: "Anything fits, you know, if you're tripping off on some trip."[11]

Be Here Now

In the midst of an early psychedelic journey, I found myself in the basement of the house where I grew up, listening to the Beatles' *Abbey Road* album. (It *is* a favorite of mine.) On this occasion, the lyric from "You Never Give Me Your Money" that riveted my attention concerned that wonderful feeling of being exactly where you are. In my highly suggestible state, these words transported me into a powerful awareness of the *Here and Now* and its accompanying sense of fullness, or perhaps completeness, along with a feeling of deep relief and release. I loved this state and wished I could find a way to be there all the time. A short time later, when a copy of *Be Here Now* appeared at The Apartment—speaking of synchronicity—I was quite curious to find out what Richard Alpert (Ram Dass) might have to say about this psychedelic phenomena. This amazing book, along with *The Psychedelic Experience,* turned out to be my first authoritative guides to these newly revealed dimensions of reality, as they were for many others. As with most literature concerning mystical and spiritual matters, confusion can easily arise over what these experiences really mean and what implications they hold for our lives. Whitehead's philosophy has been extraordinarily useful for sorting out many of these issues.

My psychedelic journeys have made it clear why so much of the interest around nonordinary states and mystical experience in one way or another concerns the notion of an encounter with the here and now.[12] This fascination with the here and now includes a variety of assertions,

11. See Solt, dir., *Gimme Some Truth.*

12. I am aware of Gilbert Ryle's attempt to explain away any mystical attributions to the notions of "I" and "now" by analyzing these and other self-referential words in terms of logic and language theory, i.e., via analytic philosophy. In *The Concept of Mind,* Ryle writes that:

> There is nothing mysterious or occult about the range of higher order acts and attitudes, which are apt to be inadequately covered by the umbrella-title 'self-consciousness.'
> ... It is worth mentioning that there is one influential difference between the first personal pronoun and all the rest. 'I', in my use of it, always indicates me and only indicates me. 'You', 'she' and 'they' indicate different people at different times. 'I' is like my own shadow; I can never get away from it, as I can get away from your shadow. There is no mystery about this constancy, but I mention it because it seems to endow 'I' with a mystifying uniqueness and adhesiveness. 'Now' has something of the same besetting feeling. (198)

ranging from the benefits derived from focused attention on immediate experience to the belief that *all* of reality is located in the present moment. Whitehead's description of the actual occasion is particularly promising for evaluating such claims.

To begin with, the moment of concrescence itself provides a metaphysical exemplification par excellence of an eternal moment—as that which is out of time and existing in-itself. In its moment of self-creation, the actual entity is outside time, contains the entire universe (in the sense of responding to all past events), and is an exemplar of the ultimate unit of reality. When nonordinary states generate an enhanced awareness of the underlying structure of the actual occasion, these metaphysical factors enter more fully into conscious experience, resulting in such assertions as: time does not really exist; the present moment contains all that is; and the here and now *is* Reality. These frequently reported insights approximate Whitehead's own metaphysical views and might easily be arrived at on the basis of mystical penetrations into the depths of a universe structured along the lines proposed by the philosophy of organism.

John Cobb Jr. provides an excellent description of the Buddhist experience of the here and now and of how we as modern Westerners attempt to ward off this fundamental Buddhist insight

> that reality is simply the immediacy of momentary being or becoming, in which each ingredient is just what it is as that ingredient in that momentary becoming. There may be memories, anticipations, and concepts, but they are features of the momentary becoming just as are emotions and sensations and intuitions. They do not remove us from the moment. When this is realized, their power to structure other aspects of experience is broken . . .
>
> The Buddhist analysis assaults our Western time-consciousness one step further. Not only can the here-now not orient itself toward an inclusive history, but in its own moment of occurrence, it is not temporal at all. Within it there is neither past nor future, neither has-been nor not-yet. The here-now is

---

To my mind, Ryle misses the crux of this issue by failing to consider that the reason the words *I* and *now* have this peculiar constancy and uniqueness is that the experiential realities they represent also possess a singular position, metaphysically and mystically. For both philosophical analysis and mystical revelation begin at the same radical point of departure: an "I" experiencing "now." Whitehead refers to this as the "subjectivist bias"; in mystical language, it is the "eternal moment" or the "here-and-now." Thus, it is not merely some odd artifact of language games that endows the words I, now, and here with a unique significance. "I-am-here-now" is, in fact, the self-definition of a conscious actual entity.

complete and perfect in itself. Furthermore, there is not some other, temporal, reality to contrast with the non-temporal here-now. What-is is always and necessarily here-now. Time exists only for the perspective that objectifies the here-now and views the succession of moments as if from without. But ultimately there is no such perspective. When this illusoriness of time is experientially realized, time is existentially dissolved.[13]

Even though the revelations from extraordinary states frequently parallel the Buddhist experience of the here and now as perfect, timeless, and empty, Whiteheadian analysis suggests that these views are incomplete, and that a more complex interpretation is required—one that can incorporate the essential insights from the here and now while also making room for those many other experiences from ordinary and nonordinary states that support the pragmatic and metaphysical existence of time and process. Cobb identifies below what is missing from the Buddhist analysis:

> Nevertheless, the Buddhist formulation, while valid, is one-sided. It is true that the here-now is a coalescence of elements which are themselves here-now. But it is also true that these elements are not simply located here-now. They witness here-now to their occurrence there-then. That is, my remembered past and the star I now see in the night sky are here-now in my present experience, but I feel them here-now as temporally past and spatially distant. For here-now to be Empty is for it to allow these elements their own integrity, which includes their having-been. They are here-now as what-has-been-there-then. It is for this reason that the Buddhist can also say that in knowing oneself one who is enlightened knows all things. But if so, then the past as the having-been of elements of the here-now coalescence is not illusory. Further, the future differs from both the here-now coalescence and the there-then as the not-yet. As claim and hope it is also ingredient in the coalescence with its own distinctive integrity.
>
> More generally, the analysis of the dependent origination of all things does not demand a doctrine of pure immanence alone. What is immanent in this vision is by the same token transcendent, for what coalesces is not the coalescence itself but the elements each with their distinctive contribution to make.[14]

Like David Hume's analysis of experience, the Buddhist theory of the here-and-now overlooks the objective status of the past events that inform

13. Cobb, *Beyond Dialogue*, 94.
14. Cobb, *Beyond Dialogue*, 115–16.

the moment of concrescence as well as the moment's necessary anticipation of the future. In a process metaphysics, each moment of self-creation *feels* the presence of the past and *aims* towards a possible future. No matter how creative and free of ego an occasion of experience may be, it still synthesizes itself out of its *response* to efficacious past events. By focusing their analysis of experience on the world as revealed through sensuous perception, the Buddhists often miss the full significance of the underlying causal influence of the past as it manifests in the here and now—the *presence* of the past—and thus tend to underestimate the past's, and the future's, inexorable impact on every moment of experience, which insures each new occasion's deep-rooted involvement in the process of universal unfoldment and the inherent meaning therein.[15]

What about the idea that all of reality exists solely in the here and now? From a process perspective, it is true that in each moment the entire world exists as your own creation; in a real sense, you are the universe. But this is only part of the story. This universe that is your moment of creative experience is composed of entities that have their *own* existence, and furthermore, your momentary synthesis of the universe is destined to be superseded by other moments of experience that will include your moment as a part of *their* universal synthesis. And *all* these momentary events also create their own universe, or more accurately, their own perspective on the universe. But it would be a mistake to think of these perspectives as mere subjective inventions. These moments of creation are more like an artistic act than dream activity, for they rely heavily on objective materials from the world to create their product. (This analogy, of course, is flawed—for dreams also create their stories partly out of material from the waking world, that is, from what Freud called the day residue, and from the input of bodily feelings and sensations, as well as from one's more distant memories.) Cobb also believes that the Buddhists place an overemphasis on the world as encountered through the mode of *presentational immediacy*, resulting in an exaggerated sense of the isolatability of the self

15. Cobb writes, "From my Whiteheadian viewpoint, Buddhism seems subtly to have exaggerated the capacity of an actual occasion of human experience to determine its own relation to its predecessors. Buddhism attributed true causality to the prehending occasion only, holding that it alone is ultimately responsible for how it prehends its predecessors. This doctrine led to the theoretical ideal of an occasion that suspends such prehensions altogether. Whitehead holds that the decisions of the past occasions inescapably play a causally efficacious role in setting the limits of the present occasion. This means that the present occasion *must* take account of past occasions and reenact aspects of them. This does not deny the possibility of a very different relation to this past from that which is normal to us. Nevertheless, from the Whiteheadian perspective, the ideal of the timeless moment is an illusion" (Cobb, *Structure of Christian Existence*, 68).

in the moment. This suggests that the Buddhist practice of detachment can be a two-edged sword—providing relief from the ego's tendency to cling to desires and resentments, but at times merely obscuring awareness of the unconscious presence of these feelings.

A Whiteheadian analysis of this kind offers a philosophical basis for understanding the transformative and revelatory potentials associated with enhanced attentiveness to the here and now. It can also provide philosophical clarification and justification for many of the ideas and claims that come out of these experiential domains. However, some of the metaphysical and cosmological deductions that have been drawn from these experiences regarding the nature of the self, time, and the world must be viewed as one-sided or as overstatement.

Be this as it may, the Buddhists are certainly justified in their belief that the human personality can be radically transformed by living more fully in the here and now, thereby eliminating much of one's emotional and intellectual over-involvement with the past and future. By reducing the limiting and organizing influence of crystallized ego structures upon the concrescent process—that is, by being more fully present in the here-and-now and receptive to the flow of things as they are—human experience can start to free itself from those largely unconscious influences feeding our habitual ego concerns, such as fears, desires, and attachments. It is wonderfully freeing to have "nowhere to go," because "wherever you go, there you are." And living intensely in the moment tends to greatly enhance one's appreciation of what is: be it color, sound, touch, taste, the presence of others—*really* taking in what is there (or here). The transformative power of being fully present to where you are is encapsulated in Gestalt therapy's "paradoxical theory of change," as formulated here by Arnold Beisser: "Change occurs when one becomes what he is, not when he tries to become what he is not. Change does not take place through a coercive attempt by the individual or by another person to change him, but it does take place if one takes the time and effort to be what he is."[16]

"Being Here"—attending more fully to the present moment of experience—can also act as a gateway to the transpersonal realm. It constitutes a critical shift away from Heidegger's *thrownness* of "Being There" and towards a reappropriation of one's essential belonging and connectedness to the universe. *Being Here*—in body, feeling, and presence—is, again paradoxically, a key to opening up to the possibility of mystical experiences involving the hidden depths of oneself, the universe, and the metaphysical reality of each moment as well. I would venture that this is partly what

16. Beisser, "Paradoxical Theory of Change," 77.

happened during my Big Trip, when I rapidly shifted from feeling like I was finally fully present to myself to opening up much more radically to the transpersonal depths.

As popularly understood, the Buddhist theory of experience tends to subtly exaggerate how much the Now can be isolated from past and future. Neither the past nor the future can (or should) be completely transcended. The present moment always involves both in its self-creative activity. Thus, living in the Here and Now is essentially inclusive of past actualities and future possibilities—but *right now*. More broadly, this inclusion of the past and future in even our mystical contemplation is crucial if we are to have a solid foundation for seriously preparing for our future, while preserving and drawing upon past achievement.

Everything Is Consciousness

The assertion that "everything is consciousness"—heard from mystics, philosophers, and laypeople alike—confounds me. The evidence of every-day experience is so to the contrary that it makes this belief seem patently wrongheaded. Some of the problem here may be due to the use of the term "consciousness" as a synonym for experience. Using these terms interchangeably badly misrepresents the vast unconscious factors that contribute to consciousness, as described by depth psychology, neurosci-ence, and most of modern philosophy. Likewise, to claim that everything is "consciousness" is quite different from Whitehead's view that reality is composed of mostly unconscious experiential events.

This sentiment might be seen as a reaction (or an overreaction) against materialism's denial of the importance of consciousness. Saying that everything is consciousness would be, in effect, a sort of post-Car-tesian reversal; instead of focusing only on the reality of extended matter (materialism), "thinking" matter is affirmed as the primary reality. Seeing the universe as composed solely of consciousness may also be appealing to those wishing to emphasize the spiritual dimensions of reality. But the most promising possibility may be that this claim is rooted in authen-tic intuitions into the deeper nature of reality, that the pathetic fallacy (ascribing human traits or feelings to nature) is *not* a pathetic Romantic error. Rather, the entire universe *is* in some important way alive and sub-jective, as Whitehead suggests.

With the philosophy of organism, Whitehead is trying to overcome the notion of *insentient* matter—literally "incapable of feeling"—that has persisted since Descartes. *Sentir* means "to feel," thus Whitehead's introduc-tion of *feeling* as a fundamental element in his metaphysics is a deft correc-tive to this problematic notion that matter lacks any sort of subjectivity. Is this really so difficult to believe? Biologists have already discovered primitive forms of subjective activity down to the molecular level, and physics postulates selective and integrative activity at the quantum level of reality—leaving little room for so-called insentient matter.[17]

A common objection to the Whiteheadian position that feeling is fundamental to reality can be summed up this way: If feeling or experience is everywhere, why don't we see the world this way? Why do rocks and tables appear lifeless, not to mention "feelingless"? Whitehead has an answer: *transmutation*. Transmutation is the way that events simplify their experiential integrations by synthesizing a multitude of feelings into a unified perception. It is a process of abstracting shared qualities from a multitude of data and then projecting them across a perceptual field. For example, we perceive a stone as a grey image occupying space, rather than experiencing millions of molecular events vibrating and radiating a certain light pattern. We feel a touch of a hand, rather than feeling the pressure of thousands of individual touch receptors.

While part of this consolidation is likely accomplished by the visual systems of the eyes and brain, the final synthesis of the multitudinous data/feelings emerging from the neural network of the vision centers requires further simplification and elaboration: namely, the synthetic abstractive process of transmutation achieved by the psyche's dominant occasions. (Transmutation is employed to some degree by all sensory modalities to simplify perception, but it is most easily described in terms of vision, where it plays such a dominant role in our experience.) There may remain in everyday consciousness a subtle sense of this data's original activity or aliveness—which can be picked up on more readily in nonordinary states—but generally this process of transmutation glosses over and obscures these underlying feeling tones. This large-scale abstraction, with its product of clear and distinct perception, is quite handy for navigating our world and surviving in it. But it has hindered philosophical analysis of reality, especially for those theoretical systems that have relied heavily on visually oriented ways of thinking.

Another principal reason that macroscopic objects like rocks and chairs seem particularly lifeless is that they are composed entirely of low-level individuals (atoms and simple molecules), which possess relatively little novelty and intensity of experience/feeling. Plants and animals, on the other hand, also contain more complex entities, such as macromolecules and cells. More sophisticated animals also possess a dominant center of integration and control—a psyche or soul, to use common parlance. With each level of additional complexity, the feeling nature of these *compound individuals*

17. For examples of the presence of primitive subjective activity throughout nature, see Griffin, *Reenchantment without Supernaturalism*, 108.

becomes more intense and easier to perceive: perception of these underlying feelings is most difficult with *aggregates* (for example, tables and stones) made up of very simple individuals; perception is less difficult with more *complex individuals* such as cells (under a microscope their self-activity is quite apparent); perception is quite easy with animals (at least to any pet owner); and self-evident with human-level events.

Returning now to the transpersonal intuition that everything is consciousness, Whitehead's philosophy suggests another reason why people might conclude that consciousness is pervasive in the world: mystical intuitions of God. On the one hand, God's primordial nature, which contains and envisions all potentialities, is immanent in all events; on the other hand, God's consequent nature receives and preserves all occasions, and might also be perceived as an overarching presence.[18] Therefore, in mystical experiences—with their heightened access to factors from the earlier phases of unconscious processing—it may be possible to intuit an underlying and surrounding Intelligence that permeates and enjoys all of reality. But God's encompassing conscious synthesis of the universe does not imply that "everything is consciousness" either. For all the events that flow in and out of God's momentary universal syntheses first have their *own* moments of reality, most of which are composed of *unconscious* feeling. Thus, God's consciousness is not all-consuming, nor are the finite events primarily conscious: most are always unconscious, and only some occasionally rise to conscious awareness. Furthermore, consciousness is not a thing-in-itself, as James famously argued in his essay, "Does Consciousness Exist?" Consciousness is a *way* or *mode* of feeling things, that is, feeling them *consciously*. Consciousness, as a thing-in-itself, is an abstraction.

For Whitehead, *experience* is an encompassing concept that includes consciousness as its occasional aspect. As Whitehead puts it, consciousness is the "crown of experience."[19] The unconscious activity of feeling and synthesizing past events is the foundation of all experience, including conscious awareness. I remind readers that Whitehead uses the term *experience* to cover a much wider field of phenomena than is typical for our culture. *Experience* describes the self-constructive activity of all actual occasions, ranging from the events constituting God to humans to cells to molecules to atomic and subatomic particles. Thus, in Whitehead's metaphysics, *conscious awareness* belongs to a peculiar phase of experience occurring sporadically in certain complex individuals:

18. Bear in mind that this dichotomy exists only in the abstract: God's lived nature is a *unity*. These functional divisions serve mainly to differentiate and highlight the various aspects of God's activities and constitution.

19. Whitehead, *Process and Reality*, 267.

> Mental activity is one of the modes of feeling belonging to all
> actual entities in some degree, but only amounting to conscious
> intellectuality in some actual entities. This higher grade of
> mental activity is the intellectual self-analysis of the entity in
> an earlier stage of incompletion, effected by intellectual feelings
> produced in a later stage of concrescence.[20]

Once again, in accord with William James's view, consciousness is not conceived of as an independently existing thing or substance but rather as an aspect of the process of self-creative experience. It is *how* part of this process is experienced, that is, *consciously*.

At times I find Whitehead's technical description of consciousness (an "affirmation/negation contrast") rather difficult to get my mind around. But I believe its essence is that consciousness involves a focused awareness of a *difference*. To be aware of something, we need to feel a contrast with what it is *not*. Thus, we have the observation that fish don't know what water is, or how humans are not generally conscious of the weight of the atmosphere.

But even if the pervasive substance of the universe is not primarily consciousness, what if all that *really* exists is the One Consciousness of God, as propounded in certain pantheistic and New Age schemes? Might not this be a viable meaning of "everything is consciousness"?

This idea of a One that is the ultimate and absolute reality is as aberrant to Whitehead as it was to James. As a result, their theologies are panentheistic: God is in everything *and* everything is in God, but everything has its *own* reality too. This differs fundamentally from most pantheistic theories, where the universe is *identical* with God. A helpful image sometimes used to describe *panentheism* is the *world as God's body*. Just as our psyche unifies the activities and events of our body, so too God provides a unified center of experience for the universe—however, God's synthesis of the universe would be vastly more complete than any integration accomplished by the human psyche. The ultimate exemplar of the category of the "One and the Many" is the flow of all events into God's being, and the flow of God's experience back into the universe. In this way, God sympathetically receives the manifold experiences of all the creatures and then offers a vision of potential creation to them as well. So, although process theology envisions an ultimate conscious unification of the universe within God's own experience, these momentary unifications are in a rhythmic interaction with the multitudes of actual finite events constituting our universe, which are mostly unconscious in nature.

I share James's and Whitehead's suspicion of theologies that advocate for an Absolute that is the *only* reality, with perceived diversity being ultimately an illusion or error. This view simply does not resonate with how

20. Whitehead, *Process and Reality*, 56.

our lives are experienced or how we live. I tried living for a while with this theory as my guide and that proved unworkable, and more importantly, dangerous and irresponsible. The idea (which some Neoplatonic doctrines seem to boil down to) that our world is filled with entities that are not fully real and yet somehow fit into levels of being that are not quite real either, seems opaque, if not nonsensical. And the notion of the universe as God playing hide-and-seek with himself appears ultimately pointless and boring, especially for God, who must already know where everyone is hiding and how they will be found.[21] Real *adventure*, Whitehead argues, is found when creativity is shared with the creatures and the future is full of open possibilities. The so-called adventures of a single totalizing Consciousness would thus seem to be the real illusion.

In sum, process philosophy rejects the assertion that everything is consciousness, both as a claim that consciousness is the fundamental nature of all entities and as a portrayal of One consciousness as the only true reality.

This Is It

One of the things I remember most vividly about getting off on acid is the moment that I would *wake up*. A strange feeling would start to come to the fore, and then I would suddenly *Be There*. It was often accompanied by an eerily familiar recognition and remembrance—like, "Oh, yeah, how did I forget about this? It's so obvious." What, exactly, was this strangely familiar state?

I wish I could summon up this feeling at will, but the best I can do is try to describe it. As I recall, it manifested as a powerful sense of being fully present in the now, combined with an enhanced openness to the world and to my deepest feelings, with all experience flowing along within a holistic awareness. Waking up included an awareness of everything unfolding vividly and transparently before me—a sense that it is all me, and at the same time there is no me. I believe this experience is similar to what Alan Watts describes in a wonderful essay titled, "This Is It"—perhaps a more evocative phrasing than "waking up" (although the Buddha *is* purported to have responded to an inquiry about who he really was with the simple answer: "I am awake").

From a process perspective, this feeling could arise out of the *metaphysical unity* of the experiential field characterizing each moment of becoming, along with a deep sense of impersonal identity that is rooted within this mode of awareness. One identifies more fully with the whole field of experience

21. Alan Watts, the famous popularizer of Asian thought in the West, is fond of describing the search for enlightenment in terms of God playing hide-and-seek. See Watts, *Book*, 14.

and feels part of everything within one's awareness. As we have seen, I *am* the world in a very real sense (and so is everyone else, of course). Identification with my body/consciousness is a partial truth, masking the greater truth that I *am* everything I see, feel, hear, touch, and experience—both in the sense of being *constituted* by it genetically and *creating* it phenomenologically. The world creates me as I create my world.

Although certainly intended as a romantic ballad, "You Are Everything," by the Stylistics, also points to an important metaphysical truth. At one level, this realization involves becoming aware that *you* (at a deep level) are creating your own experience and your reality. This is the insight so popular with many New Age and New Thought advocates. More profound, perhaps, is the realization that Reality is *creating you;* that you (your everyday self) merely emerge out of every moment as a byproduct or an observer of this creative process. But this "little" you is more connected to that deeper reality that creates your world of experience—and to those deeper feelings that flow through and form and inform you—than is ordinarily recognized. A deeper *openness* to this underlying reality and to a more transparent awareness is a fundamental dimension of waking up.

This heightened openness is closely related to *wonder.* In this state, the present moment is *less* directed by the habitual lines of force (Whitehead's *vector feelings*) arising out of conscious and unconscious ego projects that produce fixed anticipations of the future. Such an "open moment" feels *surprised* by each new occasion, as novel and unexpected feelings and ideas arise more freely from within and amazing things appear from without. The normal ego fades into the background and seems strangely absent, which can be wonderfully freeing or terrifying—and sometimes both.

Although I am *always* open, I can distort *how much,* and to *what,* I open myself. I may be open more deeply to feelings of another person, or to my past ego structures, or to nature, or to the immediate past as it is now (Buddhist openness), or to God (holy openness). The term *emptiness* has an advantage over the term *openness* to the extent that in addition to conveying the open flow of the past into the present, *emptiness* also points to the psychological state of ego-free receptiveness that predisposes a newly arising actual occasion to be responsive to events beyond the expectations of one's *personal* past experiences. Paradoxically, emptiness also implies fullness, for being Emptiness is what allows a greater Fullness of Being to arise within one's experience.

As we begin to feel our basic nature as *flow* or creative process, we may notice that our grasping onto things and people—and most fundamentally onto ourselves—is a doomed attempt to find *safety,* permanence, through the re-creation of how things *were.* This attempt to *avoid loss* flies in the face of the basic nature of reality. For, as Whitehead puts it, the ultimate metaphysical evil is that "the past fades." When we try to re-create the past *as it was* (permanence *within* time), we undermine our own capacity for creativity and novelty, thus throttling the intensity and adventure of our own experience. We also play God: for God alone can sustain true Permanence as the everlasting preservation of the past within Infinite Being.

When we *open up* to these deeper feelings, and stop trying to control them, our unimpeded emotions, intuitions, and innate guidance from the universe allow for a renewed trust in life. Then we can really relax (let go) and also stop trying to control the world. We have entered into the flow.

This temporary suspension of normal ego repressions and structures allows a heightened feeling of connection to surrounding events and entities, while at the same time diminishing our sense of a separate self. By conforming both our unconscious and conscious experience more fully to our actual world, we respond more seamlessly and appropriately to events, thereby evoking a sense of ease, oneness with life, and a fullness of being—and of being in the Now. *This is it.*

Being in the flow also creates an atmosphere of *intense interest* as each new wave of feeling *floods* into us. This flood of feeling may be the basis of the *rush,* often referred to in psychedelic circles, where successive waves of feeling reinforce and intensify the awareness of each new moment. It is also reminiscent of Cobb's description of the essence of Christian spiritual experience: each moment of experience transcending and surpassing itself in order to be more fully open to what the world and God have to offer.

I cannot end this chapter on mysticism without speaking to a problem that puzzled me for quite some time: the overlapping and seemingly ambiguous meanings of *metaphysics.* A Whiteheadian explication of nonordinary states, in my view, provides a *unifying ground* for understanding the two primary usages of this term. During extraordinary experiences, we can *transcend everyday reality* (the spiritual or mystical meaning of *metaphysical*) and experience the *basic structure of reality* (the philosophical meaning of *metaphysical*). Since the basic structure of reality is discovered, for Whitehead, by uncovering the true nature of lived-experience itself, the penetration into the unconscious depths occurring during nonordinary states constitutes a metaphysical adventure of the first order, revealing philosophical and spiritual secrets about the hidden realities lying within.

9

Psychospiritual Transformation

Sometimes I find myself cringing a bit when I hear someone talk about their "spirituality," just as I do at the mention of miracles. But since I can only describe my recovery from addiction as miraculous, I try to tread carefully in these murky waters, where it can be especially difficult to judge the depths.

What often makes both of these subjects fringe phenomena for the modern Western mind is related to some key philosophical and religious decisions made in the early days of the scientific revolution. There was significant conflict in the seventeenth century about whether to adopt an animistic (nature as in some sense ensouled) or a mechanistic framework for science.[1] A number of leading scientists of that era, including Isaac Newton, leaned towards an animistic model, but Descartes's idea of extended matter won out, in large part because the church eventually threw its weight behind Descartes's metaphysical position.

The church's primary motivation, not surprisingly, was to protect its authority and power. These in turn depended to a great extent on Jesus's unique status as the true Son of God, as well as the church's all-important role as mediator between humankind and God's forgiveness and salvation. Oddly, a mechanical understanding of causality better served their purposes, for in a material-mechanistic universe, the kind of miracles attributed to Jesus can only be explained in terms of supernatural powers. And Christ's miracles were the church's hard evidence that Jesus was not just another prophet or spiritual giant, but truly Godlike. But within an animistic worldview, action at a distance and parapsychological powers become real possibilities for all human beings. Thus, Jesus's miracles would no longer demonstrate a special

---

1. For an in-depth discussion of this topic, as well as the broader issues related to the philosophical and religious influences on the origins of the scientific endeavor, see Griffin, *Religion and Scientific Naturalism,* chapter 5.

relationship with a supernatural God, for they could instead be understood as the kind of extraordinary powers that have been ascribed to other mystics and sages throughout history. Additionally, if the universe is suffused with spiritual energies, then the church's role as sole arbiter of relations with the spiritual domains could be compromised.

For these (and other) reasons, Descartes's depiction of reality as mind versus insentient matter came to dominate the scientific paradigm. Following the contour of this radical bifurcation, spirituality was installed within the province of mind, and therefore completely separated from the physical world. Then, as modern science's materialistic approach gained full ascendancy, at least as far as being the final arbiter of the nature of reality, mind itself moved ever more into the realm of mere epiphenomenon, and spirit was likewise deprived of real efficacy and importance. Things such as miracles, spirit entities, and parapsychology quite naturally came to be widely viewed with suspicion, amusement, or disdain within this new Weltanschauung. After all, we *know* that things of this sort are not *really* real, since scientific theory has shown they are not possible. Sometimes I too fall into this line of thinking (or really, *not* thinking), despite all that I argue for in this book. This perspective on reality just seems so *normal* to me, having been raised within a materialist, mechanistic worldview. But I do try to stay open-minded!

I have already made a case for the possible reality of psychic powers. And miracles might well be understood either as parapsychological interventions or in terms of various forces in the universe working together to arrange a surprisingly good outcome for a situation. One may well ask what I mean by forces in the universe. I have in mind here a subtly complex *alignment* of events that produces a remarkable outcome. This kind of alignment would seem to require a transpersonal coordination of actions between humans and other spiritual entities, which could of course include God in some fashion, since in the process view God's persuasive powers are omnipresent (though not omnipotent). The popular recovery idea that "God works through other people" is relevant but need not be the whole story.

What miracles do *not* look like from a process perspective are supernatural interventions by God. God has only persuasive power, not coercive power, and God operates completely within the natural laws of the universe. Remember, process theology is a *naturalistic* theology: God is part of the universe, not outside it.

This is a long way around of explaining why I and probably many others have some resistance to the notion of spirituality being so freely bandied about. But obviously in a book on transpersonal experience, spirituality is a subject that calls for careful consideration. And I *am* very interested in psychospiritual transformation, by which I mean personal and transpersonal "growth and development" (to borrow part of the name of my undergraduate department at the UW–Green Bay). The rest of this chapter will consider an array of topics: psychospiritual development, illusion, enlightenment, and even something I refer to as *enlightenment paranoia.*

Enlightenment

In the last chapter, we explored how Whitehead's metaphysics can help us understand and critique some commonly voiced mystical notions. One key issue from this exploration deserves further examination: what *would* constitute a true mystical experience of enlightenment, and how might such an experience occur in a Whiteheadian universe? Leonard Gibson's speculations and Daniel Goleman's powerful personal testimony help illustrate how process philosophy can provide a *metaphysical basis* for interpreting the enlightenment process.

Gibson's primary criteria for mystical experience—along with increased depth of awareness—centers on a *profound* experience of letting go, or of acceptance. What Gibson has in mind here is a conscious experience of the concrescent process functioning in its most *fundamental* mode: its pulsation between becoming and perishing. The mystical phenomenon of death and rebirth finds its ultimate metaphysical and experiential ground in the awareness that results from letting go fully into the depths of one's own personal series of actual occasions, thereby feeling the primal oscillation between becoming and perishing that constitutes the core of all enduring existence. Gibson writes:

> In traditional theological terms, the transition from an actual occasion to its successor is death and rebirth. In Whiteheadian terms, it is perishing and becoming . . .
>
> The person, in Whiteheadian terms, is "a mere thread of continuous inheritance containing no two actual entities that are contemporaries." On some level, therefore, a person must constantly perish and be reborn. A person is not ordinarily aware of this process, but can become aware by profoundly intensifying felt experience . . .
>
> . . . The specific awareness is of the abrupt, absolute transition from one occasion of personal identity to the next. The acceptance is of the transition—by letting go of the past, letting it perish. The awareness is felt awareness, not mere intellectual comprehension. It is felt apprehension of one's own death in the face of the perishing actual occasion, which is one's person, and

which is perishing . . . If one accepts the perishing, in effect letting go of what for the moment is the totality of oneself, one
finds the mystical experience.[2]

Gibson's theory raises the intriguing possibility that part of the experience of Nirvana—of enlightenment—involves a radical penetration into
this fundamental dyad of becoming and perishing. In the following, Daniel
Goleman's vivid description of the final stages of realization of Nirvana and
its consequences appears to bear witness to Gibson's hypothesis:

> As this pseudonirvana gradually diminishes, the meditator's per-
> ception of each moment of awareness becomes clearer. He can
> make increasingly fine discrimination of successive moments
> until his perception is flawless. As his perception quickens, the
> ending of each moment of awareness is more clearly perceived
> than its arising. Finally, the meditator perceives each moment
> only as it vanishes. He experiences contemplating mind and its
> object as vanishing in pairs at every moment. The meditator's
> world of reality is in a constant state of dissolution . . .
>
> His detachment from them is at a peak. His noticing no
> longer enters into or settles down on any phenomena at all. At
> this moment, a consciousness arises that takes as its object the
> "signless, no-occurrence, no-formation": nirvana. Awareness of
> all physical and mental phenomena ceases entirely.
>
> This moment of penetration of nirvana does not, in its first
> attainment, last even for a second. Immediately following this,
> the "fruition" moment occurs, when the meditator's mind re-
> flects on the experience of nirvana just past. That experience is a
> cognitive shock of deepest psychological consequence . . .
>
> In nirvana, desire, attachment, and self-interest are burned
> out. Decisive behavior changes follow from this state of con-
> sciousness, and the full realization of nirvana actuates a perma-
> nent alteration of the meditator's consciousness per se. With the
> meditator's realization of nirvana, aspects of his ego and of his
> normal consciousness are abandoned, never to rise again.[3]

Goleman's account displays numerous surface similarities to Gibson's
Whiteheadian interpretation of the mystical experience: for example, the
meditator's extraordinarily heightened awareness of the arising (becoming) and vanishing (perishing) of each moment of experience. We might
speculate that the experience of entering Nirvana is directly related to

2. Gibson, "Mystical Experience and Psychosis," 7–8.
3. Goleman, *Meditative Mind*, 27–30.

a perception of the "space," that is, the *transition* between perishing and becoming, producing a moment of consciousness reflecting this most radical of disjunctures. But regardless of the exact nature of the mechanisms at work here, Goleman does clearly indicate that the meditator's radical penetration into the essence of experience results in a dramatic shift in ego structure and consciousness. (Readers may have noted some resemblance between Goleman's description of the "first attainment" of Nirvana and my Blue Acid experience. But if this is indeed at all the case, then apparently what Goleman identifies as the "cognitive shock" was too overwhelming for my conscious mind to absorb much of value.)

Enlightenment is sometimes portrayed more psychologically as a fundamental perishing of the ego along with a rebirth into a new way of being. Grof speaks of this death-rebirth experience in terms of tapping into the primal and archetypal dimensions of one's perinatal unconscious. The original physical process of being born can act as a prototype and gateway for *spiritual* rebirth.

Transformation

Stanislav Grof also has found that the death-rebirth experience carries with it the potential for maximal psychological transformation. In Grof's formulation, this death-rebirth process is described as an *ego death*. However, Grof is careful to point out that in ego death a person does *not* lose "one's ability to test reality and to function adequately in everyday life." Rather, "what actually dies in this process is a basically paranoid attitude toward the world which reflects the negative experience of the subject during childbirth and later in life."[4] From a process perspective, ego death involves a dramatic shift in those habitual concrescent patterns concerned with the repression and control of certain feelings and memories. In other words, this process entails a dissolution of limiting and rigid psychological patterns that normally structure the concrescent process. These patterns provide a familiar and safe level of feeling and experience, but one that severely restricts creativity, openness, and depth of experience.

The types of mystical experiences referred to above by Grof and Goleman involve a radical encounter with ego death or the Void, and therefore tend to produce profound psychological transformation. However, not all extraordinary experiences yield such a happy result. In some cases, the experiences have little or no long-term impact on the personality structure. In others, psychic disorientation or even disintegration may occur. A

4. Grof, *Adventure of Self-Discovery*, 30.

Whiteheadian perspective can shed light on this question of nonordinary states and their varying impact on psychological change.

As an initial formulation, I propose the following description of psychospiritual growth. *Psychospiritual growth* involves an enduring shift in ego structure—that is, a significant release of defensive and repressive structures accompanied by a change in habitual patterns of perceiving and understanding—which frees and opens the psyche and organism to more feeling, vitality, creativity, and range of experience. Furthermore, this long-term shift in concrescent structure must support the overall integrity of the individual organism. With this definition in mind, let us tackle the problem of why only some nonordinary states produce positive psychological transformation, that is, psychospiritual growth.

As we have seen, nonordinary states are intimately connected to the temporary dissolution of normal ego structures, especially in respect to their repressive functions. This dissolution process may happen through various means: increased flow of causal feelings, restructured symbolic-reference patterns, disrupted perceptions of presentational immediacy, or regularly implemented consciousness-focusing and -attunement techniques. Regardless of initial causal factors, as ego control diminishes, elements from the primarily unconscious phases of experience begin to exert greater influence. Such ego diminishment can produce a powerful process of psychological unfolding, as Jung indicates: "A collapse of the conscious attitude is no small matter. It always feels like the end of the world, as though everything had tumbled back into original chaos. One feels delivered up, disoriented, like a rudderless ship that is abandoned to the moods of the elements. So at least it seems. In reality, however, one has fallen back upon the collective unconscious, which now takes over the leadership."[5] This increased openness to *deep feeling* provides an opportunity for heightened experiences of one's body, emotional life, and memory. And once the concrescent process has been even more fully opened up through the further lifting of repressive barriers, the door is opened also to the possibility of transpersonal experiences of all sorts.

This communal mode of access to unconscious psychic factors accounts for the close connection between what might be distinguished as *psychological* growth versus *spiritual* growth. Assagioli makes a similar distinction between *personal* psychosynthesis and *spiritual* psychosynthesis.[6] This distinction is artificial to the extent that both kinds of growth belong to the same continuum and are experientially intermingled during

5. Jung, *Two Essays*, 7, 163.
6. See Assagioli, *Psychosynthesis*.

the process of psychic unfoldment. Nevertheless, most people would likely draw something of a Rubicon between events falling within the framework of everyday existence and experiences of the kind that Grof classifies as "transpersonal." Similarly, I find it useful to contrast psychological growth with spiritual growth as a way of indicating a shift from the biographical realm to the transpersonal realm. Such temporarily heightened access to previously hidden feelings and intuitions, however, does not guarantee successful psychic integration of this new material.

Returning to the critical issue concerning psychospiritual growth and transpersonal therapy: have any *lasting* changes in ego structure been effected by the extraordinary experience in question? It is possible for repressive patterns to relax for a short period, thereby opening the concrescent structure to deep feelings from the unconscious phases, and yet to have no significant long-term shift in the habitual ego structure as a result. (In my experience, this is frequently the case with unsupported psychedelic sessions.) Unfortunately, the possibility also exists of a premature removal of repressive structures in a personality incapable of creating novel, positive patterns of psychological organization with which to integrate an increased intensity of feeling and range of experience. The result can be a "bad trip," or in a worst-case scenario, a psychotic break, meaning that the ego becomes too overwhelmed by novel experiences and heightened feeling to maintain adequate psychological boundaries with which to function in everyday reality.[7] In addition, some individuals are able to allow a powerful flow of unconscious feeling to arise into awareness—manifesting in a wide range of psychic phenomena or transpersonal experiences—but without any significant psychological growth. For these people, this kind of opening seems to be an isolated artifact within their peculiar psychic structure. I am thinking here of those individuals who lead seemingly normal lives except for occasional episodes of psychic or transpersonal experiences, which tend to remain partitioned off from the rest of the personality structure.

In these ways and others, "spiritual" (or transpersonal) experiences may transpire without any significant corresponding psychospiritual growth. For psychological transformation to result from a extraordinary experience, that experience must evoke a structural change

---

7. Enhanced psychical openness always entails a potential threat to personal integrity, thus certain levels of repression (of memory, feeling, and the universe at large) are both important and necessary. Discovering ways to reduce this need for repressive barriers to protect the ego is a critical aspect of psychospiritual growth. We might recall here Huxley's notion of the brain as a "reducing valve," rendering the organism's huge influx of raw experience manageable according to the individual's psychic limitations. See Huxley, *Doors of Perception,* 23.

in the concrescent process that transcends (i.e., continues beyond) the nonordinary state and produces or leads to a permanent and psychologically significant shift in the habitual ego structure itself. This sort of shift is not easily accomplished and requires either a long-term effort or a particularly deep and intense experience—which is exactly why nonordinary states offer such a valuable opportunity for psychological and spiritual transformation. While there is no guarantee that an extraordinary experience will produce a permanent psychical transformation, the fact remains that nonordinary states create a potent deepening and intensifying of experience and thus offer an empowering, catalytic context for the release of repressive forces and for the positive reorganization of ego structures. This is especially true when nonordinary states are employed within some kind of long-term supportive situation or community.

However, Grof emphasizes that such outside support should do just that: *support* the nonordinary state and allow the individual's inner guidance to unfold experiences appropriate in intensity and context for the individual psyche at that time and place. This innate inner guidance must likewise be trusted to aim the psychological transformation in positive long-term directions. Grof's extensive research experience indicates that this indeed tends to be the case, especially when coordinated within the context of a reliable external support system.

We can now see why the experiences of ego death, total letting go into perishing, and the Void have such transformative power. Because they involve a descent into the fundamental levels of concrescent process, these experiences can cut through numerous layers of chronic repression—perhaps through their powerful disruption of inherited, ingrained patterns of feeling—thus radically reorganizing the basic personality structure. There does seem to be a difference, however, between the process of ego death outlined by Grof and the mystical experience as described by Goleman and Gibson. The ego-death experience releases repressive structures by opening up the concrescent process to the feelings, memories, and energies that originally initiated the repression. According to Grof's research, somatic and psychic repression begin to dissolve when the experiences that are being repressed are brought into full awareness through intensified and deepened feeling. This deep healing and restructuring of the ego requires a complete release of those experiential patterns derived from repressed memories and feelings that have become erroneously identified with one's own self. This process, therefore, is experienced as a kind of personal death, and, as such, is accompanied by the most powerful of emotions.

On the other hand, in the case of attaining mystical enlightenment of the Void or Nirvana, we are talking about a radical penetration into the basic structure of experience itself. Perhaps here psychospiritual transformation is not so much a result of psychological insight or emotional release, as it is the product of a *metaphysical reordering* of the ego and concrescent structures growing out of consciousness's ingress into the very roots of Being—or Becoming. Bringing the full fabric of concrescent process into awareness, if only for an instant, may significantly disrupt the mechanical repetition of ego structure that normally dominates psychic inheritance in the human *personally ordered* society, and which makes fundamental change so difficult. In other words, by attaining this deepest level of meditational insight, consciousness evokes an upheaval in the concrescent process that undercuts and eliminates from the ego structure many of the habitual, repressive patterns and forces through which an individual unconsciously defines and limits their reality.

Eckhart Tolle's remarkable account of psychic annihilation and awakening into the Now, as described in *The Power of Now,* delivers a dramatic example of complete spiritual transformation. One is tempted to say that in this case, Tolle experienced both an ego death/rebirth *and* a major metaphysical reordering to the very foundations of his being.

I attended a talk given by Tolle some years ago at an Omega Institute event in New York City. I did not know who he was and had planned on skipping his morning presentation to sleep in, until I discovered at the opening ceremony that the man sitting next to me had flown in from South America just to see Tolle. I figured if he was willing to fly thousands of miles, I could make the effort to take the elevator down from my hotel room! My girlfriend insisted we sit up near the front of the huge ballroom, so we were quite close when Tolle took the stage. His presence was far from imposing, almost frail. Yet as he began to speak in his soft relaxed way, I quickly noticed something odd: the corners of my eyes were "vibrating" in a way that usually only happens on psychedelics and my consciousness was definitely altered. My sense was that his intense presence in the Now was somehow creating a sympathetic field capable of inducing a nonordinary state in those around him. This encounter was quite amazing, and it is the only time that something of this sort has happened to me.

Stan Grof and Ken Wilber have differing perspectives on how spiritual transformation is best formulated and fomented. Grof's model emphasizes radical change instigated by powerful extraordinary experiences, whereas Wilber attaches more importance to transformation via long-term meditational practices. However, I suspect in practice both approaches rely upon intermittent, significant transpersonal experiences being supplemented by an ongoing process of integration and synthesis via meditation, therapy, art, and various other means to help facilitate the gradual release of ingrained experiential patterns and to usher in a more fluid way of being. Tolle might be seen as an exceptional exception to this rule, whereas I, with my thirty-plus years of therapy, support groups, and intermittent transpersonal experiences, am an exemplification of it.[8]

The ego is sometimes seen as an enemy to spiritual growth. But as an old teacher of mine used to say, one has to have a strong ego in order to transcend it. Ernst Kris speaks of "regression in the service of the ego," a releasing of ego boundaries and defenses in order to deepen pleasure and access prerational sources of creativity and imagination.[9] Perhaps here we could speak of transcendence in service of the ego, where opening to the transpersonal realms deepens and broadens the ego's range of experience, thereby making it more flexible, creative, and open to living in the flow of life.

Enlightenment Paranoia

One of my more dramatic experiences under the influence of psychedelics was a feeling of *impending illumination,* wherein I felt that people and events around me were symbolically trying to point or propel me towards the Truth. This usually unfolded along a trajectory where I felt like I was being guided toward some kind of ultimate realization, accompanied by an ever-heightening intensity of feeling and an increasingly overwhelming sense of verging on the essence of Reality.

However, in addition, there was often a more or less present element of *paranoia* in this feeling of impending enlightenment. Everything and everyone around me seemed to be directly involved in this unfolding process—conspiring together, you might say. This paranoiac element made it easy to read symbolic meanings into the situation that were extremely fanciful, on sober reflection, no matter how sympathetic one may be to the authenticity of mystical states. Here is one extravagant example.

During my second term at New College, I remember lying on a mattress on the floor of my girlfriend's dorm room, tripping heavily. Her roommate's boyfriend started urging me to take a bite of the sandwich he was eating, which did not look at all appealing in my near-peak state. However, since I was on one of these enlightenment trajectories, I became convinced that the sandwich somehow contained important knowledge that must be consumed. Now, if you knew the man involved in this scenario—who was at least several cars ahead of me on the drinking express—or could

8. Let me make clear that I am only laying claim to a very modest transformation over time, versus Tolle's sudden psychospiritual metamorphosis.

9. See Kris, "On Inspiration."

see the sandwich he was proffering, which looked like something Dagwood Bumstead or Homer Simpson might have concocted, the absurdity of this situation would be even more blatant. In spite of all that, this sense of looming revelation was so great, I felt compelled to comply. But even with my extraordinary state of openness, I was unable to glean any insight from that bite, except that it was damned hard to swallow on acid.

In retrospect, this offers a rather amusing example of what I call enlightenment paranoia: the compelling and overwhelming feeling that *all* that happens is somehow contributing to one's path to enlightenment—or, more unnervingly, that everyone else is *already* privy to the Secret, some deep mystery of existence, and are waiting for you to finally get it too. I thought this might be an aberration of my own psyche until I read a similar account by Timothy Leary in his autobiographical *High Priest* (clever title!):

> There is a second aspect of this session from which I have never recovered. The mind manipulation paranoia . . . Ever since that day I have had a recurring science-fiction paranoia which comes up in almost every LSD session. It starts like this: suddenly, with a click, I am this new level of reality. I am suddenly on camera in an ancient television show directed and designed by some unknown intelligence. I'm the pathetic clown, the shallow, corny, twentieth-century American, the classic buffoon completely caught in a world of his own making, and not realizing that the goals and ambitions he strives for, the serious games he struggles with, are simply the comic relief . . . Am I the only one who had not caught on, who has not broken through? The only one still thrashing around in egocentric isolation?[10]

Similarly, I am haunted by a reoccurring image of entering into a room containing a small group of people, who all gaze at me knowingly. I realize immediately that they have been expecting me, and that this is the moment I have been waiting for all my life: the moment I will find out what "it" is all about. I don't know where this image comes from, a dream perhaps. Or maybe it is a fantasy built out of a much deeper intuition of a primal drive towards a deeper appreciation or realization of the true nature of things.

I suspect that both this image and enlightenment paranoia may in part stem from what Whitehead calls the *initial aim*. Readers may recall that for Whitehead, every moment of experience crystallizes around a direct feeling of God's primordial nature, which holds a graded envisagement of all possibilities, that is, a weighted valuation of what God would most like to see manifested in the universe. Thus every occasion is given a

10. Leary, *High Priest*, 257.

vision of its optimal actualization, and an impulse to move in the direction of its most intense fulfillment.

Enlightenment paranoia may find its origins in a flood of causal feeling, facilitated by a nonordinary state, wherein God's persuasive drive towards creating intensity and depth of experience is distorted by the activation of primitive ego fears and defenses. Some of this psychic distortion might arise out of early childhood inferiorities and anxieties that everyone else knows what the world is really about: you are the only one in the dark. And of course, adults and older children must seem almost omniscient to a very young child just emerging into social reality. This situation finds its parallel in enlightenment paranoia when an enhanced intuition of God—or perhaps other higher spiritual entities?—triggers again this fear of being in the dark about the deeper nature of things. The primal, infantile experience of ignorance then lends a paranoid dimension to this phenomenon. Of course, this kind of experiential distortion highlights the importance of keeping the psychedelic journey primarily an *internal* one, thus avoiding contamination from the outside world—that is, projecting transpersonal intuitions and unconscious fears onto other individuals and events in the world, rather than processing them internally or via deeper penetration into spiritual realities.

Leary also speaks of the shattering realization that he is creating all of his reality: "that everything I perceive, everything within and around me is a creation of my own consciousness."[11] While this insight itself is congruent with Whitehead's metaphysics, such is *not* the case with Leary's extrapolation from his insight: "I have never quite lost the realization that I am an actor and that everyone and everything around me is stage prop and setting for the cosmic drama I am creating. LSD can be a profoundly asocial experience."[12] In this latter belief, Leary seems to take his authentic insight into the fundamental role that creativity plays in each moment of experience and then projects it onto all reality without counterbalancing it with the equally primordial insight that creativity relies on feelings of the *past world* for its raw material. The "actors" and "props" we create are created *out of real past entities*. Thus, while Leary's type of paranoia described here involves an authentic mystical intuition, his intuition is skewed by a solipsistic distortion of the implications of the sheer creativity of the concrescent process. While this caveat may seem a bit nitpicky, it is just this kind of paranoid misunderstanding that can lead to much more serious distortions of reality—both in theory and in practice.

11. Leary, *High Priest*, 256.
12. Leary, *High Priest*, 256.

This same basic principle constitutes the essence of Whitehead's correction to the solipsistic tendencies in Eastern and Western thought: *the many become one, and are increased by one*. Even though creativity and the atomic moment of experience are fundamental metaphysical realities, the fundamental *process* of creativity is the "many" (real past entities) becoming a new "one" that itself aims at a future. Thus the Now itself is constituted by a real past and some necessary future. A *real world of real entities* informs and encompasses us.

Living in the World

In these last two chapters I have attempted to show how process philosophy can help interpret and clarify some of the thorny issues that arise around mystical intuitions about the nature of reality. It is especially important to examine and sort out the moral imperatives associated with these insights, as these can have grave implications for how to live in the world—and for the survival of our world.

The Eastern theory of *maya*, commonly understood to mean that the world is an illusion, becomes dangerous when absolutized beyond the simple (but profound) message that the nature of reality tends to be obscured by our egoic desires and distortions, as well as by our limited spiritual understanding. For example, Leary's sensational insight that he is creating *everything*, that the world is a self-created illusion, could easily lead to decisions based on poor reality testing, as well as a lack of concern about the dangers facing society and our world at large.

There are real personal dangers too. Another story from my New College days may serve as a cautionary tale; it certainly became one for me.

One night during that eventful first term, I drove four friends down Highway 41 to see the movie version of Kurt Vonnegut's *Slaughterhouse-Five*.[13] It may not come as a complete surprise to hear that I was high on some psychedelic, probably MDA, since it had quite an amphetamineish edge to it. This gorgeously filmed movie is about Billy Pilgrim, who "time-trips" back and forth through various events in his life. At one point, he is abducted by aliens from the planet Tralfamadore who explain that the universe is made up of an infinite set of perfect moments, all of which have always happened, are always happening, and will always happen. Towards the end of the film, in a scene set in the future, Billy is standing at a dais in a grand lecture hall explaining this philosophy to a large audience, when as an example he mentions that there is an insane man in the audience who

13. Hill, dir., *Slaughterhouse-Five*.

is there to kill him. He tries to calm the shocked and protesting audience by observing that anyone who is upset by this has not properly understood his message, as his assassination will happen, has happened, and is always happening. Billy is then shot as he recites the Tralfamadorian salutation: hello, goodbye, hello, goodbye . . .

When I left the theater, I had taken that philosophy to heart and was relishing each perfect moment. Very soon, however, one of those perfect moments nearly killed us all. I was driving back north along Highway 41, a four-lane divided road, at about seventy-five miles per hour in a forty-five-mile-per-hour zone as I came up to a major intersection with a traffic light. The light ahead was green so I kept on rocketing down the left lane, when suddenly a car at the intersection started to make a left turn in front of me, saw our car coming and stopped abruptly, thereby completely blocking my lane. I slammed on the brakes and swerved the car to the right, tires screeching as we slid past the stopped car at high speed. I reversed the wheel and we skidded back across the highway, bounced off the center median, then drifted back across the road to hit the opposite curb, knocking off a hubcap, all in a thick cloud of smoke from the overtaxed tires. We came to a stop . . . and I asked the man next to me, an Eckankar devotee (or so he said), to retrieve the hubcap, which he did, and we proceeded back to New College. I was quite amazed and amused by the episode—which, ironically, I do not think would have turned out so happily without my heightened reflexes and perceptions due to the MDA.[14]

Back in my dorm room, the "witchy" friend—bewitching literally and metaphorically—who I had a crush on was visibly upset by what had happened. When I asked her why, she said,

"Do I really have to tell you? You could have killed everyone, and the other girls in the backseat were terrified."

I responded that what had happened on the drive home was just like what Vonnegut had portrayed in the movie: a series of perfect eternal moments—which really reflected where my head was at right then. She would have none of it, and rightly so; those "perfect" moments might just as easily have been our last. This is a sensational, but I think effective, example of why it is important to see life as *more* than a collection of temporally neutral, perfect moments of experience—or as mere illusion. Such a viewpoint, while captivating and deceptively similar to Whitehead's, is metaphysically skewed and existentially dangerous for enduring organisms, especially those with the ability to endanger the entire environment through their actions.

---

14. This is not to extol the benefits of driving under the influence of MDA, since without it, I probably would not have gotten into that fix in the first place.

It is vitally important to see the world as real, our actions as efficacious, and the future as partially undetermined. If we think our choices really do not matter, then we gravely endanger ourselves, others, and the world. While the belief that there are no coincidences may provide solace to some, suggesting as it does that there is a guiding hand at work in everything, this guiding hand must not be seen as absolutely controlling, as the phrase "no coincidences" might seem to imply. Moral responsibility *requires* freedom of choice and, for better or worse, a world that includes accidents, tragedies, and poor choices as well as victories, achievements, and right actions.

A danger of focusing on the here and now, understood as totally exclusive of the past and future, is that it can easily devolve into *presentism,* a hedonistic or amoral approach to life that ignores significant concern for the future or understanding of the past.[15] This sort of hedonism is a byproduct of misunderstanding the metaphysical constitution of the present moment.

This claim may seem at odds with the idea of the here and now as a source of serenity and fulfillment. However, the situation is more complex. At one extreme, the here-now represents crass presentism, with its narcissism, angst, and lack of responsibility; this can be understood as living too much in presentational immediacy with its correspondingly shallow level of meaning. On the other end of the spectrum, living in the here-now entails the immediate joy of being present to what is, as it *really* is. This is far different from living for the sheer disconnected moment of sensory input or pleasure. Ram Dass captures this idea simply, but beautifully, in a recent book: "The ego asks, 'Why not live *for* the moment? Eat, drink, and be merry, for tomorrow you will die.' But if instead you live *in* the moment, being here now, discovering the preciousness of life in each moment, then you are living, not as an ego, but as a soul, outside time."[16] To experience the joy and transcendence of the here-now, one must be fully present to the depth of bodily feelings (the past as *ground* of the present) and to other people, nature, and the transpersonal dimension, all as relational partners.

Being-here-now involves transcending the ego to discover the here-now is made up of the past, the world, and anticipations of the future. Thus being fully present to the moment often opens up to more dramatic experiences of transcendence involving beings and dimensions far removed from everyday experience. As Colin Wilson points out, happiness should not be understood as living fully (only) in the present, but as in a certain sense *transcending* it.[17] This is one reason why it is so difficult

15. Didsbury, *The Futurist,* 60.
16. Ram Dass, *Walking Each Other Home,* 69.
17. Personal correspondence with Colin Wilson.

to *stay* in the real here-now, for it spontaneously opens up or transforms into memories, feelings, insights, plans, and connections to the world that reengage ego involvements and interests. Perhaps this cycle is necessary for being-in-the-world—and to the good, as it keeps us from getting stuck or becoming too one-sided.

I probably do not need to say much about the New Age intuition that "everything is perfect just as it is." The obvious concern is that this attitude might easily impede one's initiative to make changes in the world—to make things better—if being "perfect" is taken to imply that things are exactly how they are meant to be now *and* in the future. That said, I am familiar with the beauty and peace inherent in this intuition of perfection. I particularly remember how I felt walking outside after a night of tripping, and being entranced by the dew on the grass, the birds singing, the sunrise colors, and the spring flowers blooming all around me. It was the epitome of Cat Stevens's song, "Morning Has Broken," whose inspirational lyrics capture perfectly this sense of everything being in harmony, fresh, and just as it should be. It is a wondrous feeling, and not one that I wish to belittle in any way. However, I do not think it should be understood essentially as a *moral* judgment of the world. From a Whiteheadian perspective, this insight or sentiment arises from heightened feelings of the inherent *aesthetic* Beauty of each moment, something that is often more powerfully available during nonordinary states. And yet, it is also true that this sense of intense beauty and harmony is often accompanied by a certain sense of the *rightness* of things, which perhaps arises out a vague but deep intuition of how the past universe has come together to create *just this* moment. Moreover, this sense of rightness may be reinforced by an intuition that God's initial aim is informing every moment, offering the perfect possibility for that occasion, and then making the best out of what has been accomplished. But this momentary sense of perfection does *not* imply we should stop aiming ourselves at a better future through our creative decisions and actions.

Some things, however, are easily perceived as being far from perfect. By my later twenties, I badly needed to start aiming *myself* at a better future. If I was to survive much past my thirtieth birthday, some kind of dramatic change in my life, or more accurately, some very deep shift in me, was going to have to happen—and soon. Miraculously, and quite synchronistically, it did.

A Personal Interlude

Putting Me Back Together

Things began to get *really* bad with my drinking during my time studying at the University of Wisconsin–Green Bay. I offer a few grim examples that painfully illustrate how things had spiraled out of control.

After a long period of throwing up nearly every morning, I began to nervously consult *Taber's Medical Dictionary* to try to diagnose which of my organs might be failing. My primary diagnostic tool was the changing color of my vomit; I will draw the line at describing what our toilet looked like. One time after unsuccessfully trying to dry myself out at the Pioneer Inn in Oshkosh, I started going into the delirium tremens (DTs) on the drive home. (Fortunately my girlfriend was driving, but that was the only good news.) I bought some malt liquor, but it was not strong enough to relieve the shakes, so I had to go back to vodka. I was reminded of this demoralizing episode when in *The Courage to Change* I read Pete Townsend's account of the frightening moment when he realized that he could not drink enough beer to stave off the DTs.[1] I mention these depressing events, which are only the tip of the iceberg, for two reasons. First, because I do not want to risk giving the impression that my alcohol and drug use was anything like a bed of roses; and, second, so readers will more fully understand the level of gratitude I have for my miraculous escape from that life.

Following several more or less helpful stays in the psychiatric ward of my hometown hospital, Four North—that spooky place where a high school classmate had been locked up after a "bad trip"—my oldest sister arranged for me to come to Sioux City, Iowa, for more focused treatment of my chemical dependency. I somehow managed to charter a small plane, as my physical state was so fragile that I feared flying commercially. This

1. Pete Townsend relates his battle with alcoholism on pages 25–38 of Wholey, ed., *Courage to Change.*

self-diagnosis was validated by the doctor, who along with my sister and brother-in-law, met me as I got off the plane in Iowa. He immediately placed me in the hospital and put me on a Valium drip (200 milligrams a day, I believe) and was pleasantly surprised when after only three days I asked for something to eat.

After about a week, I was transferred to the addiction wing of the hospital—an excellent facility that was based on Hazelden's twelve-step approach. When I finally noticed that I was the only patient not being taken through the early steps of recovery, I was informed that their primary concern was getting me healthy enough to *start* a full treatment program at the Hazelden itself in Center City, Minnesota.[2]

At some point along the way, my counselor had me fill out a survey of the drugs I had used. While I readily admitted my alcohol problem, I did not feel my drug use was *that* bad. When he reviewed my list, he said not only was it one of the most extensive he had ever seen, but he had not even heard of some of the drugs I had been using. This got my attention. I had always thought of myself as experimenting with drugs and had never experienced physical withdrawal from any *one* of them, so I believed this meant I was not addicted. Quickly, or as quickly as my foggy brain permitted, I began to grasp how alcohol had served to conceal the major negative effects from other substances. Even though what might be called my alcohol therapy, combined with moving around from one drug to another, had prevented me from experiencing significant withdrawal issues, I had to admit my near-constant use of drugs over the last eight or nine years probably *did* qualify as addictive behavior. (This stunning lack of insight on my part is just another example of the level of denial regularly encountered by addiction counselors, poor souls.)

I will save time here by simply saying that after Hazelden I was sober for about fifteen months and then relapsed at an archetypal psychology conference in San Francisco, when a pretty young woman giving me an astrological reading offered a hit of pot. And I can save more time by saying that approximately three years later, having completed a master's in psychology and my first year of doctoral studies, I found myself addicted to two of my least favorite drugs: Valium and codeine, proving once and for all (hopefully) that I can get addicted to most any mood-altering substance. Apparently, I had not been *fully* convinced of this by my treatment in Sioux City. What I discovered later was that, deep down, *I had to*

2. Hazelden was the first major alcoholism treatment center to use the twelve steps of Alcoholics Anonymous as the foundation of its treatment program. Its paradigm, the mission of which is to help patients recover from alcoholism and other addictions, has been widely copied by treatment programs throughout the United States.

become more afraid of having drugs in my life than of not having them. That critical inner shift had yet to arrive.

The final chapter of this particular saga began on my way to lunch with an Emory professor. I wanted to tell him in person that I was dropping out of school. My driving that morning was less than stellar—perhaps because I had been up most of the night having "just one more" line of cocaine—and on the way to the meeting I hit a curb, pushing the bumper into a front tire. After trying to pull the bumper back far enough to drive, I continued undaunted on my appointed task. The next thing I knew, I came to with a policeman at the window of my wrecked car. Evidently, after my little run-in with the first curb, my car was pulling to the right, and at some point I lost control—ripping out the oil pan as I went over another curb—and drove into the side of a bulldozer parked in a field. There were two large circular impact cracks in the windshield, which my head must have bounced off twice: hit bulldozer, hit windshield, fly back into seat, rebound back into windshield. Ever quick thinking, when asked if I wanted to go to the hospital, I said no, realizing they might test me for drugs there.

Well, my lawyer told me that I was the first person ever tested for drugs after a car accident at the Dekalb County Police Department (or was it the jail?), which was only just, though a bit ironic. After several hours in lock-up, as I worked my way ever deeper into the bowels of the county jail, I finally recovered sufficiently from my concussion to remember my neighbor's name so I could look up his number and issue an SOS. (My wife, Susan, was not home, and Emory showed a distinct lack of interest in my problems.) The neighbor kindly paid my bail and drove me home, where I embarked on my scheme to get off the Valium and codeine, to which I had become physically addicted. The plan was to use some recently acquired Placidyl and Tuinal to ease myself through the withdrawal period. (For those fortunately not in the know, these are two very powerful sedative-hypnotics.)

Predictably, I took too much of both and went into a three-day blackout. I came out of it lying on the loft floor of our house with the phone ringing, and then my wife yelling up that it was my mother calling and needing to talk with me. My mind cleared instantly upon hearing that my grandfather had not regained consciousness after recent surgery and that my mother wanted me to come up to Wisconsin to help out.

Fortunately, although it definitely did not seem that way at the time, Susan had hidden all of my drugs that she could find. I headed up north with the small amount of Valium and codeine that she had missed to start doing eight- to twelve-hour shifts sitting with my grandfather. He was semiconscious at best, but would start trying to pull out tubes and IVs or to get out of bed when unmonitored. We needed to have one of the family with him at all times; otherwise the hospital wanted to tie down his hands, which was clearly very upsetting to him. Thus, on and off for the next month and a half, being a night person, I would often take the late shift with my grandfather, trying my best to comfort him and prevent him from disturbing the various apparatus keeping him going. As you might imagine, this was very physically and emotionally stressful for me, especially in my already fragile state. After my shift, I would drive back to the Pfister Hotel, sometimes stop at the bar for a drink—only one or two, amazingly—and then try to get a little food and sleep.

One afternoon, when it had become clear that he was not likely to recover, my mother and I were sitting in my grandfather's room. Out of the blue, she asked how things were going in my life. Miraculously I told her the truth: I was using again; my marriage was falling apart again; I was dropping out of school again. My mother listened carefully and then pointed out that her second husband had been closely involved with Eisenhower Hospital and the Betty Ford Center. She wondered if I might want to go out there for treatment. It is hard to fully convey how good that sounded to me right then: a warm, safe place in the desert, far away from all my problems (except the ones I would bring with me), where I could get help with withdrawal and with trying to stay sober.

A few days before I went into Betty Ford, having mostly detoxed myself at their behest, my grandfather died.

I now believe that even before I got to the Betty Ford Center, what transpired in my grandfather's hospital room had synchronistically cast the die. The terrible event that had psychologically predisposed me to addiction had been re-created and redeemed. The very sudden loss of my father, and the inability to properly grieve and assimilate that loss, had left me with many unresolved emotions that eventually became frozen over. Alcohol and drugs had initially offered relief from the pervasive anxiety that kept me at arm's length from others and from my own buried feelings and had also provided a mode of access to those hidden feelings and to the world.

Then, suddenly, there I was in a desperate state—once again in a hospital room with my (grand)father dying. This time, however, my mother was able to offer me the help that I needed (through the auspices of my *step*father's benevolent work!). Perhaps most importantly, I was able to reveal honestly what was really going on inside me and *ask for help*. The old gestalt was completed, as Fritz Perls would say, and now I could begin to move forward again.

The synchronicity of getting just the help I needed continued when I got to the Betty Ford Center. The psychologist was very knowledgeable about psychedelics and took a keen interest in my recovery. I made some dear friends who to this day continue to support me in sobriety and in life. And my primary counselor, Drew, who had lived down the road from Timothy Leary and was himself a deep soul, pulled me out of the numbing confusion that surrounded me.

When I arrived in the desert, I was more emotionally and mentally burned out then I have ever been. Early on, one of the other patients asked me if I realized that I was having trouble putting together a coherent sentence. While most of the patients met with their counselors soon after their arrival, Drew waited about a week for me to clear up a bit before calling me in to talk. I felt empty and selfless—and not in the interesting spiritual sense. We talked for an hour, and Drew asked me about my life and somehow helped me *remember* who I was and what I wanted to do with my life. When I walked out of his office, it was reminiscent of that moment during my Big Trip when I knew exactly who I was. I have been following that path ever since.

Looking back, I've come realize that, along with the other events that conspired to heal my emotional wounds, another kind of healing had taken place earlier that same year. My fractured worldview and bygone belief in the possibility a loving god had been restored, or reconstructed, through my discovery of process philosophy and theology. The universe once again made sense. Soon my life would too.

It has been well over thirty years since I left the Betty Ford Center. I have been clean and sober ever since. While I have never been seriously tempted by alcohol, I still wonder from time to time if another psychedelic experience might benefit my psychospiritual condition or provide intellectual insight. But thus far I have steered clear of these special substances, which, ironically, in sobriety have been more available in more tempting ways than even during my college heyday. (My ongoing involvement with transpersonal communities leads me to many people who are just as intrigued by mind-altering substances as I ever was.) I am not really sure what holds me back, as I know of people in recovery who have made this experiment with apparent success—although others have not fared so well. One thing for certain, though, is that every time in the past when I tried to control my drug use, I failed miserably in the long run. Also, I fear this breach in abstinence might skew my feelings of *belonging* to my support groups, which have been so important for maintaining balance in my life. Of at least equal importance is my commitment to the mission that was reawakened at Betty Ford—to convey the vision I have been sharing in this book—and my resolve to *be here* for my family, friends, and colleagues.

It must be said, though, that my psychedelic experiences opened up my world in a radical, frightening, and marvelous way. I fear that without the hope of *something more* that was portended through these substances, I would not have had the impetus I needed to remain interested in life, nor the belief in deeper realities I needed to get sober. That is why I almost called this book *LSD and Me*. That is also why I want to share what I have discovered, both with those who have taken psychedelics and wonder what it all means, as well as those who have not taken psychedelics and wonder what it all means.

_____ 10 _____

Putting It All Together

In previous chapters I have focused primarily on how Whitehead's metaphysics and cosmology are relevant to mystical and transpersonal experience. Thus, it may seem that these areas represented a major focus of Whitehead's work. However, while recently reading through Lucien Price's record of conversations from late in Whitehead's life,[1] I was reminded that these ideas occupy a relatively small part of Whitehead's ruminations. In fact, his approach to psychology is deeply embedded in the human body and brain processes. Also, Whitehead's metaphysics is intentionally designed to be congruent with the major breakthroughs in physics that were emerging during the years of his mature philosophical thought, particularly relativity and quantum theory, as well as Maxwell's electromagnetic field theory, which was the topic of his research dissertation at Cambridge. Since it is a contention of this book that one of the most valuable aspects of process metaphysics is its applicability to all areas of experience, including to the full range of the scientific enterprise, I will briefly try in this chapter to indicate a few of the ways that Whitehead's fundamental ideas might be useful to current theory construction and interpretation in the sciences.

What Is Reality?

A common thread in my pivotal life experiences is that they all raised important questions about the nature of reality. Three of these events in particular brought this ultimate problem to the forefront: (1) discovering that alcohol and drugs could radically alter my experience of myself and the world, that reality was malleable; (2) encountering psychedelics and so questioning more deeply the makeup and scope of the universe; and (3)

---

1. Whitehead, *Dialogues of Alfred North Whitehead.*

experiencing my Big Trip, which forced me to take seriously the possibility of God as a real Entity.

After my Big Trip, I felt compelled to try to understand what had happened to me and how to integrate this experience into the rest of my worldview. I explored many helpful and otherwise sound theories but ultimately found them problematic in some important way. The fundamental source of difficulty with many of these approaches seemed to grow out of their reliance on Cartesian and Kantian modes of thought, which either leave the human psyche radically separated from the physical world (Descartes's two substances of mind and matter) or make mind the creator of the physical world, for all practical purposes (Kant's transcendental ego). This tends to leave us with theories that create an impassable barrier between human experience and the objective world, or ones that awkwardly conflate the two.

I recall a disconcerting conundrum proffered by one of my favorite professors during a class at UW–Green Bay. He explained that we have to find a way to live under the shadow of a disquieting epistemological dilemma. We are trapped within our own brains and can never know if there is really anything out there, since if all we have are our sense impressions, there is no way of knowing whether our senses are giving us true information about the outside world. I remember one student asking coyly, "Why do the children play?" (I assume the student was alluding to the Cat Stevens song called "Where Do the Children Play?"). The professor quickly responded: "Because they don't know about this yet!"

I now believe that our situation is not so dire. I also see that this paradox itself exhibits some faulty reasoning (as does the solipsistic position in general). If we really do not have dependable access to the outside world, then we also cannot take seriously the idea that we are trapped in our brains, since the brain is only something presented to us through our senses and our theories. How do we know that the brain is any more real than the other things our senses tell us about? Taken one step further, does it really make sense to claim that our experience is an epiphenomenon of brain processes, when it is only through our experience itself—especially memory, thought, and perception—that these theories themselves exist?

But what about being trapped inside our *own experience*, rather than just in the abstraction of our brains? Well, my moment-to-moment experience finds itself dwelling in a natural world that includes other people and all kinds of regular patterns and connections, as many phenomenologists have so carefully pointed out. So the more puzzling question would be, is there a *me* that exists independently of the flow of experience constituting my world? This is also the direction that the Buddhist analysis leads. After much searching, I have reached the conclusion that I have been sharing throughout this book: these questions and issues can best be understood by reorganizing our basic philosophical premises, categories, and methodology along the lines suggested by Whitehead.

Whitehead, recurring to "pre-Kantian modes of thought," radicalizes Descartes's critique and reverses Kant's essential insight. Instead of starting with Descartes's *thinking subject,* Whitehead starts with a moment of experience—out of which thoughts and the occasional thinker arise. Rather than Kant's synthetically unified Mind creating the relatedness of conscious experience, Whitehead hypothesizes a plurality of past events combining synthetically to create a unified experience *out of* the connections and feelings inherent to the events themselves.

Methodologically, rather than relying primarily on the data provided by the physical senses (modern science), or on this sense data combined with rational thought (modern philosophy), or on the data presented by consciousness itself (phenomenology), Whitehead champions what he calls *speculative philosophy.* Speculative philosophy draws on *all* areas of experience—scientific, rational, imaginative, religious, aesthetic, moral, mystical, irrational—and by means of generalization and deduction uncovers the most fundamental aspects and relations of our experiential universe. Why *not* draw on all experience when trying to determine the nature of reality? Our experience is the only *direct contact* we have with reality, so should not *all* of it be considered and weighed when creating models claiming to account for the nature of the universe? Whitehead's approach makes the most sense, as it has allowed me to take seriously my psychedelic adventures, the contributions of science and rational judgment, and the rest of my life experiences as well—while providing a mode of thought congruent with them all.

Science and the Whiteheadian World

A Whiteheadian foundation for the sciences can be encapsulated in this simple formula: cell theory combined with quantum theory creates the basis for a universe consisting of an interflowing hierarchy of organic societies. Charles Hartshorne argues convincingly that cell theory is one of the most significant advances in scientific understanding, and Whitehead's generalization of this theory is one of his greatest achievements.[2] All actuality can be understood within the cellular model, but it was not until the microscope that we had direct evidence of its wide applicability. Nevertheless, its revolutionary

2. Hartshorne, "Compound Individual," 210–11.

importance has yet to be fully appreciated by most philosophical and cosmo-logical models: our universe is *social* through and through.

Cell theory attains its full significance when seen through the lens of the breakthroughs of quantum theory, where the ultimate entities in the universe are momentary events. This expands cell theory into a vision of our universe as a process of interflowing momentary events that creatively interact to generate organic societies of progressively greater complexity. And unlike most theories involving higher orders of complexity, the *compound individuals* of process philosophy entail the formation of *new ongoing centers of coordination* that are themselves enduring entities.

This creative organic process is found at every level of actuality. Whitehead writes: "The community of actual things is an organism; but it is not a static organism . . . Each actual entity is itself only describable as an organic process. It repeats in microcosm what the universe is in macrocosm."[3] Thus the philosophy of organism finds its own (rational) exemplification of the ancient adage: "as above, so below." All that remains to complete this Whiteheadian cosmology is to add that the actual occasions are connected by their mutual feelings of one another, and that these feelings provide the basis for understanding the events that constitute our universe as experiential in nature.

When the philosophy of organism is merged with transpersonal psychology, we get what I like to call a *transpersonal-organic cosmology*. This integrative theory gives us a model that ranges seamlessly from the atomic level all the way through to mystical experiences of the furthest reaches of actuality. I next describe the bare bones of this worldview by starting from the bottom up, beginning with the simplest organisms and then working my way to the more complex. (Please forgive the hubris inherent in the following attempt to apply Whitehead's ideas to a variety of other fields. I was reminded of the possible folly of such an endeavor during a long-overdue perusal of Walter Miller's classic of speculative fiction, *A Canticle for Leibowitz*, when I came across this telling sentence. "In the basement, the scholar's eyes had come alight with the brash exuberance of one specialist invading the field of another specialist for the sake of straightening out the whole region of confusion."[4])

3. Whitehead, *Process and Reality*, 214–15.
4. Miller, *Canticle for Leibowitz*, 228.

Physics

The microscopic entities of particle physics represent the most primitive exemplifications of Whitehead's actual occasions—quantum moments of synthetic activity. This correspondence between the near-instantaneous events of quantum mechanics and the kind of integrative activity attributed to Whitehead's actual occasions is no coincidence. Whitehead's metaphysics is explicitly designed to incorporate quantum theory as a fundamental feature of reality. But as Michael Epperson so adroitly articulates, in Whitehead's method of analyzing the nature of these events—as centers of self-creative synthetic activity—new quantum particles arise out of primitive *decisions* about how to actualize the probability field constituted by the influence of past events.[5] The actual occasion's own inner activity of simple data selection, even at the quantum level, obviates the necessity of calling upon a outside observer to provide the necessary conditions for this "decision," thus restoring to nature the (relatively) independent status that we all naturally attribute to it. The cat is *not* dead and alive until we open the box—which was Erwin Schrodinger's point all along.[6] Going more deeply into a Whiteheadian reading of quantum theory, Epperson demonstrates a fundamental correspondence between Whitehead's phases of concrescence and the formative stages of a quantum event: "The evolutionary valuation of potentia in quantum mechanics can be correlated phase by phase, and concept by concept, with Whitehead's metaphysical scheme, such that the former can be characterized as the fundamental physical exemplification of the latter."[7]

While recently reading an online article about the physicist Brian Greene, I noticed a similarity also between string theory and Whitehead's actual occasions. What caught my attention was this brief description: "String theory posits that the fundamental ingredients of the cosmos are not point-particles, but tiny one-dimensional strings, the varying vibrations of which determine material expression. One frequency produces an

5. Epperson, *Quantum Mechanics.*

6. In Schrödinger's thought experiment, a cat is placed in a box with a Geiger counter and a small amount of radioactive material that may or may not decay enough to emit a particle over an hour's time. If a particle is emitted, the Geiger counter is set up to cause the release of a poisonous gas, killing the cat. According to quantum theory at the time, the state of the decaying radioactive particle would remain indeterminate until observed. Thus the cat would be both dead and alive for the hour until a human being looked into the box. Schrödinger intended this thought experiment to demonstrate the problems encountered when applying microlevel quantum indeterminacy at the human macrolevel. See Trimmer, trans., "Present Situation in Quantum Mechanics."

7. Epperson, *Quantum Mechanics,* 10.

electron, another produces a quark, and so on."[8] While I do not know if the notion of one-dimensional strings translates well into Whiteheadian theory, Whitehead's fundamental events are definitely "not point-particles." Furthermore, actual occasions, as patterned momentary pulsations created out of harmonic contrasts, seem to resemble string theory's postulate that the manifestation of physical reality depends on the *string's varying vibrational frequencies*. I will stop here, as I realize that it is perilous to make extrapolations about theoretical physics based merely on popular descriptions of what are ultimately mathematical formulae.

When we start with an underlying reality that possesses its own synthetic activity and fundamental interrelatedness, it becomes much, *much* easier to conceptualize the evolutionary process, the mind-body problem, and the nature of perception and conscious awareness. And let me reiterate that Whitehead's interpretation of quantum particles—namely, as events that create themselves by synthetically integrating the influence of past events—is fully congruent with contemporary quantum theory. What Whitehead's approach *is* attempting to dispel from current scientific thought (thought that today occurs largely *outside* the field of physics) are the vestiges of a materialist philosophy—such as matter viewed as insentient and inert—where these modes of thought are no longer viable. For Whitehead, quantum events are conceived as *vector flows of energy* that exhibit (extremely) primitive integrative and selective powers:

> In the language of physical science, the change from materialism to 'organic realism'—as the new outlook may be termed—is the displacement of the notion of static stuff by the notion of fluent energy. Such energy has its structure of action and flow, and is inconceivable apart from such structure. It is also conditioned by 'quantum' requirements. These are the reflections into physical science of the individual prehensions, and of the individual actual entities to which these prehensions belong. Mathematical physics translates the saying of Heraclitus, 'All things flow,' into its own language. It then becomes, All things are vectors. Mathematical physics also accepts the atomistic doctrine of Democritus. It translates it into the phrase, All flow of energy obeys 'quantum' conditions.
>
> But what has vanished from the field of ultimate scientific conceptions is the notion of vacuous material existence with passive endurance, with primary individual attributes, and with accidental adventures. Some features of the physical world can

---

8. Masterson, "Albert Camus and String Theory."

be expressed in that way. But the concept is useless as an ulti-mate notion in science, and in cosmology.[9]

Biochemistry

In the field of biochemistry, we encounter in more familiar guise Whitehead's *societies of societies* or *organisms of organisms*, which sometimes produce what Charles Hartshorne has termed *compound individuals*. When primitive entities, such as atoms and molecules, combine in such a way as to create a more complex organism in which the "many become one, and are increased by one," we have a new *compound individual*. A cell, for example, is not *just* a complex of interacting atomic and molecular events, nor reducible to their causal influence. According to this theory, a cell also contains events that provide a unifying center of experience and spontaneity of response. (Think of a cell as a much simpler version of how the human body generates a center of unified experience: the human psyche.) Whitehead does not make many definitive statements concerning which lower-level societies might qualify as Hartshorne's compound individuals, but in the following comments, David Griffin provides a helpful summary of some contemporary thinking on this topic. Compound individuals arise, Griffin suggests,

> when quarks are organized into electrons and protons, and these electrons and protons are organized into atoms and molecules, and these into organelles, and these into eukaryotic cells, and these into animals. The best clue that something is a genuine individual is that it shows evidence of spontaneity—of making a self-determining response to its environment. They can do this because the low-grade individuals making them up have given rise to a higher-level individual—which in the case of an animal we call the "mind" or "soul"—which gives the thing as a whole a unity of experience, through which it can exercise self-determination.[10]

This model offers many avenues for understanding the complex inter-actions between the atomic, molecular, and cellular influences occurring in the biochemical world. However, it also complicates research and theory by hypothesizing that purely reductionistic approaches are inadequate to the full range of organic phenomena. According to the philosophy of organ-ism, *top-down* causal factors would also come into play. The more complex

9. Whitehead, *Process and Reality*, 309.
10. Griffin, *Panentheism and Scientific Naturalism*, 29.

centers of experience in compound individuals exert a direct causal influence on the simpler events composing their "bodies."

In the human case, this kind of higher-level influence is part of daily life, for example, when we decide to change the channel or to pick up a saltshaker. From a process perspective, this same kind of top-down influence should be seen at more primitive levels of experience too, with the cell's center of experience to some degree coordinating the activities of its molecular subsocieties. Undoubtedly, there would be significant resistance to incorporating top-down causation into scientific theory. But if this kind of causation does in fact exist, then our scientific theories will prove inadequate without it—as quite clearly seems to be the case now for psychology and neuroscience.

A Sufi story is relevant here. While walking along the street one evening, a man came upon an old Sufi master down on his hands and knees looking about on the ground. The man asked him what he was doing, to which the Sufi replied that he was searching for his missing key. "Where did you lose your key?" the man asked. "Over in that alley," the Sufi replied. "Then why are you looking in the street?" the man inquired. "Because the light is better here," answered the Sufi, mischievously. Lesson: it is important to look where the key might actually be located, even if searching there is more difficult and less convenient.

While these more complex causal interactions hypothesized by Whitehead's organic realism may make research more complicated, since new scientific methods and theories built around the notion of bottom-up *and* top-down causation might be required, they could also unlock doors into new modes of understanding. And while this type of causative theory might call for some new forms of analysis, Whitehead suggests that all concrescences—just like the quantum events of physics—are organized along the lines of logical propositions and thus should be susceptible to statistical techniques. Also, the organizational influence of the dominant societies may help account for the incredible synchronization of their subsocieties—such as atoms, molecules, and macromolecules—and may also shed valuable light on the unconscious mind's influence on neural functioning and coordination. Finally, since general laws and habits may well be consistent through all levels of compound individuals—although more complexity should of course be expected within higher-order individuals—we may be able to begin formulating rules for these kinds of organic social interactions by extrapolating from simpler to more complex events, or vice versa.

C. H. Waddington, a British developmental biologist and geneticist who helped found epigenetics and evolutionary developmental biology, provides an excellent example of how Whitehead's metaphysics can make important contributions to scientific theory construction. In his book *The Evolution of an Evolutionist,* Waddington describes how Whitehead's ideas directly influenced his work:

> In the late thirties I began developing the Whiteheadian notion that the process of becoming (say) a nerve cell should be regarded as the result of the activities of large numbers of genes, which interact together to form a unified 'concrescence.' This line of thought had several ramifications . . . Influenced—probably over-influenced—by genetics I insisted that the switch must have sufficient specificity to recognize particular genes. We showed that, in these terms, the specificity resides inside the cells which react to induction—we called it 'the masked evocator' . . . If I had been more consistently Whiteheadian, I would probably have realized that the 'specificity' involved does not need to lie in the switch at all, but may be the property of 'concrescence' and the ways in which it can change. Because of course what I have been calling by the Whiteheadian term 'concrescence' is what I have later called a *chreod,* a notion which Rene Thom has explicated; and the switches are Thom's *catastrophes.*[11]

Waddington concludes: "Thus my particular slant on evolution—a most unfashionable emphasis on the importance of the developing phenotype—is a fairly direct derivative from Whiteheadian-type metaphysics."[12]

Ecology

Clearly Whitehead's organic philosophy has a natural affinity for an ecological understanding of our planet as intrinsically interconnected and interdependent, with all parts possessing inherent value. A philosophy like Whitehead's, which regards the universe as a giant organism composed of interflowing societies of societies of societies is, by its very nature, ecological at heart.

The overall thrust of the evolutionary process, within a Whiteheadian paradigm, becomes more broadly understood to encompass the ever-increasing inner complexity and intensity of actual occasions in concert with the corresponding elaboration of social organisms they form. This process is ubiquitous. Consequently this fundamental model of evolution serves to account for the process of universal unfolding from the big bang onwards.

---

11. Waddington, *Evolution of an Evolutionist,* 9–10.

12. Waddington, *Evolution of an Evolutionist,* 8.

As for the further evolutionary implications of process thought, I happily entrust readers to Charles Birch, who has written extensively on evolutionary biology and ecology from a process perspective.[13] While a process-informed evolutionary biology is similar in many regards to Darwinian theory, it does not regard current evolutionary theory as dogma. For example, many process thinkers hypothesize a general underlying impetus in the universe towards greater complexity and order that provides new potential forms and encourages their actualization. Such an impetus, however, would be understood as occurring *within* the natural order rather than deriving from an outside or supernatural influence.

Economics and Political Theory

A Whiteheadian-oriented take on economics is explored by Herman Daly and John Cobb Jr. in their 1989 book: *For the Common Good*. By placing economic theory within the larger context of the project of human civilization and the planetary matrix, they question the assumptions of unlimited resources, and whether perpetual economic growth is necessarily good or even possible within a finite world. As obvious as these points sound, one need only look at the financial news to see that economic growth is widely assumed to be society's summum bonum. In a similar vein, Cobb and Daly call into question the gross national product as an accurate indicator of social progress. Is money spent to manufacture and buy weapons, to clean up hazardous waste, or to sell tobacco products indicative of true social productivity? Or is it "gross" in a more disturbing sense?

Cobb and Daly's process approach also challenges the narrow understanding of intrinsic value and human motivation in traditional economics. This truncated, pseudoscientific perspective traditionally ignores the inherent importance and worth of the natural world and the complex social character of human civilization, envisioning self-interest as the primary driving force in society and viewing nature as an unlimited resource for economic exploitation. Given this one-sided view of reality, it is not surprising that modern economic theory has contributed to creating a society that is undermining nature and community in increasingly dangerous and alarming ways. In contrast, a Whiteheadian-informed economics would place primary importance on community and social relations, including our relationship with the natural world, which is held to be ultimately valuable as our larger social matrix and as possessing inherent value and importance.

13. See Birch and Cobb, *Liberation of Life*; and Birch, *Feelings*.

A quote from economist Cliff Cobb summarizes how Western civilization might benefit from a Whiteheadian perspective on social relations:

> The problems associated with reductionism and philosophical individualism are obvious. The U.S. now spends billions of dollars to warehouse a high proportion of its citizens in prisons. Individualist economic models repeatedly cause high levels of involuntary unemployment. Social problems are ameliorated by social workers who help individuals without addressing the root causes. Environmental disasters are worsening largely because our intellectual apparatus has ignored nature and insists on individual responsibility. We should drive less and eat less meat.
>
> ... Only a philosophy not wedded to notions of discrete, enduring entities can do justice to the ways in which human existence is simultaneously individuated and spontaneously coordinated, separate and together, chaotic and orderly ... Process thought seems best suited to provide the basis for a needed philosophical revolution.[14]

Psychology

Introducing Whitehead's metaphysical framework works wonders for clearing up many of psychology's most vexing problems. It also opens up some fascinating ways of understanding basic psychological phenomena and concepts and suggests many novel avenues of research. Since psychology is a field I have studied extensively, I will go into greater detail here to illustrate how Whitehead's philosophy could serve as a productive metatheory for working through some of the paramount issues in this field.

NEUROSCIENCE AND CONSCIOUSNESS STUDIES

We have already considered at some length how a process metaphysics can shed light on the mind-body problem, one of modern thought's most recalcitrant theoretical obstacles, and a corollary, the problem of sense perception (how does information from "out there" get "in here"?). This section looks more closely at how a Whiteheadian perspective might offer useful clues for theory construction and research in the area of neuroscience.

By conceiving the makeup of the universe in terms of momentary pulses of "feeling" (primitive experience), we obtain a model of the brain as billions of interflowing cellular events generating, and in interaction

14. Cobb, "Overcoming the Impasse," 217–18.

with, a series of far more complex moments of experience at the level of the human psyche. Not only do the neural cellular events help create these higher-level experiences of the psyche, but the feelings from the psyche's events flow *back into* the nexus of brain cells to influence them and the rest of the body. During the process of sense perception, feeling/data from the world flows into the body and through sensory systems to be modulated and synthesized by a complex array of neural events and finally integrated and unified by the body's central moment of experience. This model is conventional in that it relies on the kind of upward causation recognized by contemporary science, although the final integration into a moment of human-level awareness remains highly problematic for any materialist theory. Whitehead's proposal of a complementary downward causation is especially problematic for mechanistic-materialistic science even though this kind of intentional volition is assumed in all human activity. From the process perspective, this downward causation is easily accounted for by feelings/data from the psyche's experience feeding back into the neural circuitry (brain cell events and fields) and effecting voluntary actions by influencing unconscious neural processes.

This general picture is in many ways similar to the traditional understanding of how the human nervous system functions. The all-important differences are that the Whiteheadian view (1) grants *full reality* to human experience and (2) coherently describes the human psyche and body in terms of an interflowing system of events—events that are similar in nature but vary greatly in complexity and intensity of feeling. Furthermore, this process model lends agency to the psyche: human beings will, choose, and act at least in part through their subjective experience. The qualities of sensory experience—colors, tones, odors—are seen as originating from objects themselves, rather than as *purely* secondary additions created by the human brain, as with the physicalist explanation.

The most important implication for the psychology of perception—besides providing an epistemological grounding for perception and a basis for a correspondence theory of truth—is that the processing and synthesizing accomplished by the sensory organs and receptors, the nerve tracts, and especially the brain cells, are *supplemented* by further selection and transmutation at the level of the psyche's own moments of experience. The psyche draws upon the highly enriched and synthesized perceptual data preprocessed by the brain and nervous system, and out of this nexus prehends and unifies this array of data into one integrated perception of the world, incorporating symbolic meaning into the very fabric of the experience.

Whitehead seems to attribute much, if not most, of the synthetic integration found in sensory perception to the "final integration," that is, to the activities of the human psyche proper. Advances in neuropsychological understanding since his day suggest that the sensory systems and the brain accomplish more of this synthesis than he hypothesized. For example, many of the basic shapes and patterns found in visual experience seem to be preformed in the complex cellular formations of the visual cortex rather than entirely during the early stages of the psyche's concrescences.[15] But however much preprocessing the brain is responsible for, the theories and research paradigms for the psychology of perception will be very different once we include in our models a central occasion of psyche-level events that is intrinsically involved in the final process of synthesizing and unifying perception.

In this context, I would add that this process approach allows for neural pathways that function either more as structures (for example, more or less permanent neural interconnections) or as fields: patterns of neural events that habitually work together through direct mutual prehensions. And along with the human psyche's dominant or central occasions, there might also exist neural centers of integrative activity operating alongside the central occasion. Here I have in mind organizational centers in the brain stem or limbic system—*not* independent personalities. (The issue of multiple personalities, I think, is better addressed as aberrations within the psyche, understood as a *single* personal order of events.)

The question of how best to interpret *memory* is particularly interesting within a Whiteheadian paradigm. His notion of prehension as a direct inner connection to past events casts a whole new and unorthodox perspective on theories of remembering, but one that fits more closely with our immediate experience. This mode of memory—past events flowing directly into the human psyche itself—seems most likely as an explanation for very short-term memory, where just-past occasions seem to still be partially present to the current moment of experience. That this must in some way be the case seems apparent when listening to music: appreciation of the musical patterning requires the previous notes to be ready at hand (or ear). This kind of direct access to past events also appears in those moments where a smell or image or song will suddenly set off a vivid recall, or reliving, of a long-forgotten event. More dramatically, under hypnosis people are reportedly able to tap into a mode of memory that reveals precise details inaccessible to normal recall. As it does not seem highly plausible that *all* of one's experiences could be (so to speak) recorded in the brain in such exacting fashion, by what mechanism do these memories become suddenly accessible? There is no need to revisit here the sensational examples

15. Kandel, *In Search of Memory*, 300–302.

of transpersonal memory cited by Grof, as these more mundane examples make the point just as strongly. However, it should be noted that what might be termed Whiteheadian prehensive recall[16] answers precisely Grof's appeal for a theory that provides a coherent understanding of what Grof refers to as "memory without a material substrate."[17]

But is most memory solely of this variety—that is, a direct accessing of the original event? I have my doubts. While working on this book, I read through Eric Kandel's fascinating intellectual autobiography about his Nobel Prize–winning research into the biological basis of memory. (In its title, *In Search of Memory,* one suspects an allusion to Proust's *In Search of Lost Time,* more commonly known as *Remembrance of Things Past.*) While I take exception to his adamant belief that memory can be *fully* explained at the cellular level through purely reductionistic methods, it also seems certain that the brain is intimately and deeply involved with many facets of what we think of as memory.

Kandel's research indicates that short-term memory tends to be functional in nature—changes in the synaptic connectivity—while the transition to long-term memory involves more permanent changes in the synaptic structures themselves. I hope that by now I have conveyed why it seems unlikely that this is the whole story. As an alternative general hypothesis, I suggest that memory is a variable activity that involves a number of closely related processes. First would be what Kandel refers to as *procedural* mental processes that organize perceptual and motor skills at an unconscious level.[18] These processes may well occur primarily at the neural level. Similarly, rote learning is also implanted in memory through massive repetition and may be embedded or retained largely at the cellular level. More complex forms of ongoing memory may involve something best described as an intercellular field phenomenon: something like Sheldrake's "morphic fields,"[19] which are easily accommodated by a Whiteheadian approach. Other kinds of memories seem to rely primarily on direct prehensions of past events, but it's likely that these memories are often "cued" by marker-like changes in the brain. These cues might resemble what Kandel calls a *core memory:* "Recall of memory is a creative process. What the brain stores is thought to be only a core memory. Upon recall, this core memory is then elaborated

16. Whitehead discusses memory as the direct perception of past events in several places in *Process and Reality,* including pages 120, 122, and 239.

17. See Grof, *Beyond the Brain,* 44.

18. Kandel, *In Search of Memory,* 374.

19. Rupert Sheldrake most fully develops his theory of morphic resonance in Sheldrake, *Presence of the Past.*

upon and reconstructed."[20] Finally, we have those occasional recall episodes that entail pure prehensions of past events that may supersede neurology entirely. Kandel describes something similar as "so-called flashbulb memories, memories of emotionally charged events that are recalled in vivid detail . . . as if a complete picture had been instantly and powerfully etched on the brain"[21]—or perhaps rather, from a Whiteheadian perspective, as if in certain memories neural mechanisms are somehow transcended, and the emotional intensity of a past experience is accessed directly.

Clearly these last paragraphs have involved a significant amount of speculation. These speculations could be viewed as illustrating how Whitehead's philosophy can help guide theory construction in science and so open up new avenues of thinking and research. Please bear with me as I speculate a bit further along these lines.

While wrestling with the question of how the elemental units of reality can generate the complex phenomena of memory and conscious experience, Kandel writes, "All life, including the substrate of our thoughts and memories, is composed of the same building blocks."[22] In this vein, Kandel notes the amazing parallels between the kinds of inhibitory and excitatory actions that occur at both the molecular and cellular levels.[23] Interestingly enough, according to Whitehead, these same operations take place in the early stages of concrescence when the initial feelings of past events are selected for intensification (adversion) or attenuation (aversion). Perhaps human memory is basically an expanded and supplemented form of a more primitive prehensive activity—which is present at the molecular and cellular level in rudimentary form—amplified by the power of the human actual occasion and supplemented and reinforced by simple representations stored via neural mechanisms such as "synaptic markers" and the production of new synaptic terminals.[24] I think the idea of cells as subjects would appeal to Santiago Ramón y Cajal (1852–1934), who Kandel says "is arguably the most important brain scientist who ever lived,"[25] and about whose drawings Charles Sherrington wrote: "He treated the microscopic scene as though it were alive and were inhabited by beings which felt and did and hoped and tried as we do."[26]

20. Kandel, *In Search of Memory*, 281.

21. Kandel, *In Search of Memory*, 265.

22. Kandel, *In Search of Memory*, 236.

23. Kandel, *In Search of Memory*, 264.

24. See Kandel, *In Search of Memory*, 267–70 and 274–76.

25. Kandel, *In Search of Memory*, 61.

26. Kandel, *In Search of Memory*, (For the source of the Sherrington quotations, see

By drawing on Whitehead's notion of reality as composed of societies of organisms—all sharing the same underlying elements of momentary events of synthetic feeling—we can draw closer to Kandel's goal to "join radical reductionism, which drives basic biology, with the humanistic effort to understand the human mind, which drives psychiatry and psychoanalysis."[27] Kandel candidly admits that reductionistic techniques for biology are woefully inadequate, at least so far, to the task of explaining human subjectivity and the unity of consciousness. And although Kandel argues that research can and should move forward with these standard methodologies, he cites Thomas Nagel's claim that the explanation of consciousness will depend on discovering "the elements of subjective experience," which will require a "revolution in biology and most likely a complete transformation of scientific thought."[28] A Whiteheadian approach provides a metapsychological model capable of addressing these most vexing issues for neuroscience and consciousness studies: namely, the unity of consciousness and human subjectivity. While some might protest that it is poor methodology to construct a theory around the metaphysical hypothesis that subjectivity is a fundamental aspect of reality, I would argue that trying to derive the unity of consciousness and subjectivity from a metaphysics that *denies* their existence (materialism) is futile, while trying to *explain away* the most intimate aspects of human existence (epiphenomenalism) is folly.[29]

The foundation and vision for Nagel's revolution and transformation is here at hand in Whitehead's philosophy of organism. It offers a general framework for understanding human biology and psychology that is much more adequate and coherent than any other available theory—whether materialist or information-processing, mind/brain correlates or identism. As a coup de grace, Whitehead's metaphysics is congruent with quantum

---

Kandel's notes on page 457.)

27. Kandel, *In Search of Memory*, 375.

28. Kandel, *In Search of Memory*, 381–82.

29. Here is a side note: The Whiteheadian emphasis on subjectivity arising out of prehensions of past events would seem to preclude the possibility of true computer consciousness. Even quantum-level circuitry would appear incapable of the kinds of primitive perception that inform all actual occasions in Whitehead's scheme, and which provide the possibility of subject experience. Of course, if organic or living elements could be introduced into computer technology, this might cast a different light on the matter. Olaf Stapledon, in *Last and First Men*, describes "silos" filled with neural material that generates conscious superbrains—who eventually take control of the world. However, these organic "computers" come to realize that their enormous powers are ultimately limited by their lack of a biological bodily matrix, which could function as a source for the kind of deep feeling attunement necessary for those higher mystical intuitions capable of probing the ultimate dimensions of reality.

physics, providing a direct connection between biochemistry and the most primitive dimensions of reality. Of course, endless details and intricacies must be worked out—but that is wherein the adventure lies.[30]

While the philosophy of organism is valuable as a unified big picture of our universe, it was never intended to be the last word. Speculative philosophy, according to Whitehead, is ever evolving as new facts come to light and better concepts are divined. One of the most important functions of such a system is to provide the basic concepts that the sciences can then use to coordinate and organize their collective efforts and develop new avenues of research and theory building. Reciprocally, as new evidence and theories arise that challenge the general philosophical paradigm, modifications may be required—and at times the entire system must be reconceived. Nothing is written in stone. Speculative philosophy, like science, is an ongoing, self-correcting endeavor that seeks to draw ever closer to understanding the nature of reality and the universe.

Along with procedural mental processes, Kandel describes two other types of unconscious processes: the dynamic unconscious and the preconscious. This brings us into the realm of the *depth unconscious,* which seems to rely more directly on the activities of the human psyche than on the neural processes themselves.

THE UNCONSCIOUS

In developing a rudimentary Whiteheadian theory of the unconscious, I will first suggest how a process approach might help clarify Jung's theory of archetypes and the collective unconscious. Jung states that "the collective unconscious, being the repository of man's experience and at the same time the prior condition of this experience, is an image of the world which has taken aeons to form"[31] Jung's notion of an active, collective aspect to the psyche has been rejected by much of the scientific community because there has been no theoretically admissible way of conceptualizing how experiences from the distant past could form this kind of active psychic foundation. For example, current evolutionary theory has no mechanism

---

30. Jason Brown has had some success in applying Whiteheadian concepts to brain functioning through his theory of *microgenesis.* While his system does not fully cohere to Whitehead's metaphysical principles, Brown has illustrated how many of these ideas might be beneficially employed. His evaluation of the shortcomings of conventional approaches to psychopathology, through his extensive knowledge of neurophysiology and brain disorders, is quite revealing. See Brown, *Mind and Nature*; and Brown, *Microgenetic Theory and Process Thought.*

31. Jung, *Two Essays,* 95.

by which individual subject experience could be directly passed on to future generations. As Sheldrake succinctly puts it: "Jung's idea of the collective unconscious simply does not make sense in the context of the mechanistic theory of life; consequently it is not taken seriously within the current scientific orthodoxy."[32] However, by grounding Jungian psychology in a Whiteheadian metaphysics, the psyche's depth dimensions—individual and collective—can be understood *as its past*. John Cobb Jr. believes this approach might prove mutually beneficial: "Both traditions could be enriched if Whiteheadians realized more fully that the past is the depth of each occasion of human experience, and if Jungians realized that the depth of the psyche is the whole of what Whitehead calls its 'actual world.'"[33]

Fleshing out this idea, Cobb goes on to write:

> In Whiteheadian terms, we can roughly correlate the "mental pole" of an occasion of experience, including perception in the mode of presentational immediacy, with its surface. The term *surface* must not be used derogatively in this context, because mentality is an extremely important aspect of reality. Yet in any occasion of experience it is still a minor part. Overwhelmingly predominant is the physical pole, which corresponds to the experience's depths. The physical pole is the actual world, or the past, as it is constitutive of the present. It is almost entirely, and almost necessarily, unconscious.[34]

Cobb's formulation fits in well with Ira Progoff's schematic of Jung's theory of the personality:

> On the surface was consciousness; below that the Personal Unconscious; and further below that, the Collective Unconscious. The best analogy for this view is a cross-sectional drawing of a geologic formation. At the top is a thin layer of surface rock; this is consciousness. Just below that is another layer, thicker than the first, but still relatively thin; this is the Personal Unconscious. And below these two strata, as a deep formation of rock extending back to the Plutonic core of the earth itself, is the Collective Unconscious. This is really quite an apt analogy for the structure of the personality in terms of levels of depth.[35]

32. Sheldrake, *Presence of the Past*, 251.

33. Cobb, "Eternal Objects and Archetypes," 127.

34. Cobb, "Eternal Objects and Archetypes," 127.

35. Progoff, *Death and Rebirth of Psychology*, 146. Progoff does go on to say that Jung was not fully satisfied with the static nature of this analogy and later in life attempted to construct a more dynamic and unified approach to his theory of the unconscious (see 146–47).

A process perspective adds a *dynamic* dimension to these layers of depth, in that these layers of experience are placed within the context of the synthetic, psychic activity occurring within each human-level momentary event. We thereby obtain a view of the structures or depths of the human personality *constantly arising out of the psyche's own creative process,* in contrast to a static or stratified image of the unconscious.

According to the Whiteheadian theory of experience, only the tip, or the "crown" of each momentary concrescence contains the potential for consciousness, while the vast majority of each human event is composed of unconscious experiential activity. Constituting the depths of this unconscious experience is each occasion's "actual world," that is, the entire past universe from that occasion's particular vantage point. But since the past is a completed pattern, it must be *dynamically reconstructed* by each new moment of experience. The structure of the human unconscious is created and maintained through this same dynamic process of receiving and reconstituting direct feelings of past events. As Cobb writes, "There are continuities within the unconscious, but they are the kinds of continuities to be found within a process. What is to be affirmed, in affirming the unconscious, is a succession of experiences in which continuity is established by reenactment rather than by static identity."[36] An individual's unconscious preserves its idiosyncratic structure by constantly re-creating its own defenses or patterns of repression, as well as by favoring certain positive prehensions and higher-level symbolic unifications.

In its most comprehensive sense, the "Unconscious"—as the unconscious portion of every human concrescence—represents a perspective on all of the universe's past occasions of experience. This vast sea of experience, or "ocean of feeling," can be usefully subdivided for conceptual purposes.

To start with, there are the once-conscious feelings and memories belonging to the personal order, which are now repressed, forgotten, or simply not consciously remembered in the present moment. This level of a Whiteheadian unconscious equates with the personal unconscious widely described in psychoanalytic theory. However, a process view of the personal unconscious emphasizes a dimension that tends to be neglected in much of psychoanalytic theory: the human body. The bulk of the feelings determining most moments of concrescence are those flooding in via the sensory systems, the brain, and other organic processes. (From the discussion of the brain's contribution to memory in the previous section, I hope it is apparent that neural cellular events are also intimately involved in the psyche's unconscious processes, though of course from a Whiteheadian

36. Cobb, *Structure of Christian Existence,* 32.

perspective, not solely responsible for them.) Naturally, the degree of bodily involvement in the dominant occasion varies greatly, depending upon the activity at hand: compare a moment of making love with a moment of vivid recall of a complex, intellectual insight. But whatever the human body's moment-to-moment contribution may be, a Whiteheadian theory of the unconscious must consider the feelings from the physical body to be an important component of the personal unconscious. In this regard, it is important to note that Stanislav Grof's research suggests that the historical odyssey of the body, especially episodes of physical trauma, play a more significant role in determining ongoing unconscious dynamics than many psychological systems acknowledge.

Another division of the human unconscious corresponds to Jung's concept of the collective unconscious. This level would contain so-called archetypal phenomena as understood within a Whiteheadian framework: that is, humanity's collective patterns of experience that have been reinforced throughout the past, producing prototypical patterns of behavior, feeling, imagery, and symbols. While I am inclined to locate these patterns within a shared collective field of human experience, they might also somehow be encoded in the human organism itself, with the "core memory" cues (mentioned above) utilized as a mode of access to the patterns latent in the field of past human events. These hypotheses are *very* tentative. Even with Whitehead's help, it is difficult to discern the best interpretation for these Jungian concepts and phenomena.

Grof's data indicate that beyond this collective level of the unconscious lies another domain that might be referred to as the transpersonal unconscious proper, as it transcends both the personal aspects and the shared experiences of the human race. To start, we might delineate an individual dimension of the transpersonal unconscious. This dimension would transcend the limits of the personal unconscious (as generally understood) in two ways: first, by extending the individual's personal order into the realms of perinatal and past life experiences; second, by incorporating the energies and fields of the subtle body. In addition, this individual dimension would include the unconscious components of parapsychological phenomena.

Another part of the transpersonal unconscious would encompass the collective feeling patterns of other animal species here on earth, as well as the morphic fields and habitual energy patterns belonging to earth's other natural phenomena. This might be designated as the *planetary* dimension of the transpersonal unconscious. (It may be more appropriate to conceive of all or part of the planetary dimension as a *deeper aspect* of the human collective unconscious—as its natural ground or depth, perhaps.)

Thirdly, the transpersonal unconscious might have an extraterrestrial dimension consisting of the psychical contributions made by any individuals or groups of physical entities existing beyond the earth's boundaries during any point in our universe's past. Grof's evidence also suggests the existence of a *historical* dimension that entails an objective rendering of events relating to our planet's and the universe's natural and historical unfoldment. And lastly, the transpersonal unconscious possesses a *spiritual* dimension made up of God's primordial and consequent natures, as well as any other purely spiritual entities that may exist.[37]

A final point concerning a Whiteheadian conception of the unconscious is related to the notion of *openness*—and this in several ways. We have already seen how the Whiteheadian unconscious opens directly into the experience of all past events. This transcendence of individual boundaries is strikingly different from the Freudian view of the unconscious as "clearly bounded, containing only the personal past and the instinctual drives of the individual."[38] On the other hand, as Catherine Keller further points out, this idea of an "open" unconscious means that each individual's unconscious (and conscious) experience flows out into the world, where it influences the experience of other individuals, collective humanity, the universe, and God.

> If it is true that in its depths our unconscious bottoms out, flooding into the world, as it floods into us, the influence is not unilateral: our conscious, individual and communal experiences and actions can and do make a difference, affecting   however gradually—the collective unconscious itself.
>
> ... The archetypal perforations in the individual's life, through which collective life flows in and the individual input flows out, are at the same time windows to the sacred.[39]

Thus, the openness of the Whiteheadian unconscious means not only that human experience is open in its unconscious depths to all past experience; in addition, human experience enters into and influences all *future* occasions of experience (at an unconscious level).

Before moving on to a process notion of repression, I want to reemphasize a crucial implication that this Whiteheadian notion of an open unconscious holds for transpersonal psychology. A human unconscious

---

37. I would be remiss if in this context I did not mention Steve Odin's extraordinary theory of the collective unconscious. Odin envisions it in terms of a syncretism between Jungian, Whiteheadian, and Buddhist "psychologies." On this topic, see especially part 3 of Odin, *Process Metaphysics and Hua-yen Buddhism*.

38. Keller, *From a Broken Web*, 101.

39. Keller, *From a Broken Web*, 115.

that can receive feelings from all past events and exert an influence upon future occasions means that the human psyche itself should be regarded as a *psychical organ of perception and projection,* intrinsically endowed with the potential for a multitude of parapsychological faculties, as well as other exceptional capabilities.

REPRESSION

Whitehead's philosophy offers the basis for a coherent psychophysical understanding of repression in its muscular, neural, and psychological manifestations. What follows is only one example of what such a theory might look like. However, I am convinced that the freedom to move so seamlessly between the activities and structures of the body, brain, and psyche—which Whitehead's metaphysics makes possible—affords significant advantages for all theory construction in this area.

Drawing upon neo-Reichian theory, we can hypothesize that the *physiological* roots of repression are correlated especially with chronic tensions in the musculature and breathing apparatus, which obstruct the flow of certain problematic emotions and related memories. These habitual unconscious physical blockages have in fact been created for this very purpose: avoidance of painful thoughts and feelings. It seems likely that this muscular level of repression is supported and reinforced at the neuronal level by weakened or strengthened neural connections that help fortify certain memory and emotional patterns and blockages. Repressive forces would also be operative within the psyche's own concrescent activity: specifically, through intensifications and attenuations of past experiences in the earlier phases, and via habitual patterns of contrast in the higher phases—in other words, through selective memory and the ego defense mechanisms. These habitual repressive patterns gain force over time, with the psyche re-creating them moment to moment, thereby establishing a normal mode of feeling and perceiving the world and oneself. From a process perspective, the best way of initiating a new concrescent order is by somehow circumventing these repressive processes and thereby accessing lost memories and reviving suppressed modes of feeling.

In Whitehead's scheme, *order* is necessary for eliciting the depth dimension of experience. However, "it is not true that in proportion to the orderliness there is depth. There are various types of order, and some of them provide more trivial satisfaction than do others."[40] Experience with nonordinary states indicates that the types of order provided by normal

40. Whitehead, *Process and Reality*, 110–11.

ego structures are not especially conducive to intensive depth experiences. In part, this is due to the human psyche's evolutionary and social conditioning, which tends to attune conscious attention to the mundane realities of survival and social interactions.

Along with this "evolutionary" inhibition, however, is a layer of surplus repression made up of the excessive physical and psychological armoring related to overly repressive ego structures. These structures are often remnants of defenses erected in early childhood to protect the individual from overwhelming psychic distress. Although important to the child's survival, these same defenses in adulthood tend to obstruct avenues for healing and growth. While acting to shelter the individual from internal and external threat, these excessively rigid defenses also isolate the ego from a fuller contact with the world, and the deeper self, by blocking off access to direct influx of feeling.[41]

Some ramifications of such surplus repression are described here by Catherine Keller, in more Whiteheadian terms:

> The degree of complexity achieved by the entity in its moment of becoming depends upon its *openness* to that in-flowing world. The influences of its own past and of the environment are the materials it works into the creative contrasts patterning the final "complex feeling." The more the individual represses its feelings, the fewer materials it will have to work with; indeed, it will not know those it *does* have for what they are.[42]

Generally speaking, the more repressive the order imposed upon the concrescent process by the ego structures, the less depth and intensity of feeling in the final satisfaction or conscious experience. On the other hand, an ordering pattern that is sensitive to the immediate requirements of synthetic integration and the coordination of the variety and intensity of feelings arising from the unconscious phases can provide maximal depth and richness

41. Keller describes some of the ramifications of this "psychic isolationism": "The in-flowing other must feel to a defensive ego like an aggressive intrusion, a threat to its self-containment. So it will redouble its fortifications and can justify its own aggression as defense . . . Relation to others, once ousted from the self's inside and so experienced as external, must be *kept* outside by a policy of psychic isolationism. Thus the ego denies the streams of influence entering into it and tries to control—and so to possess—their sources. Only by subduing and possessing the Other can it feel truly in possession of itself. Externalizing relation, it in fact projects both the threats and comforts of relationship onto the Other . . . And so in a bizarre sense, by objectifying the Other the subject compensates for a lack that it does not really have—for it is only the feeling, not the reality, of isolation that cuts it off from the in-flowing other." (Keller, *From a Broken Web*, 27)

42. Keller, *From a Broken Web*, 189–90 (italics original).

in conscious awareness. This type of order must in large part organize itself creatively in the moment around the demands of the data at hand and the contingencies of the particular concrescent process. Spontaneity and flexibility are crucial. Thus, any stylized patterning of experience based on rigid ego structures—and their neurophysiological correlates—will tend to have a dampening effect not only on one's emotional intensity and availability, but also on the possibility of experiencing mystical and transpersonal states.

THE SELF

We have already looked at the concept of *the self* from various psychodynamic and transpersonal perspectives. Here I will summarize the various ways this central feature of human experience might find explication within a Whiteheadian metaphysics.

As a starting point, the human psyche would be understood as a series of mostly unconscious momentary events that draw upon feelings from the brain, the body, the psyche's past, and the environment at large in their process of self-creation. Thus one notion of the self would be the totality constituted by the entire historical flow of these occasions of experience: "An enduring personality . . . is a route of occasions in which the successors with some peculiar completeness sum up their predecessors."[43] For Whitehead, the "mind with its perceptions" is an abstraction from the more fundamental metaphysical reality of a multitude of serially ordered moments of creative experience. Moreover the subject, or "thinker," as a persisting thing-in-itself, represents a further abstraction from this series of events involving conscious thought and perception. In *Modes of Thought*, Whitehead examines this fundamental notion of the self or the "I":

> Descartes' "Cogito, ergo sum" is wrongly translated, "I think, therefore I am." It is never bare thought or bare existence that we are aware of. I find myself as essentially a unity of emotions, enjoyments, hopes, fears, regrets, valuations of alternatives, decisions—all of them subjective reactions to the environment as active in my nature. My unity—which is Descartes' "I am"—is my process of shaping this welter of material into a consistent pattern of feelings. The individual enjoyment is what I am in my role of a natural activity, as I shape the activities of the environment into a new creation, which is myself at this moment; and yet, as being myself, it is a continuation of the antecedent world. If we stress the role of the environment, this process is

43. Whitehead, *Process and Reality*, 350.

causation. If we stress the role of my immediate pattern of active
enjoyment, this process is self-creation.[44]

In contrast to the modern Cartesian view of a person as a conscious self
who is sharply independent from nature, the body, and other human beings, Whitehead understands a person to be a unifying "natural activity"—
creatively integrating the feelings derived from its entire environment into
moments of "active enjoyment."

Two central features make Whitehead's approach especially useful for
psychology. First, every human being is in immediate experiential contact
with nature and other people: a human being's very moment-to-moment
existence is founded on its unconscious intuitions of its entire environment. This suggests that Western civilization's pervasive sense of alienation,
existential angst, and solipsistic isolation is not so much a product of the
sophisticated mind's encounter with the reality of the human condition as
it is a psychological and historical artifact of our current modes of being in
the world. This reassessment offers a road map for more meaningful and
concrete ways of encountering the world. For if this analysis of the nature of
experience and the self is accurate, it indicates that at least some of the wide
range of psychospiritual methods available today *do* provide important tools
capable of producing real and fundamental changes to help us relate to the
universe and one another in ways that are more fulfilling and more sensitive
to the true nature of our common world. Second, the idea of a self that is
re-created each moment describes a model of the psyche that holds great
potential for psychospiritual growth and change. The possibility of deep
transformation is literally only a moment away.

Whitehead's philosophy suggests a multifaceted understanding of the
self that contrasts its sheer momentary subjective events with its continuously re-created structures. Thus a Whiteheadian notion of self would include a number of interlocking dimensions or aspects, the point not being
to craft a precise definition but rather to illustrate the complex relations
between ego, personality, sense of identity, and deeper self. First, the *ego*
might be thought of as the aspect and sense of self that emerges out of the
habitual patterns of enhancement and attenuation that have developed over
the life span: those stubborn patterns that guide or canalize the normal flow
of conscious and unconscious experience. Then there is the essential quality
of experience or awareness that emerges in each successive moment. This is
what all sentient entities have in common, the centrality of which is emphasized especially in Buddhist thought. To this we might add the conscious

44. Whitehead, *Modes of Thought*, 166.

sense of *identity* that arises spontaneously when we reflect on our situation, or when desire appears: *I* want, *I* need, *I* will, *I* wish.

Our personal sense of identity is largely reliant on the established self-image that emerges out of the unconscious compromises crystallized by our habitual repressive structures—that is, the face presented by our defense mechanisms. It could be said that *who we are* (or who we *think* we are) at any point in time is determined largely by those things we fear or avoid the most. By this I mean that our sense of self is unconsciously regulated by our avoidance structures, which funnel our flow of feeling into safe and predictable patterns. This is one reason why, when repression is lifted suddenly, there is both a feeling of increased freedom *and* of not quite knowing who you are anymore. This disorientation and freedom reflect how strongly our identity is related to the long-term repressive structures that delineate habitual emotional, thought, and experiential patterns.

For Whitehead the *enduring personality* "is a route of occasions in which the successors with some peculiar completeness sum up their predecessors."[45] Since this kind of *summing up* is rarely anywhere close to fully accessible to conscious awareness, one's sense of this greater identity is ordinarily fragmentary and vague. However, at times we may have greater access to what we might call a *higher* self, the *deep* self, or more colorfully, our Big Self, which is the sum of all we have been—rather than being primarily based on what we have been avoiding. A strong experience of this higher self might resemble what I felt during my Big Trip just before entering my dorm room: "there is a moment in every man's life when he knows exactly who he is." In this mode of being, one's past feels fully available, but at the same time one is fully open to the world, drawing on the more distant past only to maximize the richness of each new experience.

Going one step further still, we can say that the *True Self* is ultimately the Creativity that is exemplified in every moment. From this perspective we are essentially a creative process that continuously arises out of and flows back into the entire universe, like waves upon the ocean. To add yet another dimension of depth, this ultimate notion of Self might also involve a sense of how our process of becoming arises in every moment out of a direct intuition of God's being and purpose. This could lead to the mystical insight that "Atman and Brahman are One." However, a Whiteheadian take on this deep intuition upholds both the unity *and* the discreteness of God and Self.

So, who am I? In one mode I am each creative occasion of experience unfolding moment to moment. I am also the "peculiar summing up" of these personal moments, the full pattern that embodies the essence of my

---

45. Whitehead, *Process and Reality*, 350.

history. I am also the sense of ego identity that pervades my experience, largely based upon what I still avoid and repress out of fear, guilt, and just plain habit. And at my furthest reaches, I am the depths of the universe out of which I arise in every new moment, shaped (more or less) by the guidance of a caring Universe.

I will put this another way, drawing on a dream I had while working on this chapter. In this dream, I was explaining to a class how our everyday moment-to-moment awareness is not who we really are. Although this me feels like all I am, there lies behind it all of our unconscious psychic processes, all the underlying activity of our brain-and-body nexus, and our entire personal and evolutionary histories. Thus we are like the tip of an iceberg, floating on this great sea of past experience and bodily activity. And if you add in Whitehead's most general understanding of reality, then *who we are* originates out of an even greater ocean of feeling: the entire past universe.

TRANSPERSONAL PSYCHOLOGY

Whitehead's metaphysics does not prove the veracity of any mystical intuitions or confirm the theories of transpersonal psychology per se. But his organic theory does offer a unified interpretive model that provides a coherent interpretation of most transpersonal phenomena and places transpersonal psychology within the same frame of reference as the findings of contemporary science and the realm of everyday experience. The interpretive versatility of this framework of fundamental ideas furnishes a range of possible ways for understanding complex transpersonal phenomena and nonordinary states, giving a welcome flexibility that helps counter dogmatic tendencies. Perhaps most importantly for transpersonal psychology, Whitehead's cosmology portrays the universe as a *layered organic environment that is intrinsically penetrable by primitive perception, with depths that are fully accessible to human awareness.* By introducing an experiential mode of access to all actualities in the universe—through his revolutionary notion of prehension as direct intuition of past events—Whitehead's philosophy opens up a world of potential parapsychological abilities, direct intuitions of nature's inner workings, and meaningful insights into the more subtle dimensions of reality.

When viewed within the context of a Whiteheadian model, the phenomena investigated by transpersonal psychology no longer need be excluded from serious scientific examination. Nor can they simply be dismissed as anomalies, since the primary reason for this rejection is that they are theoretically impossible. As Grof has provocatively remarked,

anomalies are "what is left after we apply a bad theory."[46] Along with
providing a framework hospitable to the reality and importance of many
so-called anomalous transpersonal phenomena, the philosophy of organism offers a rationally coherent understanding of the basic processes of
ordinary existence—in contrast to many other philosophical schemes
whose major inconsistencies and inadequacies in this regard are so frequently overlooked. So even though my emphasis here has been on how
Whitehead's metaphysics can contribute a foundation and an interpretive
framework for transpersonal psychology, of at least equal significance is
process philosophy's ability to fuse the transpersonal field with the rest of
psychology, science, and everyday life. Remember Whitehead's observation: philosophy "attains its chief importance by fusing the two, namely,
religion and science, into one rational scheme of thought."[47]

46. From page xxii of Grof's Introduction to Laszlo, *What Is Reality?*

47. Whitehead, *Process and Reality*, 15. I feel compelled to add a few words about
one of the other major contemporary theorists of transpersonal psychology, Ken
Wilber. Wilber has done exemplary work to advance transpersonal psychology and
has made a Herculean effort to create a unified theory of . . . well, nearly everything.
However, brilliant as it may be, I find crucial parts of his thought confusing, and confused. I believe the central problem lies in Wilber's attempt to use holons (whole/part
relationships) as the metaphysical core of his system. (I have been advised recently
that Wilber has moved much closer to Whitehead's position of late. If this is so, please
read my critique as applying primarily to the philosophical positions articulated in his
earlier voluminous writings.)

A number of years back, I wrote a journal article comparing and contrasting Whitehead and Wilber's metaphysics. Rather than reinventing the wheel, let me simply give
the crux of my critique written about twenty years ago, when my mental faculties were
more finely honed:

> One could argue that Wilber's holonic theory is essentially Whitehead's philoso-
> phy of organism made obscure by removing temporal atomicity and prehensive
> experience from the actual entity. I believe that Wilber's emphasis of an eclectic
> "holonic" metaphysic over key elements of Whitehead's philosophy of organism
> constitutes a critical philosophical miscalculation. By making an abstract rela-
> tionship more fundamental than actual experience, Wilber's metaphysics loses
> touch with immediate reality and thus commits what Whitehead calls the "fallacy
> of misplaced concreteness": placing greater reality in an abstraction than in the
> concrete entities or beings from which those abstractions arise . . .
>
> Wilber's conflation of the flow between the one and the many into the simul-
> taneous whole/part holon [Wilber, *Sex, Ecology, Spirituality,* 502] eliminates the
> temporal interplay between the individual actual entities and their societies and
> thus turns reality into a universe of "sliding contexts" with little basis for differ-
> entiation of structure. (Wilber cannot fully acknowledge the primacy of the tem-
> poral flow between actual moments of experience because this would "privilege"
> process and individuals rather than the whole/part relation.) This, in turn, forces
> Wilber to compensate by becoming excessively rigid and stratifying in describing
> his pervasive levels of reality and consciousness. Furthermore, Wilber neglects to

It would take an entire book (which I hope to write one day) to even begin to do justice to the wide-ranging implications and applications of Whitehead's philosophy for the field of psychology: for example, for neuropsychology, physiological psychology, evolutionary psychology, cognitive psychology, artificial intelligence, animal behavior, developmental psychology, personality theory, counseling, and more. The potential here is extraordinary, as is evidenced by the ever-growing literature in this field.

Whitehead likens his method of philosophical speculation to taking an imaginative flight above the realm of particular observations in order to obtain original generalizations that may display hidden patterns and relationships lurking within the empirical world below. These generalizations are of true philosophic import only if their application is found to extend beyond their field of origin—that is, only if they shine light on other fields and disciplines as well.[48] In this chapter, I have tried to show how Whitehead's ideas could be beneficial for the academic and scientific domains, especially psychology. In the next chapter, we will take flight into some highly speculative ideas about the larger nature of reality and our cosmos.

---

systematically offer any "connective tissue" for these endless levels of whole/part relationships. Even though Wilber writes of "cascading whole/parts all the way up . . . rushing forward ceaselessly in time . . ." (p. 628), the mechanism behind this rushing forward is missing: namely, prehensive connection whereby a new moment (individual) creates itself out of the flow of past feeling. We are left, I believe, with a monistic mass of whole/parts requiring no temporal mode of connection, but allowing no means of real interaction or differentiation. (Buchanan, "Whitehead and Wilber," 238, 240–41)

Perhaps more importantly, an emphasis on process, rather than on levels or quadrants, means for me that the spiritual journey does not have a predefined end or some higher level to attain. Rather, it is just that: a journey. This journey may have peaks and valleys, discoveries and losses, but it is based on self-awareness and kindness. And hopefully, if one is fortunate, some moments of enlightenment and other peak experiences will appear along the way.

48. See Whitehead, *Process and Reality*, 4–5.

─── 11 ───

A Vision for You

Human beings instinctively attune themselves to the ultimate nature of reality, or more precisely, to what they believe that reality to be. It follows that our entire way of being and orienting in the world hinges upon our worldview. Here David Griffin describes the key role played by our cosmological perspectives and explains why we require a *new* guiding vision in order to change our civilization's problematic trajectory:

> A basic failure of modern thought has been to underestimate the extent to which we are *religious* beings. By this I mean that we seek *meaning* (however unconsciously), and that we do this by trying to be *in harmony with the ultimate nature of the world,* as we perceive it. Modern thought has suggested that religion was a mere transitory state, something we are now outgrowing. Modernity hence ignored the degree to which the *modern cosmology* would create a *new kind of human being,* a new way of being human ... Modernity has even come up with a derogatory name—"the naturalistic fallacy"—for the idea that our ethic should be based upon our cosmology, that how we *ought* to live should be based upon our view of the *nature* of things. Having dubbed this a fallacy, moderns could cheerfully continue propagating the fragmented, disenchanted, power-based, competitive worldview of modernity, releasing themselves from all responsibility for the behavior of the people to whom this new way of seeing reality is spread.
>
> ... We will not overcome the present disastrous ways of ordering our individual and communal lives until we reject the view of the world upon which they were based. And we cannot reject this old view until we have a new view that seems more convincing.[1]

1. Griffin, "Peace and the Postmodern Paradigm," 143–44.

Griffin also delineates a number of fundamental ways that modernity's worldview has dangerously skewed our notion of reality. The modern paradigm emphasizes coercion over persuasion, materialism over spirituality, consumerism over self-actualization, independence over relationship, and isolation over interconnectedness.[2] These tendencies engender a type of human self-understanding and a cultural framework that have steered Western civilization to the brink of disaster. Having fallen under the spell of this problematic modern vision of reality, the public has become widely inured to the dangers facing their families, community, and world, and is unable to fully perceive, much less adequately address, overpopulation, resource depletion, pollution, climate change, international conflicts, and the many other critical issues that threaten our civilization and the planet.

The notion that human beings are motivated primarily by self-interest, around which modern economic theory is constructed, has turned into a self-fulfilling prophecy. John Cobb Jr. identifies a general historical progression in dominant world paradigms, moving from religionism to nationalism to the situation today where *economism* rules.[3] When the central concern of governments and political policies is "the economy," money and possessions come to dominate the cultural psyche, and personal gain *does* seem to be humanity's primary motivating drive. John Lennon's song "Imagine" exemplifies this progression quite beautifully, artistically rendering how Cobb's first three stages of human society might be *transcended*, as well as how the next phase might be sharing and preserving the planet through *Earthism*.

A postmodern cosmology and ethos of Earthism would recognize the inherent value of all life and processes on the planet, as well as human society's fundamental dependence on a flourishing ecosystem. Joseph Campbell envisioned something similar for a new guiding myth of Western civilization. The early photos of Earth taken from space, displaying our planet as a beautiful blue-green ball floating in an infinite black sea, provided Campbell's inspiration.[4] This image is reminiscent of the culminating sequence of the film *2001: A Space Odyssey*—a fetus/newborn floating through space in a transparent womblike sphere, gazing intently at the sight of the approaching planet Earth—symbolizing humanity's rebirth into the next stage of human evolution. The question is: Is humanity capable of fully recognizing the catastrophic nature of our planetary dilemma and of making the changes and sacrifices necessary to transition successfully into this next stage?

2. Griffin, "Peace and the Postmodern Paradigm."

3. For example, see Cobb's *Sustaining the Common Good*. In *The Earthist Challenge to Economism* Cobb lays out this historical progression more directly but uses the term "Christianism" rather than "religionism."

4. For example, see Campbell, *Power of Myth*, 41.

Will Beardslee, who readers may remember introduced me to process thought, also had an intriguing idea about hope for the future and the mature use of the past. The symbol of the *child* can be used to draw us back into the past in an attempt to rehabilitate and restore a lost paradise, or the image of the child can serve as a symbol of hope for the possibility of future adventures. In more personal terms, this is the difference between laboring endlessly in therapy to heal one's inner child and being inspired to improve the world after holding your child or grandchild in your arms. Obviously, I am not at all opposed to freeing up the unconscious depths from old blocks and limitations, but the focus of this healing process should be to enrich the present, in service of a greater future.

The implication for society is this: our aim must be towards the future. We must relinquish the hope that returning to the dogmas of the past will save us. While the past does provide wisdom and fertile possibilities to draw upon, radically new situations call for novel solutions, not old, familiar ones—comforting though they may sound.

Along with furnishing a general framework for orienting our world towards a novel and hopefully better future, the other vital role of a cosmological vision is providing inspiration and hope. I recently read a fine book outlining what needs to be done in order to adapt to the environmental crises. It contained a keen analysis of the problems we face, and the author's writing skills left me envious indeed. However, the concluding sections were so stark—for example, accepting the end of our civilization and muddling through as best we can, while preserving as much of our culture and humanity as possible—that it is hard to imagine it having much of a positive influence for change. Strangely enough, this alarming verdict is not really what I objected to, as I think he paints an unfortunately accurate picture of our situation. What I found truly disheartening was the last chapter's vision of our universe as a soulless, material wonder, evolving purely out of causal necessity with no greater or inherent meaning of any kind.[5] This is the same vision of reality advanced by the narrator of the planetarium show in *Rebel Without a Cause,* and I don't believe that this disenchanted worldview will work any better for us today than it did for those troubled teenagers back in 1955.

---

5. Although Roy Scranton includes the vagaries of human experience in his overview of our civilization's plight, and its likely demise, his vision is mostly that of a scientific materialist (see "Coda: Coming Home," 111–17).

Tell Us a Story

My hope and belief are that Whitehead's philosophy—especially when augmented by the spiritual dimensions and methods articulated by transpersonal psychology—can serve as a cosmological corrective for the Western world. Of course, any unifying story must be able to coordinate *all* major elements of a society, including scientific theory in a culture such as ours. As we have seen, Whitehead's metaphysics is equal to the task of this type of broad integration. But process philosophy does something more, which I think is vitally important: it infuses an *inner subjectivity* to all things and to the universe at large.

While I admire the efforts of Thomas Berry and his adherents in their bold endeavor to create and narrate the "Universe Story"[6]—the truly amazing scientific account of our universe's journey from the big bang to this moment on earth—I believe something vital is missing here. In colorfully moving terms, Berry and his followers describe the evolution of our universe as an integral part of the human spiritual adventure. But where, one wonders, is the subjectivity and spirituality that informs the *universe at large* and precedes and transcends humanity? The account told by the physical sciences covers only the *objective* dimension of this evolutionary story; it examines only the husk, as it were. Even adding in human subjectivity as the current conclusion, or culmination, of this process still renders a cosmological vision that feels too "thin," in William James's sense of being spiritually shallow or impoverished, not to mention notably humancentric. In a Whiteheadian universe, we don't need to wait for human consciousness to come along and bestow meaning and value. For Whitehead, every event and entity is itself valuable and vibrant, and *already partaking* in the Adventure of the Universe.

Perhaps in a reasoned and well-intentioned effort to reach a wider audience by making their vision more compatible with current scientific thought and modern sensibilities, Berry's followers have chosen to downplay the kind of subjectivity that pervades the universe in Whitehead's cosmology. Still, I think it is a mistake to *desubjectivize* Berry's wonderful characterization of the universe as a "communion of subjects,"[7] for it is this very intuition of subjectivity that makes our experience of the universe most alive and radically open to a wide range of spiritual possibilities. Real wonder needs spiritual depth and a *universe of subjects* with whom to share this adventure.

6. See Swimme and Berry, *Universe Story.*

7. Berry, *Evening Thoughts,* 17.

When we combine a pervasive subjectivity with the spiritual opportunities suggested by transpersonal psychology, we arrive at a much "thicker" (James again) vision of existence than the evolutionary story of the physical universe as told by modern science. I will be the first to admit that many of the additional spiritual dimensions that are discussed below are *highly* speculative—and that even without them the Universe Story is still exciting and deeply moving. But like Olaf Stapledon, I suspect that only a spiritually inspired vision of our cosmos such as Whitehead's will offer the sense of deep Adventure necessary to galvanize the human race's full engagement with its next stage of exploration and evolution.[8]

I am *not* denying the importance of the kind of wonder for this amazing universe that visionaries such as Thomas Berry and Brian Swimme attempt to instill. But the sort of deep transpersonal awe evoked by Stapledon and Grof's articulation of a *spiritual adventure* is also necessary for real hope, joy, and purpose. Wonder may then find itself transforming into *awe*.

A Transpersonal-Organic Cosmology

The importance of imaginative elaborations on Whitehead's philosophical system is concisely captured here by Frederick Ferré: "Indeed, one of the urgent tasks for defenders and extenders of Whiteheadian theory lies precisely in continuing to identify and explore vivid imaginative images or metaphors by which they and others may clothe this powerful scheme of

---

8. In the 1930s, sensing the impending crisis in civilization, Olaf Stapledon sought to create a "modern Myth" to guide the world into a new kind of future. This myth is embodied in his magnum opus, *Star Maker*. Although widely recognized as one of the most powerful influences on the field of science fiction, it is far more than that. It is also a philosophical, psychological, and spiritual exploration of what Stapledon believed to be the most promising ideas for a new vision of reality and our universe: a worldview capable of inspiring and guiding civilization through its critical passage into psychospiritual maturity.

In his Foreword to the fiftieth-anniversary edition of *Star Maker*, Brian Aldiss writes that Stapledon did not consider *Star Maker* to be a "novel at all. True, it more resembles an attempt to create myth on the grandest possible scale—a myth for our time that will appease both the scientist and the mystic in us." (Stapledon, *Star Maker*, ix) It may also be worth noting again that John Lilly, that most intrepid explorer of transpersonal realms, states on the back cover of that edition that *Star Maker* is the only book with a vision large enough in scope to incorporate all that he has experienced.

It is important to emphasize that Stapledon's *Star Maker* represents only *one possible example* of a Whiteheadian-based myth for the "new age." As impressive as they may be, none of Stapledon's particular speculations or characterizations—including his crescendoing higher-level compound individuals—is necessary for, nor definitive of, a Whiteheadian, transpersonal cosmology.

ideas."[9] In this section, I explore one such speculative elaboration, with the caveat that there are many other valid and interesting ways to develop the potential spiritual dimensions of process thought.

The universe, as imagined through this interface between transpersonal psychology and process philosophy, might resemble in significant ways the Fechnerian cosmology championed by William James late in his career.[10] Along with a generally ensouled cosmos, Gustav Fechner postulates the existence of various levels of what might be termed higher-order *compound individuals*. In this passage, James summarizes this hierarchy of consciousness:

> The vaster orders of mind go with the vaster orders of body. The entire earth on which we live must have, according to Fechner, its own collective consciousness. So must each sun, moon, and planet; so must the whole solar system have its own wider consciousness, in which the consciousness of our earth plays one part. So has the entire starry system as such its consciousness; and if that starry system be not the sum of all that *is*, materially considered, then that whole system, along with whatever else may be, is the body of that absolutely totalized consciousness of the universe to which men give the name of God.[11]

While James and Fechner jointly offer a spiritually compelling vision of our universe, a more contemporary and, in my view, more useful combination would pair Whitehead and Olaf Stapledon—with Whitehead providing the philosophical framework and Stapledon supplying the transpersonal imaginative speculation. It is no coincidence that Stapledon's writings find a Whiteheadian cosmology so congenial. In the following, Susan Anderson displays the high regard between these two men of genius: "In *Philosophy and Living* Stapledon calls Whitehead's thought 'the most brilliant, most comprehensive, most significant, though also most difficult, metaphysical system of our time.'"[12] Stapledon's cosmic vision is similar (though by no means identical) to Fechner's in postulating a hierarchy of increasing complex beings arising out of a rich and diverse array of intelligent entities. Stapledon's hierarchy differs from Fechner's in that it is

9. Ferré, "Contemporaneity, Knowledge, and God," 113.

10. "The analogies with ordinary psychology, with certain facts of pathology, with those of psychical research, so called, and with those of religious experience, establish, when taken together, a decidedly *formidable* probability in favor of a general view of the world almost identical with [Gustav] Fechner's" (James, *Pluralistic Universe*, 309–10; italics original).

11. James, *Pluralistic Universe*, 152–53.

12. Anderson, "Evolutionary Futurism," 123.

somewhat more constructive and evolutionary in nature. For example, in Stapledon's scenario, planetary consciousness arises in the form of a group mind based upon the individual minds of the planet's sentient inhabitants. In Fechner's scheme, planetary consciousness is closer to an angelic presence that draws upon the entire planet's resources—perhaps falling somewhere between J. E. Lovelock's Gaia hypothesis and the planetary beings of C. S. Lewis's space trilogy.[13] Stapledon does, however, postulate the existence of stellar and nebular beings who function independently of any such nexus of intelligent minds.[14]

Here Stapledon describes an unfolding series of higher-level compound individuals: where individual minds unite into a world mind, world minds into a planetary-system mind, and these system minds into a galactic mind.

> Constellation after constellation, the whole galaxy became visibly alive with myriads of worlds. Each world, peopled with its unique, multitudinous race of sensitive individual intelligences united in true community, was itself a living thing, possessed of a common spirit. And each system of many populous orbits was itself a communal being. And the whole galaxy, knit in a single telepathic mesh, was a single intelligent and ardent being, the common spirit, the 'I,' of all its countless, diverse, and ephemeral individuals.[15]

Stapledon extends this progression into the emergence of a *cosmic* mind, formed out of an assembly of galactic minds. Even this cosmic mind, however, discovers itself far surpassed by the "Star Maker," the Ultimate Entity. While Whitehead does not argue in favor of the actual existence of the higher-level compound individuals hypothesized by Fechner and Stapledon (except for God), these kinds of entities could rather easily be integrated into his cosmology.

---

13. For the Gaia hypothesis, see Lovelock, *Gaia*; Lewis's space trilogy includes *Out of the Silent Planet*, *Perelandra*, and *That Hideous Strength*.

14. The notion of a planetary being has generated significant support in modern times; for example, see Lovelock, *Gaia*; and Russell, *Global Brain*. Much more recent (2021) examples of interest in the possibility of experience outside the animal realm can be found in the volume 28 issues of the *Journal of Consciousness Studies*. For instance, issue 1–2 covers plant sentience, and issue 3–4 covers cosmology and consciousness, among other topics. On plant sentience, see Nani et al., "Sentience With or Without Consciousness." On cosmology and consciousness, see Sheldrake, "Is the Sun Conscious?"

15. Stapledon, *Star Maker*, 178.

Whitehead's philosophy boasts a unique metaphysical apparatus capable of addressing those critical questions that inevitably arise regarding the "compounding of consciousness," recurring to William James's apt expression. According to Reck's formulation of the problem:

> The insuperable task for the mystic is to explain why and how the simple unity fractures into multiple stories of being.
> The task for the realist is to explain how the different levels or kinds of being can be related in a hierarchically ordered cosmos. This task is nothing short of explicating the bond of being.[16]

Part of the answer to Reck's task for the mystic lies in Whitehead's "Category of the Ultimate," as it concerns the endless flow between the One and the Many. According to this category, the Many must necessarily combine into a new One, which then becomes a part of the Many waiting to be united into more Ones—and so on into eternity. Why *this* is the basic metaphysical principle of the universe, and what God's exact motivations might be for promoting a pluralistic hierarchy, remain unknowns. But Whitehead does argue that God seeks intensity of experience, and that intensity is fomented by the specialized societies that are able to flourish in a universe arranged as an organic hierarchy of structured societies—such as we find expressed in our universe through atoms, molecules, cells, and animals.

Reck's other question concerns *how* these various levels of being can be related. According to Whitehead, it is via the connections established by each occasion's feelings of past actualities, and the synthetic, creative activity of unification that occurs during the formation of every new event. A critical point concerning these interentity connections or relations is that Whiteheadian compound individuals do not share *instantaneously* in the subjective process of their parts or *subordinate societies*.[17] For example, a cellular-level event does not feel its molecular events *as* they occur, but rather only *just after* they occur. In contrast, when simultaneous sharing or *overlapping* of experience is hypothesized, it obscures any coherent notion of a plurality of real individuals. For instance, if all actualities are said to exist totally and only *within* God's experience, as is the case in some pantheistic systems, this would seem to negate the full reality of the finite entities' personal experience. They would be swallowed up (so to speak) by God. In Whitehead's metaphysics, however, the feelings synthesized by a compound individual are feelings derived from the (immediate) *past* experiences of its parts (subsocieties). Thus

16. Reck, *Speculative Philosophy*, 81.

17. Whitehead discusses subordinate societies (or sub-societies) in *Process and Reality*, 99–100, 103, 104.

the parts have of their own moments of actuality, which are only later felt by the more subsuming whole. Consequently, the process notion of hierarchy in no way conflicts with a true pluralistic interpretation of the universe, for all entities have their own moment of experience *before* their feelings enter into the experience of another being.

This is the strength of Whitehead's approach, and it is the source of the "bond of being" (Reck). By combining atomic moments of creative activity with direct sensuous contact between individual moments, Whitehead's philosophy provides the basis for both real independent existence and true connection between individuals and their societies. We have already seen in detail how this scheme provides a coherent understanding of the relationship between brain and mind, with the psychic and neuronal events working in constant, intimate interaction.

For some decades now, scientific speculation has been more seriously considering the possibility of higher-order levels of intelligent or organic being, as well as the idea of the universe as a living process. For example, Rupert Sheldrake hypothesizes a series of *morphic fields* (i.e., nonmaterial organizational patternings that regulate behavior and communication) of increasing complexity or expanse that parallel Stapledon's hierarchy of experiencing entities. According to Sheldrake, a "natural extension of the morphic field approach would be to regard living ecosystems as complex organisms with morphic fields that embrace the communities of organisms within them, and indeed to regard entire planets as organisms with characteristic morphic fields, and likewise planetary systems, stars, galaxies, and clusters of galaxies."[18] The notion of a "living universe" is highlighted by Briggs and Peat in their discussion of Jantsch's theory of an evolving universe: "In Jantsch's scenario, the universe as a whole is the ultimate of all dissipative structures—*feeding off the far-from-equilibrium environment of itself.* 'Life appears no longer a phenomenon unfolding in the universe—the universe itself becomes increasingly alive.'"[19] And in the following, the physicist Paul Davies outlines some novel ideas on the possibility of life occurring within highly unusual environmental matrices and the implications these possibilities hold for the notion of a *universal* mind.

> There is a growing appreciation among scientists that neither mind, nor life, need be limited to organic matter. In a recent extremely speculative but thought-provoking book—*Life Beyond Earth*—the possibilities for extraterrestrial life are reviewed by the physicist Gerald Feinberg and the biochemist Robert

18. Sheldrake, *Presence of the Past,* 300–301.

19. Briggs and Peat, *Looking Glass Universe,* 203 (italics and quote marks original).

Shapiro. They argue the case for life based on plasmas, electromagnetic field energy, magnetic domains in neutron stars and a variety of other bizarre systems. Now consciousness and intelligence are software concepts; it is only the pattern—the organization—that counts, not the medium for its expression. Taken to its logical conclusion, it is possible to imagine a supermind existing since the creation, encompassing all the fundamental fields of nature, and taking upon itself the task of converting an incoherent big bang into the complex and orderly cosmos we now observe; all accomplished entirely within the framework of the laws of physics. This would not be a God who created everything by supernatural means, but a directing, controlling, universal mind pervading the cosmos and operating the laws of nature to achieve some specific purpose.[20]

While Davies's "software" metaphor does not seem to be particularly helpful—especially in light of Whitehead's more encompassing organic approach that extends sentience to all actuality—the rest of his ideas regarding a "universal mind" bear a striking resemblance to Whitehead's and Stapledon's speculations on this subject. Davies's image of God, on the other hand, appears to lack some of the qualities that Whitehead—and Stapledon, in a somewhat different way—attribute to God's primordial nature. But Davies's notion of a universal mind, pervading the cosmos while working from within as a persuasive influence, is *very* Whiteheadian, especially if we view the cosmos as the body or the organic matrix of this universal mind. Even though God occupies the zenith of the hierarchy of beings in Whitehead's scheme, and God consciously feels all existence in its totality, God is *not* everything. Rather, God is one enduring individual among many, existing in the flow of process, and communicating with all other entities in existence.

The Whiteheadian, transpersonal universe that I am outlining is envisioned as an ensouled, organic hierarchy of entities and clusters of entities, interacting at all levels through mutual feeling or prehensive interconnection. Feeling and experience are pervasive, as is God's conscious synthesis of all actuality, but consciousness is not a facet of every subjective process—nor is everything consciousness.

While at first blush this cosmology might smack of primitive animism, crucial differences exist between a Whiteheadian approach and other animistic systems. Griffin has enumerated three ways in which this Whiteheadian "animism" differs from most premodern forms:

---

20. Davies, *God and the New Physics*, 210.

First, the power of perception and self-movement is not attributed to things such as rocks, lakes and suns. A distinction is
made between individuals and aggregates of individuals. Only
true individuals are self-moving, perceiving things . . .

A second way in which this postmodern animism differs
from most premodern forms is that radically different levels
of *anima* are assumed. To have experience is not necessarily to
have *conscious* experience, let alone *self-consciousness* . . .

Third, whereas most premodern animisms (Buddhism
was an exception) thought of the basic units of the world as
enduring souls, postmodern animism takes the basic units to
be momentary experiences. The ultimate units are "occasions
of experience."[21]

(What is referred to above as "postmodern animism" is elsewhere in this essay—as well as in Griffin's other writings—usually called *panexperientialism.*)

Finally, spiritual experience constitutes at least a threefold concept in
this Whiteheadian, transpersonal cosmology. Most generally, spiritual experience involves an increased apprehension of the value and importance
that lies in the depths of experience and which permeates all existence. This
dimension of spirituality continues to increase in intensity and breadth as
it matures, developing into a more conscious and consistent appreciation
of the beauty and excellence of each moment of experience—both in itself
and for the Whole. Secondly, spiritual experience describes a slow, or rapid,
heightening of feelings from the mode of causal efficacy—a heightening that
brings into one's everyday world a vivid sense of aliveness and connection
with all existence. And, thirdly, the notion of spiritual experience points to
the myriad potential encounters with entities, energies, and dimensions of
the transpersonal realm that await in the depths of our own being.

The Crisis at Hand

The core of the crisis we now face perhaps resembles nothing so much as
that of *addiction* on a massive, cultural scale.[22] In Whiteheadian terms,
the planetary organism is under siege by one of its subsociety's unbridled
pursuits. (And in a universe composed of *organisms of organisms,* the notion of a planetary body is no mere metaphor.) The Western world—and
increasingly, the rest of the human race—is treating the planet the same

21. Griffin, *God and Religion,* 88 (italics original).

22. See LaChapelle, *Sacred Land, Sacred Sex,* especially chapter 3, for a provocative
discussion of the relationship between capitalism and addiction.

way that an addict treats his or her body. The addict exploits and pollutes the body's resources to create a brief and artificial sense of vitality and well being, with a blind eye to the long-term damage being done to body and soul. Modern civilization is ravaging its environment, the world-body, yet somehow remains dangerously oblivious to this perilous situation—to the ever more apparent fact that its desperate pursuit of pleasure, excitement, escape, and so-called safety is rapidly pushing many systems of our organic matrix beyond the point of recovery. In other words, we are burning up our social and planetary resources for a short-term high, and we are in major denial of the full consequences that our actions hold for the planet, our civilization, and our souls.[23]

Page Smith explains this addictive phenomenon in terms of *presentism*, which can be seen as a long-term ramification of a worldview based on David Hume's analysis of experience:

> One of the most striking consequences of presentism is the swelling power of greed. If there is nothing but the transitory present, the impulse to seize and devour everything in sight is irresistible. Greed then becomes truly monstrous. Not simply greed for money . . . but greed for experience of every kind in every form—greed for sex, for drugs, for "things," for baubles, for transitory pleasures and exotic places, greed for any titillation of the senses.[24]

The disappearance from Western metaphysics of the philosophical reality of subjective experience and temporal process appears to have resulted finally in a culture with an insatiable craving *for* experiences, as well as a pronounced inability to truly comprehend the long-term impact this compulsive grasping is having upon our society and the world around us.

But even through our addictive denial, the writing on the wall intrudes—and the future looks bleak indeed. We must ask, with Ebenezer Scrooge,

> "Are these the shadows of things that Will be, or are they shadows of the things that May be, only?" . . .
> "Men's courses will foreshadow certain ends, to which, if persevered in, they must lead," said Scrooge. "But if the courses

---

23. It appears the modern world has become unconsciously allied with the "forces of death," as Stapledon might put it, instead of with the forces of life—in large part by powering its explosive growth with fossil fuels.

24. Smith, *Killing the Spirit*, 294.

be departed from, the ends will change. Say it is thus with what you show me!"[25]

"Certain ends" now appear foreshadowed for the human race, too. *Unless*, like Scrooge, our civilization can undergo a major redemptive process that reshapes our mode of being in the world, thereby altering the fatal trajectory upon which we seem bent.

Various attempts to correct or modify the Western worldview—as excessively materialistic, atheistic, scientistic—have been largely ineffective. Take, for example, the work of the Romantics, the transcendentalists, and the vitalists. In the last century, efforts to blunt the juggernaut of modern civilization have succumbed, on the whole, to hegemony. The insights and creative possibilities offered by sociology, anthropology, psychoanalysis, psychology, and the arts have mostly been absorbed and appropriated by mainstream Western culture without effecting a truly significant alteration in society's direction—or lack thereof. Some variation of the organismic-transpersonal cosmology outlined in this chapter may be one of our civilization's final opportunities to avoid social and ecological disaster. By generating a new coordinating vision capable of unifying and directing our scientific, social, and spiritual energies and values, this Whiteheadian, transpersonal cosmology could represent our last (or at least best) chance to redeem our future.

A Second Maturity

Placed within a proper historical perspective, this crisis in Western culture and planetary civilization can be reenvisioned as an opportunity for evolutionary advance. The traumatic times in which we now find ourselves may be reflective of a monumental reworking of the human psyche on a cultural or planetary scale. And, as Whitehead cogently notes, these periods of major transition are very disturbing to the civilizations involved: "It is the first step in sociological wisdom, to recognize that the major advances in civilization are processes which all but wreck the societies in which they occur."[26]

A number of authors have proposed theories relating to an impending psychosocial shift, or transformation, into a new phase of civilization. Nicholas J. Yonker speculates that humankind may be on the verge of entering into a "planetary age," which will constitute the fifth stage of human awareness: the four earlier stages being "the primitive age, early civilization,

25. Dickens, *Christmas Books*, 87.
26. Whitehead, *Symbolism*, 88.

the axial age, and modernity."²⁷ Stapledon conceives of this type of transition as a movement into sanity or maturity:

> We were inclined to think of the psychological crisis of the
> waking worlds as being the difficult passage from adolescence
> to maturity; for in essence it was an outgrowing of juvenile
> interests, a discarding of toys and childish games, and a dis-
> covery of the interests of adult life. Tribal prestige, individual
> dominance, military glory, industrial triumphs lost their ob-
> sessive glamour, and instead the happy creatures delighted in
> civilized social intercourse, in cultural activities, and in the
> common enterprise of world-building.²⁸

This notion of the evolution of consciousness immediately brings to mind Gerald Heard, an author that Jean Houston introduced me to many years ago. Heard was a polymath and leading figure in the formative years of the psychedelic and Eastern spirituality movements in the United States, being a major influence on Aldous Huxley, Bill Wilson, Alan Watts, and Houston Smith, among many others.²⁹ In his remarkable work *The Five Ages of Man*, Heard similarly envisions human history in terms of five stages: namely, the preindividual, the protoindividual, the midindividual, the total individual, and the postindividual, or leptoid man—the latter referring to a "leap" into a new depth awareness of being.³⁰ However, Heard views this movement into a fifth age of humanity not as a step into simple maturity but rather as a quantum jump into a *second* or full maturity. This second maturity represents a leap beyond the total individual—the "humanic, self-sufficient man"—into the postindividual, or what we might call the *transpersonal human*.

Might it not be possible that this "leap" from the self-sufficient individual to the postindividual requires a return to or reappropriation of the unresolved or repressed elements of the previous developmental stages? A regression in the service of transcending the ego, so to speak, may be necessary to achieve the level of psychological integrity required for the next evolutionary jump. Of particular importance here, according to Heard, is the crisis immediately preceding our current age, which involved the transition from an ascetic, adolescent mode of being into the modern, self-sufficient individual. In the Western world, this shift is epitomized by

27. Cobb, *Beyond Dialogue*, 38.
28. Stapledon, *Star Maker*, 132.
29. For the little-known relationship between Heard, Huxley, and Bill Wilson, see Lattin, *Distilled Spirits*.
30. Heard, *Five Ages of Man*.

the end of the Middle Ages, the establishment of the Renaissance, and the scientific revolution. The critical change in pattern occurs in the fifteenth century: the fall of Constantinople dramatically marks this shift.[31] This also marks the period when the rise of science, and the emergence of the modern attitude, began to exert a repressing influence upon most animistic, psychical, and spiritistic theories and phenomena.

In order to complete the spiral of its passage into full maturity, our culture must recover those elements and dimensions of experience that were lost during this last major upheaval in consciousness. Notably, these repressed and missing aspects of experience can be found today in Whitehead's philosophy and in the theories and techniques of transpersonal psychology. By helping to restore these lost elements of experience, a transpersonal-organic cosmology can offer much of the inspiration, vision, and methodology that Heard believes is necessary for the transcendence of humanic individuality, if we are to make the leap into the unknown realm of the human race's second maturity. I cite here some of Heard's final thoughts (written over fifty years ago) on the prospects of humankind:

> Hence, humanic man has to end. For his specific age, that was to complete man's coming of age, the age of the completely rational, analytic, objective individual, has become the age of anxiety, the age of fear, pervasive, indefinable, inexpressible, unmentionable . . .
>
> This must end in intensifying isolationism as this modernic man explores the ever expanding vastness of the macrocosmos shown by his radar telescope, and the hyperintensity of the microcosmos revealed by his hyper-X-ray electro microscope . . . He has to face the awe-ful discovery that as his mind grows he can and must apprehend how large a part he takes in composing his cosmoi. The simple dualism of the macrocosm and the microcosm was but a beginning symptom of his mind's expansion . . .
>
> Finally, this matrix mind of ours, which is in this expanding play with its matrix, the macro-environment, discovers this hyper-environ is far more like the supermind that today we find enfields our full selves than it is an unconscious machine. At the highest reach of our transpersonal mind we discover we are in percolative-osmotic, transfusive contact with a hierarchy of integrated mind-circuits. These pass up in ever intensified frequencies and through constantly increased dimensions, going beyond discrimination, definition, and the all-various

31. Heard, *Five Ages of Man*, 58–59.

modalities of time. Such a compelled conviction alone can now
deal with *Angst,* and all fear, by restoring awe. But in that vision
the human mind, made for ecstasy and infinitude, experiences a
reverence which alone can give purpose to every experience and
meaningful delight to every act.[32]

A powerful vision, indeed.

I believe that the Whiteheadian, transpersonal cosmology, as outlined
in these pages, can encompass just such a vision of human existence, of our
world, and of the universe. It is a vision capable of restoring awe, reverence, and hope, and of empowering and guiding our civilization through its
journey into the next evolutionary stage. By restoring humanity's sense of
the *universe as Home,* this revolutionary cosmology could endow us with a
renewed sense of meaning and a deeper perspective on our place in nature
and our role in the universal adventure.

According to Brian Swimme, our lack of a meaningful cosmic perspective is the central cause of the current world crisis: *"all our disasters
today are directly related to our having been raised in cultures that ignored
the cosmos for an exclusive focus on the human."*[33] This neglect of the larger
environment—and the complementary emphasis on the human level, or
on the human individual—is the final reductio ad absurdum of Humean
doubt (and Cartesian substance), resulting in the complete bifurcation of
self from the world. Ironically, we are obsessed with a self that modern
thought tells us does not really exist.

Douglas R. Hofstadter, in *Gödel, Escher, Bach,* attempts to demonstrate that all self-referencing activity must ultimately lead to paradox. In
the subliminal metaphysics of modern Western culture, with its solipsism
of the present moment, there exists only the momentary self, with no real
others. Therefore, paradoxes resulting from self-referencing systems turn
up everywhere as the metaphysical implications of our culture's philosophy are worked out with relentless precision: for example, in the hermetic
hermeneutic circle, the deconstruction of all foundations and authority,
the "observer effect" in physics, and the relativizing of all values in theories of culture and education. In our lived social psychology, it appears as
ever-increasing levels of selfishness, anxiety, loneliness, and meumingless-
ness—for if all we have is our present isolated self, then how can we know
what else is important or where we belong?

A massive shift in thinking and feeling will be needed to break free
of our culture's addictive isolation and self-centeredness and to prepare for

32. Heard, *Five Ages of Man,* 381–83.
33. Swimme, "Cosmic Creation Story," 49 (italics original).

the great adventure ahead. And this will be a *major endeavor:* namely, the adventure of transforming ourselves and our civilization in order to create a new kind of relationship between cultures and peoples, an organic relationship with our planetary matrix, and a new sense of our place in the cosmos. Whitehead's philosophy is capable of forming the foundation for just such an enterprise. When combined with the depth insights and experiential methods of transpersonal psychology, this new cosmological vision of the universe can inspire and illuminate our civilization and help direct and sustain us through the challenges and crises that lie ahead.

But if this image of an addictive culture is accurate, then how might our addictive pattern be broken? How will we effect the shift out of adolescent regression, and existential despair, into full maturity? With alcohol and drug addiction, real transformation is usually instigated in one of two ways: (1) through intervention, or (2) by hitting bottom. At the cultural level of addiction, effective intervention from the outside becomes a curious notion. Perhaps a debilitating nuclear incident or an encounter with an alien race might produce the kind of shock necessary to force a serious reevaluation and a change in our habitual beliefs and lifestyle. As far as hitting bottom goes, one wonders just how desperate our plight must be before our society will seriously undertake the fundamental changes and sacrifices that are essential for the survival of our civilization. This question becomes more troubling with every day that passes. Pressing this analogy of denial a little further, we find in the Big Book of Alcoholics Anonymous this chilling observation: "The persistence of this illusion is astonishing. Many pursue it into the gates of insanity or death."[34]

The critical idea, however, regarding recovery from addiction is the notion of a *spiritual awakening*. For regardless of how the addictive pattern is disrupted, a spiritual awakening is the key to true recovery and a transformed life. This same principle should hold for cultural levels of addiction. Our civilization will need a spiritual awakening, a transformation to the roots of our collective being, to survive the impending crisis and to pass on into the "second maturity" (Heard) of a planetary age.

In the following, Grof's description of *hitting the cosmic bottom* during powerful nonordinary experiences exemplifies the kind of transformation that might be involved in this process of spiritual awakening:

> After the subject has experienced the very depth of total annihilation and "hit the cosmic bottom," he is struck by visions of blinding white or golden light and has the feelings of enormous decompression and expansion of space. The general atmosphere

34. Alcoholics Anonymous World Services, *Alcoholics Anonymous,* 30.

is that of liberation, redemption, salvation, love, and forgiveness. The individual feels cleansed and purged, as if he has disposed of incredible amounts of "garbage," guilt, aggression, and anxiety. He experiences overwhelming love for his fellow men, appreciation of warm human relationships, solidarity, and friendship. Such feelings are accompanied by humility and a tendency to engage in service and charitable activities. Irrational and exaggerated ambition, craving for money, status, prestige, or power appear in this state to be absurd and childish desires.[35]

How might this type of spiritual experience be promulgated widely enough to make a fundamental tidal shift in societal attitudes? Interestingly, one possibility is suggested by the story of Bill Wilson, the cofounder of Alcoholics Anonymous, whose famous spiritual awakening was at least partly related to psychedelics. The hospital treatment he was receiving for alcoholism at that time included a mixture containing belladonna and henbane, both of which have psychedelic properties. Bill Wilson later had a number of LSD sessions, which he found valuable enough to consider including psychedelic sessions as an adjunct to the AA program as a way of fostering a transformative spiritual experience.[36] The current psychedelic renaissance might just be the catalyst our civilization needs for a change of mind and a change of heart. Of course, the context within which psychedelics are used and by which these experiences are integrated and understood is also vitally important.

David Griffin has suggested that the techniques found in transpersonal psychology are especially well suited to the task of supplementing subjectivity's "self-correction by consciousness," which Whitehead argues can be attained though proper philosophical reflection.[37] Put another way, philosophy furnishes the intellectual basis for consciousness to expand beyond its limited perspective and to gain insight into its own aboriginal depths of experience; transpersonal psychology provides various experiential modes of access capable of illuminating these normally unconscious elements. By joining the depth insights and psychospiritual methodology of transpersonal psychology with the metaphysical system and cosmological vision of Whitehead's philosophy, we just might shift our society's trajectory enough to make it through the impending cultural, environmental,

35. Grof, *Realms of the Human Unconscious*, 139.

36. See Lattin, *Distilled Spirits*, 190–200, for details of this surprising facet of the history of Alcoholics Anonymous.

37. Griffin, "What Is Consciousness?," 69–70.

and spiritual crises and into an entirely new mode of relating and being in the universe, and with one another.

These kinds of psychospiritual tools are desperately needed. For even though process and transpersonal perspectives both suggest that a transformation in consciousness could in some ways be shared psychically as a general shift throughout all of humanity, much of the transformative work will have to be done individual by individual. Thus, while it is exciting to dream of a psychic transfiguration spreading through the world via the ether, such as we find in Arthur Clarke's *Childhood's End* or perhaps in Teilhard de Chardin's "noosphere," we must also be prepared to trudge our own roads of happy destiny.

Adventure and Peace

In concluding *Adventures of Ideas*, Whitehead sums up why transcendent values and intuitions are necessary for a full rendering of the notion of civilization:

> The concept of Civilization, as developed up to this stage, remains inherently incomplete . . .
>
> The incompleteness of the concept relates to the notion of Transcendence, the feeling essential for Adventure, Zest, and Peace. This feeling requires for its understanding that we supplement the notion of the Eros by including it in the concept of an Adventure in the Universe as One [i.e., God's consequent nature]. This Adventure embraces all particular occasions but as an actual fact stands beyond any one of them . . . In this Supreme Adventure, the Reality which the Adventure transmutes into its Unity of Appearance, requires the real occasions of the advancing world each claiming its due share of attention. This Appearance, thus enjoyed, is the final Beauty with which the Universe achieves its justification. This Beauty has always within it the renewal derived from the Advance of the Temporal World. It is the immanence of the Great Fact including this initial Eros and this final Beauty which constitutes the zest of self-forgetful transcendence belonging to Civilization at its height.[38]

Pulsing at the heart of Civilization at its most complete manifestation is an awareness or an intuitive sense of the immanent presence of a Higher Power flowing in from the depths of reality. This immanent sense of God's being, which saves and unites all past experience into a vision of untold excellence,

---

38. Whitehead, *Adventures of Ideas*, 295–96.

provides a feeling of excitement and joy that leads beyond the self and into the greater possibilities of this adventure of existence.

What then, according to this cosmology, shall be our attitude—our mode of being and of action—regarding this Adventure? First we might re-envision our systems of morality by moving away from rigid notions of good and bad, or of perfect justice, and towards the realization of the aesthetic ideals of beauty, truth, adventure, and peace, as they manifest themselves in the harmonious complexity of intense experience. The true rewards may well be found in full participation in, and appreciation of, the great adventure of universal experience; while the true punishments are the sins of being cut off from—of blocking—one's own intuition and intensity of feeling, and of denying the world the benefits of one's inherent creative and connective potentialities. Even though the universe may be a "very beautiful and very terrible" place, as Stapledon claims, these powerful oppositions appear necessary for the intensity, novelty, and depth required of a universe characterized by a meaningful and participatory Adventure.

This idea of a *participatory adventure*—one in which all beings contribute—is of critical importance at this juncture in history. For our civilization needs both a greater spiritual imperative than can be found in the remnants of our modern Western culture, and a greater call to action in the world than that offered by most so-called New Age paradigms. If our culture were to adopt, for example, the kind of cosmological vision once voiced by Willis Harman, that "the world of matter-energy is as a dream in universal mind,"[39] then we would be in danger of falling into the predicament that Stapledon speaks of as undervaluing the life-world to such an extent that the vitality necessary for carrying on the battle of life against death is critically sapped or lost.[40] The danger posed by a withdrawal into the transcendent is especially great at this point in time. Our civilization requires not only increased spiritual awareness but also great vitality and a strong belief in the importance of Life, in order to face with courage, wisdom, and fortitude the plethora of social and planetary problems that confront us. To maximize our efforts, we must have a vision that empowers our activities in the world and imbues them with human and cosmic meaning. All the truth, beauty, and peace found in the various New Age philosophies are available within the Whiteheadian paradigm—but so is real adventure in *this* world, as well as grounding for the value, creativity, and freedom of the individual.

Aside from the more specific actions and transformations necessary to resolve humankind's current spiritual and planetary crises, what are the

39. Harman, "Postmodern Heresy," 126.
40. See Stapledon, *Last and First Men,* 298.

more general attitudes and activities appropriate to human beings within this cosmological envisionment? In *Odd John*, Stapledon suggests that the ultimate calling for a spiritual life and community is world-building and intelligent worship; while in *Last and First Men*, he writes, "And this is the goal of all living, that the cosmos may be known, and admired, and that it may be crowned with further beauties."[41] Stapledon also delineates two modes of being in the world, which he adjudges to be the "supreme achievements" of spirit: these are the "art of ecstatic fatalism"—that is, a transcendent appreciation of the beauty and ultimate rightness of everything that is—and "loyalty to the forces of life embattled against the forces of death."[42] These dual spiritual attainments, transpersonal detachment combined with passionate hope and commitment, will be crucial for meeting the challenges of the twenty-first century.

Stapledon's "ecstatic fatalism" and "loyalty to the forces of life" resemble two modes of *hope*, as delineated by William A. Beardslee: *ecstasy* and *future fulfillment*. These sources of hope both find their origin within Whitehead's analysis of the actual entity, and therefore are deeply rooted in reality. Ecstasy arises out of a mystical intuition connected to the synthetic creativity of an accomplished event. This ecstatic nature flows from "a recognition that its limited unification of the reality available to it is analogous to God's unification of reality. For this reason, there is a tendency to cling to such moments and to imagine that their indefinite prolongation would be the ultimate fulfillment."[43] Mystical and transpersonal experiences certainly can be exhilarating and alluring. Aspects of my Big Trip fall into this general category of ecstasy, and I know well the desire to rediscover this state and entertain all that it holds.

Beardslee's other mode of hope arises out of an occasion's *aim towards a goal*—its orientation towards what it is trying to become—which inherently entails an aim beyond its own satisfaction. Hope for the future finds its locus here. Beardslee describes these two sources of hope as "two possibilities for centering experience: the occasion as a detached satisfaction, or the occasion as dynamic and reaching towards a goal."[44] From a process perspective, one points to the infinity residing within each moment, the other to a never-ending future of an "infinitely enriched infinity."

These two ideals of Stapledon's—ecstatic fatalism and life-affirming enterprise—are also similar in nature to Whitehead's notions of peace and

41. Stapledon, *Last and First Men*, 284.
42. Stapledon, *Last and First Men*, 298.
43. Beardslee, *Margins of Belonging*, 115.
44. Beardslee, *Margins of Belonging*, 116.

adventure, respectively. In the final chapter of *Adventures of Ideas*, Whitehead struggles to clarify his meaning of the term *Peace*.

> The Peace that is here meant is not the negative conception of
> anæsthesia. It is a positive feeling which crowns the 'life and
> motion' of the soul. It is hard to define and difficult to speak of.
> It is not a hope for the future, nor is it an interest in present de-
> tails. It is a broadening of feeling due to the emergence of some
> deep metaphysical insight, unverbalized and yet momentous in
> its coördination of values. Its first effect is the removal of the
> stress of acquisitive feeling arising from the soul's preoccupation
> with itself. Thus Peace carries with it a surpassing of personality.
> There is an inversion of relative values. It is primarily a trust in
> the efficacy of Beauty. It is a sense that fineness of achievement
> is as it were a key unlocking treasures that the narrow nature
> of things would keep remote. There is thus involved a grasp of
> infinitude, an appeal beyond boundaries.[45]

But as beautiful and inspirational as this notion of Peace may be, Whitehead
yet cautions against making Peace a goal in itself. For true Peace is not attained by escaping life or subduing strong feeling. Rather, the active creation
of value should constitute one's primary aim, until one's ever-expanding
scope of activities and awareness opens into a natural transcendence of self:

> The experience of Peace is largely beyond the control of purpose.
> It comes as a gift. The deliberate aim at Peace very easily passes
> into its bastard substitute, Anæsthesia. In other words, in the
> place of a quality of 'life and motion,' there is substituted their
> destruction. Thus Peace is the removal of inhibition and not its
> introduction. It results in a wider sweep of conscious interest.
> It enlarges the field of attention. Thus Peace is self-control at its
> widest,—at the width where the 'self' has been lost, and interest
> has been transferred to coördinations wider than personality.[46]

The human aim, in Stapledon's vision—that is, social, cosmological,
and spiritual exploration and creation, crowned by intelligent worship—
converges with Whitehead's Adventure of creating intense, harmonious
experience embodying Truth and Beauty and tempered by transcendent
intuitions of Peace, and their revelations of ultimate meanings and of the
everlasting Value of all that is, and all that has been.

This, then, is one view of how a Whiteheadian, transpersonal cosmology might help inspire the actualization of a new order of civilization.

45. Whitehead, *Adventures of Ideas*, 285.
46. Whitehead, *Adventures of Ideas*, 285.

This cosmology offers a unifying metaphysical grounding for all human experience and activity, an expanded cosmological picture of a spiritually informed universe, and an enlarged and deepened perspective on the meaning of human existence. In addition, a Whiteheadian, transpersonal cosmology has the potential to provide the vision and the means required for humankind's transformation into its second maturity—something deeper, wiser and kinder than anything we have yet known.

A Final Interlude

Some of my fondest holiday memories are of helping decorate our Christmas tree and then basking in its ethereal glow. The childlike wonder that rapidly subsided as I entered my teens was restored first through the warm haze of alcohol intoxication and later by the more vivid enhancements provided by pot and other drugs. But in all these modes of appreciation, I found profound joy in the host of ornaments, the glistening tinsel, and the strings of lights—blinking lights especially, which cast an ever-changing tenor of color and nuance—all somehow unified into a comforting perfection by the tree itself. This image of our Christmas tree can also throw some metaphoric light on an important way that Whitehead's philosophy diverges from classic cosmological thought.

The great chain of being, the ancient theory of a hierarchical ordering of material and spiritual beings culminating in God, offers a prime example of the difference between a classical perspective and a process approach to the metaphysical and cosmological order of things. Could it be that intuitions of the great chain of being, and Huxley's and Ken Wilber's perennial philosophy of "Wholeness," are at least partly derived from a metaphysical intuition of the concrescent process, rather than solely from insights into the organization of the greater Cosmos? Is the vision of a subsuming fusion of all reality into a perfect and timeless whole, culminating in pure Being, really the ultimate picture of the universe? Or might this image be more reflective of the inner structure of the actual entity itself—as the out-of-time synthesis of the past universe into a new momentary whole—which is then projected as the eternal nature of God and Cosmos?

Returning to my holiday memory, the customary depiction of the great chain of being rather resembles a traditional Christmas tree, with the chain's higher and higher levels of being displayed aesthetically in the tree's complex patterns of decoration. In the ornaments, lights, and tinsel, we have

represented the greater and lesser spiritual beings, the stars and planets, the
streaking comets, all brought together in a beautiful unification—with God's
angelic presence at the top, presiding over All.

In a Whiteheadian rendering of this vision, the elaborately decorated
Christmas tree would symbolically convey *both* the concrescent process of
the momentary actual entities *and* the various orders of the universe's enduring societies, with God once again unifying the entire tree. However, in
a Whiteheadian cosmology, the tree would be *turned on its side,* indicating
the shape (so to speak) of every concrescence—sometimes represented as a
large wedge, open to the left, where past feeling flows directly into the newly
forming event, condensing toward the small tip of the actualized experiential occasion at the right—as well as reflecting that this "great chain" also
instantiates itself as a momentary event, which must re-create itself everlast-
ingly. The higher orders of Whitehead's organic societies, with their greater
integrating complexities, can also be represented statically by a vertical tree,
once again proceeding up towards the pinnacle occasions of God. On the
other hand, because all these societies are interflowing and in constant flux,
a horizontally aligned tree is a necessary correlate to fully capture the dynamic aspects of this universal process.

12

What Are We Going to Do?

In Chapter 10, I related how Whitehead's metaphysics, along with transpersonal psychology, helped me make sense of my third big crisis: What is reality? The rest of this chapter explores how these same ideas have helped me make sense of my other four pivotal life events.

On Purpose

Let us return once again to that dramatic moment from my blue acid trip, where immediately after watching a clock's second hand come slowly to a stop, I suddenly found myself clutching my friend's shirt and imploring him: *"What are we going to do?"* When we grasp the full nature of our dilemma, that does indeed become the question: What *do* we do? In the case of the blue acid, the question seemingly emerged out of an unexpected encounter with the abyss and the resultant confusion and terror about what one does in the face of Nothingness. However, this question also urgently reflects on the whole of one's life and our collective existence as well. How does one find, or create, meaning and purpose in one's existence—with the Abyss looming ahead of us all?

These problems first came sharply into view when my father's death made me question the purpose and value of life. As I would later come to see, there were several interweaving issues here: these included discovering a purpose in life, finding reconciliation with a universe that could be capricious and cruel, and developing a spiritual worldview that could accommodate the many, often conflicting, elements that make up our existence.

It took several years just to regain some semblance of psychological footing and emotional balance after my father's death. My first intuition of a greater purpose, you may remember, was when the thought suddenly popped into my head that *making other people happy* could be my goal. This idea is certainly far from revolutionary, but it came to me like a revelation. That this insight felt so novel is rather surprising, since it so closely resembles what you might call our family motto: *be nice*. In my teens and twenties, I may have made light of this simple axiom—which, if practiced without an open heart, can of course become merely a shallow gesture. But really, this idea is not so different from the conclusion of the lama's moving speech in the film *Lost Horizon*, when he describes the community of Shangri-la as "a way of life based on one simple rule: Be Kind!" This aim is also the essence of Jesus's message of love and the Buddha's ideal of compassion, is it not? Though once again, these attitudes and actions need to be grounded in depth of insight and understanding, as does true kindness.

The next step in my search for purpose was considerably more self-centered. Experimenting with alcohol, I realized that I could make myself *feel* and *be* very different—and I liked it a lot. During these early drinking experiences, I felt freer, more empowered, more alive, and more at ease than I ever remembered feeling in my life. I had discovered the secret to being happy, or so I thought.

This was my second shock and the real beginning of my epistemological musings. What does it mean for who we are that simply by drinking alcohol or taking drugs we can radically change our perception of ourselves and of the world? How do these nonordinary states work, and can they provide real knowledge or real change—or true satisfaction?

Process thought offers a useful way of clarifying these issues. Humans, indeed all entities, *cocreate* not only their own reality but the rest of the universe as well. The crucial caveat here is that the past universe also powerfully shapes every event. All events draw upon the influence of the past as they create their new perspectives on the world. That is why we are both cocreators of the world *and also* subject to so many constraints on how our creativity actually impacts the world. While we humans have great leeway in how we imaginatively influence our own experience, especially in nonordinary states, our ability to directly influence other entities is much more limited. I will not again rehearse the details of the Whiteheadian theory of perception and the creation of experience, which I have already described at some length. Suffice it to say that Whitehead's metaphysics, by making us cocreators of our experience, helped me understand how in nonordinary states we can radically alter our perception of the world in ways that are sometimes purely imaginary (though nonetheless fascinating), and at other times provide real insight into subtler aspects of a larger reality.

This epistemological insight has ramifications for the questions arising out of my three remaining pivotal events. First, if the universe is made up entirely of entities that cocreate reality, then it may be useful to think of God as a *co*creator as well. Second, the notion of all entities having creative influence on the world has important consequences for the problem of evil. Third, if humans cocreate their world, then the well-being of the Earth and its creatures must be at least partly our responsibility. Before describing my own resolution to the question of purpose, I will consider the possibility of a *higher power* and how evil and loss might be reconciled with such a notion.

A Higher Power?

A surprising and important revelation emerged out of my search for a comprehensive worldview. I discovered that it is not only plausible that psychic experiences convey *real* information about the world; it is even likely that this is the case. Even more importantly, I found that mystical experiences, including those of God, can be compatible with a scientific and rational understanding of the nature of the universe. In light of my third shock regarding the amazing depth and power of spiritual experience, in concert with the realization from my fourth pivotal event that these experiences could include compelling intuitions of a Higher Power, this discovery was especially significant. With Whitehead's philosophy in hand, I now had a rationally coherent way of grounding these spiritual insights, which before had appeared so contrary to those guiding principles of modern thought that I had been brought up with.

We have already seen how, in Whitehead's philosophy, mystical intuitions might emerge via direct prehensions of past events outside one's own personal order—that is, through direct nonsensory perceptions of other entities—and could thus theoretically access *any* spiritual beings that might exist, including God. This type of intuition would arise out of the depths of one's own experience, flooding consciousness with illumination and insight of a numinous nature. Mystical experiences of a more impersonal nature are also possible: for example, when an individual reaches into the experiential depths *as such* and discovers that the essence of one's own experience consists of the same kind of openness and creativity that characterizes all actuality. This insight represents the Buddhist enlightenment experience, par excellence. Finally, there is the mystical intuition that this same spiritual activity informs all entities in the universe, and that all of creation is thereby hallowed—this is the animistic revelation of a spirituality imbuing all reality.

These kinds of mystical experiences tap into three of the ultimates that have so far been delineated by process theology: God, Creativity, and World. Not coincidentally, these are also three *metaphysical* ultimates of process philosophy. Establishing an intelligible system of basic ideas that can help interpret and locate mystical experiences within a coherent universal framework is a central task of speculative philosophy:

> If you like to phrase it so, philosophy is mystical. For mysticism is direct insight into depths as yet unspoken. But the purpose of philosophy is to rationalize mysticism: not by explaining it away, but by the introduction of novel verbal characterizations, rationally coordinated.
>
> Philosophy is akin to poetry . . . Poetry allies itself to meter, philosophy to mathematical pattern.[1]

Along with this aim of rationalizing mysticism, Whitehead also seeks to create a coherent frame of reference adequate to science and religion more generally, and all other kinds of experience as well. The current controversies about religion and science, between religions, and between atheists and believers make a few words on this topic even more critical.

Even though process theology has been studied most thoroughly from a Christian standpoint, it is inherently pluralistic in that it recognizes the validity and importance of a wide range of mystical experiences and their corresponding Ultimates. Also (and one cannot emphasize too strongly the importance of this point), process theology is *naturalistic*. There are neither supernatural forces nor entities acting outside the natural order in a Whiteheadian universe. Of course, as we saw in the previous chapter, what we might call the natural order of a Whiteheadian cosmology is potentially far grander than that of the physical universe as commonly conceived today. While he came to believe that God, as a central source of order and novelty, is an intrinsic and necessary element in the universal process, Whitehead also ensured that in his philosophy God is a *part of the natural order* and acts within the laws governing the evolving cosmos. God exists *within* the ebb and flow of the universal advance. Finally, process philosophy provides a metaphysical understanding of the universe and reality that makes possible an in-depth discourse *between* all religions and the sciences as well. There is ample room in this conversation for nonbelievers too—a number of prominent process thinkers are nontheistic or atheistic. Process thought lives under an expansive roof.

Before considering how a process notion of God helps overcome Whitehead's ultimate evil—*perpetual perishing*—I want to comment on the current preoccupation with contrasting spirituality with religion: "I am spiritual, but not religious." Besides indicating a lack of participation in the activities and beliefs of a particular religion, I think this dichotomy is often drawn in response to adverse early experiences with one's

---

1. Whitehead, *Modes of Thought*, 174.

religious upbringing, or as an avenue of escape from modernity's logical and scientific critiques of religion and God. But religion at its best is *spirituality in community*: a spiritual community. Since from a process view humans are essentially beings-in-community, it is antithetical to have an authentic spirituality that does not take community seriously into account. Also, spirituality practiced in isolation faces many dangers, not the least of which is narcissistic distortion, a problem recognized and addressed by spiritual communities throughout history, be they Buddhist temples, Christian monasteries, or yogic ashrams.

I do not mean to imply that distancing oneself from religion is in any way unacceptable. Whitehead saves some of his toughest criticism for religion and its dogmas. (He is equally hard on scientism and its dogmas.) Furthermore, early on in *Religion in the Making*, Whitehead famously writes: "Religion is what the individual does with his own solitariness."[2] Here, I believe, Whitehead is pointing to the personal spiritual dimension and the direct experience of religious sentiment and truth. But notice that he still calls it *religion*. What the world needs now is not more individuals honing their own idiosyncratic spirituality, but rather spiritually informed people working together in community to help solve our world's problems. And that effort I think of as religious.

I will make one more comment in defense of religion, which so often seems to take the rap for many of the evils of civilization. While it is true that religion has to bear much responsibility for many dark turns in history, so do science and technology, nationalism, economism, and (so-called) rationality: consider Hiroshima, the world wars of Europe, and the devastation of Indigenous people, all of which were considered rationally justifiable at one time. Religion admittedly needs to incorporate new modes of thought into its worldview and morality, drawing especially from paradigmatic breakthroughs in scientific knowledge and rational understanding. But modernity in turn needs to more fully recognize the vital importance of values, spirituality, and community. This is where speculative philosophy can make a significant contribution, as it finds its "chief importance" in fusing science and religion into a coherent worldview.[3]

2. Whitehead, *Religion in the Making*, 16. Grof makes a similar claim about the personal nature of spirituality: "Spirituality involves a special kind of relationship between the individual and the cosmos and is, in its essence, a personal and private affair" (Grof, "Revision and Re-enchantment," 158).

3. The phrase "chief importance" comes from Whitehead, *Process and Reality*, 15: "It attains its chief importance by fusing the two, namely, religion and science, into one rational scheme of thought."

I should also note that I have not attended church with any regularity since I was a teenager despite my obvious interest in spiritual matters. The ceremonies and rituals no longer touch me in a deep way—though I do still love hearing the hymn "Harvest Home." I since have found groups outside of the church that fulfill needs for shared spirituality and community. I suspect that our world will need many such multiform spiritual communities, coordinated by a shared vision and common goals, working alongside recognized religious bodies in order to adequately address the planetary crisis now facing us.

The Final Problem

If there is a God—in particular, a loving God—how do we reconcile this fact with a world filled with dissolution and loss? This question takes me back to where I started, to my first great shock: my father's sudden death.

This problem is deeply intertwined with the inevitable loss of things through time: "The ultimate evil in the temporal world is deeper than any specific evil. It lies in the fact that the past fades, that time is a 'perpetual perishing.'"[4] Because of the essential structure of the creative advance, each new moment fades away into the mists of time.[5] The evil of this perpetual perishing is poignantly expressed in the final words spoken by Roy, the last surviving renegade "Replicant" in the film *Blade Runner*. Struggling against his imminent demise, Roy mourns the extinction of his remembrances of the many fantastic events he has beheld: "All those moments will be lost in time, like tears in rain."[6] Death is merely an extreme case of this constant fading away.

Existentially we can try to take comfort in the ever-new adventures that are the corollary of the fading past, and relish that we had these passing experiences. As Dr. Seuss is reputed to have observed: Don't cry because it's over—smile because it happened. Whitehead, however, felt that a deeper resolution of this ultimate evil was required if the universe was to be understood as the truly *friendly* place that William James hoped for. A story from my mother comes to mind here—one she told me about her Great Decisions discussion group (a group in an ongoing program of foreign-affairs

---

4. Whitehead, *Process and Reality*, 340.

5. What quickly perishes is every event's *subjective immediacy*. Cobb also notes that perpetual perishing is the "ultimate" evil in Whitehead's scheme in the metaphysical sense—that is, it is inherent to the nature of things (Cobb, *Whitehead Word Book*, 71–72).

6. Scott, dir., *Blade Runner*.

discussion groups) back in the 1950s. At the end of their sessions together, the leader asked, "When the last fire of the last tribe of humans goes out, will it all have been worthwhile?" She was the *only* one who answered yes. Along with revealing my mother's innate optimism, I believe this story is indicative of the despair of the modern mind deprived of a sense of some kind of higher redemptive process—some kind of enveloping sense of meaning.

Whitehead's resolution to this problem is found in God's consequent nature: that is, God's conscious reception, transmutation, and preservation of all that occurs. *Ultimately,* nothing is lost, for all is saved and transformed within God's being. The experiences of the universe's myriad entities not only enrich God, but they also serve as creative possibilities for future events, when newly arising occasions draw upon God's inspiration for their own becoming. Objective immortality, or permanence, then is the final remedy for the bitterness of a world filled with inevitable loss.

This sentiment captures that deep human desire to know that there is some aspect of reality that includes a genuine sense of *forever*—something transcending the flux and process of the World and its attendant uncertainties and insecurities. For Whitehead, this Forever is found in the "Everlastingness" of God's consequent nature, which preserves and cherishes all that has been. Whether or not this preservation includes a *subjective* participation in God's being is something yet to be revealed, but in the meantime, we may be consoled by the knowledge that our existence contributes not only to those beings sharing our contemporary world, and to future generations, but also to that ultimate and eternal Adventure: God, the Universe as One. Whitehead concludes *Adventures of Ideas* with this very sentiment:

> At the heart of the nature of things, there are always the dream of youth and the harvest of tragedy. The Adventure of the Universe starts with the dream and reaps tragic Beauty. This is the secret of the union of Zest with Peace—That the suffering attains its end in a Harmony of Harmonies. The immediate experience of this Final Fact, with its union of Youth and Tragedy, is the sense of Peace. In this way the World receives its persuasion towards such perfections as are possible for its diverse individual occasions.[7]

In these final thoughts, Whitehead points to a human-level answer to the problem that *the past fades.* This answer is played out in every unfolding moment, each of which recapitulates cosmic creation as a whole. Each moment of our becoming arises out of God's creative love, has its adventure of self-creation, and ends with its reception by God's compassionate

---

7. Whitehead, *Adventures of Ideas,* 296.

and preserving love. And more than that, it contributes also to the future of all beings. Thus, by drawing on the relevant past to creatively transform the present and contribute to a better future, we participate in the Great Adventure that is life's counter-valence to the necessity of lost relationship and achievement.

My father's death ushered me into these considerations earlier than many, and sadly, later than some. Given all this time and study, have I learned to live with the knowledge of the inevitability of death and loss? Recently my youngest sister, two very dear friends, and a beloved dog—four beings that truly seemed to love me unconditionally—all died suddenly and more or less unexpectedly. I was greatly saddened and mourned them all, and was very grateful for having them in my life. Perhaps some part of this acceptance was merely due to something like what William Powell relates to Lauren Bacall in *How to Marry a Millionaire.* When Bacall is taken aback by how calmly Powell's character handles her standing him up at the altar, Powell explains, "No, that's just one of the few advantages of age. Disappointments become a normal part of life."[8] I hope that my acceptance is based much more on having a greater appreciation of this universal process in which we live than merely on an acquired resignation to the inevitability of loss. And I like to think that what I have learned from Whitehead and transpersonal psychology has helped me come to accept loss without having my faith in the goodness of life and the universe too badly shaken.

Here are two of the more appealing alternatives I have encountered concerning that great final Mystery: what, if anything, comes next? Charles Hartshorne, one of Whitehead's greatest students, thought that our existence should be understood as a limited temporal process occurring within the larger universal process, as life cycles that naturally have a beginning and an end, as our allotted time of adventure within the Great Adventure. This process-friendly way of coming to terms with death as our subjective end might be thought of as a kind of Whiteheadian stoicism. Regardless, this stoic acceptance of our finitude is softened by the understanding that all our achievements are preserved fully within God's memory—even after death we continue to contribute to the creative advance of the universe.

On the other hand, David Griffin has taken another tack by carefully examining the empirical evidence for survival of physical death. In his remarkable *Parapsychology, Philosophy, and Spirituality,* Griffin first makes the philosophical case for the possibility of the human psyche or soul existing outside its bodily matrix, as this seems a prerequisite for any survival hypothesis. Whitehead himself suggests on occasion that purely spiritual

8. Negulesco, dir., *How to Marry and Millionaire.*

entities are a possibility within his metaphysics (but *not* a necessity, unless God is characterized as such). After demonstrating from a process philosophical perspective how the psyche might exist outside the body, Griffin then combs through the evidence from cases involving mediums, possession, reincarnation, apparitions, and out-of-body experiences, all of which bear directly on this issue. Griffin's keen analysis of the implications of the weightiest evidence from these categories leads him to conclude that four of them (*not* possession) "contained phenomena that were in themselves strongly suggestive of survival," and that "taken together they provide an even stronger case."[9] (This, by the way, is a good example of how the findings of transpersonal psychology can make an important contribution to Whitehead's cosmology—by deepening and broadening our understanding of the spiritual dimensions of our universe.)

Both Griffin's and Hartshorne's views seem reassuring in their own ways. With Hartshorne, we have a stoic acceptance of the natural cycle of life imbedded within a universal meaning. In Griffin, we find a rationally arrived at hope for more adventures yet to come awaiting us in the Unknown.

And what of the reality of my own death? I will not pretend that when the specter of my demise once again suddenly appears over my shoulder that I will not frantically hope to escape one more time. Yet, in my more reflective and peaceful moments, I sometimes return to one of my earliest memories from my time at The Cottage, my grandparents' cozy house on the shores of Green Bay. I am walking at night with my family down a country lane; there are trees and a few houses along one side and a small woods on the other. The moon and stars are shining brightly—it is all magical, and I stare in wonder. This is how I like to imagine death: being surrounded by loving companions in whom you have total trust, facing the vast universe in Awe.

The Problem of Evil

A cosmology that includes a fully evolving universe and an involved cosmic intelligence, in the manner set out by Whitehead, is also helpful for making sense of the problem of evil. For along with the metaphysical evil of Loss, there are the manifold individual evils that befall our world, such as natural disasters, tragic accidents, individual cruelties and wrongdoings, and the myriad forms of ill health. Understandably, many are led to question the reality of God, for it is difficult to reconcile so much tragedy and suffering happening under the purview of a loving Higher Power. From a process perspective, these evils are understood to be a necessary

9. Griffin, *Parapsychology, Philosophy, and Spirituality,* 264, 266.

correlate to the real freedom and creativity afforded to the universe's many creatures. Olaf Stapledon cogently expresses the essence of this viewpoint in *Star Maker*, where he writes, "Whereas in former ages tragedy had been commonly thought of in terms of physical pain and premature death, now it was conceived more readily as resulting from the clash and mutual yearning and mutual incompatibility of diverse personalities."[10] This is another reason why Stapledon describes the "nature of existence" as "very beautiful, though also terrible."[11]

In the following, John Cobb Jr. clarifies this process view regarding the necessity of evil in a universe containing real novelty, freedom, and complex beings:

> If God is understood as that factor in the universe which makes for novelty, life, intensity of feeling, consciousness, freedom, and in man for genuine concern for others, and which provides that measure of order which supports these, we must recognize that he is also responsible in a significant way for the evil in the world. If there were nothing at all or total chaos, or if there were only some very simple structure of order, there would be little evil—there would instead be the absence of both good and evil. Earthquakes or tornadoes would be neither good nor evil in a world devoid of life. Only where there are significant values does the possibility of their thwarting, their conflict, and their destruction arise. The possibility of pain is the price paid for consciousness and the capacity for intense feeling. Sin exists as the corruption of the capacity for love. Thus God by creating good provides the context within which there is evil.[12]

As Cobb points out, however, God *also* works to inspire the world so as to strengthen the good, while sharing in the suffering that evil brings. Also, it is vital to bear in mind that since God, from a process perspective, always acts persuasively and never coercively, God *cannot* act unilaterally to prevent evil acts or events, much less cause them directly.

A rather similar view on the problem of evil comes out of Stanislav Grof's psychedelic cosmology, where evil is seen as necessary for the advancement of the cosmic adventure: "The final understanding of evil always seems to involve its appreciation and acceptance as an indispensable instrument in the cosmic process. The recognition that evil is the price that has to be paid for the creation of the existing experiential realities, and

10. Stapledon, *Star Maker*, 135.

11. Stapledon, *Last and First Men*, 285.

12. Cobb, *God and the World*, 96.

that it is not only a useful, but necessary ploy in the universal drama tends to bring forgiving and reconciliation."[13]

Whitehead's philosophy differs sharply from some existentialists' assessment of the *absurdity* of human existence: that is, the view that our lives are unjust, lead only to death, and are ultimately meaningless. For from a Whiteheadian perspective, this bleak outlook is rooted in several of modernity's questionable assumptions—for example, the metaphysical isolation of the Humean individual and the "death of God." Therefore this assessment is essentially a reaction to a skewed or misguided view of existence rather than reflecting the true nature of things. (As we have seen, the Whiteheadian human being is very different from the "Humean being.") According to the philosophy of organism, each moment of existence is essentially an achievement of value and meaning both for the event in question and for future entities as well. Simply to exist, or to be, is to be valuable, to create value for others, and to contribute value to the universal Adventure. Furthermore, all entities are in a continuous *intimate relationship* with their world and all other beings, including God, even though much of this depth connection often occurs outside of conscious awareness.

However, there will still be elements of absurdity to human existence. Charles Hartshorne points out the kind of absurdity or irony that naturally goes along with increasing levels of human freedom and awareness:

> As just depicted, our life is not necessarily absurd in the sense that nothing matters because it all ends in nothingness. Even the extermination of life on this planet would, some of us believe, destroy nothing of the already actualized experiences of animals through billions of years as preserved in cosmic awareness. Nor is life absurd because no perfect justice, meaning no exact system of rewards and punishments, obtains. For such justice is in principle itself an absurdity, not a valid ideal. It assumes no freedom unless that of God, dealing with mere lifeless puppets for whom there would be no problem of justice and indeed no problems. Life cannot be absurd simply because an absurd ideal would render it so.
>
> Life is absurd only in the relative sense that the opportunities afforded by highly reflective creatures must be paid for (and this is a logical must) by the risks of the extra degree of freedom inherent in such reflectivity.[14]

13. Grof, "LSD and the Cosmic Game," 10.

14. Hartshorne, *Insights and Oversights,* 335–36.

I believe the latter is a species of absurdities that we can all learn to live with, though sometimes awareness of these associated "risks" is hard to bear.

Once my sense of existential (and drug-related) angst had been largely relieved, and my sense of meaning and connection began to be restored, another major challenge emerged. What contribution could I make to the larger Adventure?

My Final Problem

The final problem of my youth was *what to do* once I had gotten sober, now that I was no longer exploring (and escaping) reality through mind- and mood-altering substances. I found, as many people in recovery do, that the adventure of life itself, which in my addiction had come to seem rather pointless and empty, was now brimming with meaning and purpose. I felt similar to how George Bailey felt in *It's a Wonderful Life* after witnessing what the world would have been like without him. All that one had found essentially flawed and lacking becomes imbued with importance and beauty.

But that does not mean that life is easy. In early recovery, my mother sent me M. Scott Peck's book *The Road Less Traveled*, whose opening line is, "Life is difficult." Sobriety is certainly no exception to that rule. For one thing, I went through an extended withdrawal period of many months, primarily due to the Valium I had been taking. But as a friend of mine in Atlanta was fond of saying: Recovery is *not* an easy way of life, but it *is* a better way of living.

"A Vision for You," a chapter in the Big Book of Alcoholics Anonymous,[15] ends with the phrase "as you trudge the Road of Happy Destiny."[16] For a long time, I found this a rather grim way of portraying the journey of sobriety, until one day when I discovered it can mean "to walk with purpose." Then I understood. One thing that has made my trudging easier is having at hand the Whiteheadian, transpersonal worldview described in this book. It has helped me to think through problems more clearly, to more accurately assess my feelings and intuitions, and to evaluate situations with greater balance and composure—if I do say so myself.

Having always been curious about the big picture, I could not help but wonder about the broader *practical* implications of what I have learned. How might these ideas from process philosophy and transpersonal

---

15. Alcoholics Anonymous World Services, *Alcoholics Anonymous*, 151–64. This work is often casually referred to as the Big Book because of the physical size of the first edition.

16. Alcoholics Anonymous World Services, *Alcoholics Anonymous*, 164.

psychology, which helped me to understand my experiences and to reconcile my place in the universe, also help our civilization with the intellectual, social, and global problems it now faces? Without a guiding and orienting vision and a basic sense of how reality works, it is difficult to know how best to proceed. Process philosophy and transpersonal psychology have provided the map and compass I needed.

John Cobb Jr., who has far more experience and expertise in employing this process compass than I do, has been warning the world about the environmental crisis since the early 1970s. Perhaps his most evocative way of communicating the nature of our ethical and practical dilemma is his *runaway train* analogy, a precursor of sorts to the recent Korean film *Snowpiercer*.[17]

Cobb likens our global situation today to that of a group of people who are traveling across country enjoying a comfortable train ride. To their dismay, several of the passengers discover that the train has become a runaway. Making matters all the more dire, they also learn that somewhere ahead the railway bridge over a deep gorge is out. If the train reaches that chasm, it will mean complete disaster for all on board. So as not to alarm the other, unknowing passengers, they quietly investigate various ways to stop the train— but to no avail. This leaves the faction who knows about the train's dangerous situation divided over what to do next. Some want to immediately alert the rest of the passengers in the hope that as a group they can find a way to at least minimize the impending catastrophe. Others argue that since it seems that nothing can be done, they should let the people onboard enjoy their trip as long as possible and not cause a pointless panic—and, who knows, perhaps something will come along to save everyone! At this stage of the environmental crisis, we might add that there are also those trying to convince everyone that the bridge really isn't out at all, and the train is not a runaway. Or even if the worst is true, it is just "nature's way" or God's will.[18]

---

17. In his writings, Cobb uses a similar analogy involving an ocean liner in danger of sinking. By highlighting the unequal conditions existing between the various classes on board, Cobb also elucidates how climate change imposes a disproportionate burden on individuals and countries with fewer economic resources, as well as how existing social problems are exacerbated in a unfolding crisis situation. See, for example, Cobb, *Sustainability*, 127–29.

18. Let me add that I am not in sympathy with the perspective I sometimes hear bandied about, even from friends I highly respect, that they are not overly concerned about the future of our world, because even if there is a horrible collapse, Nature will eventually recover. "Eventually" indeed! This cavalier attitude upsets me greatly: how can such an appalling degree of tragic and unnecessary loss of evolutionary achievement be acquiesced to so easily, be taken so lightly?

From the perspective of addiction, these various attempts to avoid reality all fall under the rubric of *denial.* As is the case with individual addiction, this kind of denial can have lethal consequences. The way out of denial and addiction is to acknowledge reality, seek help, and take constructive action. So, like Cobb, I believe the responsibility of those on the train who are in the know is to try to make the rest of the passengers fully aware of their plight and to marshal everyone's combined efforts towards creating the best outcome possible, no matter how desperate things may appear.

Our civilization *is* aboard a runaway train of global climate change, the potential disaster being accelerated by ever more damaging levels of pollution, resource depletion, and overpopulation. As if that is not worrisome enough, one must factor in the threat posed by weapons of mass destruction, which governments will certainly be tempted to employ as their own people struggle more and more with the cumulative effects of these other problems. Any one of these challenges could turn out to be what knocks out that bridge ahead of us. Taken together, the outlook is grim.

But there is *hope.* John Cobb likes to say that he is not optimistic, but he is hopeful. His hopefulness comes from his faith that God is always working to help make the best out of whatever happens. But we humans, as cocreators of our world, must do our part too. And here we need to take the role of *protagonist,* especially as we have already excelled in the part of antagonist in this tragedy.

An unusual transpersonal experience many years ago warned me that Western *men* in particular should step up to the plate. This is because we have been responsible for most of the past miscalculations that are now leading to global disaster, and also because many of us are *still* turning a blind eye to the crisis that is staring us squarely in the face.

Ritual at Hollyhock

One of my most compelling nondrug experiences occurred near the end of a three-year training group in holotropic breathwork led by Stan and Christina Grof. This particular retreat was being held on a remote island in Desolation Sound, between Vancouver Island and mainland British Columbia. Towards the end of our twelve days together, Stan suggested that the women in the group put on a ritual for the men, and the men reciprocate for the women.

I don't recall all of the ritual that the women created for us. The parts I do remember were surprisingly powerful, especially since I do not usually fall into trance or enter altered states easily—at least not without a lot of chemical assistance. At one point in the ceremony, the men were seated in a circle, facing outward; the women sat down in front of us, slowly moving around the circle to encounter various partners. The women were dressed up in diverse attire, creating a curious atmosphere, given that this was taking place inside a dome-like structure in the woods, which lent a tribal feel to the proceedings. As they progressed around the circle, some of the women applied makeup to the men or interacted in other ways that emerged out of the process. With two of the women in particular, something remarkable happened. As I watched ever more intently, their faces and clothes transformed into other guises belonging to foreign times and places. One woman became a Turkish harem girl, while the other changed into an American Indian. Their faces melted and shifted before my eyes to create different personas of various ages. The encounter with the American Indian princess was particularly significant for me.

As she decorated my face, I seemed to experience an opening into the psychological depths of tribal life, which threw light on traditional gender roles. I directly intuited that the primal function of males in tribal society has been to protect and provide for the group—to make sure that the tribe is safe from outside threats and well cared for as a whole. Although such gender stereotypes may now appear quaint or even offensive, I had the sense that this function is deeply embedded within the primordial human psyche. As this insight crystallized in my awareness, I suddenly understood at least part of why men today are often confused and frustrated about their lives, and why women are often angry, scared, and bitter towards men. We all sense at some deeper level that our society and environment are falling apart, and that no one is adequately addressing these life-threatening problems. We are *not* safe; the men are not doing what needs to be done to protect the tribe.

These ideas flooded my mind as I watched this beautiful woman in front of me become all women, everywhere, who need men's help in preserving our world and our civilization. Men have lost their vision and their mission and are failing their people. Their impotence and misdirected anger come from not rightly seeing the reality before them, and thus not knowing how to adequately protect and serve their tribe. Perhaps some of the current culture wars and battles over religion can in large part be read as misguided efforts to defend one's own tribe out of parochial sentiment. Unfortunately, by diverting attention and energy in often unproductive directions, these actions can indirectly exacerbate the fundamental threats to the planet and to humanity at large: to our *planetary tribe*.

I should emphasize that my vision of the tribal role of men is pertinent only for understanding some of the complex unconscious dynamics that are making it difficult for society to confront and face the challenges threatening our world. The work of saving our civilization and the planet is a task that will require a grand unified effort of women and men, of all races and creeds and nationalities, joined together in the willingness to sacrifice and toil for the common good.

Most of what has seemed to work so well in the past for modern Western Civilization is now destroying us. Modernity has become unconsciously allied with the "forces of death," as Stapledon might put it, instead of with the forces of life.[19] The deadly nature of our addictive dependency on a no-longer-viable way of life is a difficult thing to realize—and even harder to change. If we are to face head-on the enormous problems that confront and confound us, we must mobilize all our resources and create a new vision for the future and a plan capable of attaining that future. To voice what should by now be obvious—at least surely to our leaders—we must clearly see and define the dangers before us, find the courage to understand and do what must be done, and bravely accept the necessary sacrifices for the sake of future generations and our world. No matter what these sacrifices may entail, I am convinced we will be happier and more truly satisfied facing reality squarely and living in tune with that deeper reality.

If this sounds like a drum call for altruism, it definitely is—altruism for all those future generations yet to come. And real altruism does exist. Attempts to brand all human actions as ultimately selfish or self-serving seem wrongheaded to me, and often involve circular reasoning, such as the position that if any enjoyment or satisfaction is obtained from one's deeds, this means that it was *really* done from selfish motives. Just because an action involves some form of enjoyment does not mean that it is not *also* altruistic. Enjoying each moment of creative contribution is completely natural. For Whitehead, *enjoyment* is essential to the nature of experience—the manifold forms of pleasure are all manifestations of a more primary value arising out of the appreciation of the feeling of sheer becoming. Whitehead calls the culmination of an occasion its *satisfaction* for the same reason that he refers to actual occasions and the creative advance in terms of enjoyment and adventure: these terms are descriptive of paradigmatic

19. By powering its explosive growth with fossil fuels, the modern world has invited our own destruction. Grof shares this intriguing psychedelic insight into how these substances, as frozen death, are now releasing that death onto the planet: "I understood that petroleum—immense deposits of mineralized fat of biological origin—had escaped the mandatory cycle of death and birth that the world of living matter is subjected to. However, the element of death was not completely avoided, it was only delayed. The destructive plutonic potential of death continues to exist in petroleum in a latent form and waits for its opportunity as a monstrous time-bomb" (Grof, *Adventure of Self-Discovery*, 64).

dimensions of experience. Contributing to the future of other events always includes our own future as *one* of those others, but that does not significantly undercut the altruistic motives also associated with many of our actions. Raising one's children is the most obvious, and perhaps the best, example of how we can derive enjoyment through altruistic contributions to the future. The effort is immense and the reward is primarily the enjoyment of paying forward the process of life.

So what am I to do; what are *we* going to do? First and foremost we need a change of heart and a change of mind. By a change of heart, I mean a spirituality capable of carrying us through the difficult times ahead. This must be a spirituality that is lived and felt, not detached principles or an abstract morality. We must feel a moral compass rising up from the depths, and a spiritual feeling that inspires and enlivens our actions and our thinking alike. But we also need a vision and a guiding paradigm to galvanize and coordinate our efforts and our planning.

Process thought offers the most useful guiding paradigm I know of. A vision that can fully inspire us to the task ahead is still being incubated, but I believe it may resemble something like the one offered by Olaf Stapledon in his great work of speculative fiction, *Star Maker*. (See Chapter 11, above, for one possible version of this vision.) And a sophisticated lived spirituality, providing experiential access to an ensouled cosmology, could be nurtured and articulated through the methods of transpersonal psychology. This chapter concludes by exploring some elements of a postmodern spirituality that might result from drawing on a process, transpersonal understanding.

Spirituality

The second step of Alcoholics Anonymous (AA) reads, "Came to believe that a power greater than ourselves could restore us to sanity." Newcomers who may have trouble accepting any conventional notion of God as a "higher power" are often advised that they can choose almost anything as their higher power: a mountain, a tree, a river, or their AA group itself. The aim is to initiate a move away from self-centered isolation. This is an apt recommendation for the world at large, which has experienced a progressive erosion of community, loss of connection to nature, and a corresponding shift towards the individualistic values of economism, as in, "It's the economy, stupid."

In a particularly bitter irony, that sense of belonging, community, and connection to oneself and the world—what the addict often seeks so desperately through drugs and alcohol—is precisely what is stripped away by the addicting substances that once seemed to fulfill those longings so brilliantly. What once gave pleasurable release slowly turns into the mere avoidance of pain. As Whitehead insightfully points out, the constant seeking of "peace" rapidly devolves into a diminution of feeling: *anesthesia*.[20]

In her book *Shikasta*, Doris Lessing evocatively refers to the world's sorely diminished feeling of deep connectedness in terms of the loss of SOWF, "substance of we feeling." This might also be thought of as a lack of belonging, of not feeling at *home* in the world, as a paradise lost, or simply as *alienation*. (In an ironic twist, Lessing portrays beings from another world or dimension—"aliens"—as the ones trying to help restore Earth's supply of SOWF.) I have described this problem of isolation as essentially a lack of depth of *feeling*, in Whitehead's metaphysical sense. This is one of the reasons I am so respectful of psychedelics: they have the potential to open up our psyches to much greater *depths of feeling*, granting access to a world that feels like Home, like heaven on earth.

After one night of heavy tripping, I wandered out into the backyard of my childhood home, basking in the afterglow. The simple act of watching the sunrise was transformed into an exquisite, almost painfully beautiful experience. It is impossible to adequately convey the feeling of joy and sense of beauty evoked by the dew upon my feet, the singing of the birds, the vibrant colors in the sky, the tiny violets poking out from the grass. Our yard at dawn became an archetypal exemplification of the sentiment expressed in "Morning Has Broken": an embodiment of paradise in its ever-renewing glory.

A similar sentiment can also manifest in a more general form, when Jesus's admonition to "love one another" becomes a natural mode of being.[21] When you trust everyone you meet like they are family; when you care for all things like they are your own cherished belongings; when you treat nature like it is your beloved garden to tend and enjoy, and wild animals as though they are your dear pets (to be loved and respected and, of course, protected as wild creatures): then wherever you go, you are always at Home.

It may sound somewhat fanciful to opine that a shift in "feeling" could bring about such a dramatic kind of reevaluation or transformation of our place in the world. Stanislav Grof, however, has repeatedly seen exactly this type of psychic modification occur throughout the course of his psychotherapeutic research.

20. "The deliberate aim at Peace very easily passes into its bastard substitute, Anaesthesia" (Whitehead, *Adventures of Ideas*, 285).

21. John 15:12: "This is my commandment, that ye love one another, even as I have loved you" (King James Version).

> In the most general sense, emotional and psychosomatic symp-
> toms indicate a blockage of the flow of energy and ultimately
> represent potential experiences in a condensed form that are
> trying to emerge . . .
>
> The manifest clinical condition of an individual is not a
> global reflection of the nature and over-all amount of that per-
> son's unconscious material . . . How the individual experiences
> himself and the world is much more dependent on a specific,
> selective focus and tuning, which makes certain aspects of
> unconscious material readily experientially available. Individ-
> uals who are tuned in to various levels of negative biographi-
> cal, perinatal, or transpersonal governing systems perceive
> themselves and the world in a generally pessimistic way and
> experience emotional and psychosomatic distress. Conversely,
> those persons who are under the influence of positive dynamic
> governing systems are in a state of emotional well-being and
> optimal psychosomatic functioning.[22]

One's entire approach to life can change remarkably as the result of a shift
from a "negative governing system"—a dominant constellation of negative memories, emotions, and energies, similar to a Jungian complex—to
one more positive in nature.[23] These governing systems seem often to be
rooted psychodynamically in life's earliest experiences, especially those
involving life in the womb and from the birth process itself. Changing
the deeply set habitual attitudes founded on these primordial unconscious
patterns can have a tremendously transformative and revitalizing impact
on the adult psyche.

Western civilization could benefit deeply from a profound psychological reorientation along these lines to help aim our efforts and our way
of being itself in directions that protect and cherish our world, and one
another. Having a mode of being in the world that takes satisfaction in
appreciating life's basic gifts would not hurt either; in fact, it is probably
vital to our survival:

> When one experiences the shift from negative to positive
> perinatal matrices, the general degree of zest in life and the
> ability to enjoy life increases considerably. It becomes possible
> to draw satisfaction from the present moment and from many

22. Grof, *Beyond the Brain*, 355, 350.

23. Grof explains his theory of governing systems on pages 350–51 of *Beyond the
Brain*, and describes some of the psychological and social implications related to nega-
tive and positive governing systems and perinatal matrices in his epilogue to *Beyond the
Brain*, especially pages 429–31.

ordinary situations and functions, such as eating, sex, simple human interactions, work activities, art, music, play, or walks in nature . . . In this state of mind, it becomes obvious that the ultimate measure of one's standard of living is the quality of the experience of life and not the quantity of achievements and material possessions.

Together with these changes, the individual develops a deep sense of the critical importance of synergy, cooperation, and harmony, as well as natural ecological concerns . . . The concept of human existence as a life-and-death struggle for survival gives way to a new image of life as a manifestation of the cosmic dance or divine play.[24]

These major psychological shifts described by Grof were observed at the individual level of the human psyche. Impacting the wider culture will require a much larger-scale effort, such as a widespread use of experiential psychotherapeutic and psychospiritual techniques. Many of these methods are already widely available, including a variety of traditional spiritual practices and modern psychotechnologies.

Transpersonal psychology is important for teaching us how we can *feel* and *live* this new cosmology—not only for charting it. Techniques from the old and new mind-expansion technologies are vital to this new spiritual vision. It is not enough to understand that the universe is the "kingdom of God"; we must also *feel* that it is our Cosmic Home. Accessing those subtle feelings from the depths is what grants us real openness to a spiritual presence and guidance, God's love and compassion, a sense of connection to all things, and an intuition of the sacredness of all that is. Without these deep feelings, our religious and moral convictions ring hollow and can become intolerant, rigid, self-serving, blind, or reduced to a set of rules and judgments. Direct encounters with the kinds of transpersonal experiences Grof describes offer one powerful source of inspiration for the work ahead by showing us an ultimate meaning behind it all, and within it as well. Given the nature of the crisis facing our civilization, the discerning use of psychedelics may well be necessary in order to reach enough people in time and with sufficient power, both for healing and for transformation.

As David Ray Griffin has suggested in *Parapsychology, Philosophy, and Spirituality*, an experiential spirituality approach could help reinvigorate religion. Such a revival is especially needed in the liberal Protestant tradition, which has lost touch with so much of the experiential depths and transpersonal dimensions of spirituality. Incorporating this kind of

---

24. Grof, *Beyond the Brain*, 430–31.

experiential methodology and mystical depth could make religion once again a lived *spiritual adventure.*

Spiritual adventure is a deep human craving; Jung spent much of his career making just that point. Much of the drug use in our society can be seen as a search for new modes of perceiving and feeling reality in order to transcend our current worldview's inadequacies and failures. However, drugs can also become an escape from reality and a substitute for life. Both are true: we can learn much from drug-enhanced experiences—*and* these drug-induced feelings can lead to avoidance of life, loss of reality, and addiction. While drugs may well have an important role to play in spiritual exploration, it is vital for nondrug techniques and practices to also be recognized as technologies of the sacred. It is far too easy to become overly dependent on chemicals, both physiologically and psychologically, thereby evading tangible psychospiritual effort.

I hasten to add that many valuable experiences of these deeper feeling occur in guises other than of the mystical or transpersonal variety. For example, all of the following experiences and activities can help convey our deep connection to the causal feelings lying below the surface of the sensory world. *Memory,* both short- and long-term, when experienced keenly, gives a direct feeling of the presence of the past. *Intimate human relationships* often tap into deep bodily sensation and feelings of intense emotional connection. In *painting,* contrasts and harmonies of color and form evoke the essence of depth. *Music* is particularly effective at transmitting powerful feelings of causal efficacy in vibrational form. During *inspiration/ insight,* the creative unification of feelings from the depths frequently rises dramatically into conscious awareness. And, of course, nature itself can stimulate a powerful sympathetic response to its own deep resources of beauty, interconnection, aliveness, and inherent *value.*

Whitehead's understanding of the essence of each event as an actualization of *value* suggests several dimensions to this facet of spirituality: (1) an appreciation of the inherent value and depth of each individual, (2) an ecospirituality recognizing the deep value of the whole in relation to all its parts, and (3) a Buddhist-like spirituality where, resting in the moment of our own experience, we find it is "sufficient unto itself": that it is overflowing with Beauty, Adventure, and Peace. This last facet may seem to rely primarily on an appreciation of the reality revealed through the present moment itself. But to be complete, it must also include intuitions of the past and future.

To feel the immediate presence of the past and the future, oddly enough, one must first learn to live deeply in the present, where both past and future actually reside. Until then, they are just illusions, or abstractions, obscuring full contact with reality. In Whiteheadian terms, when one's focus is tied up with past events themselves, one is less aware of their *potential contribution* to the present situation. When one's focus is fixed on fantasy future events, then it is difficult to *aim the current moment* towards a better future. But when one's focus of awareness is rooted deeply in the Now, one can be open to receiving the possibilities of accomplished experience and synthesizing these possibilities into realistic future aims. Without this concern about future achievement, the value of the present moment itself is diminished. As John Cobb Jr. writes, "If one concentrates only on immediate attainment without regard to its consequences, that immediate attainment is impoverished . . . Whitehead's view is that the only locus of value is the present moment, but that the richness of that value depends on anticipation of its value to others."[25]

In *The Structure of Christian Existence*, Cobb traces the evolution of human experience and delineates the novel patterns that emerged in key epochs, including in ancient Greece and in Prophetic times, and the emergence of Buddhism. Within these general types of psychospiritual existence, one can discern very different intellectual and spiritual manifestations, as well as ways of accessing particular ranges of experience. I find Cobb's pluralistic understanding of the "evolution of consciousness" to be more inclusive and accurately descriptive than models based on linear growth or on reaching higher levels of consciousness.

Drawing out the implications of this pluralistic theory, Cobb defines Christian spirituality in a way that makes real sense to me for the first time: as *self-transcending spirit*. As self-transcending spirit, each new moment is as fully open as possible to the flow of the universe, creating itself in the pattern that best serves the world at that point in time. And each new occasion *surpasses* the one before it, rather than holding onto old avoidances and attachments from the past or forging new ones. What most clearly distinguishes this spirituality from some forms of Buddhism is whether this openness is attained through a spiritual self that is continually transcending itself, or through the annihilation of the self.

> Here we must think of a reflective consciousness in which the seat of existence is capable of changing. Furthermore, we must think of this changing center as itself responsible for this changing, and thus transcendent from the locus from which it organizes the whole. Finally, we must conceive this transcendent center as capable of retaining its transcendent identity and of refusing to identify itself with any other aspect of the psyche.

25. Cobb, "What Is the Future?," 5.

... Thus, spiritual existence is radically self-transcending existence.[26]

This act of ongoing self-transcendence cannot be accomplished solely through the resources of the self that is to be transcended. Something *more* is required. This is where those familiar maxims of the recovery movement come into play: We "let go and let God" so that God can "do for us what we could not do for ourselves." For the guidance from God's initial aim always stands ready to help us find the next moment of self-actualization that will create maximal value, beauty, and intensity. We can find this guidance residing within the depths of our own being—if only we are open to it.

In these pages, I have appealed to extraordinary experience and complex systems of ideas as a context for some very simple notions, things that should be evident to anyone who has eyes to see. The world is alive and precious, and in great danger. Our civilization's current modes of thought are threatening the basic web of life on our planet, and we are part of the web that is being perilously compromised. Major changes are needed, and are coming—either guided by our best thinking and through adapting to these challenges, or thrust upon us in unpredictably destructive ways. To successfully face the challenges ahead, we need a radically new direction for our world. Towards this end, we will require a powerful "technology of the sacred"[27] to evoke spiritual experiences and promote evolution of the human psyche. And we will need a guiding vision.

The broad thrust of this book has been that Whitehead's philosophy offers the best approach available for constructing a new cosmology for the twenty-first century, especially when enriched by transpersonal psychology's insights into the depth dimensions and psychospiritual elements of our universe. This new worldview is desperately needed, for it has become more and more starkly apparent that the current problems threatening planetary survival—overpopulation, the nuclear threat, resource depletion, ecological collapse—cannot be solved in time through traditional educational, political, or technological strategies. A major shift in consciousness or psychospiritual orientation is required to supplement and transcend our present efforts—a leap beyond the self-centered, striving ego and into Heard's "Second Maturity." I believe that a Whiteheadian, transpersonal cosmology can help reinstill meaning and hope into the human adventure and provide the inspiration, conceptual framework, and direction necessary for us to come to grips with the greatest crisis ever to confront the human race.

26. Cobb, *Structure of Christian Existence,* 123–24.

27. Grof frequently uses this term to describe transpersonal methods and techniques. See for example Grof, *Way of Psychonaut,* 2:222, 274, 286.

Glossary

This glossary offers guidance on some of the words and technical terms found in this text. The definitions provided here refer to how these concepts are used in the context of this book; they do not necessarily reflect the more general usage of these words.

In assembling the Whiteheadian entries below, I consulted the glossary found at the end of Donald Sherburne's *A Key to Whitehead's "Process and Reality,"* as well as John B. Cobb Jr's *Whitehead Word Book.* Both of these sources should prove useful to readers who wish to explore these terms in more depth.

actual occasion (moment of experience):

> Whitehead's term for the basic units of actuality. Actual occasions are momentary subjective events that form themselves by *feeling past feeling*, then contribute to future occasions by a similar process. Actual occasions correspond to what William James calls "drops" or "pulses" of experience and to the quantum events of physics.

birth trauma:

> The physical and emotional distress and pain associated with the struggle to be born, as well as the repressed memories of these primal experiences.

COEX system:

> "Systems of condensed experience," as described by Stanislav Grof. Similar to Jung's psychological complexes, COEX systems

are interconnected webs of past experiences of an emotional, psychological, and physical nature, often originating out of a traumatic episode.

—governing systems: The comprehensive, unconsciously driven attitudes and perspectives on life that arise from a powerful COEX system.

concrescence:

The "growing together" of the constituents of a newly forming moment of experience. Whitehead analyzes this process of self-formation into four stages. First, receiving feelings of past events; second, feeling the experiential possibilities related to these original feelings; third, synthesizing these various feelings into a new perspective and purpose; fourth, further refining and combining these feelings to create more complex levels of experience, at times involving conscious awareness. (This final stage only occurs in certain higher-level events.)

contrast:

How elements within a newly forming event are brought together into a new unity. The elements are not eliminated by these contrasts, but rather are combined and compared to create greater intensity and depth of experience. For example, the various colors in a painting or sunset complement and accentuate one another to create a more potent aesthetic composition.

cosmology:

Study and description of the entities, forces, processes, and structures that populate and occupy the universe.

creative advance:

The general process of the universe's movement "forward" in evolutionary creativity. The everlasting process of the past fueling the rise of newly forming events across the universe.

creativity:

> All fundamental events arise from the integration of multitudinous data into a novel "drop" of experience. This integration of many influences into a new whole is the essence of the process of creativity, the ultimate metaphysical principle according to Whitehead. Creativity is that fundamental process whereby the many feelings of past events are synthesized into a new momentary occasion of experience—into a new subjective event. There may be significant, or minimal, novelty involved within this creative activity.

data:

> The information from past moments of experience that enters into a new occasion. The newly forming actual occasion draws feelings or information from past events as it creates itself; what it draws into itself during this process Whitehead calls data.

dominant occasion:

> In certain complex organisms, a series of occasions emerges that functions as what might be thought of as a psyche or soul. These momentary events draw on the feelings of the entire organism and its environment, planning and coordinating its activities.

ego death:

> The collapse of many or most of one's habitual psychological structures may be experienced as an impending death, due to the powerful feelings of loss and disorientation that arise. However, if one is able to see the process through to completion, it can result in a psychic rebirth of epic proportion.

eternal objects:

> Whitehead's term for the pure potentials or possible forms by means of which events organize their process of self creation. Eternal objects are the forms of definiteness through which the feelings of past events are actualized, for example, qualities such as redness or sadness or roundness.

event:

> For Whitehead momentary experiential events, rather than enduring substances, are the primary actualities of our universe. Most of these events—"actual occasions"—are made up of nonconscious experience. Also, these momentary events tend to combine to form various kinds of organic societies, creating the microscopic and macroscopic entities that populate our universe.

> Whitehead does not always use the term *event* in this technical sense, sometimes using event more broadly to indicate the kind of large-scale happenings that occur in everyday life. But I will generally use *event* synonymously with "actual occasion" and "moment of experience."

everlastingness:

> Whitehead describes God's consequent nature as an ongoing, never-ending process. This is in contrast to "eternal," understood in terms of timelessness or an unchanging reality.

experience:

> Experience is Whitehead's favored term for what characterizes all actuality. Moments of experience are what make up the quantum occasions of physics, as well as pulses of actuality from the atomic, molecular, cellular, and animal levels. All of the experience of less complex occasions is considered to be nonconscious. Until shown to be otherwise, Whitehead grants conscious awareness only to complex animals.

extraordinary (nonordinary) experience or state:

> I generally use the term *extraordinary* with "experience" and *nonordinary* with "state" in line with Grof's contention that not all nonordinary states generate experiences of a spiritual, transpersonal, or growth-producing nature. While Grof often uses the term *holotropic* to refer to this class of spiritual states and experiences, I will primarily be using "nonordinary" to indicate states of awareness that fall outside the normal range and "extraordinary" to indicate experiences of a spiritual or transpersonal nature.

fallacy of misplaced concreteness:

> Whitehead's term for mistaking an abstraction for a more fundamental reality. "The map is not the territory."

feeling (see prehension):

> This is a key metaphysical concept for Whitehead. It refers to the process whereby data from another event, or an aspect of a past occasion, is grasped and absorbed into a new event or part thereof. The following are some of the most important species of feelings or prehensions discussed in Whitehead's system:
>
> —physical feeling: The direct grasping of feelings or data from the past to create a new event.
>
> —conceptual feeling: Feeling of a pure potential or sheer possibility.
>
> —intellectual feeling: A higher order feeling, involving complex integrations within a new event, sometimes including conscious awareness.
>
> —hybrid physical feeling: Direct unconscious perceptions of the higher order integrations of a past event.

God's primordial nature/consequent nature:

> For descriptive purposes, in Whitehead's later work, God possesses a *dual nature:* a primordial nature containing an ordered valuation of all potential or possibility; and a consequent nature that directly interacts with all finite "creatures" (a term Whitehead uses often) or events. (For Whitehead, God was a single everlasting entity. In this book, I treat God as an everlasting *series* of actual occasions, in accord with Whitehead's view that God should exemplify metaphysical principles.)

holotropic:

> Grof's descriptor for extraordinary experiences of a transformative nature, in contrast to those nonordinary states that are spiritually insignificant, therapeutically irrelevant, or even pathological. Literally, *holotropic* means "seeking the whole."

holotropic breathwork:

> A nondrug technique for producing holotropic states through enhanced breathing, evocative music, therapeutic bodywork, and group processes.

immortality:

> Objective Immortality: the objective endurance of past moments of experience as data to be felt by future events. Whitehead also speaks of an *objective* immortality where the achieved experience of human beings (and all other actuality) is preserved forever in God's nature or memory. This is in contrast to *subjective* immortality where an individual's personal existence would continue beyond bodily death. Whitehead's philosophy is neutral regarding this possibility.

initial/subjective aim:

> Each event arises out of feelings of the past universe, which includes feelings of God's primordial nature. These feelings of God offer an ideal direction of unfoldment for that particular event: its "initial aim." How the actual occasion takes up this guidance from the initial aim is called its "subjective aim."

metaphysics:

> Study and description of the fundamental elements, factors, or patterns that make up the universe. Account of the most general characteristics of the entities that constitute reality.

mystical:

> Relating to spiritual experience of deeper realities, transpersonal entities, or other normally veiled dimensions of existence.

nonordinary/altered state of consciousness:

> Events that fall outside the realm of everyday experience and beyond the usual ego boundaries. Grof favors the term *nonordinary* over *altered*, as the latter can imply that everyday awareness is the standard of normality by which other realms of experience should be evaluated.

parapsychology/PSI/psychic phenomena:

>   Experiences that usually, though not always, involve some kind
>   of "action at a distance," such as telepathy, telekinesis, clairvoy-
>   ance, precognition, or remote viewing. The study of these expe-
>   riences is referred to as *parapsychology.*

perception, modes of:

>   Whitehead describes three interrelated ways we perceive the
>   world.

>   —causal efficacy: This fundamental mode represents an unme-
>   diated intuition or unconscious perception of past events. It is
>   the direct flow of feeling from the past into the present.

>   —presentational immediacy: Pure conscious sensory
>   perception.

>   —symbolic reference: The union of the first two modes, creat-
>   ing our normal experience of a world filled with meaningful
>   objects.

perinatal:

>   Feelings and events related to the infant's experiences around
>   birth.

>   —perinatal matrices: Grof describes these events in terms of
>   four basic experiential stages: the intrauterine period; the
>   initial period of contractions; the struggle through the birth
>   canal; and the emergence into the world.

perpetual perishing:

>   The inevitable fading away of the subjective immediacy of each
>   new moment of experience. Loss.

philosophy:

>   The general search for a more or less systematic understanding
>   of the nature of life and the universe.

prehension (see feeling):

> The direct incorporation of data from past events. Feeling the feeling of others. The flow of feeling and data between and within events. Whitehead uses the term *feeling* analogously with "positive" prehensions (that is, prehensions that involve the transfer of feeling/data). "Negative" prehensions are those that block or exclude data.

process philosophy:

> The universe is seen primarily as a flow of events rather than a world of beings who go through changes. Becoming is more primary than Being. The world is understood as event-based rather than substance-based. There is a becoming of continuity, not a continuity of becoming.

propositions:

> How data and a potential way of feeling that data are brought into complex relationship. Through propositions, the feelings derived from past events are examined under the lens of particular organizing patterns. Only more complex actual occasions generate these "contrasts of contrasts" through which conscious levels of experience become possible. (Simpler moments of experience are usually limited to a repetition of past organizing patterns, terminating in what Whitehead calls a "physical purpose.")

psyche:

> The series of events that make up the soul or mind of a human being or other complex animal. The psyche consists of both unconscious and conscious experience, drawing on the brain, the body, and the universe at large for its data.

psychedelic:

> A descriptor for experiences associated with substances such as LSD, mescaline, DMT, and other mind-expanding drugs. Literally means "mind manifesting." Some authorities prefer the term *entheogen*, implying "spirit manifesting" or "enthused with god."

satisfaction:

> The final stage of each actual occasion is called its *satisfaction*. Having reached its satisfaction, the event immediately passes into its career as an object for future events to draw upon for data.

societies:

> The simple, momentary events that form the basis of our universe tend to evolve into more elaborate social groupings, such as *personally ordered* or *corpuscular societies* such as electrons, and *structured societies* such as cells or animals, which exist as complex organisms involving various levels of closely interacting subsocieties.

speculative philosophy:

> A philosophical method employed by Whitehead and others. The attempt to discern the common patterns and structures and entities that underlie and characterize all reality—and then to create a rational system of fundamental, interdependent ideas that describe these basic entities and processes.

subject/superject/object:

> Events in their moment of self-creation are subjective in nature. Accomplished (completed) events take on what Whitehead calls their function as "superjects": they become objects exerting an influence on newly arising events.

subjective form:

> Whitehead's term for *how* another event, its data, or other feelings are prehended. The "feeling tone" by which data is grasped and integrated into a new moment of experience.

transmutation:

> The process whereby many individual feelings or data that share some characteristic(s) are brought together to generate a unified and simplified large-scale experience—such as perceiving a red ball rather than millions of red molecules or thousands of retinal pixels.

transpersonal:

> Phenomena or events that occur beyond the ordinary range of everyday consciousness. Transpersonal experiences fall outside the normal ego boundaries, for example: telepathy, near-death experiences, mystical and meditative states, and psychedelic experiences.

value:

> Every event arises through the integration of past feelings into a new aesthetic whole. Whitehead says that this achievement of self-creation is intrinsically valuable. Every actual occasion is valuable for what it is in itself, as well as for the contributions it makes to future events, including God.

worldview:

> Overall understanding of the meaning and constitution of life and the universe. One's complete perspective on existence, both conscious and unconscious.

Bibliography

This bibliography is divided into two sections: books and articles; and film, television, and music.

Books/Articles

Alcoholics Anonymous World Services. *Alcoholics Anonymous.* 3rd ed. New York: Alcoholics Anonymous World Services, 1976.

————. *Twelve Steps and Twelve Traditions.* New York: Alcoholics Anonymous World Services, 1953.

Anderson, Susan A. "Evolutionary Futurism in Stapledon's 'Star Maker.'" *Process Studies* 5/2 (1975) 123–28.

Anthony, Piers. *Macroscope.* New York: Avon, 1969.

Assagioli, Roberto. *Psychosynthesis.* New York: Penguin, 1976.

Bayard, Pierre. *Who Killed Roger Ackroyd? The Mystery behind the Agatha Christie Mystery.* Translated by Carol Cosman. New York: New Press, 2000.

Beardslee, William A. *Margins of Belonging: Essays on the New Testament and Theology.* American Academy of Religion Studies in Religion 58. Atlanta: Scholars, 1991.

————. "Process Thought on the Borders between Hermeneutics and Theology." In "Personal Reflections on Process Thought." Special issue, *Process Studies* 19/4 (1990) 230–34.

Beisser, Arnold R. "The Paradoxical Theory of Change." In *Gestalt Therapy Now: Theory, Techniques, Applications,* edited by Joen Fagan and Irma Lee Shepherd, 77–80. Gouldsboro, NC: Gestalt Journal Press, 2006.

Berry, Thomas. *Evening Thoughts: Reflecting on Earth as Sacred Community.* Berkeley, CA: Counterpoint, 2006.

Birch, Charles. *Feelings.* Sydney: University of New South Wales Press, 1995.

Birch, Charles, and John B. Cobb Jr. *The Liberation of Life: From the Cell to the Community.* Cambridge: Cambridge University Press, 1981.

Briggs, John P., and F. David Peat. *Looking Glass Universe: The Emerging Science of Wholeness.* New York: Simon & Schuster, 1986.

Brown, Jason W. *Microgenetic Theory and Process Thought.* Exeter, UK: Imprint Academic, 2015.

————. *Mind and Nature: Essays on Time and Subjectivity.* London: Whurr, 2000.

Buchanan, John H. "Whitehead and Wilber: Contrasts in Theory." *Humanistic Psychologist* 24 (1996) 231–56.

Campbell, Joseph, with Bill Moyers. *The Power of Myth.* Edited by Betty Sue Flowers. New York: Anchor, 1991.

Cassirer, Ernst. *An Essay on Man: An Introduction to a Philosophy of Human Culture.* Garden City, NY: Doubleday, 1944.

Chamberlain, David B. *Babies Remember Birth: And Other Extraordinary Scientific Discoveries about the Mind and Personality of Your Newborn.* Los Angeles: Tarcher, 1988.

Clarke, Arthur C. *Childhood's End.* New York: Harcourt, Brace & World, 1953.

Cobb, Cliff. "Overcoming the Impasse in Political and Social Theory." In *Putting Philosophy to Work: Toward an Ecological Civilization,* edited by John B. Cobb Jr. et al., 189–224. Toward Ecological Civilization Series 15. Anoka, MN: Process Century Press, 2018.

Cobb, John B., Jr. *Beyond Dialogue: Toward a Mutual Transformation of Christianity and Buddhism.* Philadelphia: Fortress, 1982. Reprint, Eugene, OR: Wipf & Stock, 1998.

————. *The Earthist Challenge to Economism: A Theological Critique of the World Bank.* New York: St. Martin's, 1999.

————. "Eternal Objects and Archetypes, Past and Depth: A Response to Stanley Hopper." In *Archetypal Process: Self and Divine in Whitehead, Jung, and Hillman,* edited by David Ray Griffin, 125–28. Evanston, IL: Northwestern University Press, 1989.

————. *God and the World.* Philadelphia: Westminster, 1969. Reprint, Eugene, OR: Wipf & Stock, 2000.

————. *The Structure of Christian Existence.* New York: Seabury, 1979.

————. *Sustainability: Economics, Ecology, and Justice.* Maryknoll, NY: Orbis, 1992. Reprint, Eugene, OR: Wipf & Stock, 2007.

————. *Sustaining the Common Good: A Christian Perspective on the Global Economy.* Cleveland: Pilgrim, 1994.

————. "What Is the Future? A Process Perspective." In *Hope and the Future of Man,* edited by Ewert H. Cousins, 1–14. Philadelphia: Fortress, 1972.

————. *Whitehead Word Book: A Glossary with Alphabetical Index to Technical Terms in "Process and Reality."* Claremont, CA: P&F Press, 2008.

Cobb, John B., Jr., and Franklin I. Gamwell, eds. *Existence and Actuality: Conversations with Charles Hartshorne.* Chicago: University of Chicago Press. 1984.

Daly, Herman E., and John B. Cobb Jr. *For the Common Good: Redirecting the Economy toward Community, the Environment, and a Sustainable Future.* Boston: Beacon, 1989.

Davies, Paul. *God and the New Physics.* A Touchstone Book. New York: Simon & Schuster, 1984.

Dickens, Charles. *Christmas Books.* The Works of Charles Dickens 18. New York: Collier, n.d.

Didsbury, Howard F. "Hedonists vs. the Future." *Futurist* 33/10 (1999) 60.

Doody, Tim. "The Heretic." *Utne Reader* (Nov-Dec 2012) 66–71, excerpted from *The Morning News,* July 26, 2012. https://themorningnews.org/article/the-heretic/.

Epperson, Michael. *Quantum Mechanics and the Philosophy of Alfred North Whitehead*. American Philosophy Series 14. New York: Fordham University Press, 2004.

Everett, Walter. *The Beatles as Musicians: "Revolver" through the "Anthology."* New York: Oxford University Press, 1999.

Fechner, Gustav Theodor. *Religion of a Scientist: Selections from Gustav Th. Fechner*. Edited and translated by Walter Lowrie. New York: Pantheon, 1946.

Fedor-Freybergh, Peter G., and M. L. Vanessa Vogel, eds. *Prenatal and Perinatal Psychology and Medicine: Encounter with the Unborn*. Carnforth, UK: Parthenon, 1988.

Fenton, John Y. "Mystical Experience as a Bridge for Cross-Cultural Philosophy of Religion: A Critique." *Journal of the American Academy of Religion* 49 (1981) 51-77.

Ferré, Frederick. "Contemporaneity, Knowledge, and God: A Comment on Hurley's Paper." In *Physics and the Ultimate Significance of Time: Bohm Prigogine, and Process Philosophy*, edited by David Ray Griffin, 110-14. Albany: State University of New York Press, 1986.

Gael, Sara. "Understanding and Working with Difficult Psychedelic Experiences." *Psychedelic Science*, MAPS Special Edition Bulletin (Spring 2017) 34–35.

Gibson, Leonard. "Mystical Experience and Psychosis: A Whiteheadian Model of Their Relation." (This unpublished sixteen-page essay may be obtained from the library of The Center for Process Studies, 680 State Street, Salem, OR, 97301.)

Goleman, Daniel. *The Meditative Mind: The Varieties of Meditative Experience*. New York: Tarcher, 1988.

Griffin, David Ray. "Charles Hartshorne." In *A New Handbook of Christian Theologians*, edited by Donald W. Musser and Joseph L. Price, 200–213. Nashville: Abingdon, 1996.

———. *God and Religion in the Postmodern World: Essays in Postmodern Theology*. SUNY Series in Constructive Postmodern Thought. Albany: State University of New York Press, 1989.

———. *Panentheism and Scientific Naturalism: Rethinking Evil, Morality, Religious Experience, Religious Pluralism, and the Academic Study of Religion*. Toward an Ecological Civilization Series. Claremont, CA: Process Century Press, 2014.

———. "Parapsychology, Philosophy, and Religion: A Whiteheadian Postmodern Perspective." (Unpublished paper). A revised version of this essay has been published in the *Journal of the American Society for Psychical Research* 87.3 (July 1993) 217–88, as "Parapsychology and Philosophy: A Whiteheadian Postmodern Perspective." (The original essay may be obtained from The Center for Process Studies, 680 State Street, Salem, OR, 97301.)

———. *Parapsychology, Philosophy, and Spirituality: A Postmodern Exploration*. SUNY Series in Constructive Postmodern Thought. Albany: State University of New York Press, 1997.

———. "Peace and the Postmodern Paradigm." In *Spirituality and Society: Postmodern Visions*, edited by David Ray Griffin, 143–54. SUNY Series in Constructive Postmodern Thought. Albany: State University of New York Press, 1988.

———. "Process Theology as Empirical, Rational, and Speculative: Some Reflections on Method." *Process Studies* 19/2 (1990) 116-35.

————, ed. *The Reenchantment of Science: Postmodern Proposals.* SUNY Series in Constructive Postmodern Thought. Albany: State University of New York Press, 1988.

————. *Reenchantment without Supernaturalism: A Process Philosophy of Religion.* Cornell Studies in the Philosophy of Religion. Ithaca, NY: Cornell University Press, 2001.

————. *Religion and Scientific Naturalism: Overcoming the Conflicts.* SUNY Series in Constructive Postmodern Thought. Albany: State University of New York Press, 2000.

————. "Steiner's Anthroposophy and Whitehead's Philosophy." *Revision* 14/1 (1991) 1–22.

————. "What Is Consciousness and Why Is It So Problematic?" In *Cultivating Consciousness: Enhancing Human Potential, Wellness, and Healing,* edited by K. Ramakrishna Rao, 51–70. Westport, CT: Praeger, 1993.

Griffin, David Ray, et al. *Founders of Constructive Postmodern Philosophy: Pierce, James, Bergson, Whitehead, and Hartshorne.* SUNY Series in Constructive Postmodern Thought. Albany: State University of New York Press, 1993.

Grof, Stanislav. *The Adventure of Self-Discovery: Dimensions of Consciousness and New Perspectives in Psychotherapy and Inner Exploration.* SUNY Series in Transpersonal and Humanistic Psychology. Albany: State University of New York Press, 1988.

————. *Beyond the Brain: Birth, Death and Transcendence in Psychotherapy.* SUNY Series in Transpersonal and Humanistic Psychology. Albany: State University of New York Press, 1985.

————. *The Cosmic Game: Explorations of the Frontiers of Human Consciousness.* SUNY Series in Transpersonal and Humanistic Psychology. Albany: State University of New York Press, 1998.

————. "LSD and the Cosmic Game: Outline of Psychedelic Cosmology and Ontology." This is a revised and expanded version of a paper of the same title originally published in the *Journal of Consciousness Studies* 5/2 (1972–1973) 165–93. Please contact John Buchanan to request a copy of this paper, which is not widely available.

————. *LSD Psychotherapy.* Pomona, CA: Hunter House, 1980.

————. *Realms of the Human Unconscious: Observations from LSD Research.* New York: Dutton, 1976.

————. "Realms of the Human Unconscious: Observations from LSD Research." In *Beyond Ego: Transpersonal Dimensions in Psychology,* edited by Roger N. Walsh and Frances Vaughan, 87–99. Los Angeles: Tarcher, 1980.

————. "Revision and Re-enchantment of Psychology: Legacy of a Half a Century of Consciousness Research." *The Journal of Transpersonal Psychology* 44 (2012) 137–63.

————, et al. *The Way of the Psychonaut: Encyclopedia for Inner Journeys.* 2 vols. Santa Cruz, CA: Multidisciplinary Association for Psychedelic Studies (MAPS), 2019.

Harman, Willis W. "The Postmodern Heresy: Consciousness as Causal." In *The Reenchantment of Science: Postmodern Proposals,* edited by David Ray Griffin, 115–28. SUNY Series in Constructive Postmodern Thought. Albany: State University of New York Press, 1988.

Harner, Michael. *The Way of the Shaman.* New York: HarperSanFrancisco, 1990.

Hartshorne, Charles. "The Compound Individual." In *Philosophical Essays for Alfred North Whitehead*, edited by Otis H. Lee, 193 220. London: Longmans, Green, 1936.

———. *Creative Synthesis and Philosophic Method.* Lanham, MD: University Press of America, 1983.

———. *Creativity in American Philosophy.* Albany: State University of New York Press, 1984.

———. *Insights and Oversights of Great Thinkers: An Evaluation of Western Philosophy.* SUNY Series in Systematic Philosophy. Albany: State University of New York Press, 1983.

Heard, Gerald. "Dromenon." In *The Great Fog and Other Weird Tales by H. F. Heard*, 156–204. Lexington, KY: Wildside, 1944.

———. *The Five Ages of Man: The Psychology of Human History.* New York: Julian, 1963.

Hesse, Hermann. *Magister Ludi: The Glass Bead Game.* Translated by Richard Winston and Clara Winston. New York: Holt, Rinehart & Winston, 1969.

Hofstadter, Douglas R. *Gödel, Escher, Bach: An Eternal Golden Braid.* New York: Vintage, 1980.

Huxley, Aldous. *The Doors of Perception*, and *Heaven and Hell*. Harper Colophon Books. New York: Harper & Row, 1963.

James, William. *Collected Essays and Reviews.* London: Longmans, Green, 1920.

———. *A Pluralistic Universe.* Introduction to the Bison Books edition by Henry Samuel Levinson. Bison Books ed. Lincoln: University of Nebraska Press, 1996.

Jung, C. G. *The Structure and Dynamics of the Psyche.* 2nd ed. The Collected Works of C. G. Jung 8. 5th printing, Princeton: Princeton University Press, 1981.

———. *Two Essays on Analytical Psychology.* The Collected Works of C. G. Jung 7. 2nd ed. Princeton: Princeton University Press, 1966.

Kandel, Eric R. *In Search of Memory: The Emergence of a New Science of Mind.* New York: Norton, 2006.

Kapleau, Philip, ed. *The Three Pillars of Zen: Teaching, Practice, and Enlightenment.* A Beacon Paperback. Boston: Beacon, 1967.

Keller, Catherine. *From a Broken Web: Separation, Sexism, and Self.* Boston: Beacon, 1986.

Kris, Ernst. "On Inspiration." *International Journal of Psychoanalysis* 20 (1939) 377–89.

LaChapelle, Dolores. *Sacred Land, Sacred Sex: Rapture of the Deep.* Silverton, CO: Finn Hill Arts, 1988.

Laing. R. D. *The Politics of Experience.* New York: Ballantine, 1968.

Laszlo, Ervin. *What Is Reality? The New Map of Cosmos and Consciousness.* New York: SelectBooks, 2016.

Lattin, Don. *Distilled Spirits: Getting High, then Sober, with a Famous Writer, a Forgotten Philosopher, and a Hopeless Drunk.* Berkeley: University of California Press, 2012.

Leary, Timothy. *High Priest.* New York: New American Library, 1968.

L'Engle, Madeleine. *A Wrinkle in Time.* 1962. Reprint, Harrisonburg, VA: Donnelley, 2007.

Lessing, Doris. *Shikasta: Re, Colonised Planet 5.* New York: Vintage, 1981.

Lewis, C. S. *Out of the Silent Planet.* Paperback ed. New York: Macmillan, 1965.

———. *Perelandra.* Paperback ed. New York: Macmillan, 1965.

———. *That Hideous Strength.* Paperback ed. New York: Macmillan, 1965.

Lovelock, J. E. *Gaia: A New Look at Life on Earth*. New York: Oxford University Press, 1979.

Lowe, Victor. "Alfred North Whitehead." In *Encyclopædia Britannica* 15th ed. (1988), 12:635–37.

Lowen, Alexander. *Bioenergetics: The Revolutionary Therapy That Uses the Language of the Body to Heal the Problems of the Mind*. Hammondsworth, UK: Penguin, 1977.

Masters, Robert, and Jean Houston. *The Varieties of Psychedelic Experience: The Classic Guide to the Effects of LSD on the Human Psyche*. Rochester, VT: Park Street, 2000.

Masterson, Andrew. "What Do Albert Camus and String Theory Have in Common?" *Cosmos: The Science of Everything*. (Feb. 22, 2016) web. https://cosmosmagazine.com/physics/what-do-albert-camus-and-string-theory-have-common/.

McKenna, Terence, and Dennis McKenna. *The Invisible Landscape: Mind, Hallucinogens, and the I Ching*. San Francisco: HarperSanFrancisco, 1994.

Miller, Walter. *A Canticle for Leibowitz*. Philadelphia: Lippincott, 1959.

Myers, Gerald E. *William James, His Life and Thought*. New Haven: Yale University Press, 1986.

Nagel, Thomas. "What Is the Mind–Brain Problem?" In *Experimental and Theoretical Studies of Consciousness*, 1–13. CIBA Foundation Symposium Series 174. New York: Wiley, 1993.

Nani, Andrea, et al. "Sentience With or Without Consciousness." *Journal of Consciousness Studies* 28/1–2 (2021) 60–79.

Odin, Steve. "Postmodernism and Aesthetic Symbolism in Japanese Shingon Buddhism." In *Sacred Interconnections: Postmodern Spirituality, Political Economy, and Art*, edited by David Ray Griffin, 193–215. SUNY Series in Constructive Postmodern Thought. Albany: State University of New York Press, 1990.

———. *Process Metaphysics and Hua-yen Buddhism: A Critical Study of Cumulative Penetration vs. Interpenetration*. SUNY Series in Systematic Philosophy. Albany: State University of New York Press, 1982.

Ostrander, Sheila, and Lynn Schroeder. *Psychic Discoveries behind the Iron Curtain*. Introduced by Ivan T. Sanderson. Englewood Cliffs, NJ: Prentice-Hall, 1970.

Peck, M. Scott. *The Road Less Traveled: A New Psychology of Love, Traditional Values and Spiritual Growth*. A Touchstone Book. New York: Simon & Schuster, 1978.

Pollan, Michael. *How to Change Your Mind: What the New Science of Psychedelics Teaches Us about Consciousness, Dying, Addiction, Depression*. New York: Penguin, 2018.

Progoff, Ira. *The Death and Rebirth of Psychology: An Integrative Evaluation of Freud, Adler, Jung and Rank and the Impact of Their Insights on Modern Man*. McGraw-Hill Paperbacks. New York: McGraw-Hill, 1973.

Ram Dass. *Be Here Now, Remember*. San Cristobal, NM: The Lama Foundation, 1971.

———. *Walking Each Other Home: Conversations on Loving and Dying*. Louisville: Sounds True, 2018.

Reck, Andrew J. *Speculative Philosophy: A Study of Its Nature, Types and Uses*. Albuquerque: University of New Mexico Press, 1972.

Russell, Peter. *The Global Brain: Speculations on the Evolutionary Leap to Planetary Consciousness*. Los Angeles: Tarcher, 1983.

Ryle, Gilbert. *The Concept of Mind*. 1949. Reprint, Chicago: University of Chicago Press, 1984.

Scranton, Roy. *Learning to Die in the Anthropocene: Reflections on the End of a Civilization.* San Francisco: City Lights, 2015.

Sheldrake, Rupert. "Is the Sun Conscious?." *Journal of Consciousness Studies* 28/3-4 (2021) 8-28.

———. *The Presence of the Past: Morphic Resonance and the Habits of Nature.* New York: Times Books, 1988.

Sherburne, Donald W., ed. *A Key to Whitehead's "Process and Reality."* 1966. Reprint, Chicago: University of Chicago Press, 1981.

Smith, Page. *Killing the Spirit: Higher Education in America.* New York: Viking, 1990.

Stapledon, Olaf. *Last and First Men: A Story of the Near and Far Future.* With a foreword by Gregory Benford and an afterword by Doris Lessing. Los Angeles: Tarcher, 1988.

———. *Odd John & Sirius: Two Science-Fiction Novels by Olaf Stapledon.* New York: Dover, 1988. [First printing, 1972].

———. *Star Maker.* Los Angeles: Tarcher, 1988.

Swimme, Brian. "The Cosmic Creation Story." In *The Reenchantment of Science: Postmodern Proposals,* edited by David Ray Griffin, 47–56. SUNY Series in Constructive Postmodern Thought. Albany: State University of New York Press, 1988.

Swimme, Brian, and Thomas Berry. *The Universe Story.* San Francisco: HarperOne, 1994.

Taylor, Eugene. *William James on Exceptional Mental States: The 1896 Lowell Lectures.* Reprint, Amherst: University of Massachusetts Press, 1984.

Tolle, Eckhart. *The Power of Now: A Guide to Spiritual Enlightenment.* Rev. ed. Vancouver, BC: Namaste, 2004.

Trimmer, John D., trans. "The Present Situation in Quantum Mechanics: A Translation of Schrodinger's 'Cat Paradox' Paper." *Proceedings of the American Philosophical Society* 124 (1980) 323–38.

Waddington, C. H. *The Evolution of an Evolutionist.* Ithaca, NY: Cornell University Press, 1975.

Walsh, Roger N., and Frances E. Vaughan, eds. *Beyond Ego: Transpersonal Dimensions in Psychology.* Los Angeles: Tarcher, 1980.

Watts, Alan. *The Book: On the Taboo against Knowing Who You Are.* New York: Vintage, 1972.

Whitehead, Alfred North. *Adventures of Ideas.* 1st Free Press paperback ed. New York: Free Press, 1967.

———. *The Concept of Nature: The Tarner Lectures Delivered in Trinity College, November, 1919.* Cambridge: Cambridge University Press, 1964.

———. *Dialogues of Alfred North Whitehead.* As recorded by Lucien Price. Westport, CT: Greenwood, 1977.

———. *The Function of Reason.* Beacon Paperbacks. Boston: Beacon, 1958.

———. *Modes of Thought.* A Free Press Paperback. New York: Free Press, 1968.

———. *Process and Reality: An Essay in Cosmology.* Corrected ed. Edited by David Ray Griffin and Donald W. Sherburne. New York: Free Press, 1979.

———. *Religion in the Making.* A Meridian Book. New York: New American Library, Meridian, 1974.

———. *Science and the Modern World.* A Free Press Paperback. New York: Free Press, 1967.

————. *Symbolism: Its Meaning and Effect.* New York: Fordham University Press, 1985.

Wholey, Dennis, ed. *The Courage to Change: Personal Conversations about Alcoholism with Dennis Wholey.* Warner Books ed. published by arrangement with Houghton Mifflin. New York: Warner, 1988.

Wilber, Ken. *Sex, Ecology, Spirituality: The Spirit of Evolution.* Boston: Shambhala, 1995.

Wilson, Colin. *Below the Iceberg: Anti-Sartre and Other Essays.* 2nd ed. Milford Series 34. San Bernardino, CA: Borgo, 1998.

————. *New Pathways in Psychology: Maslow and the Post-Freudian Revolution.* New York: Taplinger, 1972.

Yonker, Nicholas J. *God, Man, and the Planetary Age: Preface for a Theistic Humanism.* Corvallis: Oregon State University Press, 1978.

Film/Television/Music

The Beatles. "Here Comes the Sun," "You Never Give Me Your Money," "Sun King," "Golden Slumbers/Carry That Weight." *Abbey Road.* EMI CPD 7-46446-2, 1987, CD. Originally released in 1969.

————. *Magical Mystery Tour.* Capitol Records SMAL 2835, 1967, LP.

Bong, Joon-ho, dir. *Snowpiercer.* 2013. Based on *Le Transperceneige,* by Jean-Marc Rochette et al. Starring Chris Evans et al. DVD. Beverly Hills: Anchor Bay Entertainment, 2014.

Brahm, John, dir. "The Cheaters." *Thriller.* Season 1, Episode 15. Adapted by Donald S. Sanford from a story by Roland Bloch. Aired on December 27, 1960, on NBC.

Emerson, Lake, and Palmer. *Emerson, Lake, and Palmer.* Atlantic Records CD-19129-2, 1987, CD. Originally released by Island in 1971.

Fleetwood Mac. "Dust." *Bare Trees.* Reprise 2278-2, 1987, CD. Originally released in 1972.

Hill, George Roy, dir. *Slaughterhouse-Five.* Based on the novel by Kurt Vonnegut Jr. Screenplay by Stephen Geller. Starring Michael Sacks et al. Produced by Paul Monash. 1972. DVD. Universal City, CA: Universal Pictures, distributed by Universal Studios Home Entertainment, 2004.

Jarrott, Charles, dir. *Lost Horizon.* Based on the novel by James Hilton. Screenplay by Larry Kramer. Starring Peter Finch et al. 1973. DVD. Culver City, CA: Sony Pictures Home Entertainment, 2011.

Lennon, John. "Imagine." *Imagine.* Capitol Records 5099990650222, 2010, CD. Originally released by Apple in 1971.

Loggins and Messina. "Back to Georgia." *Kenny Loggins with Jim Messina "Sittin' In."* Columbia Records C 31044, 1971. LP.

The Moody Blues. "Question." *A Question of Balance.* Decca 820 211-2, 1986. CD. Originally released by Threshold in 1970.

Negulesco, Jean, dir. *How to Marry a Millionaire.* Screenplay by Nunnally Johnson et al. Starring Marilyn Monroe et al. 1953. DVD. Beverly Hills: 20th Century Fox, 2012.

Pink Floyd. "Brain Damage." *The Dark Side of the Moon.* Harvest SMAS 11163, 1973, LP.

Ray, Nicholas, dir. *Rebel without a Cause.* Screenplay by Stewart Stern et al. Starring James Dean et al. 1955. DVD. Burbank, CA: Warner Home Video, 2005.

Schlesinger, John, dir. *Marathon Man*. Screenplay by William Goldman. Starring Dustin Hoffman et al. 1976. DVD. Los Angeles: Paramount Pictures, 2001.

Scott, Ridley, dir. *Blade Runner*. Screenplay by Hampton Fancher et al. Starring Harrison Ford et al. 1982. Hollywood, CA: Warner Bros., 2020.

Senensky, Ralph, dir. "This Side of Paradise." *Star Trek,* Season 1, Episode 24. Written by D. C. Fontana et al. Aired in March 1967, on NBC.

Solt, Andrew, dir. *Gimme Some Truth: The Making of John Lennon's "Imagine" Album*. Starring John Lennon et al. DVD. Hollywood, CA: Capitol Video 2000.

Stevens, Cat. "Morning Has Broken." *Teaser and the Firecat*. A&M Records 4313, 1987, CD. Originally released by Island in 1971.

———. "Where Do the Children Play?" *Tea for the Tillerman*. A&M Records SP 2480, 1970 LP.

Strawberry Alarm Clock. "Incense and Peppermints." *Incense and Peppermints*. UNI Records 73014, 1967. LP.

The Stylistics. "You Are Everything." *The Best of the Stylistics*. Amherst Records AMH-9743, 1985, CD. Originally released in 1975.

Tourneur, Jacques, dir. *Curse of the Demon*. Originally called *Night of the Demon*. Screenplay by Charles Bennett et al. Starring Dana Andrews et al. 1957. DVD. Culver City, CA: Columbia Tristar Home Entertainment, 2002.

The Who. "Amazing Journey." *Tommy*. MCA Records MCAD 2-10005, 1984, CD. Originally released by IBC in 1969.

Yes. "Perpetual Change." *The Yes Album*. Atlantic Records 19131-2, 1988, CD. Originally released in 1971.

Index

Abbey Road (album), 109–10, 112, 144, 145
Absolute, 50, 153–54
abstractions, 105–6. *See also* fallacy of misplaced concreteness, Whitehead
absurdity of human existence, 243–44
acausal ordering principle, 141–43
acceptance, 159, 240–41
action-at-a-distance, 104
actual entity, 92, 146, 182, 206n47, 228
actuality
    cell theory, 181–82
    and God, 50, 99, 141
    mystical intuitions, 235
    and Oneness, 141
    sense perception, 102
    Whitehead's metaphysics, 42, 46–49, 56–58, 63–64, 84, 128–29, 216–17
actual occasions (moment of experience), 46–49
    as atomic, 67–68, 169, 216
    and Christianity, 187
    computer consciousness, 194n29
    concrescent structure of, 58, 97, 124, 146–48, 193, 197
    and connectedness, 61–63
    conscious awareness, 119, 152
    creative synthesis, 58–59, 82–84, 119, 140–41, 148
    Creativity, 129, 138, 168–69
    and ecology, 187

    and emptiness, 138, 155
    and enjoyment, 248–49
    and enlightenment, 159–60
    and hierarchy, 216
    human complex amplifier, 84–89
    and illumination, 124
    and memory, 57, 191, 197
    metaphysical knowledge, 138
    and mysticism, 119, 134–60
    and parapsychology, 104
    philosophy of organism, 182
    and physics, 183–85
    and reality, 180–81
    sense perception, 190
    Sine Waves experience, 55–64
    spiritual experience, 218
    and time, 66–70
    transpersonal experience, 101–2, 106, 119
    and the unconscious, 197
    See also dominant occasions
actual world, 196–97
addiction, 60–61, 174–75, 218–19, 244, 246, 249–50
addictive culture, 223–24
adventure, 132, 154, 156, 211–12, 223–24, 226–30, 238–41, 242–44, 248–49, 253
Adventures of Ideas (Whitehead), 226, 229, 239
aesthetic theory, 91–92, 172
Afghanistan, 20–22
agency, 190

aggregates, 152
alcohol, 4–5, 17–19, 29, 173–77, 179,
        224, 234
Alcoholics Anonymous (AA), 61,
        174n2, 224–25, 244, 249
alienation, 63, 141, 203, 250
alignment of events, 158
All is One, 139–41
Alpert, Richard. See Ram Dass
altered states of consciousness.
        See nonordinary states of
        consciousness
altruism, 248–49
The American School in Switzerland
        (TASIS), 76
analytic philosophy, 40
Anderson, Susan, 213
anesthesia, 250
animal body, 86–87
animism, 157–58, 217–18, 235
annihilation of the self, 254–55
anomalies, 205–6
Aquinas, Thomas, 29
archetypes, 34, 67, 75, 111–12, 118, 161,
        195–96, 198
Arons, Myron ("Mike"), 41, 79
Assagioli, Roberto, 90, 162–63
asymmetrical theory of time, 68
atomic events, 48–49, 62, 67, 185, 216
attunement, 90, 104, 144
authentic spirituality, 237
avoidance structures, 155–56, 204
awareness. See conscious awareness
awe, 5, 212, 222–23

bad trips, 163
Bayard, Pierre, 118n15
Beardslee, William A., 41–42, 71, 73,
        210, 228
Beatles, 16–17, 109–11, 144
becoming and perishing, 159–61
behaviorism, 31–32
Be Here Now (Ram Dass), 145
Being Here, 145–50, 171–72
Beisser, Arnold, 149
belonging, 149, 177, 249–50
Berggren, Douglas, 33
Bergson, Henri-Louis, 51

Berry, Thomas, 211–12
Betty Ford Center, 43, 60, 176–77
Big Trip, 116, 177, 204, 228
biochemistry, 185–87, 195
Birch, Charles, 188
birth process, 80, 116–18, 118n14, 251
birth trauma, 116–18
Blue Acid experience, 55, 64–70, 233
bottom-up and top-down causation, 62
boundaries, 22, 72, 76–78, 95, 123–24,
        134, 163, 166, 199
brain. See neuroscience
"Brain Damage" (song), 71–72
breaking through, 20–28, 100
Briggs, John P., 216
Broad, C. D., 95
Brown, Jason W., 195n30
Buddha, 154, 234
Buddhism, 34, 37, 70, 90, 102, 128, 138,
        146–50, 180, 203, 235, 254

Campbell, Joseph, 110, 209
Cartesian mode of thought, 49, 180, 203
Cassirer, Ernst, 39, 75
Castalia seminar, 75–78, 108, 134
Category of the Ultimate, Whitehead,
        102, 138, 215
causal efficacy, 85–89, 91, 97–101, 105,
        138, 218, 253, 263
causal feelings, 140, 162, 253
causal influences, 143, 148, 185–86
causality, 82–83, 104, 141, 148n15, 157
causation, 46–47, 62, 104, 131, 142–43,
        186, 190
cell theory, 47, 181–82
cellular functioning, 38
Center for Process Studies, 43
central coordinating influence, 130
central occasion, 191
chakras, 79
child, symbol of, 210
Christian spirituality, 156, 254–55
church, 157–58
civilization, 52, 208–10, 212n8, 220–25,
        226–30
clairvoyance, 69
Claremont School of Theology, 43
Cobb, Cliff, 189

Cobb, John B., Jr.
  Buddhism, 146–48, 148n15
  Christian spirituality, 156, 254–55
  economic theory, 188, 209
  environmental crisis, 245–46,
    245n17
  on evil, 242
  perpetual perishing, 238n5
  receptive awareness, 100
  unconscious, 196–97
cocaine, 20
cocreation, 234–35
COEX systems (systems of condensed
    experience), 115–18
cognitive psychology, 33–35
coherence in Whitehead's metaphysics,
    45, 50, 52
coincidences, 141–45, 171
collective unconscious, 34, 47n9, 114,
    162, 195–200
common good, 248
complex amplifier, 75, 84, 94–96
complex individuals, 152
compound individuals, 61–62, 151–52,
    182, 185–86, 212n8, 213–15
conceptual feelings, 97–98
concrescence
  and biochemistry, 186–87
  Buddhism, 146–49
  Christmas tree example, 231–32
  defined, 258
  and enlightenment, 159
  fireworks example, 58
  four phases of, 118n15
  and illumination, 123–24
  and memory, 191, 193
  and music, 91
  mystical intuitions, 168
  nonordinary states of consciousness,
    97–101
  and physics, 183
  and repression, 200–202
  and transformation, 161–65
  transpersonal experiences, 105, 121
  and the unconscious, 197
conformity, 131
connection. See interconnectedness
conscience, 130–31

conscious awareness, 1, 57, 67, 86,
    93–95, 98–99, 101–2, 105–6,
    119, 124, 137, 152, 184, 202,
    204, 243, 253
consciousness
  computer consciousness, 194n29
  Cosmic Consciousness, 124–26
  and ego, 155–56
  and enlightenment, 159–61
  everything is consciousness, 150–54
  evolution of, 221–22, 254–55
  extraordinary experiences, 112
  James on, 213
  and Kandel, 194
  New College experiment, 33–36
  and phenomenology, 37–39
  planetary consciousness, 214
  range of possible states of, 17–19
  and symbolism, 80, 90–91
  transpersonal psychology, 2, 225–26
  Whiteheadian theory, 48, 58, 64,
    97–101, 121, 181, 211, 217–18
  See also causal efficacy; conscious
    awareness; conscious sensory
    perception; nonordinary states
    of consciousness; unconscious
conscious sensory perception, 60, 67,
    85–89. See also presentational
    immediacy
conscious vision, 126
consequent nature of God, 120, 124–26,
    128–29, 139, 141, 152, 199, 239
constructive postmodernism, 6n6,
    135–36, 209. See also process
    thought
Continental philosophy, 39
core memory, 192–93, 198
correspondence theory of truth, 190
Cosmic Consciousness, 119, 124–26
cosmic mind, 214
cosmology, 44–45, 44n3, 52–53
  cosmological knowledge, 137–38
  cosmological shock, 4, 24, 29, 113
  defined, 258
  of Earthism, 210
  and evil, 241–43
  and experience, 48–49, 58, 205
  organismic, 212–20, 222

cosmology (*continued*)
  and panpsychism, 64
  philosophy of organism, 182
  transpersonal psychology, 252, 255
  vision of God, 130
  Whiteheadian vision, 52–53, 211–18, 222–30
creativity, 169, 215–16
  activity of actual occasions, 64, 67–68, 84, 101
  and cocreation, 234–35
  creative advance, 53, 58–59, 69–70, 120, 125, 238–40, 248–49, 258
  creative entities, 62–64, 148
  creative synthesis, 119, 140–41
  defined, 259
  ecstatic fatalism, 228
  and enjoyment, 248
  and evil, 132, 242
  and God, 121
  and Leary, 168
  mystical experiences, 138, 235–36
  primordial embodiment of, 126
  process of, 155–56
  and the self, 202–5
  self-creative experience, 150, 153
  and spirituality, 253
  Whitehead's metaphysical notion of, 120, 128–29, 154
cultural relativism, 105–7

Daly, Herman, 188
Darwinian theory, 188
data or feelings
  causal efficacy, 88–89, 98, 100
  complex amplifier, 93–96
  downward causation, 190
  knowledge through nonordinary states of consciousness, 137–38
  from past occasions of experience, 46–47, 62–63, 69, 97–98
  speculative philosophy, 181
  transmission of, 83–85
  transmutation, 151
  transpersonal experiences, 101–3, 105
  See also sense data
Davies, Paul, 216–17

death, 238–41
  absurdity to human existence, 243
  death-rebirth experience, 118, 159–61
  ego death, 70, 112, 161, 164–65
  and enlightenment, 159–61
  existential crisis, 4
  father's death, 4, 24, 40, 117, 233, 238–40
  Houston's workshop on, 77
  and modernity, 248, 248n19
  psychedelics, 24
  and purpose, 233
  unconscious, 114
deep feeling, 60, 72, 91, 162–64, 194n29, 250, 252–53
defense mechanisms, 95, 116–18, 200–201, 204
Demiurg, 119–24
denial, 219, 224, 246
depth unconscious, 53, 74, 94, 96–97, 113–14, 195
Descartes, René, 157–58, 180–81, 202–3
Desolation Sound retreat, 246–49
detachment, 149
developmental psychology, 33–34, 207
difference, 153
dipolar God, 124–26, 128. *See also* consequent nature of God; primordial nature of God
direct contact, 181
direct influence, 56–57
directionality of time, 68–69
direct physical prehensions, 102
"Does Consciousness Exist?" (James), 152
dominant occasions, 84–85, 151, 259
Doody, Tim, 95
The Doors of Perception (Huxley), 95
downward causation, 190
Dream Power (Faraday), 33
drugs/drug use, 4–5, 18–28, 29, 36, 60–61, 173–78, 249–50, 253. *See also* LSD; nondrug methods
dualism, 49
dual-nature God. *See* dipolar God
dynamic reconstruction, 197

Earthism, 209

Eastern philosophy and religion, 34–35,
    38–40

ecology, 187–88

economics and political theory, 188–89

economism, 209

ecospirituality, 52–53, 253

ecstasy and future fulfillment, 228

ecstatic fatalism, 228–29

ego
    boundaries, 22, 72, 76–78, 95, 163,
        166
    in Buddhism, 34, 148–49
    complex amplifier, 94–95
    ego death, 70, 112, 161–65
    and enlightenment, 161
    and Kant, 83
    nonordinary states, 100
    and openness, 155–56
    and repression, 200–202
    transcendence of, 171–72
    Whiteheadian notion of self, 203–5

Einstein, Albert, 57

Emory University, 41–42

emotions
    causal efficacy's emotional basis,
        87–89
    COEX systems, 115–16
    and deep feeling, 59–60, 77, 91, 156,
        162
    ego death, 164–65
    and intuitions, 104
    and repression, 200–202
    and symbolism, 79–80, 90–91

emptiness, 90, 127–29, 138, 141, 155

enduring personality, 84, 202–4

enjoyment, 202–3, 248–49

enlightenment, 107, 159–61, 164–65,
    235

enlightenment paranoia, 107, 159,
    166–69

entropy, 68

epistemological shock, 4, 17, 29, 234–35

epochal theory of time, 67–68

Epperson, Michael, 183

Esalen Institute, 44

essential unity, 125

eternal moment, 146

event. See actual occasions (moment of
    experience)

everyday awareness, 8n12, 78,
    80–81, 100, 151, 205. See
    also nonordinary states of
    consciousness

everything is consciousness, 150–54

evil, 131–32, 235, 238, 241–43. See also
    perpetual perishing

evolution, 106, 106n15, 187–88, 195–96,
    201, 211–12, 221

The Evolution of an Evolutionist
    (Waddington), 187

evolution of human experience, Cobb,
    254–55

existential crisis, 4, 14–15

experience, defined, 260. See also
    actual occasions (moment of
    experience); extraordinary
    experiences; mystical
    experiences

experience, Hume's analysis of, 219

experiential psychological techniques,
    115

external relations, 140–41

extraordinary experiences, 2, 4, 8n12, 44
    and awareness, 98
    and Buddhism, 147
    defined, 260
    and metaphysics, 156
    and mysticism, 135, 137–39
    past feeling, 80
    psyche, 102–3
    psychospiritual growth and
        transformation, 161–65
    theological shock, 113
    Void, 127
    See also nonordinary states of
        consciousness

extrasensory perception, 64

extraterrestrial dimension, 199

extreme doubt, Hume, 82

Fadiman, James, 95–96

fallacy of misplaced concreteness,
    Whitehead, 6, 206n47

fallacy of the perfect dictionary,
    Whitehead, 46

Faraday, Ann, 33–34
father's death, 4, 13–16, 24, 40, 117, 233, 238–40
Fechner, Gustav, 51, 213–14
feelings. *See* prehensions (feelings)
fellowship and community, 61
Fenton, John, 73–74
Ferré, Frederick, 212–13
Firesign Theatre, 28–29
The Five Ages of Man (Heard), 221–23
flow of feeling, 50, 91, 140, 155–56, 163, 204
forever, 239
For the Common Good (Daly and Cobb), 188
fossil fuels, 248n19
Four North, 173–74
freedom and awareness, 243
freedom and choice, 69, 131, 142, 171
free will, 131–32
Freud, Sigmund, 14, 79–81
Freud and Philosophy (Ricoeur), 79
full maturity. *See* second maturity
future occasions, 56, 68–69, 140, 143, 148–50, 169, 171–72, 199–200, 210, 228–29, 239–40, 248–49, 253–54. *See also* actual occasions (moment of experience)

Gael, Sara, 11n15
gender roles, 247
generalizations, 46, 136, 181, 207
Georgia, 39–41
Gestalt therapy, 149
Gibson, Leonard, 159–60, 164
Gimme Some Truth (film), 144–45
God
    and actuality, 50, 99, 141
    consequent nature of, 120, 124–26, 128–29, 139, 141, 152, 199, 239
    and creativity, 121
    as dipolar, 124–26, 128
    enlightenment paranoia, 169
    everything is consciousness, 152–54
    Hartshorne's modification of Whitehead's notion of, 47, 47n9, 49–50
    hating or doubting, 14

hierarchical ordering, 231–32
    as Higher Power, 226–27, 234–43
    and James, 49–50
    and Jesus, 157–58
    and miracles, 157–58
    mode of perception, 139
    notion of Self, 204, 255
    and openness, 155–56
    persuasive nature of, 131–32, 142, 158, 168, 217, 242
    primordial nature of, 120–21, 124–29, 130, 132–33, 152, 167, 199, 217
    process theology, 49–50, 99, 129–33, 143
    theological shock, 113, 129
    as transcendent, 102, 139
    transpersonal experience, 101–2, 119–29
    vision of, 74, 130
    in Whitehead's metaphysics, 119–21, 124–32, 215–17
Gödel, Escher, Bach (Hofstadter), 223
Goleman, Daniel, 159–61, 164
governing systems, 251
Great Adventure, 240
great chain of being, 231–32
Greene, Brian, 183
Griffin, David Ray, 45n4
    animism, 217–18
    Claremont School of Theology, 44
    compound individuals, 185
    constructive postmodernism, 135–36, 209
    cosmological perspectives, 208–9
    death, 240–41
    evil, 132
    on the Holy, 73
    hybrid physical feeling, 119
    nonordinary states of consciousness, 99
    perception, 81
    religion and spirituality, 252
    transpersonal psychology, 225
Grof, Christina, 43–44, 50, 246
Grof, Stanislav, 2, 39–41, 43–45, 74
    amplified processes, 93–94
    anomalies, 205–6

Cosmic Consciousness, 124–26
cosmological knowledge, 138
evil, 242–43
  and feeling, 250–52
  fossil fuels, 248n19
  and God, 101–2
  and memory, 192
  nonordinary states of consciousness,
    25, 50–51, 119–24, 224–25
  past feeling, 80
  psychedelics, 79–80, 113–18
  spiritual adventure, 212
  spirituality, 237n2
  supracosmic and metacosmic void,
    126–29
  theory of the unconscious, 113–20,
    198–99
  transformation, 161–66
  See also holotropic breathwork

habitual formations, 96–97
habitual repressive patterns, 200, 204
hallucinations, 67, 102
happiness, 171–72
Harman, Willis, 227
harmonic contrasts, 91–92, 124, 184
Harner, Michael, 6–7
Hartshorne, Charles, 46, 47n9, 49–50,
    61n9, 91, 129n43, 181, 185,
    240–41, 243
Hatha Yoga, 18
Hazelden, 174, 174n2
Heard, Gerald, 97n6, 221–23, 255
Heidegger, Martin, 39, 88, 149
here and now, 145–50, 171–72
"Here Comes the Sun" (song), 109–11,
    110n1, 144
Hesse, Herman, 76
hierarchy, 181, 213–17
Higher Power, 129, 226, 235–38, 241,
    249
higher self, 204
highly complex forms of prehensions,
    84
High Priest (Leary), 167–68
historical dimension, Grof, 199
history of the individual, 137

hitting the cosmic bottom, 224–25
Hofstadter, Douglas R., 223
Hollyhock, 246–49
holotropic breathwork, 44, 50, 91, 100,
    117, 118n14, 246
holotropic states, 8n12, 137, 137n4
holy, 73
hope, 16–20, 63, 210, 228–29, 246
Houston, Jean, 36, 75–77, 107, 123
human body, 52, 75, 84–89, 94, 96, 179,
    185, 197–98
human existence, absurdities of, 243–44
human nervous system, 38, 190
human perception, 83, 85
Hume, David, 81–82, 140, 219, 223, 243
Husserl, Edmund, 37
Huxley, Aldous, 95, 163n7
hybrid physical feeling, 119, 127, 261
hyperconnectivity, 144
hypercosmical light, 122
hypnosis, 18, 191

ideal impulses, 49
ideals, 130, 131n44
identity, 29, 154–55, 203–5
illumination, 99, 121–24, 128
immortality. See objective immortality
impending illumination, 166
"Incense and Peppermints" (song),
    16–17
independent center of experience, 61
individual knowledge, 137–38
ineffability, 40, 71–74
inevitability of loss, 4, 240
initial/subjective aim, 96, 131, 144,
    167–68, 172, 228, 255
inner activity, 49, 183
inner archetypal vision, 111–12
inner guidance, 27–28, 164
inner subjectivity, 211
inner synthetic processes, 140–41
In Search of Memory (Kandel), 192–94
insentient matter, 48–49, 57, 89, 150–51,
    158, 184
intellectual feelings, 98–99
intelligent worship, 228–29
intense interest, 156

interconnectedness, 24, 60–61, 63–64,
        66–68, 139–41, 209, 216,
        252–53. *See also* belonging;
        coincidences
interdisciplinary tendencies, 3, 29–30,
        36, 40
internal relations, 141
interrelationship, 61
intimate relationships, 243, 253
intuitions. *See* causal efficacy; mystical
        intuitions
The Invisible Landscape (McKenna), 6
isolation, 61, 141, 249–50

James, William, 49–52
        consciousness, 152–53
        drops or pulses of experience, 47, 56
        evolution, 106, 106n15
        human subjectivity, 211–12, 213
        loss, 16
        process thought, 2
        scientific and philosophic openness,
                114
        truth and meaning, 3, 3n4
Jantsch, Erich, 216
Jesus, 157–58, 234, 250
Jung, Carl, 33–35, 75, 115–17, 141–43,
        162, 195–96, 198, 253

Kandel, Eric, 192–95
Kant, Immanuel, 4, 37, 82–83, 180–81
Karloff, Boris, 26–27
Keller, Catherine, 199, 201
Kris, Ernst, 166

Laing, R. D., 138
language, 71–73
Last and First Men (Stapledon), 194n29,
        228
Leary, Timothy, 77, 122–23, 167–68,
        169
L'Engle, Madeleine, 16
Lennon, John, 144, 209
Lessing, Doris, 60–61, 250
Lewis, C. S., 111
liberal Protestant tradition, 252–53
living symbol, 78
living universe, 216

long-term memory, 192, 253
loss, 13–16, 132, 155–56, 238–40
Lovelock, J. E., 214
loyalty to the forces of life, 228
LSD, 1, 4–5, 20–25, 29, 32, 50, 54–56,
        76–77, 93, 121–23

Magical Mystery Tour (album), 16–17
mandala art, 90, 92, 106
Maslow, Abraham, 39, 141
Masters, Robert, 36, 75–76, 123
materialism, 150, 158, 184
maya, 169
McKenna, Terrance and Dennis, 6
meaning perception, Wilson, 82, 85–86
meditation techniques, 101, 102, 160–61
memory/memories, 59, 79–80, 82,
        96, 115–16, 137, 164, 191–93,
        197–98, 200, 253
mental pole, 143n8
Merleau-Ponty, Maurice, 39
mescaline experience, 19
metacosmic Void, 126–27
metaphysical crisis, 4, 29
metaphysical knowledge, 102, 138
metaphysical reordering of the ego, 165
metaphysical ultimates of process
        philosophy, 235–36
metaphysics, 129, 156, 194–96, 219–20.
        See also Whitehead, Alfred
        North
Miller, Walter, 182
Mind Games (Masters and Houston), 36
miracles, 157–58
modernity, 141, 208–9, 237, 248
modes of being in the world, 203, 228
Modes of Thought (Whitehead), 63,
        131n44, 135, 202–3
morality, 171, 227, 249, 252
moral shock, 14
morphic fields, 192, 198, 216
music, 26, 91, 109–11, 191
Myers, Gerald, 3n4
mystical experiences, 71–74, 113,
        119–23, 124–26, 129–33, 136,
        137–39, 145, 149, 159–61, 182,
        228, 235–36. *See also* symbolism

mystical intuitions, 49, 72, 74, 119,
    121–23, 126, 130, 137 39, 140,
    152, 168, 228, 235
mysticism, 134–56

Nagel, Thomas, 194
naturalistic theology, process theology
    as, 50, 132, 158, 236
natural order, 188, 236
natural phenomena, 198
natural transcendence of self, 229
negative governing system, 251
neuroscience, 37–38, 58n4, 59–63,
    83–86, 151, 180, 186, 189–95,
    195n30, 200–202
New Age thought, 40, 64, 74, 139–56,
    172, 227
New College, 33–36, 108–9, 144, 166,
    169–70
new ongoing centers of coordination,
    182
New Pathways in Psychology (Wilson),
    81
Newton, Isaac, 157
new whole, 48
Night of the Demon (film), 24
Nirvana, 160–61, 164–65
nonconscious experience, 48, 58, 260
nondrug methods, 44, 246, 253. See also
    holotropic breathwork
nonordinary states of consciousness
    causal efficacy, 97–101
    and cocreation, 234
    conscious awareness, 93–94, 96–97,
        102, 105–6, 140
    defined, 262
    enlightenment paranoia, 168
    and God, 125–26
    Grof's theory of, 25, 44, 51, 114,
        119, 224–25
    heightened ability to follow ideas
        and questions, 54n1
    here and now, 145–47
    and Houston, 36
    hyperconnectivity, 144
    and intuition, 172
    LSD trip, 71
    and memory, 115–16

    and order, 200–201
    spiritual experiences, 224–25
    and symbolism, 91
    and synchronicities, 66–67
    and transformation, 162, 164–65
    and transmutation, 151
    transpersonal psychology, 205
nonphysical causation, 104, 142
North Shore Country Club, 17

objective immortality, 115n11, 239
obscurantism, 21–22, 46
ocean of feeling, 49, 61, 197, 205
Odd John (Stapledon), 228
Odin, Steve, 90–91, 106, 199n37
omnipotence, 132
One and the Many, 62, 68, 83, 97, 102,
    128, 138, 139–41, 153, 169, 185,
    215. See also transmutation
One Consciousness of God, 153–54
Oneness, 134–35, 139, 141
Ontological Principle, 130
openness
    Buddhism, 254
    concrescent process, 141
    Creativity, 129, 138
    mystical intuitions, 235
    nonordinary states of consciousness,
        105–6, 162
    psyche, 63, 252
    psychical openness, 163n7
    surplus repression, 201
    waking up, 154–55
    Whiteheadian unconscious, 199
order, in Whitehead's scheme, 100,
    130–31, 200–202, 236
ordinary existence, 206

panentheism, 50, 153
panexperientialism, 48, 64, 218
panpsychism, 48, 64
pantheism, 50, 153, 215
pantheistic intuitions, 101
paradoxical theory of change, 149
paranoia. See enlightenment paranoia
parapsychology, 80–81, 83–84, 96,
    103–5, 143, 157–58, 198–200,
    205, 263

*Parapsychology, Philosophy, and
    Spirituality* (Griffin), 240–41,
    252–53
participatory adventure, 227
past events or occasions
    Buddhist thought, 147–50
    causal efficacy, 85–87, 105
    and cocreation, 234
    concrescence, 97–98, 193
    conscious awareness, 152, 204–5
    and creativity, 129, 168–69
    feeling/prehensions in Whitehead's
        metaphysical scheme, 46–49,
        56–58, 67–69, 83–87, 102, 119,
        181, 194n29
    future achievements, 254
    God of process theology, 49–50
    and Grof, 79–80
    here and now, 171
    hope for the future, 210
    past lives, 115, 115n10
    and physics, 183–84
    preservation of, 156
    and the psyche, 62–64, 93–97, 104
    and synchronicity, 143
    and the unconscious, 196–200
    Whitehead's theory of perception,
        130–31, 138–39
    See also actual occasions (moment
        of experience); memory/
        memories; transmutation
past fading problem, 132, 156, 238–40
past feeling, 47, 80, 84, 85, 96, 232
peace, 226–30
Peat, David, 216
Peck, M. Scott, 244
perception, 263
    All is One, 139–41
    Hume's theory of, 140
    psychology of, 190–91
    and self, 202
    and self-creation, 234
    sensory perception, 63–64, 67,
        101–2, 124, 190–91
    and symbolism, 90
    and transmutation, 151–52
    Whitehead's theory of, 80–89, 93,
        130

See also causal efficacy;
    presentational immediacy;
    process thought; psyche;
    symbolic reference
Perelandra (Lewis), 111
perfection, 172
perinatal psychology, 80, 116–18, 161,
    198
perishing and becoming, 159–61
"Perpetual Change" (song), 29, 140
perpetual perishing, 236–38
personality, 116–17, 149, 161–64, 196–
    97. *See also* enduring personality
personal narratives, 7, 72
personal psychosynthesis, 162–63
personal unconscious, 34, 197–98
persuasive influence of God, 131–32,
    142, 158, 168, 217, 242
phenomenology, 37–38, 39, 51, 89,
    121–23
philosophy, 1–3, 31–32, 34–36, 37–38,
    39–40, 51, 64, 88–89, 135–36,
    206, 225. *See also* specific types
    of philosophy
philosophy of organism, Whitehead, 44,
    52, 138, 139, 143, 146, 150–51,
    182, 185–86, 194–95, 206, 218,
    243
physical causation, 104, 142–43
physical traumas, 114–18, 198
physics, 183–85
physiological roots of repression, 200
Piaget, Jean, 34
piety, 130
Pink Floyd, 71–72
planetary age, 220–21
planetary beings, 214, 214n14
planetary consciousness, 214
planetary crisis, 218–19, 227–28. *See
    also* Earthism
planetary dimension, 198
planetary tribe, 247
Plato, 49, 131
pluralistic hierarchy, 215–16
pluralistic monism, 49, 139
postindividual, 221
postmodern animism, 218
potential contribution, 254

The Power of Now (Tolle), 165
prehensions (feelings), 46–48, 55, 58–
    60, 64, 84–89, 93–94, 98–100,
    102, 104, 106, 119, 123–24, 127,
    131, 191–93, 197, 205, 235, 261,
    264. *See also* deep feeling; past
    feeling
prescribed perspective, 55
presentational immediacy, 85–86,
    88–89, 90, 98, 101, 106, 148–49,
    162, 171, 263
presentism, 171, 219
present moment, 67–68, 92, 119, 146,
    149–50, 155, 171, 197, 223,
    253–54
presymbolic reality, 105
previously accomplished events, 69
Price, Lucien, 179
primitive experience or feeling, 47–48,
    58, 60, 85, 87–88, 90, 98–99,
    102, 105–6, 123, 186, 189
primordial nature of God, 120–21,
    124–29, 130, 132–33, 152, 167,
    199, 217
procedural mental processes, 192–95
Process and Reality (Whitehead), 3, 45–
    46, 49, 53, 136, 143n8, 192n16,
    215n17
process philosophy, 44–45, 50–53,
    62–63, 72, 81, 96, 142, 154, 159,
    177, 182, 211, 213, 244–45, 264
process theology, 49–50, 99, 129, 132–
    33, 143, 153, 158, 235–36
process thought, 2, 52, 63, 130, 136, 141,
    188, 234, 237, 249
Progoff, Ira, 196, 196n35
psi phenomena, 103–5
psyche
    Cartesian and Kantian modes of
        thought, 180
    cellular functioning, 38
    complex amplifier, 93–94
    compound individuals, 62
    creative psyche-level integration, 98
    defined, 264
    extraordinary experiences, 102–3
    God's synthesis of the universe, 153
    Grof's theory of, 74, 114, 116, 252

individual knowledge, 137
neuroscience, 63, 106, 190–91
openness of, 83–84, 106
and parapsychology, 104
process philosophy, 96
psychedelic experiences, 72
psychospiritual growth and change,
    203
quantum theory, 57–58
and repression, 200–202
second maturity, 220
sensory perception, 60
transpersonal experience, 22
and the unconscious, 195–200
psychedelic(s), 1–7, 54–55
    in Alcoholics Anonymous, 225
    Being Here, 145–50
    Big Trip, 108–13
    Blue Acid experience, 64–69
    breaking through, 19–28
    Castalia experience, 75–78
    COEX systems, 117–18
    defined, 264
    depth of feeling, 250
    enlightenment paranoia, 107,
        166–68
    Grof's theory of the unconscious,
        113–18
    ineffability, 71–72
    and memory, 79–80
    New College, 33–36
    new cosmology, Grof, 242, 252
    and reality, 28–30, 179–80
    recovery, 176–78
    Sine Waves experience, 55–64
    time distortion, 69–70
    transpersonal phenomena, 94–96
psychical causation, 143
psychical transformation, 161–66
psychic isolationism, 201n41
psychic phenomena, 103–4, 162–63
psychoanalytic theory, 51, 197–98
psychological transformation, 161–64,
    251–52
psychology, field of, 35–38, 51–52, 58,
    189–95, 203, 207
psychology of perception, 190, 191
psychophysical approach, 36, 116, 200

psychospiritual transformation and
        growth, 157–72
    and enlightenment, 159–61
    enlightenment paranoia, 166–69
    experiential techniques, 225–26,
        252–54
    holotropic states, 137
    living in the world, 169–72, 203
    new cosmology, 255
    psi abilities, 105
    psychical openness, 163n7
    psychological transformation,
        161–66
    spiritual entities, 143
    and symbolism, 90

quantum theory, 47, 55, 57–58, 57n3,
        151, 181–82, 183–84, 183n6,
        194–95
"Question" (song), 108

radical empiricism, James, 135
Ram Dass, 28, 145, 171
Ramón y Cajal, Santiago, 193
Rank, Otto, 51, 116
Realms of the Human Unconscious
        (Grof), 51
receptive awareness, 100
Reck, Andrew J., 215–16
recollective-biographical realm, 114–15
recovery, 43–45, 173–77, 224, 244, 255
reductive methodology, 38
Reich, Wilhelm, 51, 113–14
Reid, Thomas, 81
religion, 3, 15, 74, 136, 236–38, 252–53.
        See also Buddhism
Religion in the Making (Whitehead),
        143n9, 237
religious art, 90–91
religious experiences, 53, 91, 130
religious symbolism, 136
repression, 60
    ego death, 161–65
    second maturity, 221–22
    self-image, 204–5
    surplus, 95, 201
    transmutation, 106
    unconscious, 114–17, 197

Whiteheadian metaphysics, 200–202
rhythmic patterns, 56
Ricoeur, Paul, 39, 79, 81
rightness, 172
The Road Less Traveled (Peck), 244
Romantic tradition, 60, 88, 220
rote learning, 192
rush, 156
Russell, Bertrand, 2
Ryle, Gilbert, 145–46n12

sacrifices, 224, 248
safety, 155
Santayana, 80
satisfaction, 228, 248, 265
science, 15, 21, 181–207
    biochemistry, 185–87
    and Eastern thought, 34, 39–40
    ecology, 187–88
    economics and political theory,
        188–89
    panexperientialism, 64
    and philosophy, 32, 88
    physics, 183–85
    psychology, 189
    and religion, 3, 15, 136, 206, 236–37
    scientific rationality, 21–22
    scientism, 21
    sense perception, 190
    transpersonal psychology, 205–6
    See also neuroscience
search for meaning and purpose,
        14–16, 54–55, 233–34. See also
        philosophy
second maturity, 220–26, 230
self, 202–5, 223
    annihilation of, 254–55
    self-creation, 57, 146, 148, 150, 153,
        183, 202–3, 234, 239–40
    self-interest, 188, 209
    self-transcending spirit, 254–55
sensation, 57, 59, 72, 87, 253
sense data, 81, 181
sensory-barrier phenomena, 114
sensory perceptions, 59–60, 64, 67,
        75, 84–89, 101–2, 124, 130,
        189–91. See also presentational
        immediacy

serially ordered societies, 61
settled events, 68
Sheldrake, Rupert, 192, 196, 216
Sherrington, Charles, 193
Shikasta (Lessing), 60–61, 250
short-term memory, 82, 99, 191–92
Sine Waves experience, 55–64
Slaughterhouse-Five (film), 169–70
Smith, Page, 219
sobriety, 43, 174–77, 244
social relations, Whiteheadian
    perspective on, 189
societies, 61–62, 215–16, 232, 265
societies of societies, Whitehead, 185–
    87, 194
solipsism, 80–81, 141, 168–69, 223
Sorge, 88
soul, 63, 85, 151, 171, 185, 219, 229, 240
SOWF (substance-of-we-feeling),
    60–61, 250
spatiotemporal events, 49
specific data, 101–2
speculative philosophy, 2–3, 42, 107,
    136, 181, 195, 236–37, 265
spirituality, 113, 249–55
    authentic, 237
    Christian, 156, 254
    in community, 237
    ecospirituality, 52–53, 253
    psychospiritual transformation,
        157–59
    and religion, 236–37, 252–53
    spiritual adventure, 212, 253
    spiritual awakening, 224–25
    spiritual crisis, 4
    spiritual dimensions, 55, 126, 150,
        199, 211–12, 237
    spiritual experiences, 163–64, 218,
        225, 235–38
    spiritual growth, 162–63, 166
    spiritual psychosynthesis, 162–63
    spiritual rebirth, 161
    spiritual transformation, 164–66
Stapledon, Olaf
    computer consciousness, 194n29
    hierarchy, 213–17
    maturity, 221
    modernity, 248

participatory adventure, 227–29
Star Maker, 44n3, 74, 122, 212n8,
    242, 249
subjectivity, 212
    on the universe, 4–5, 24
Star Maker (Stapledon), 44n3, 74, 122,
    212n8, 242, 249
Star Trek, 36, 60
Strawberry Alarm Clock, 16–17
string theory, 183–84
structuralism, 40
structured societies, 215
The Structure of Christian Existence
    (Cobb), 254–55
structure of experience, 101–2, 165
Stylistics, 155
subjective immediacy, 68, 238n5
subjectivity, 57, 64, 102, 150–51, 190,
    194, 211–12, 225, 265. *See also*
    initial/subjective aim
subordinate societies, 215, 215n17
substance-of-we-feeling (SOWF),
    60–61, 250
suffocation experiences, 117
summing up, 204–5
Sunyata, 138
superject, 94, 265
Supracosmic Void, 119, 126–29
surplus repression, 95, 201
survival, 95, 201, 224, 240–41, 251–52
Swimme, Brian, 212, 223
Switzerland, 76–77. *See also* Castalia
    seminar
symbolic reference, 85–89, 90–91, 106,
    263
symbolism, 78–81
    of the child, 210
    enlightenment paranoia, 166
    illumination, 124
    phenomenology, 39
    religious, 106
    symbolic order, 105–6
    symbolic unifications, 197
    symbolization process, 75
    and transformation, 90–92
    visual phenomena, 67
Symbolism (Whitehead), 81
synchronicity, 66, 141–45, 176–77, 186

systems of condensed experience
(COEX systems), 115–18

TASIS (The American School In
Switzerland), 76
technology of the sacred, 255
telekinesis, 104
telepathy, 102, 103–4, 119, 138, 143
temporality, 61, 67–69
theistic determinist theories, 69
theological shock/crisis, 4, 113, 129
theological speculations, Whitehead's,
124–25
theoretical systems, 39–40, 151
"This Is It" (Watts), 154
Thriller series (Karloff), 26–27
Tibetan Buddhism, 15–16
time, 64–70
Tolle, Eckhart, 165–66
top-down causation, 62, 185–86
transcendence, 156, 171, 229, 254–55.
See also openness; transpersonal
human; transpersonal
unconscious
transcendent, God as, 102, 139
transcendent values and intuitions,
226–27
transformation, psychospiritual, 159,
161–66
transformation, symbolic, 78–81, 90–92,
106
transformative work, 224–26
transmutation, 58, 89, 106, 151, 239,
265
transpersonal human, 221
transpersonal phenomena, 95, 97, 114,
205–6
transpersonal psychology/experiences,
2–3, 5–6
complex amplifier, 93–97
concrescent process, 162
cultural relativism, 105
death-rebirth experience, 118
defined, 266
at Green Bay, 38
and Grof, 44–45, 51, 74, 119, 120,
125–26
and James, 49, 93–97

and loss, 240
mystical experiences of God, 129–30
new cosmology, 211–12, 244–45,
255
and obscurantism, 22
philosophy of organism, 182
process thought, 141, 249
psi phenomena, 104
psychological shifts, 165–66, 252
recovery of feeling, 60
and religion, 136
second maturity, 220–26
spiritual transformation, 163, 205–6
and time, 69
transpersonal amplifier, 93–96
transpersonal unconscious, 199
value-laden feelings, 87
and the Void, 126–29
Western men, 246
at West Georgia College, 39–40
and Wilson, 81
transpersonal unconscious, 198–99
treatment. See recovery
truth. See correspondence theory of
truth
Twelve Steps and Twelve Traditions, 21
2001: A Space Odyssey (film), 209

unconscious, 195–200
actual occasions, 48, 64
concrescent process, 162–63
conscious awareness, 93–94, 119
depth unconscious, 53, 74, 94,
96–97, 113–14, 195
developmental psychology, 34
downward causation, 190
and ego, 149, 155–56
everything is consciousness, 150
God's being, 126, 139
Grof's theory of, 51, 113–18
and identity, 204
and illumination, 123
mystical experiences, 152
negative governing system, 251
phases of concrescence, 99–100
and repression, 200–202
and symbolism, 90–91
and time, 66–67

Whitehead's approach, 83
unifying felt contrast, 97–98
unitary transcendental ego, Kant, 83
universal adventure, 223, 227, 243
universal mind, 124–26, 128, 213–17
universal of universals. *See* creativity
universal process, 49, 56, 140, 232, 236,
       240
universal syntheses, 148, 152
"Universe Story" (Swimme and Berry),
       211–12
University of Wisconsin–Green Bay,
       37–38, 173, 180

vacuous actuality, 49, 57, 63
value, 87–89, 101, 125, 229, 243, 248,
       253–55, 266
The Varieties of Psychedelic Experience
       (Masters and Houston), 36,
       75–76
Varieties of Religious Experience (James),
       49, 75
vector flows of energy, 184–85
vibratory events, 61–62, 104, 111, 112
vision of God, 74, 130
visual phenomena, 67, 98, 111–12,
       151, 191. *See also* sensory
       perceptions
Void, 119–20, 126–29, 161, 164
Volin, Michael, 108

Waddington, C. H., 186–87
waking up, 154–55
Watts, Alan, 154
The Way of the Shaman (Harner), 6–7
West Georgia College, 39–41, 79
Whitehead, Alfred North
       approach to organizing nonordinary
              states of consciousness, 101–3
       Being Here, 145–50
       and biochemistry, 185–87
       Center for Process Studies, 43–45
       and civilization, 226
       and cocreation, 234
       and coincidences, 142–43
       complex amplifier, 93–97
       and consciousness, 98–100, 150–54

cosmological vision, 52–53, 211–18,
       222–30
creative advance, 59
       and ecology, 187–88
       economics and political theory,
              188–89
Emory University, 41–42
enjoyment of experience, 248–49
and enlightenment, 159–61
and evil, 241–43
and experience, 71–73, 75, 98–100,
       181
fallacy of misplaced concreteness, 6
foundation for the sciences, 181–82
and God, 119–21, 124–32, 215–17
initial aim, 167–68
on interest, 7
introduction to philosophy of,
       45–53
and loss, 16
McKenna brothers, 6
and memory, 80, 191–93, 192n16
metaphysical notion of creativity,
       120, 128–29, 154
and mysticism, 134–36, 138, 156,
       236–38
"Nature Alive," 63–64
nature of our universe, 63–64
and neuroscience, 189–95
objective immortality, 115n11
and obscurantism, 21–22, 21n5
One and the Many, 62, 68, 83, 97,
       102, 128, 138, 139–41, 153, 169,
       185, 215
and Oneness, 139–41
and parapsychology, 104
past events or occasions, 115,
       115n10, 148n15
and peace, 228–29
perpetual perishing, 238–41
as philosophical foundation for
       transpersonal psychology, 2–3
philosophy of organism, 38, 143,
       143n9, 194–95
       and physics, 183–85
       and psychology, 189–207
       and repression, 200–202

Whitehead, Alfred North (*continued*)
　　revolutionary possibilities
　　　offered by, 5
　　and science, 179
　　self or the "I," 202–4
　　symbolic reference, 90–91
　　theory of perception, 81–89
　　theory of the unconscious,
　　　195–200
　　and time, 67–70
　　and transition, 220
　　transpersonal psychology, 205–7
　　and value, 253–54
　　West Georgia College, 41
　　and Wilbur, 206n47
　　See also actual occasions
　　　(moment of experience);

concrescence; prehensions
　　(feelings)
Wilber, Ken, 39–40, 165–66, 206n47
Wilson, Bill, 21, 225
Wilson, Colin, 81–82, 85–86, 141, 171
wonder, 155, 211–12
world-building, 228
worldview, 3, 22, 50, 73, 113, 140,
　　　157–58, 208–10, 219–20, 233,
　　　235–37, 253, 255, 266
A Wrinkle in Time (L'Engle), 16, 107

Yellowstone National Park, 14
Yes (band), 29, 140
Yonker, Nicholas J., 220–21
"You Are Everything" (song), 155